D0202869

PACIFIC ISLANDS
1942-45

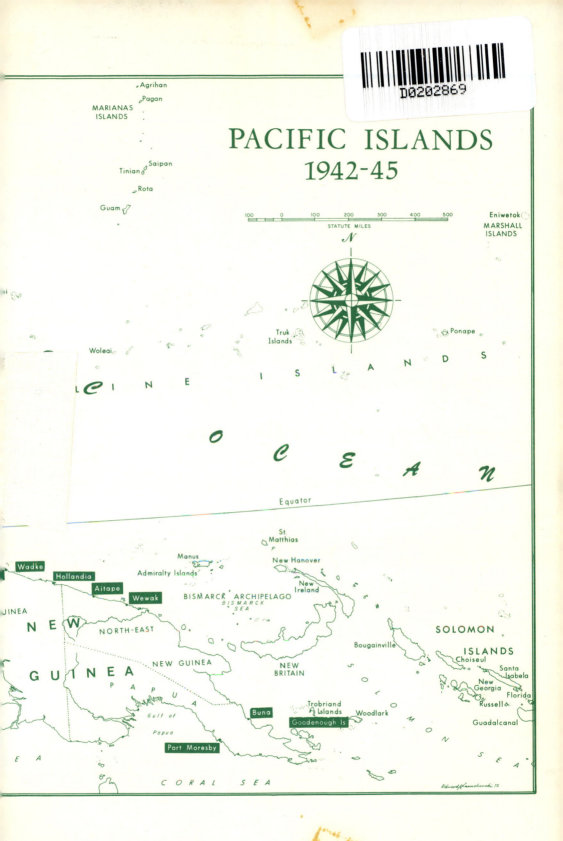

MARIANAS
ISLANDS

Agrihan

Pagan

Tinian Saipan

Rota

Guam

100   0   100   200   300   400   500
STATUTE MILES

N

Eniwetok
MARSHALL
ISLANDS

Truk
Islands

Ponape

Woleai

LINE ISLANDS

C I N E   I S L A N D S

O C E A N

Equator

St.
Matthias

Wadke

Hollandia

Aitape

Wewak

Manus

Admiralty Islands

New Hanover

New
Ireland

BISMARCK ARCHIPELAGO
BISMARCK
SEA

SOLOMON

ISLANDS
Choiseul

GUINEA

NEW

NORTH-EAST

Bougainville

Santa
Isabela

GUINEA

NEW GUINEA

NEW
BRITAIN

New
Georgia

Florida

Russella

PAPUA

Trobriand
Islands

Woodlark

Buna

Goodenough Is

Guadalcanal

Port Moresby

Gulf of
Papua

Papua

SEA

CORAL SEA

Edward Gasnobarski 72

Dear Miss Em

Johnny Florea-LIFE Magazine © Time Inc.
Miss Em and General Eichelberger

CONTRIBUTIONS IN MILITARY HISTORY, NUMBER 2

DEAR MISS EM
General Eichelberger's War in the Pacific, 1942–1945

Jay Luvaas, Editor

L.C.C.C. LIBRARY

GREENWOOD PRESS, INC., PUBLISHING DIVISION
WESTPORT, CONNECTICUT

Library of Congress Cataloging in Publication Data

Eichelberger, Robert L
    Dear Miss Em.

    (Contributions in military history, 2)
    Includes bibliographical references.
    1. World War, 1939-1945 — Pacific Ocean.
    2. World War, 1939-1945 — Personal narratives, American.
    I. Eichelberger, Emma Gudger. II. Luvaas, Jay, ed.
    III. Title. IV. Series.
    D767.E37   940.54'26'0924 [B]   71-176429
    ISBN 0-8371-6278-5

Copyright © 1972 by Jay Luvaas
All rights reserved. No portion of this book may be reproduced,
by any process or technique, without the express written consent
of the author and publisher.

Library of Congress Catalog Card Number: 71-176429
ISBN: 0-8371-6278-5

First published in 1972

Greenwood Press, Inc., Publishing Division
51 Riverside Avenue, Westport, Connecticut 06880

Printed in the United States of America
Designed by Laurel Brown

Contents

List of Illustrations

Preface

Although I could not realize it at the time, this book was conceived during the summer of 1954, when I was courting General Robert L. Eichelberger's papers for the Duke University Library. I was engaged in developing an already impressive collection of printed and manuscript materials in Southern history, and, given my own military interests, it was inevitable that sooner or later my gaze would fall upon the former commander of the U.S. Eighth Army, then living in retirement in Asheville. If his career did not properly belong to Southern history, the normal parameters of my "search and preserve" mission, I had no difficulty in rationalizing any efforts to acquire his papers. His wife, after all, came from a prominent North Carolina family, he was living comfortably south of the Mason-Dixon line, and his father (I later learned) had even fought in the Civil War.

Through the good offices of Daniel K. Edwards, his former aide and more recently the mayor of Durham, I made contact with the General. He had indeed saved everything from his long and varied career and a hasty reconnaissance to Asheville uncovered all sorts of treasures — diaries, official reports, newspaper clippings, photographs, and personal correspondence — tucked away in trunks and boxes in his attic.

By far the most intriguing portion of his papers was the letters to Miss Em, for as his friend and classmate, General George S. Patton, Jr., Eichelberger wrote at least once a day to his wife whenever they were separated. These were conversational, candid letters that revealed his hopes and frustrations, experiences and opinions during his years in Siberia and the Pacific. Although aware that one day his letters would have historical value, Eichelberger did not write with the notion that historians would peer over Miss Em's shoulder. "History is still in the making right here," he explained at the close of the war, "and I want you to see all sides of it."

General Eichelberger placed many of these letters at the disposal of the writer who collaborated in producing *Our Jungle Road to Tokyo,* which was published in 1949 and serialized in the *Saturday Evening Post.* His main interest then, however, was to see that history took notice of the accomplishments of his Eighth Army, which had operated throughout the Pacific war in the heavy shadow of General Walter Krueger's Sixth Army. Only about twenty percent of the present volume duplicates passages quoted in *Jungle Road.*

After the emotional binge that accompanied General Douglas MacArthur's abrupt dismissal in 1951, Eichelberger became increasingly annoyed with attempts to deify his old chief. He was conspicuously absent from the coterie of dedicated followers who surrounded MacArthur upon his dramatic return from Korea and he bristled at some of the assumptions in the rhapsodic biographies by Frazier Hunt and Major General Charles A. Willoughby. Hunt, declared Eichelberger, "tried to be very friendly to me in his book" but "Willoughby indulged in some half truths which I didn't like." Both volumes were "far too one-sided to have any historical value," a judgment echoed by some disinterested critics far removed from the MacArthur circle. Hanson Baldwin, for example, warned that historians "will have to sift carefully through a mass of subject chaff" to get much of value out of Willoughby's *MacArthur 1941-1951,* and General S. L. A. Marshall described Hunt's *The Untold Story of Douglas MacArthur* as "strictly the front view, seen by a friend through the eyes of the advocate," of a figure who "comes out like implacable Mars garmented as Uncle Sam."[1]

For a while Eichelberger was tempted to write a second volume that would adjust reputations a little, but as the years passed and his golf game improved he lost any desire he once had to refight the war. He continued to read and react to literature on the war and to assemble source materials for his memoirs — or rather for some interested historian after he himself had "gone on to his reward."

At first I had no plans to do anything with the collection myself. My interests were concentrated on the Civil War, and when I left this overworked field it was to study military thought abroad. During my frequent trips to Asheville, however, I did become intrigued by what I learned of MacArthur and his lieutenants as we searched Eichelberger's attic and his prodigious memory. When the time came for me to remove the papers to Duke University, the General tried to reread each letter, not for fear that something would get out that should remain private, but because each letter seemed to revive suggestive memories. He would

1. *The New York Times Book Review,* October 3, 24, 1954.

set aside a pile of letters retrieved recently from a trunk and explain: "I get a kick out of reading these old letters. I'll see that you get them next time." And then characteristically he would add: "How much do you need to take back today to make it look good with your bosses?"

Usually at this point Miss Em would intervene, whispering to me: "If you and Bobby don't go through these things any faster you will never finish. No matter what he says, he will never take time to read them. You distract him with a few letters and we'll just take the rest to the car." In this unceremonious way the Eichelberger papers, by detachments, were marched off for the library.

The best part of this characteristic procedure was that there was always need for another trip, and every few months I returned for additional treasures. Our conversation during these visits usually centered on sports or military events, topics which I gather did not greatly interest many of General Eichelberger's retired friends. On those frequent occasions when I did not know enough about operations in the Pacific to converse intelligently, I fell back upon the simple expedient of pretending I was interviewing Stonewall Jackson and framing my questions accordingly. What was it like to lead a corps in battle? What books or men had influenced him during his career? How would he rate his subordinate commanders? How would he compare the American and Japanese soldier? How good was the generalship on the other side? Did his own superiors ever intervene in tactical decisions?

His staunchly loyal secretary, Mrs. Virginia Westall, frequently came to my aid. "Get Sir Robert to tell you about the time MacArthur offered him Sutherland's job," she would suggest in her distinctive Oklahoma twang. On the next trip she might volunteer: "The General has Fred Irving on his mind a lot these days." And after each visit, General Eichelberger would dictate his aroused recollections and impressions, a habit he had formed shortly before my first trip to Asheville. Ultimately there were some five hundred typed pages of his panoramic and often pungent commentary on all sorts of matters touching his career and public figures he had known.

In 1957 I left Duke for a teaching position, but at General Eichelberger's request I remained in command of his papers to protect them from being exploited by anyone with an eye for the sensational. I still had no intention of using the collection myself and it was not until 1961, when I was in England working on another book, that General Eichelberger brought up the subject. Could I visit him upon my return in the fall? Sensing some urgency and of course delighted at the prospect of seeing him again, I rearranged my home journey to include a side trip to Asheville. After the usual polite preliminaries between friends, he took me aside and came straight to the point. Had I given any thought to using his papers for a book? I had not. Would I be interested?

He had continued to dictate his thoughts on MacArthur, George Catlett Marshall, Eisenhower, and other "great men" he had known. "Some of these historical data are controversial," he admitted, and he was anxious that someone with historical training would make use of the material, disregarding those passages that were based on insufficient or faulty evidence or were manifestly inaccurate or unfair.

Although inundated with other work and aware of my own limitations in what for me would be virtually a new field, on the spur of the moment I promised him that as soon as present obligations were fulfilled I would do something with his papers. I asked him if he would object to my editing his personal letters to Miss Em. Not at all, he replied, although Miss Em would probably insist that her letters would be too personal to be made public. He would want me to honor her wishes in the matter. (Thus when she insisted that her own letters be destroyed because they would have no historical value, I felt obliged to comply.) That settled, we rejoined the ladies and the rest of our brief visit was purely social. He seemed a little pensive when we left the next day, but I assumed that this was because he knew he had to face major surgery the following week.

I had only one more communication from him. "With luck," he wrote from the hospital, "it should prove to be more or less minor but it is nothing I would cry for. Virginia has been busy as a bee getting her Marshall data together and other things. I have made some dictations about General Richardson who backed out of his Australian detail and who changed my life very radically. Have also dictated about my life in China and important people I knew there including Sun Yat Sen. Send the questions along and we shall get on them with life." Four days later General Eichelberger was dead.

That Christmas, when I visited Asheville to arrange for the dispatch of the stray papers to the library, I assured Miss Em that I would do everything within my power to see that General Eichelberger's views, as well as his accomplishments, would one day become a matter of historical record. This book is the result of that promise. I did not find time to commence work on it until 1965, when I spent the better part of a sabbatical wading through the two hundred and fifty odd boxes of correspondence, documents, and pictures that comprise the Eichelberger Papers. I emerged with some four hundred single-spaced typed pages of excerpts from General Eichelberger's daily letters to Miss Em, selected because of what they revealed of the personalities, the campaigns, and the atmosphere of the Pacific war.

I next asked three friends to mark those passages that to them had some special interest. General Clovis E. Byers, Eichelberger's gifted Chief of Staff, indicated the material that in his judgment would be essential for a proper understanding of the story. Colonel Thomas E. Griess, who fought with the Sixth Army in the Philippines and is currently Professor and Head of the History Department at West Point, drew my attention to episodes which he thought would merit inclusion or further investigation. And Miss Karin Arentzen (Mrs. William K. Stahl), my capable student assistant for two years, marked those passages that she was convinced would interest the general reader. Once I had made my own selections I weighed the recommendations of these good people and it was astonishing the degree to which our interests had overlapped. They are in no way responsible for any errors of judgment on my part, but each, viewing the story from a special vantage point, powerfully reinforced my own feelings about the kind of material that should be included.

I have tried throughout to be impartial in investigating General Eichelberger's opinions and the "facts" as he communicated them to Miss Em. Wherever I have found his views in conflict with others or his facts subject to change in light of information not known to him at the time, I have so indicated.

In order to provide continuity and maintain a lively and trim literary style, I have resorted to several unconventional editorial practices. Because General Eichelberger rarely had time to write a complete letter at one sitting, but was forced to dictate snatches at slack moments throughout his busy day, his letters to Miss Em rarely were compact and carefully composed. I have therefore redeployed passages within each letter to avoid excessive redundancies, to give his full thoughts on an important subject, and to maintain some continuity of thought. I have also deleted entire paragraphs and inserted his marginal comments and postscripts into the regular text. I can assure the reader that none of the sentences thus transplanted are in an environment where the context has been changed, which obviously would lead to distortion, and that I have not tampered with the wording except to expand abbreviations into words familiar to the general reader, like changing CP to command post. On the rare occasions when I have combined elements from two letters I have designated the hybrid passage.

To avoid overloading the text with excess impedimenta I have made only limited use of ellipses. Where words have been deleted or a sentence cut short I have so indicated, but I did not think it necessary to insert ellipses when entire passages (or pages), or even complete sentences that belong to paragraphs quoted, have been omitted. Nor have I denoted which paragraphs have been rebuilt from sentences scattered throughout a rambling letter. The reader should understand that only a small portion — perhaps fifteen percent — of General Eichelberger's daily letters to Miss Em have been included and that most entries are distilled from one, two, and sometimes even three letters written on any given day. And because most of these were dictated in haste and under conditions where concern for consistency in spelling and punctuation was second to other considerations, I have simply made the changes necessary to please the copy editor without activating the overworked *sic.*

As editor I had one other function. Although his letters were subject to military censorship, General Eichelberger felt at liberty to comment upon personalities (never upon operations until they had been completed) by the simple expedient of inventing nicknames for the major characters. Consequently his letters are filled with terms such as Sarah, Old Heart of Gold, your Leavenworth friend, your old Palsy Walsy, and the Kemper football coach. Miss Em of course knew the identity of each, and thanks to General Eichelberger's diary and General Clovis Byers' memory, the reader too can share the secret. Otherwise this book would contain as many blank spaces as the most scurrilous of eighteenth-century political tracts.

My friendship with General Eichelberger did cause one difficulty that I had not anticipated: his personality kept getting in the way! I found myself responding to a desire to resurrect one of the most colorful and attractive individuals it has been my good fortune to meet. General Eichelberger had a rare way with people. I have seen him captivate a class of sophomores, charm aristocratic ladies at a United Fund luncheon into inviting a black worker to share their table, admonish a student who griped about the eggs in a cafeteria line, and entertain a two-year-old (who called him Bobby) while enjoying meatballs in our all-purpose kitchen. He used to delight in introducing me to friends who held political views opposite from mine and then walking away, after giving them the target and the range. While generally conservative he made a point of trying to understand all points of view. He enjoyed people — all kinds of people — and because of his lively curiosity, vitality, and basic optimism, he never became an old man. Above all he was honest. He possessed a magnetic sense of humor, sturdy integrity, and a lofty concept of duty and patriotism. So without any conscious effort on my part, what began as a book giving General Eichelberger's view of the war and the men who fought it became also a testament to his own vigorous character and personality.

Many have been indispensable in preparing this volume. Colonel Thomas E. Griess introduced me to several officers who had served with General Eichelberger; Miss Arentzen compiled a subject index to the sprawling dictations, which enabled me to work with this important source without excessive loss of time. Dr. Mattie Russell, Curator of Manuscripts, The Perkins Library, Duke University, went far beyond the call of duty to enable me to make the best possible use of the limited time I could spend with the Eichelberger Papers, while other good friends, Dr. Richard Pearse, Professor Theodore Ropp, and "Colonel" Charles S. Sullivan generously provided quarters during my visits to Durham. General Clyde Eddleman was kind enough to lend this stranger his copy of General Krueger's book and Dr. Forrest Pogue provided helpful information on General Marshall's views of Eichelberger and the Pacific war. The Hon. Tracy S. Voorhees placed at my disposal his correspondence with General Eichelberger while Under Secretary of the Army.

I am particularly indebted to a number of former associates of General Eichelberger, each of whom has added a dimension to my own understanding. From General Jacob L. Devers, a classmate, and Colonel Russell P. (Red) Reeder, Jr., who knew him later at West Point, I was able to broaden my perspective about Eichelberger in the pre-war days. General George H. Decker, Chief of Staff, Sixth Army, and Dr. Roger Egeberg and Brigadier General Paul W. Johnston of MacArthur's staff helped me to fathom the sensitive relationships between Eichelberger and his superiors — they would not necessarily agree with all of the comments to Miss Em about their respective chiefs, but they would recognize and respect the man who emerges from these letters. Brigadier General John R. Jannarone, Assistant Engineer, Eighth Army Headquarters Staff, and presently Dean of the Academic Board at West Point, Major General F. S. Bowen, Jr., the dedicated and energetic "Billy" who was Eichelberger's indispensable G-3, and Major Generals Frederick A. Irving and Clarence A. Martin, two of Eichelberger's favorite division commanders, shared freely their recollections. They showed me how the commander of I Corps and Eighth Army appeared at the time to his subordinates.

No man, it is said, is a hero to his valet. Perhaps this is true of military aides as well, but not so with Colonel William H. (Tommy) Tomlinson, who served Eichelberger as an aide during the closing months of the war and afterwards in Japan. His respect and affection for "the Old Man" prompted him to bring several points to my attention and, despite heavy family responsibilities of his own, moved him to continue to attend Miss Em throughout her long, final illness. More than any words could convey, his unselfish actions give meaning to what I heard so often in my interviews: Eichelberger treated his staff as his family. Obviously they reciprocated.

By far my greatest debt is to the "kid brother" of this military family, General Clovis E. Byers, who was indispensable in many ways. His reactions to my original notes, his helpful suggestions during memorable conversations, his candid and patient answers to questions that lesser men would have considered impertinent, his unrivalled understanding of the man Eichelberger and of the General's problems, his detailed letters that made history of fleeting references in the Eichelberger correspondence, and his gentle criticisms — which were free of any intention to influence what I might want to write — have added immeasurably to this volume. General and Mrs. Byers opened their home to me whenever I was in Washington, and the conversations that went long into the night — and often far afield from the subject of these letters — greatly broadened my outlook in things military. I now know why Eichelberger placed such a high value upon his services.

And almost in the same breath, I would like to acknowledge the availing help of Virginia Westall, the General's friend and secretary. By making order of his dictations, providing assistance in locating missing papers and former subordinates, and answering cheerfully all cries for assistance, she too has been indispensable. Like Tommy Tomlinson, she continued to serve Miss Em long after General Eichelberger had died.

I am indebted (and without generous financial support from Allegheny College, it would be in more than one sense) to Mrs. K. K. Robertson who typed the final manuscript with unerring accuracy and something more than a professional interest; to Mr. Edward J. Krasnoborski, Cartographer, Department of History, West Point, for preparing the fine maps that are indispensable in a book of this kind; and especially to Mr. Roy E. Larson, Vice Chairman of *Life,* who made it possible for me to include the superb Strock pictures that speak even louder than Eichelberger's words of the terrible conditions at Buna.

Finally I would express my thanks to two unusual ladies. My wife, who suffers sometimes from the illusion that she is a Civil War widow, encouraged me to set aside domestic chores in the hope that the finished product might be in Miss Em's hands while she was still able to enjoy it. She was as fond of the General as I and we both regret that Miss Em died before the book was published. For her part, I would thank Miss Em for her trust. Never once did she ask that anything be deleted or censored: it was enough for her to know that I was at work on the book and obviously enjoying it.

It is fitting that this volume, like the letters themselves and the life of the man who wrote them, be dedicated to Dear Miss Em.

Jay Luvaas

Dear Miss Em

CHAPTER ONE

Introduction

We have difficulty in following the satellites of MacArthur, for like those of Jupiter, we cannot see the moons on account of the brilliance of the planet.... Many of us would like to know who the agents are that execute the well laid plans of the boss. Even the Gods were alleged to have their weaknesses.[1]

The recipient of this letter, written toward the end of World War II by a retired American general, was one of many unknown soldiers who served under MacArthur. General Robert L. Eichelberger successfully led the I Corps and later the U.S. Eighth Army throughout the war in the Southwest Pacific. After the surrender he remained in Japan as head of the Army of Occupation until the summer of 1948, when he retired from active service to write his memoirs, *Our Jungle Road to Tokyo*. Except for a brief period as Consultant to the Secretary of the Army on Far Eastern affairs during the Korean War, when his knowledge of "the MacArthur personality and of the idiosyncrasies of his principal staff members" came into play,[2] General Eichelberger spent his last years in comparative retirement in his wife's hometown of Asheville, North Carolina. "Retirement" is perhaps a misleading word, for he was perpetually active in civic and educational affairs, he wrote and lectured widely on current political and military issues, and his lively interest in the world about him kept him from ever becoming an "old" soldier. He died in Asheville on September 27, 1961. He was seventy-five.

To General MacArthur, Eichelberger was always "one of the army's most brilliant commanders." Other high-ranking officers knew him as an outstanding commander, leader, and administrator, and one prominent member of his military family spoke for many whose careers had touched his when he observed, "it was through his rare human understanding that he attained his greatest stature."

This was apparent even to those who were not privileged to know him closely. When news of his death reached Yokohama, a retired ricksha-man solemnly presented the United States Consulate there with 3,000 yen in order to send flowers to the family. "If I only had one million yen," he explained, "I would go to Asheville." He could not forget the tall, friendly man who had given him permission to keep his ricksha in front of Eighth Army Headquarters, and who after leaving Japan had never failed to send a package at Christmas time.[3]

Robert Lawrence Eichelberger was born in Urbana, Ohio, on March 9, 1886.[4] His father was a prominent lawyer who had served for a time in the Union army; his mother was a Southern girl who could remember the ravages of war when the armies had clashed near her family home in Port Gibson, Mississippi. The youngest of five surviving children, Robert Eichelberger spent a happy boyhood on the farm built by his grandfather before the Civil War. Upon graduation from Urbana High School, he attended Ohio State University for two years before entering the Military Academy at West Point in 1905. He graduated in 1909, sixty-eighth in a class of one hundred and three.

There were twenty-eight members from this class who would become general officers, including two Chinese students who later served in their own army. Several attained supreme distinction during World War II. General Jacob Devers commanded the United States Forces in North Africa and later the Sixth Army Group in southern France and Germany. General George Patton won undying fame with his Third Army and another less-heralded classmate, General William Simpson, earned respect as commander of the Ninth Army. Major General Edwin Forrest Harding took the Thirty-second Division to New Guinea, and Major General Horace Fuller led the Forty-first Division until it got bogged down on Biak; both were replaced by Eichelberger when he commanded I Corps, acts that caused him considerable pain and embarrassment and led to some bitter feelings on the part of other classmates.

Lieutenant Eichelberger's first assignment after leaving West Point was with the Tenth Infantry at Fort Benjamin Harrison, Indiana. I Company, he later recalled, "had everything from quiet, nice chaps to jail birds and drunks." The only man in the outfit with so much as a high school education was the company clerk who had served a hitch in the penitentiary after absconding with funds from the bank where he had worked. The men gambled and drank away their money on payday and often were worthless for several days afterwards, but they could shoot, they had developed a rough kind of pride "which made them march to exhaustion rather than fall out on long hikes or night forced marches," and, in Eichelberger's later judgment, if properly commanded they "would have been valuable in combat."

He was quick to learn a basic lesson in leadership. "About my first experience with these men was a long annual 200-mile practice march. My uniform shoes were new and I was soon walking on blisters. If I had fallen out I do not believe I would ever have gained the respect of these men. One officer who rode in an ambulance after his feet began to hurt never had any standing... after that." The officers who did stand high in the estimation of the troops were those who looked after the men and paid strict attention to duty, providing an example which Eichelberger claimed had assisted him throughout his career.

In March 1911, when the situation in Mexico threatened to involve units of the United States Army stationed on the border, the Tenth Infantry was sent to San Antonio, Texas, to join the so-called Maneuver Division. (There were no regular divisions in the army at this time, and the 11,000 troops assembled near San Antonio for maneuvers represented the largest concentration since the Philippine Insurrection.)[5] For six months the regiment lived in tents. "There were maneuvers, long practice marches and many of the dull things that made up camp life in those days," Eichelberger later recalled. Many of the older officers had seen fighting in the Spanish-American War and the Philippine Insurrection, and much of their conversation was taken up with stories of life in Cebu, Malabang, Zamboanga, Jolo, and Davao. The young lieutenant who listened wide-eyed to stories of Moro attacks could little dream that one day he would command an army that would liberate these far-off places from the Japanese: it seemed remarkable enough at the time that he would end his tour in command of I Company.

In September the regiment was sent to Panama, where Eichelberger first encountered the jungle. This time, however, it was the jungle itself that had to be conquered, for during his stay in Panama the canal was completed. The camp where Eichelberger was stationed was on the edge of the great cut, and so he had "intimate and daily knowledge of this gigantic engineering feat." Lieutenant Franklin Sibert, who would later command a corps on Mindanao, was one of his friends in the Tenth; Sibert's father, Colonel William Sibert, was in charge of the construction of the Gatun Locks, and gave Eichelberger a marvelous opportunity to satisfy his curiosity and follow the progressive construction of these great locks. "Those were interesting and exciting days," he wrote later. When the first ship steamed through the canal, Lieutenant Eichelberger was aboard.

It was in Panama also that he met Emma Gudger, the lovely and cultivated daughter of Judge H. A. Gudger, Chief Justice of the Canal Zone. She appeared one day as Eichelberger and a number of other interested bachelors of the Tenth were calling on the daughter of Colonel William C. Gorgas, the conquerer of yellow fever in the Canal Zone. What followed can only be described as a whirlwind courtship. The competition was fierce, but with typical zest and determination, and making the most of his infectious charm, the lieutenant pursued "Miss Em" to the altar. They were married on April 3, 1913, and during their years together no couple could have been happier and more devoted. Eichelberger's admiration and affection are expressed in every letter and were evident in each gesture. Emma's staunch loyalty and agonizing concern for her husband's welfare were no less apparent, constituting throughout his career an unusual source of strength, and occasionally of worry. She was always his companion, confidante, and ardent champion, while he never outgrew his need for her, or his boyish desire to please his "dear old doll."

In 1915 Eichelberger was assigned to duty with the Twenty-second Infantry, then stationed on the Mexican Border. He enjoyed border patrol duty: the varied and almost limitless terrain in Arizona was a welcome contrast to the jungle, and it was here that he first witnessed live combat. When the Mexican insurgent leader, Francisco "Pancho" Villa, attacked government troops at Agua Prieta, just across the border from Douglas, Arizona, Eichelberger viewed the fight from the doorway of an old slaughterhouse about a thousand yards distant. "Men were wounded and men died and we had been ordered not to give any water to the Villa forces, but many a canteen was filled at our spigot near the doorway. It is hard to deny water to wounded men." Among the men who passed by the doorway was Rodriguez, one of Villa's principal leaders. "He looked like a Hollywood soldier, with his wide silver-embroidered sombrero, his bolero and pearl handled pistols. He looked us over with hatred such as I never saw again until I tried to give water to a wounded Japanese boy in a jungle at Hollandia, Dutch New Guinea."

Eichelberger remembered the occasion as "a fine fight," and he never got over the fact that some of his fellow officers had elected to remain in the Officers' Club to play cards. "Wouldn't one think that any officer who had taken up the military as a career would have wanted to see the Mexican Army at close hand? To hear the crack of a bullet fired in anger? And yet for several days, the officers crowded around a poker table when permission had been granted for them to go up to the front and see what was going on." Even when the regiment was in reserve, one had only to go three-quarters of a mile to reach the slaughterhouse, where it was possible to stand in perfect safety "and see the effect of fire coming out of Agua Prieta and gauge the enthusiasm of Villa's men for combat." He would witness a similar indifference several years later in Vladivostok, when fierce fighting broke out near the American head-quarters and 1,100 men were massacred in a nearby railroad station. "Many didn't bother even to look out of the window."

To Eichelberger, whose lively curiosity has been likened to that of an energetic cat upon entering a strange room, it was incomprehensible that any officer should fail to take advantage of an opportunity to learn some-thing more about his profession. Had they been studying for the ministry, he snorted, no one would have given the matter any thought. But the soldier's profession was apt to involve fighting, and to his way of thinking, preparation for combat of any kind was a necessary part of the job.

In September 1916 Eichelberger was named professor of Military Science and Tactics at Kemper Military School in Boonville, Missouri. Upon the completion of that academic year he joined the Twentieth Infantry at Fort Douglas, Utah, and, with the expansion of the army made possible by the National Defense Act of 1916, he soon found him-self a captain, in command of a battalion of the Forty-third Infantry. After a brief stint as instructor at the Third Officers' Training Camp in Camp Pike, Arkansas, he went to the War Department General Staff in Washington.

Here he served in the office of Major General William S. Graves, executive assistant to the Chief of Staff. When General Graves left the War Department to command the Eighth Division at Camp Fremont, California, in July 1918, Eichelberger went along as his G-3 (Opera-tions). Although the division originally had been slated for service in Europe, Graves instead was ordered to select a few officers and 5,000 enlisted men — "strong, hardy, [and] fit for service intended" — to form a part of the expeditionary force that was about to sail for Siberia. After months of pressure from allies, the United States government had agreed to joint military action in Siberia, ostensibly to help save some 70,000 Czech soldiers, former Russian prisoners of war and deserters from the Austrian army who had worked their way across Siberia after the Bolshevik revolution. Lacking the necessary transportation to leave Vladivostok for France, where they hoped to continue the fight, the Czechs expanded their control of Eastern Siberia, and so the original purpose of the American intervention had been achieved before any of the allied contingents had landed. There were of course other mo-tives, ranging from an official suspicion of Japanese intentions in the area to a rather hazy hope of stabilizing "any efforts at self-govern-ment or self-defense in which the Russians themselves may be willing to accept assistance." America's allies unfortunately pursued more ambitious policies, and in the ensuing months Major Eichelberger received an advanced education in geography, politics, and the capri-cious behavior of his fellow man.

As Assistant Chief of Staff and later as Chief Intelligence Officer, Eichelberger enjoyed a panoramic view of life in Siberia. Vladivostok was a virtual Babel, with Czech, Cossack, Japanese, American and other allied troops mingling with Chinese coolies, displaced Koreans, German and Turkish prisoners of war, and all sorts of "ungodly looking people." Eichelberger's principal amusement was to sit in a cafe drinking tea, listening to the music and observing the various types of vaudeville characters that drifted by. "I haven't seen a decent looking woman in the town," he assured Miss Em. "The Bolshevikis must have scared them away. All the inhabitants are dirty and smell like Billy Goats." There was certainly here the makings of a good comic opera.[6]

During working hours things were not always so amusing. Eichelberger got caught in a cross fire involving Graves' Chief of Staff, whom he identified in his letters to Miss Em as the "Great I." "As popular as the itch to an armless beggar," this unfortunate officer intrigued unsuccessfully to have Eichelberger sent home, and he so bullied the rest of the staff that ultimately Graves had to relieve him and reduce his rank. Eichelberger was not involved directly in this row, a "rotten thing in every way"; when everyone "took a crack" at the Great I, Eichelberger sadly wrote Miss Em that he had grown "tired of the whole darn bunch."[7]

He became even more disgusted with many of the allied officials he met, particularly after he began work in intelligence. While his descriptions of unusual characters were as colorful as the Cossacks themselves, underlying most of his comments to Miss Em was growing distaste for intrigue and the battle of personalities that he saw being waged at every level. "It is a great life for a poker player."[8]

Eichelberger was particularly incensed by the attitude and actions of the Japanese, who were conducting an aggressive anti-American campaign. Many of the White Russian leaders were puppets of the Japanese or at least were openly supported by them, and it became increasingly evident that the Japanese army intended to gain control of Eastern Siberia and the Chinese Eastern Railway. Numerous incidents revealed a deep-seated hostility toward the Americans. Japanese soldiers often failed to show respect to American officers (Eichelberger was treated rudely on a number of occasions) and even Japanese school children would jeer at their allies. The effect on Eichelberger was pronounced. "This is the best school in Americanism I have ever seen," he informed Miss Em. "Nearly any half-American coming over here would be turned into a real patriot because some of the biggest liars and crooks in the world are assembled here and they are all knocking us."[9]

In later life Eichelberger frequently mentioned that it was in Siberia that he had learned to hate Japanese militarism. There is ample contemporary evidence that this was so, for his letters in 1919 betray almost as strong a dislike for "the monkeys" as any written from New Guinea twenty-five years later.

Eichelberger's daily letters to Miss Em would fill a separate book. Perhaps his description of the attack by General Sergei Rozanoff and his White Russians against troops representing the Siberian National Directorate on 17 November 1919 will convey some sense of the frustrations experienced by Graves and his staff. The action occurred at the railroad station in Vladivostok.

> The big fight ... continued through the night. We had everything from a bombardment by torpedo boats to a lot of artillery fire. Grenades were banging but the worst thing was a machine gun in the corner by our back garden.... There were 21 bodies around it this morning.
>
> Things got too hot for General Gaida [commanding the troops of the National Directorate] — he had his headquarters at the railroad station. They were surrounded and towards morning his men began to surrender. When I went down ... the prisoners (hundreds of them) were being marched away.... When I reached the railway station the last batch of prisoners were lined up against the wall to be shot.... It was a sad blow to democracy as these murderous cutthroats backed by the Japanese are in full control....
>
> From a military standpoint, the Russian student officers and noncoms trained in a British School on Russian Island were the determining factor for Rozanoff. They had discipline, training and equipment while Gaida's men ... were without organization.... I hope this is another step in our early withdrawal."[10]

> November 19, 1919
> Everything is very quiet here now — the debris of the fight is being cleaned up and the bodies recovered. Wild rumors of all kinds are flying around, most of them hinging on the word that the Japanese joined in the fighting against the Gaida troops after dark. I rather doubt this but the Japanese contended that in the interests of humanity the fight should be limited to the railway yards and vicinity, and as the monarchists had machine guns on all the high points the democrats were cooped up and couldn't get out. In addition the ... line of Japanese troops put behind the Rozanoff crowd undoubtedly gave them encouragement. At any rate the Japanese scored a victory over America because Democracy is killed in Eastern Siberia and the Rozanoff crowd being only a small group with all the arms can be controlled by the Japanese, giving them unlimited economic control....
>
> I have collected evidence of Rozanoff troops shooting *wounded prisoners some time after they had surrendered, and then the little minds claim that that bunch should be supported by America because they are anti-Bolsheviki.*
>
> *Women come here pleading to save them and their husbands but we can do nothing. It is a dirty place for Americans to be.*[11]

Eichelberger found himself in many dirty places before he left Siberia. As chief intelligence officer he made frequent and extended trips into the field to keep his outstretched fingers on the pulse of the Japanese as well as the rival Russian factions. He also witnessed most of the fighting in which American soldiers were engaged. Once he was captured by the White Russians and for a few long hours his life appeared to be in jeopardy. On another occasion he led a company in an expedition to root out the partisans on the Suchan plain. A Russian newspaper described what happened when Eichelberger's flanking detachment was discovered. "The bullets begin to whistle in quick succession. The soldiers lie down on the ground. Only Colonel Eichelberger and Major Graves remain standing. After a while, the left flank of our line occupies a hill, from whence it keeps up a fire upon the Partisans.... In this battle, the Americans and Japanese fought side by side for the first time."[12]

"Now that my trip up in the hills is over," Eichelberger reported to Miss Em, "I realize that I had a wonderful time — I also proved to myself that I could stand up and laugh while bullets were passing and other men, old enough to know better, had eyes as big as full moons.... I enjoyed our little engagement thoroughly."[13] He would react similarly at Buna, the first battle the Americans carried to the Japanese in New Guinea. "You will be glad to know that... my nerves are not shot in any way," he wrote to Miss Em soon after assuming command at Buna. "Some of the boys were having a hard time lighting a cigarette and... my hands are steady."[14]

The experience was instructive in another sense, for Eichelberger quickly learned to respect the rugged qualities of the Japanese soldiers. "Their patrolling was meticulous and all points within rifle fire of the main body were carefully covered," he later recalled. "In that fight it was the Japanese rear elements advancing down the ridge who cleared the Reds... and permitted us to resume our advance." Compared to American troops, he found the Japanese "decidedly better trained and certainly better disciplined." Given "equally good leadership... the Japanese would defeat us in battle."[15]

The Siberian experience proved also to be a hard-boiled school in leadership. General Graves had been instructed not to meddle in the civil war, but British and French officials desired to support the anti-Bolshevik forces even after the Armistice was signed in Europe. In their view, Graves was an obstacle as long as he adhered to orders. Even members of the State Department criticized Graves' attitude and occasionally his actions, accusing him of being sympathetic to the Bolsheviks. The Ambassador to Japan contended that he was not friendly enough to the Japanese.[16]

Eichelberger always admired Graves for his tireless efforts to walk a straight path in the midst of intrigue, suspicions, misunderstandings, and growing hostility, with allies that could not always be trusted and with the State Department and the War Department occasionally working at cross-purposes. Graves was a shining example of integrity, courage, and honesty, "a big man in every way." "How he can settle so many questions day after day without having it get on his nerves is more than I can see — he sleeps all night, gets his exercise and gains weight. Even at this critical time, he is cheerful as you please."[17]

Eichelberger's own staff might have posed the same question throughout the Pacific war, and there can be no doubt that the future army commander learned much from Graves not only by the example he set, but from the long and frank discussions that animated their daily walks in the nearby hills. At such times the General would analyze the situation "from every angle," much in the same way that Eichelberger would later confide his most intimate thoughts to his own chief of staff, General Clovis Byers. The only part of his experience in 1919 that he had to learn over again concerned the inevitable "play of personalities." He should have seen and heard enough in Siberia to have learned not to expect too much of his fellow man and yet, to judge from his later reactions, he was surprised to find that "the Great I" — or his equivalent — was apt to show up in any organization.

In March 1920, Miss Em arrived in Vladivostok and soon afterward the couple departed for Japan, where he served on temporary duty until assigned as Assistant Chief of Staff, Military Intelligence, Philippine Department. In October of that year Eichelberger was sent to report on the unsettled conditions in China, and while his specific concern was the Tientsin area, where a United States infantry regiment was stationed, he was free to travel pretty much where he wished. The Eichelbergers found life in China pleasant, varied, and intensely interesting. "No young officer," he later reflected, "ever had a better job or one under more interesting conditions." Among the many fascinating people that Eichelberger encountered in China was Joe Stilwell, whose career was inextricably tied up with that turbulent country; the two would be thrown together again briefly during the closing days of World War II.

Eichelberger's next job was with the Military Intelligence Division in the old War Department. Here his responsibilities continued to be China, the Philippines, and Siberia, and when the conference on the limitations of armaments was held in Washington during 1921 and 1922, his knowledge of the Far East probably won him the assignment as liaison officer with the Chinese delegation. In 1924, primarily because the chances of eventual promotion to general rank seemed brighter, he transferred to the Adjutant General's Department.

The next year he went back to school. In 1926 Eichelberger was at the top of a list of "Distinguished Graduates" of the Command and General Staff School at Fort Leavenworth (Dwight D. Eisenhower stood number one in the class), where he remained for three more years as

Adjutant General and instructor. He then attended the Army War College in Washington, earning a superior rating, and in August 1931 he returned to West Point as Adjutant and Secretary of the Academic Board.

In July 1935, Lieutenant Colonel Eichelberger became Secretary to the War Department General Staff. The Chief of Staff at that time was already a household word, Major General Douglas MacArthur, and in later days Eichelberger reminisced frequently about his associations with the most publicized and controversial American soldier in modern times.

His first memory of MacArthur was in 1911, when both were in San Antonio as part of the Maneuver Division. "A handsome young captain of Engineers," MacArthur impressed Eichelberger as "a fine looking, upstanding officer" whose reputation as a coming leader was enhanced by his ability to "strike attitudes to impress the spectators." Eichelberger's most vivid recollection was seeing MacArthur in front of a drugstore one night, "standing a bit aloof from the rest of us and looking off in the distance with what I have always considered in other people to be a Napoleonic stance."

In 1933 MacArthur delivered the commencement address at West Point, and Eichelberger was impressed by the impassioned attack he launched on that occasion against pacifist organizations and other politicians who would sacrifice national defense in the name of economy. He remembered in particular MacArthur's eloquent plea not to break faith with those who had met death on top of a trench, "gentlemen unafraid." The Chief of Staff spoke to a national audience on the radio. "It took courage to face facts as he did that day," and Eichelberger had only praise for this fellow officer and distinguished spokesman for the Military Academy. "Those who criticized him that day spoke of his theatrical attitude in the way he let his voice quiver ... during the impressive parts of his talk. This made no impression on me at the time."[18]

In his new position Eichelberger found MacArthur "very friendly and extremely courteous. His mind was scintillating. At times he would show great dramatic ability." He was bothered somewhat by MacArthur's unconventional hours, which made it difficult to maintain a regular work schedule, but his impressions of MacArthur during this period were distinctly favorable. "He told me many of his troubles as Chief of Staff so that I could carry over this information to the new regime that might arrive. Many times he talked to me at length about what he called the conspiracy between the Navy and the National Guard to reduce the army to nothing but a bunch of inspectors. He mentioned individuals by name and I am sure in his own heart he felt it was the truth." There would be similar conversations when he joined MacArthur in the Pacific.

For his part, MacArthur was "particularly impressed" with Eichelberger's "comprehensive grasp of the Army's major problems, and of the War Department functioning." Two days after he was officially named Military Adviser of the Commonwealth Government of the Philippines, MacArthur paid tribute to Eichelberger's "tact, loyalty, intelligence and initiative. I shall watch your future career," he promised, "with keen interest."[19]

MacArthur's successor was General Malin Craig, "a wise and understanding mentor." With Craig, Eichelberger enjoyed the same kind of association that had characterized his years with Graves, except that instead of the long walks that he had shared with Graves, he now listened to the troubles of his chief over the lunch table. "I always sat facing a large portrait of William Tecumseh Sherman, and soon I felt I knew what made the grim-faced Sherman grim."[20]

As the war clouds began to darken over Europe, Eichelberger thought increasingly of transferring back to the infantry. His efficiency reports from his tour at West Point indicated that he was considered qualified for command of an infantry division, and Craig from time to time would volunteer the comment, "You ought to be with troops in case of war." Finally, in the summer of 1937, Eichelberger submitted a one-line letter: "I request that I be transferred to the infantry." He continued as Secretary to the General Staff for another year, when he attended the Infantry School at Fort Benning, and then assumed command of the Thirtieth Infantry, which was stationed at the Presidio of San Francisco.

This was "one of the proud moments" of Eichelberger's life. It also provided the kind of experience necessary for higher command, for at maneuvers, which at one time involved three divisions, Eichelberger "served as just about everything" from division commander to chief of staff. (Two of these divisions, the Fortieth and the Forty-first, were National Guard units that later came under his command in the Pacific.) And as Assistant Division Commander of the Third Division he acquired valuable experience during the amphibious exercises in Monterey Bay.

Obviously the years spent behind a desk had not impaired Eichelberger's effectiveness as a leader. He inherited a serious morale problem in the Thirtieth, but an improved atmosphere in the Officers' Club and careful attention to the needs of the enlisted men paid big dividends. Eichelberger worked hard to improve the barracks, supported every regimental athletic team, and insisted that his officers place the interests of the soldier ahead of their own comforts. "I found it helped if I turned out in the rain every morning to show that the plight of the men was known to me." Before long, most junior officers joined the "Dawn Patrol."

Like many officers who went on to achieve high rank, Eichelberger probably enjoyed his days as regimental commander as much as any subsequent service. It brought him into close touch with the men, and his record with the Thirtieth caught the attention of his superiors. One of his fondest memories was the farewell review: the tears of the old noncommissioned officers as they shook hands after the ceremony "was perhaps the greatest reward that I ever have attained in the army."

Fortunately there were other and more tangible rewards. In October 1940 Eichelberger was promoted to brigadier general and soon afterwards he was appointed Superintendent of the Military Academy. He always had a special place in his heart for West Point and during his years in the Pacific he used to dream occasionally of the possibilities of returning there in some capacity when the fighting was over. From the Philippines, the beauty and sheltered atmosphere of West Point must have tugged hard at cherished memories.

To hear Eichelberger talk in later years, one could easily come away with the impression that his most important accomplishment at West Point had been to recruit Earl Blaik to rebuild Army's football fortunes. His main mission, however, was to produce officers fit to command in modern war, and to accomplish this Eichelberger introduced a series of reforms to bring both the training and the education in line with what the times demanded. He introduced fatigue uniforms, expanded the time devoted to military training and instruction, and arranged for the cadets to maneuver with National Guard units in New Jersey. He also cut back drastically on horseback riding so that the cadets could devote more time to developing skills relevant to the "gasoline age." He made a special effort to make the cadets air-minded, even to the extent of devising a plan that would permit those who were interested to obtain their wings upon graduation.

Replacing the horse with the airplane antagonized a few old sabers in the cavalry, but none could deny that Eichelberger "left behind him a West Point that was far better prepared to cope with the challenge of total war than the Academy of 1917–18." Not the least of his accomplishments was his vigorous fight to preserve the four-year course of instruction in the face of pressures to accelerate the program in order to produce more officers. This had been done with harmful effects in World War I, and although the course ultimately was cut back to three years, the educational program was not seriously impaired. Thanks to Eichelberger, it was merely put on a war footing.[21]

When Japan struck at Pearl Harbor, it was time for Eichelberger himself to go on a war footing. Upon request for a command in the field, he was assigned in January 1942 to command of the Seventy-seventh Division, which was then being organized at Fort Jackson, South Carolina. While the principal officers of the new division attended brief courses at the appropriate military schools (for Eichelberger and certain of his staff this meant a return to Fort Leavenworth for several weeks), a cadre of experienced officers and enlisted men was taken from an active division to organize and train the recruits. The Seventy-seventh was activated in March 1942, and applying the same techniques that had worked so well with the Thirtieth Infantry, Eichelberger and his staff soon had the division whipped into such good shape that in June he was asked to stage a demonstration calculated to convince Sir Winston Churchill and his military advisers of the ability of the United States to raise an army capable of fighting alongside the experienced British in Europe. It was "a stirring show," a "competent, professional performance" in the judgment of Churchill's Chief of Staff, who also "ventured the opinion that it would be murder to pit them against continental soldiery." But Churchill was impressed with the ability of his American allies to mass-produce an army as well as the necessary materiel.[22]

Even before this demonstration, Eichelberger was a marked man. Early in June, he had been ordered to form the XI Corps in Chicago. Within two weeks, he was in Washington, where plans were afoot to give him command of a proposed amphibious corps for use in the forthcoming North African landings. On 22 June, he was named commander of I Corps, and early in August, while observing amphibious exercises of the Ninth Division in the Chesapeake Bay, he received a sudden summons to the office of General George Catlett Marshall.

There had been an abrupt change of plans. The officer originally designated for a corps command in the Southwest Pacific Area, Major General Robert C. Richardson, objected to serving under Australians. Eichelberger and his staff were available; they had some acquaintance with amphibious forces; and Eichelberger had got on well with MacArthur when the latter was Chief of Staff. Accordingly Eichelberger and I Corps headquarters were ordered to proceed to Australia without delay. After ten days of preparation and briefing, General Eichelberger and a few of his staff boarded a B-24 bomber bound for Australia, where General MacArthur was organizing his forces for a counteroffensive against the Japanese in New Guinea.

"When there is a war," Miss Em observed quietly, "you always seem to go to the queerest places." This time she had special reason for feeling apprehensive: General Malin Craig had already communicated his fears for the career of a friend and protégé now sent to serve under a man considered by many in the old army as selfish and at times vindictive. As the next four years — and the following letters — would testify, these were no idle worries, but if such thoughts preyed upon the mind of General Eichelberger as he and the excited members of his staff flew to Sydney, he kept them to himself.

There is no need here to tell the story of what happened to General Eichelberger during the war; that was, after all, the original intent of his letters to Miss Em. But the significance of his accomplishments does require brief comment, if only to place his activities in some sort of historical perspective.

At Buna, to put it bluntly, he pulled MacArthur's chestnuts out of the fire. Prior to his intervention, the American forces had become bogged down in the swamps and were rapidly falling victim to the mosquitoes as well as the Japanese. The American soldiers were not adequately trained and equipped for this kind of warfare; their morale was shot, their leaders were at wit's end, and lateral contact among the units on separate fronts was extremely difficult. On the other hand, the Japanese were well fortified, easily reinforced, and they enjoyed good lateral communications. Their soldiers, to quote Eichelberger, "were a commander's dream. They never exposed themselves unnecessarily, they never fired until they had a good target, and they obeyed the orders of their officers while taking perfect cover."[23] One might add that thus far in the war they had not been driven from their own positions.

Eichelberger's arrival is described by his immediate superior, General Sir E. F. Herring, as "a very pure breath of fresh air" that "blew away a great deal of the impurities that were stopping us getting on with the job."[24] He analyzed the situation quickly, reorganized and regrouped the badly intermixed forces, improved the supply problem, strengthened the chain of command, and provided the dynamic leadership necessary to infuse new life and spirit into the operation at every level. The capture of Buna only a month after assuming command gave Eichelberger the first victory won over Japanese forces fighting to hold a fortified position since the allies first began their offensive at Guadalcanal.[25] And the possession of Buna and Sanananda gave MacArthur the necessary sites for airstrips so vital to any further advance along the New Guinea axis. Finally, Buna has given subsequent generations of soldiers a convincing demonstration of vigorous and efficient leadership. Normally for the tide of victory to be changed some new element must be inserted — more troops, better equipment, or a change in command.[26] There were no reinforcements to speak of even after Eichelberger took over at Buna and he never had what he needed by way of artillery or air support; the difference between victory and defeat on this occasion was simply Eichelberger. It is for this reason that Buna remains as a case study of the corps commander in modern battle in the leadership course at the United States Army Command and General Staff College, Fort Leavenworth.

Eichelberger's next battle was Hollandia, the largest amphibious landing up to that time in the Southwest Pacific. Because this was the first operation where MacArthur dared to reach out beyond range of land-based fighter cover, the Japanese were caught completely by surprise. Consequently, logistics rather than tactics became the main consideration, and in the quick and efficient way that Eichelberger established his forces ashore and constructed the bases and airfields necessary to support forthcoming operations at Wakde-Sarmi and Biak, he performed what his Chief of Staff later styled "a logistical miracle."[27] This is not the kind of work that wins headlines, but failure to maintain a rigorous schedule, and in the face of unforeseen difficulties, would have meant a severe setback for MacArthur's further plans.

Scarcely was the situation in hand at Hollandia when Eichelberger was sent, again at the eleventh hour, to accelerate operations that were behind schedule at Biak. Again, as at Buna, it was necessary to reorganize the forces, devise new tactical plans, and put life into a sagging offensive. A week after his arrival the main objectives had been captured and the critical phase of the battle was over, giving MacArthur a vital site for the construction of heavy bomber fields.

Known widely for his administrative abilities even before the war, Eichelberger's next achievement was to prepare the new Eighth Army staff, most of which he inherited, for the complex and demanding operations that lay ahead. It was a first-rate staff — in his estimation the best — and throughout the Philippine campaign it astonished Pacific veterans with its versatility and the tempo of the operations it planned and staged. In one span of forty-four days, for example, the Eighth Army conducted fourteen major landings and twenty-four smaller operations; by 1 May 1945, it was involved in operations simultaneously on all of the major and numerous of the smaller islands in the central and southern Philippines. The new staff "worked out, intelligently and with mathematical accuracy, the hazards and supply realities of our landings. Never once were its calculations seriously in error. Never once were we forced to resort to the airdrop of supplies because of the failure, or congestion, of seaborne transport."[28] Eichelberger freely gave the credit to the "pick and shovel boys" who accomplished such marvels, but it was "the old man" himself who provided the leadership, the example, and the atmosphere of mutual confidence which inspired loyalty in all of his subordinates. In dealing with MacArthur, Eichelberger could never be sure exactly how much his own difficulties may have been due to the actions of MacArthur's chief of staff. No such confusion existed among Eichelberger's subordinates. Even though General Byers enjoyed his complete confidence and support, he never inserted himself as a third force between the commander and another officer.

Byers remembers the staff as a happy military family and in this sense, at least in the Pacific war, it was unique. Eichelberger treated Byers as a kid brother and the rest of the immediate family as favorite sons. He took a personal interest in them and their problems, he trusted them as one would members of his own family, and there was never any "generation gap" in communications. He always asked opinions and backed the decisions of his subordinates. Each man knew where he stood and had confidence in "Uncle Bob's" ability to make the right decision. "He had the happy faculty of looking over your shoulder without making it appear that he was doing so," General Frank E. Bowen has stated. "He could get along with everybody and his brother." Consequently there were few who served under Eichelberger who did not have the highest regard for him, and his staff was fiercely loyal. It probably would not have surprised them to learn that after the war, when General Eichelberger was offered an opportunity to become Assistant Chief of Staff at the Pentagon, he remained in Japan because he wished to protect and advance the careers of "his boys."[29]

Eichelberger's crowning achievement in World War II was the part his Eighth Army played in the liberation of the Philippines. General MacArthur described the Visayan operations as "a model of what a light but aggressive command can accomplish in rapid exploitation." General Marshall wrote of the "lightning speed" of Eichelberger's amphibious thrusts at Panay, Cebu, and Mindanao. MacArthur used Eichelberger to accelerate the drive for Manila and he planned a leading role for the Eighth Army in the projected invasion of Japan. "No army of this war," he proclaimed, "has achieved greater glory and distinction. . . ."[30]

This much can be deduced from the published histories, even though the Eighth Army runs a poor second to General Walter Krueger's Sixth Army in the attention it has received. To publicize the achievements of the men he commanded, "the ordinary, muddy, malarial, embattled," and overburdened GIs, Eichelberger in 1949 collaborated with a professional journalist to produce *Our Jungle Road to Tokyo,* which was also serialized in *The Saturday Evening Post.* Although his own feelings are frequently revealed, the tone of his criticisms is subdued even though he had left Japan in order to write without MacArthur peering over his shoulder. Had Eichelberger been intent on telling his own story, there would have been little justification for publishing *Dear Miss Em.* One did not have to be around him very long to appreciate his restraint in print.

He unburdened himself to Miss Em, whom he wrote faithfully every day and sometimes as often as four times a day, depending upon the amount of time he could spare. "I don't know how often you have been separated from Marie for long periods of time," he remarked to his chief of staff as they were about to depart for Austrialia, "but the matter of writing is most important! When I went to Siberia Miss Em and I realized that if you wrote every couple of weeks there was nothing you dare tell because of censorship. If you wrote every week it was a little better, but if you wrote every day there was so much of interest to tell that it was hard to find time to tell it. Then when we got back together, we had shared so much that the gap in our lives did not appear to be so great as it otherwise would have been."[31]

And in trying to plug this gap General Eichelberger made his letters "as interesting as possible" without violating the rules of the military censor. "Everything I see or do brings the thought, 'I wonder how Miss Em would like that,' or 'I wish Miss Em could see that'."[32] For a few minutes each day he could share his emotions and experiences with Miss Em. Her letters, which unfortunately have been destroyed, searched for his hopes and fears and occasionally sounded warnings of some real or imagined threat to his career. In turn he explained what he could about his campaigns, revealing an almost boyish pride in his growing accomplishments, and kept her well posted throughout on the shifting personal relations with MacArthur and the others at General Headquarters. Sometimes to clarify a previous statement or to put at rest some rumor, he wrote trenchantly about his colleagues, and to focus on this aspect of his letters would suggest that Eichelberger spent much of his time sulking in his tent.

Nothing could be further from the truth. Although his personal letters during the dark days of 1943 reveal hurt feelings, occasional bitterness, and a growing frustration at the thought that the war was moving away from him, along the New Guinea coast, while he administered a training command in Australia and was denied several opportunities to command armies elsewhere, to anyone outside of his intimate military family he exuded optimism and good cheer. Indeed, one of the themes that jumps out of his letters was the striking way in which Eichelberger overcame discouragement and set aside bitterness to triumph in every sense of the word. To show him as he usually appeared to his subordinate commanders, as a man whose own mental outlook seemed always optimistic and good-natured, would be to deny one of his great strengths, his ability to "cultivate the habit of happiness." "It is hard to get a fellow down who has a grin on his face."[33]

At the risk of making Eichelberger appear at times a vain and dissatisfied man, which most assuredly he was not, his criticisms of the other generals are included because of their unusual historical interest. Anything about General MacArthur is apt to be significant, and he so dominated the scene that the general public to this day has only a hazy impression of the other "satellites." In fairness to Eichelberger, it should be noted that his comments do not always reflect full knowledge of the facts in a given situation, nor is it to be assumed that they represent his final verdict as he reflected about the war in later years. Sometimes he merely repeated a story for Miss Em's amusement; most of the high-ranking officers were people she had known long before the war, and any incident that might have contributed to her insight into the behavior of MacArthur and the others was apt to be included in the letters.

To avoid passing such juicy tidbits to the censor, Eichelberger used a primitive code whenever he dealt in personalities. He would praise General MacArthur, refer frequently to the "Big Chief," and write frankly of "Sarah" (Sarah Bernhardt). Similarly whenever he mentioned "your palsy walsy," "old heart of gold," and "molasses in January," Miss Em knew that he meant General Walter Krueger. If an old acquaintance turned up unexpectedly, Eichelberger would identify him not by name but by associating him with an event or place that would mean something to Miss Em. If any doubt remained, he would casually identify him by name in the next letter, assuming that the story had already slipped quietly by the censor. In this way he felt few inhibitions in sharing his thoughts of the moment, and the letters contain many refreshing, candid, and fascinating descriptions of the leading personalities in the Pacific.

General Eichelberger did not communicate any closely kept or explosive military secrets, for he was too scrupulous to write anything that conceivably could be of help or comfort to the enemy. He did try, however, to educate Miss Em as to what she might expect next in New Guinea and the Philippines, and in teaching her about the problems to be overcome in logistics and air power he also unwittingly instructs the general reader in the peculiar nature of the Pacific war. Frequently he explained what had happened after some landing, when the news had already appeared in the papers back home, but his letters to Miss Em are scarcely sensational even when he reveals something of the "inside story."

He seems at times to have been obsessed with publicity. Eichelberger was not averse to recognition and praise: he had a pardonable touch of vanity and he resented the way in which MacArthur managed the publicity, making an unknown soldier of Eichelberger and any other general who served in the area. But Eichelberger was every bit as anxious to publicize and reward the achievements of his men as he was to gain recognition for himself, and as the war dragged on he merely wanted Miss Em to know more than the press handouts from GHQ would reveal of what he and his "lads" had been doing. He also came to view publicity as a necessary weapon in the fight to obtain the supreme command for MacArthur in the final drive against Japan, and he learned — the hard way — that as long as "Sarah" occupied the stage no figures were going to "rise up between him and his place in history." For Miss Em, with names like Patton in the headlines every day, this was always a difficult situation to accept, but Eichelberger, much as he would have liked to have had the accomplishments of the Eighth Army given more play, came to view personal publicity of the sort he had enjoyed after Buna as something fully as dangerous as a rattlesnake in his pocket. "If I would get all the publicity you would like. . . . I would never get the chance to fight in the battle of Japan," he cautioned, "and you know that is a fact."[34] Certainly it was a reasonable fear.

Eichelberger had an unusual sense of history. He read widely, and his knowledge of the past enabled him to view himself and the men and events around him in a historical perspective. He kept meticulous notes, sometimes to the extent of having his chief of staff draw up his own memoranda of conversations with MacArthur so that the two might compare notes. His diary in the early years was simply a record of his activities, but by 1944 he began to record things that he dared not write to Miss Em because of the censor. Always aware that "history is . . . in the making right here," Eichelberger wanted to be sure that Miss Em could "appreciate the historical significance" of what was happening. He kept all letters that seemed of special importance, and his files contain frequent memoranda of conversations, some of which were recorded during battle. Even the photographs and pictures he preserved are annotated.

The result is not only a detailed record, but an intimate picture of a vibrant personality. War has grown so immense and impersonal that rarely do we have the opportunity to become acquainted with the main actors. Most memoirs written by top-ranking generals tend to be so crowded with the details of battles and campaigns and so restrained in the handling of personalities that we get a superficial impression of the man with the stars on his shoulder.

The letters to Miss Em, however, preserve a colorful and attractive figure. Eichelberger was endowed with a rich sense of humor that never left him, even in times of hurt and disappointment. His insight was both vivid and profound, and his language was always picturesque: one general was a "cuff snapper," another "has no more dash than a circus elephant," and the conflict between personalities maneuvering for power reminded him of a poker game "where the cuspidor was put on the center of the table because no one dared look away to spit."[35] We learn how the man reacted to a visit with the wounded (who could see only the disciplined face of the commander), his thoughts as he takes a last, lingering look at the military cemetery filled with men who had obeyed his orders, his mental preparations aboard ship in a convoy steaming toward the far shore and its hidden perils. We see him anxious to prod one sluggish subordinate and fighting hard to revive the career of another. We can share his joy when the dark days that followed Buna began to brighten and one successful campaign followed another. We can understand his frustrations, his concerns and his hopes and we are privy to his initial observations and opinions recorded within hours of some memorable event. In this respect *Dear Miss Em* provides us with an inside view of the men who fought the war in a remote and relatively unpublicized theater. Certainly if one compares these letters with the *Rommel Papers,* which was drawn from similar materials, we see less of the tactics and strategy of the campaigns, but a great deal more of the man who was commander. But then, Rommel was never known for his sense of humor![36]

The general reader will gain some appreciation for the special character of the Pacific war, the problems of amphibious warfare, the exorbitant demands upon logistics, and the rigors of life in the jungle. He will get more than a glimpse of interservice rivalry, the management of news, and the manipulation of casualty statistics, and he will probably develop ambivalent feelings toward MacArthur the man, while sharing Eichelberger's respect for the strategist who pried a determined enemy from one strong position after another. It was a savage war, and the emotions it aroused will seem foreign to a generation that has adopted, for its standard, a symbol of peace. The young may have difficulty even in understanding Eichelberger's concept of duty, which guided him throughout life and which he states on several occasions with simple eloquence.

For the military reader, the book is an object lesson in leadership. Eichelberger possessed in abundance the essential ingredients of good leadership — integrity, loyalty, sound judgment, knowledge, courage, and human understanding. Watch him operate at Buna and Biak; observe the general in his dealings with subordinates on the staff and in the field; listen to what he says to the men.

Eichelberger insisted on personally verifying conditions in every situation, which is why he and many of his staff spent so much time in the field. On the Mexican border this meant a short walk to a place where as a neutral he could observe the fighting; in Siberia it took him far into the field; and in the Pacific, whether by jeep, on foot, in a launch, or in his converted bomber, Eichelberger was always present to determine the exact nature of the problems his men confronted. For this reason he never stampeded over rumors. His success as commander underscores the old maxim, "Time spent in reconnaissance is never wasted."

"The personal appearance of General Eichelberger on the various battlefields had a profound effect," one of his division commanders has testified. "In many cases it caused operations to be speeded up and it insured early success. Leaders and troops cannot but be impressed and inspired to have their commander in their midst. And he coupled reports with first hand information to make decisions where they were required."[37] Eichelberger always welcomed the suggestions of those principally concerned with some specific problem. Never once after Biak did he "take over" in a tactical situation, but he was always on hand to provide support and to see for himself what was going on. "This demonstration of confidence in his subordinates drew them to him" because they knew that he would never relieve a commander without personally verifying the situation. On one occasion, General Byers recalls, Major General G. A. Vasey, commanding the Australian Seventh Division, wanted to relieve Brigadier General Jens A. Doe, "whose 163rd Infantry of the 41st Division wasn't moving fast enough. Bob suggested that Vasey go with him to visit Doe's front line. They went and on their return Vasey thanked Bob for preventing him from making one of the worst mistakes a commander can make. Doe's forces had captured the offending position while Bob and Vasey were there and Vasey saw for himself the fine work that was being done. Many learned of the incident — not from Bob — and they never forgot it."[38] Some of Eichelberger's criticisms of other senior cammanders was that they did commit such mistakes, and his support of Major General Frederick A. Irving after the latter had been relieved on Leyte indicates his conviction that a real injustice had been done.

Eichelberger was also conscious of the impact of his visits upon morale. Here too he applied lessons that he had grasped early in his career, when he learned that blister or no, an officer marched with his men. At least a leader does.

After one of his inspection tours in Siberia he wrote scathingly of a friend who "has himself beautifully fixed up with a bedroom, sitting room, bath and office. In fact everyone *but his men* were very comfortable."[39] Eichelberger's desire to be seen during moments of discomfort and depression among his men had led to the "Dawn Patrol," with the Thirtieth Infantry, and in New Guinea this was responsible for one of the truly rare moments that he lost his temper with his chief of staff. The occasion was one of his first visits to the front at Buna. General Byers, fearing (with good reason that a Japanese sniper might put an end to it all, began a diverting conversation on the need for vitamin pills (General Eichelberger was a great believer in pills) as he pretended to straighten the General's collar, meanwhile removing, unnoticed, the telltale insignia. That evening when they returned and Eichelberger was fuming about having misplaced the pin of stars, Byers confessed. Eichelberger nearly exploded. "I want the boys to know I'm here with them," he insisted. "Hell, what's the use of my going up front if I go incognito?" Without the insignia, the risks he had taken may well have been wasted.[40]

Eichelberger also made it a point to speak to troops whenever possible, particularly as they moved into combat. Pétain at Verdun had found this an effective technique for rebuilding morale, and Eichelberger gave so many talks to "the lads" that he almost felt "destined to become an inspirational speaker of the Billy Sunday type." "It wasn't what he said," another has written, "it was the way he said it.... His speech — if it could be called a speech — was a package of cajolery, pats on the back and a firm boot in the pants all wrapped into one.... When he finished the reserves went in and did a wonderful job. Nothing could stop them."[41]

Eichelberger's presence also assured speed and flexibility in all Eighth

Army operations. In spirit he belonged among the successful exponents of *Blitzkrieg* in his insistence upon rapid exploitation and in the unexpected thrust and sustained tempo of his operations. Often quoting General Ulysses S. Grant to the effect that a commander must never take counsel of his fears, Eichelberger firmly believed that speed and constant pressure upon the enemy in the long run would save lives, and his operations follow a consistent pattern — strategic and tactical surprise in the amphibious assault, quick exploitation to seize key objectives and to keep the enemy off balance, and the final mopping up, which usually he left to the Philippine guerillas as he shifted forces for still another landing. It was a new kind of war that he conducted in the Philippines; the obvious difference between Eichelberger and the famed desert generals in North Africa was that he may be suspected of having webbed feet!

Miss Em of course was aware of his superb contribution all the time; she knew much more than she read in the papers.

So apparently did his old friend and classmate Patton, who confessed: "In my limited experience with amphibious attacks, I found them the most dangerous form of sport yet devised." With the fighting over in Europe, Patton was spoiling for further opportunities in the East. "If I should be so fortunate, I am going to sit at your feet and learn how to do it."[42]

Notes

The Eichelberger letters have been deposited with the Flowers Collection, The William R. Perkins Library, Duke University, Durham, North Carolina. All citations to his personal correspondence, unless otherwise indicated, refer to these letters.

1. Maj. Gen. William D. Connor as quoted in Gen. R. L. Eichelberger to Mrs. Eichelberger, 31 May 1945. Eichelberger Papers, Duke University.
2. W. J. Garvin to Tracy S. Voorhees, 9 June 1965, Eichelberger Papers.
3. "He Lost an Old and Dear Friend," Durham *Morning Herald,* 1 October 1961; Obituary, *New York Times,* 27 September 1961; *The Phi Gamma Delta,* November 1961.
4. All information pertaining to the early career of General Eichelberger is taken from his voluminous dictations, 1952-60, a complete copy of which is deposited in The William R. Perkins Library. Hereafter cited as "Eichelberger Dictations."
5. D. Clayton James, *The Years of MacArthur,* vol. I, *1880-1941* (Boston: Houghton-Mifflin, 1970), p. 106.
6. Eichelberger to Miss Em, 4 September 1918, 16 January 1919.
7. Ibid., 29 November 1918, 22, 23 September 1919.
8. Ibid., 15 February 1919.
9. Ibid., 4 May 1919.
10. Ibid., 18 November 1919.
11. Ibid., 19 November 1919.
12. "Newspaper Summary" from *Echo,* 12 July 1919. Eichelberger Papers.

13. *Eichelberger to Miss Em, 9 July 1919.*

14. *Ibid., 5 December 1942.*

15. Eichelberger Dictations, 23 September 1957.

16. Betty Miller Unterberger, *America's Siberian Expedition, 1918-1920.* (Durham, Duke University Press, 1956), pp. 124-125.

17. Eichelberger to Miss Em, 5 March 1919.

18 Later MacArthur told Eichelberger that he had been called to the White House by President Roosevelt and reproved for his remarks. See also James, *Years of MacArthur,* pp. 431–432.

19. MacArthur to Eichelberger, September 20, 1935, Eichelberger Papers; Eichelberger Dictations, March 28, 1955. In his *Reminiscences,* MacArthur first mentioned Eichelberger as an officer "already noted for his administrative ability." Douglas MacArthur, *Reminiscences* (New York: McGraw-Hill, 1964), p. 157.

20. Robert L. Eichelberger, *Our Jungle Road to Tokyo* (New York: Viking Press, 1950), p. xvii.

21. Ibid., pp. xviii–xxi; Thomas J. Fleming, *West Point: The Men and Times of the United States Military Academy* (New York: William Morrow & Co., 1969), pp. 320–321.

22. Eichelberger, *Jungle Road,* pp. xiv–xv; Forrest C. Pogue, *George C. Marshall,* vol. 2, *Ordeal and Hope, 1939-1943* (New York: Viking Press, 1965), pp. 334–335; Hastings L. Ismay, *The Memoirs of General Lord Ismay* (New York: Viking Press, 1960), pp. 256–257.

23. Eichelberger Dictations, 25 July 1960.

24. Gen. Sir E. F. Herring to Eichelberger, 27 January 1943.

25. The Marines landed on Guadalcanal on 7 August 1942, but the campaign was not over until 9 February 1943. The American forces did not begin their attack against Buna until 19 November and in forty-five days of hard fighting Buna Mission was taken.

26. Clovis E. Byers, "Combat Leadership." *Marine Corps Gazette,* November 1962.

27. Clovis E. Byers to the editor, 2 July 1968.

28. Eichelberger, *Jungle Road,* pp. 200, 202.

29. Interview with General Clovis E. Byers, 17 May 1965; with Major General F. E. Bowen, 26 April 1971.

30. Historical Section, Eighth U.S. Army, *The Amphibious Eighth* (n.p., n.d.), pp. 9, 27.

31. Clovis E. Byers to the editor, 2 April 1971.

32. Eichelberger to Miss Em, 15 June 1943.

33. Ibid., 12 December 1943.

34. Ibid., 8 April 1945.

35. Ibid., 22 March 1943.

36. This at least was the opinion of General von Mellenthin, who served on Rommel's staff in the desert in 1942. Personal information.

37. Major General Clarence A. Martin to General Clovis E. Byers, 12 May 1971.

38. Clovis E. Byers to the editor, 22 August 1968.

39. Eichelberger to Miss Em, 15 October 1918.

40. Captain Robert M. White to Mr. Thom Yates (Public Relations Office, U.S.M.A.), 7 March 1943; interview with General Clovis E. Byers.

41. Robert M. White to Thom Yates, 7 March 1943. Eichelberger Papers.

42. General G. S. Patton, Jr., to R. L. Eichelberger, 25 May 1945.

CHAPTER TWO

A Soldier's Call

San Francisco
August 15, 1942

Dearest Miss Em

On Monday I shall be leaving you and it will be a very difficult parting for us both. If the thought that I have never loved you more since I first met you over 30 years ago is any consolation, then you may be sure of that fact. . . .

I *expect* to come back to you so that we may spend many more years together. My lucky star tells me that. If I do not, I know you will be consoled by the thought that a soldier's training demands certain risks which I am glad to offer to my country. "Defense of country" seems a trite phase in peace time and yet as a professional soldier it must be near and dear to us when our country is in danger.

I shall . . . keep you informed of my impressions which will be of course tempered by the knowledge that my letters will be subject to censorship.

When Eichelberger arrived in Australia at the end of August 1942 as commander of I Corps, he established his headquarters at Rockhampton, a friendly city located midway between Brisbane and Townsville on the eastern seaboard. The Forty-first Division was stationed there, and nearby were suitable training areas for exercises in jungle fighting, river crossings, and amphibious landings.

At this time the main threat to Australia was the Japanese force in northeast Papua, where projected Allied movements had been forestalled by enemy landings on 21-22 July 1942. The immediate objective of the Japanese was Port Moresby, a vital strategic site and a key Australian base in New Guinea. A naval thrust against Port Moresby had already been turned back on 4-8 May, in the battle of the Coral Sea, and about the time Eichelberger assumed his new duties at Rockhampton the Japanese renewed their efforts. In a two-pronged pincers movement, one force pushed over the Owen Stanley Mountains along the Kokoda Trail while another landed at Milne Bay, on the southeast tip of New Guinea.

By late September, both Japanese offenses had been blunted. The force that hit Milne Bay had been compelled to evacuate on 5 September after a severe and costly fight, and on 17 September the drive over the Owen Stanleys was halted by the Australians at Imita Ridge. These failures, coupled with more recent reverses on Guadalcanal, prompted Japanese Imperial General Headquarters to subordinate all operations to the retaking of Guadalcanal. Gradually the weary and emaciated Japanese who had negotiated deep rivers, abrupt cliffs, and dense jungle fell back to the Buna-Gona beachhead, where they constructed defenses to enable them to hold on until the hoped-for victory at Guadalcanal would make available fresh troops to resume the offensive in New Guinea.

Now it was MacArthur's turn. On 14 September he summoned Eichelberger to his apartment in the Lennon's Hotel in Brisbane for a briefing. "He was in his bathrobe," Eichelberger recalled, "and Mrs. MacArthur was present. As usual, he walked the floor constantly. . . . He talked for about 45 minutes. In effect, I was to be a task force commander to go to New Guinea about the first of October. One regiment [was] to go over . . . the Kokoda Trail, and the remainder of the 32d Division to Milne Bay reinforced by the 8th Marines. The latter group [was] to go by boat up the north shore by secret hops at night using luggers, landing boats, etc. My mission was to 'take Buna and Gona.' If successful, I would be recommended to be Lt. General. All plans [were] to be made by me. . . . My Command Post might be at Abau or Milne Bay, independent of Australian high command. He said his staff was lukewarm regarding this as they had been licked once at Bataan but he was determined to do this. I asked him if General [Richard K.] Sutherland [MacArthur's Chief of Staff] had been told and he said, 'No, but I'll tell him tomorrow morning.' Nothing came of this. Sutherland told me next day that it was off."[1]

MacArthur, it turned out, was not to get the Marine regiment, and his lack of confidence in Australian troops, together with deep anxiety on the part of the Australian War Cabinet and Advisory War Council about the deteriorating military situation, resulted in Field Marshal Sir Thomas Blamey's being sent to New Guinea to take command personally. Elements of the Thirty-second Division entered the campaign early in October. During the following weeks the Australians fought their way back over the Kokoda Trail and

American troops pushed along the Kapa Kapa Trail, while other units approached the Japanese beachhead by air and by sea.

Eichelberger, however, was not directly involved during the first weeks of the Papuan campaign. The troops of I Corps came under Australian control once they reached New Guinea and he was not permitted to accompany the Thirty-second Division even for the purpose of learning at firsthand what the problems were so that he and his staff could "plan intelligently a training program to fit other troops for combat."[2] He poured out his frustrations in a personal letter he wrote — but never sent — to a friend in the War Department after the campaign was over.

Prior to November 30 I had been treated more like a lieutenant than a lieutenant general by the GHQ Chief of Staff [Sutherland]. My staff had from the beginning been made to understand our relative unimportance in the big picture. In fact, prior to November 30 the disintegration of my staff had begun. General MacArthur had pointed out that my staff was larger than his, which may or may not be true as this question would depend on whether one considers the USASOS [United States Army Services of Supply — Southwest Pacific Area] as an integral part of his staff. This latter organization, under General [Richard] Marshall, takes up many of the functions of the staff while General MacArthur's headquarters proper is organized as an inter-allied staff. All indications were that had I not been ordered to New Guinea, my staff, designed primarily as the staff of a combat corps, would have been torn to pieces. With the hope that it would be possible to retain my key men, steps had already been taken to assign approximately one-quarter of my original staff to the two divisions. This number approximated the additional officers which had been recommended to the War Department as being necessary to carry out the corps duties in combat.

In order to obtain first hand information and to acquaint the members of my staff as to the problems encountered in New Guinea, I had asked and secured approval for members of the staff to visit New Guinea on inspection trips. The main purpose was to enable the staff to plan intelligently a training program to fit our troops for combat against the Japanese. Having received from General MacArthur and General Sutherland specific approval for me to go to New Guinea to see the condition of our troops, I arrived there about the middle of November. My time of arrival as indicated by the attitude of the Chief of staff was most unfortunate, as this was the time the American and Australian troops were supposed to make their triumphant entry into Buna and Gona. It was to have been the first American Army victory over the Japanese. In my talk with General MacArthur I learned that I would not be allowed to visit the troops. Later, General Sutherland gave me a directive to return to the mainland at four o'clock the next morning. A further point in this connection was the fact that the plane on which I was returning, while passing over my headquarters en route, was not permitted to land but instead was to continue to Brisbane where I would be left to make my own arrangements to retrace my steps. General Sutherland, in explaining to me the general role to be conducted by our staff, carefully pointed out that it was to be a training role. . . . As a result, I established my headquarters and concentrated on training the 41st Division.[3]

Even this early, Eichelberger wrote after the war, "one could see the play of personalities and the lack of broad vision. . . . On November 14, when General Sutherland ordered me out of New Guinea in the name of General MacArthur, in spite of the terrible storm which was going on that day he directed that I fly at 4:00 in the morning on the Lockheed courier plane. In the hundreds of flights I have taken, I have never been in such a storm nor have I ridden in a more dilapidated plane. When we arrived out of the storm and darkness into Townsville in the morning, the pilot then told me that he had been ordered not to take me to Rockhampton, over which the plane would pass en route to Brisbane, but was to abandon me there . . . or take me through to Brisbane in my jungle clothes. A fly may not know when its wings are being pulled off but I did."[4]

Eichelberger revealed none of this to Miss Em at the time, although his letters did suggest disappointment that he was not playing a more active role as the Australian and American troops completed their build-up before Buna.

November 3, 1942

Dearest Miss Em

Had a long talk with "the Chief" yesterday and I wish that there were something I could do to help him — he is a grand leader. This morning the the papers quote Washington papers that he may be given a larger, more inclusive command.[5]

November 7, 1942

You need not try particularly to use nicknames because I think the censors have decided very wisely that letters from home are not important. At least none of your letters have been censored and certainly you know no military secrets. . . .

You mentioned . . . that you thought you detected some disappointment. I do not know what kind of mood I was in at the time I wrote, but I had hoped to be in a more active place perhaps at this time, but I am a firm believer in my own good luck and I know that if I have been detained in some certain places it is because the Goddess of Luck is hovering over me. I think I can say in all modesty that those immediately around me are working efficiently and happily. For those not immediate to me, I believe I can state in all sincerity that I have their friendship.

November 9, 1942

We were very much interested in the first radio reports of what Ike is doing.[6] If I had not come out here I would be with him. The first press reports of course are very meager but you are undoubtedly getting full coverage at home. I do feel that the whole situation for our side looks more favorable than it has for a long time, so I hope you will relax and not worry. The time must come when the balance of power as well as the influence of Lady Luck will turn against those who so richly deserve a good licking.

November 12, 1942

We heard broadcasts in English from America, England, Tokyo and Berlin. This is the first time I have heard the Tokyo broadcast which introduces war prisoners as a means of getting an audience. I can understand the Japanese speaking English much better than I can the British soldiers. I was impressed by the fact that the Germans had very little to brag about this time....[7] The Japanese were telling how deceitful we Americans are. It seems to make little difference that they are the most treacherous enemy that we have ever had to deal with.

November 22, 1942

Naturally I am chafing at the bit to get into more active service, but being lucky I am naturally not going to worry overmuch about those things.

I took Clovis, [Brig. Gen. Clovis E. Byers, Chief of Staff] with me to call on the Australian Chief of Staff[8] the other day. He is a very frank, natural person with whom I could get along for the rest of Time.

Eichelberger liked the Australians. The inhabitants of Rockhampton impressed him "as being very simple, fine people, in whom patriotism and piety are strong traits," and he did not find the Australian officers "much different from other Britishers I have known."[9]

"Shortly after I arrived in Australia," Eichelberger later recalled, "General MacArthur ordered me to pay my respects to the Australians and then have nothing further to do with them. This order I carried out to a very large extent throughout my service in or near Australia. I imagine that General Krueger, when he took command of the Sixth Army in May, 1943, was given similar orders because he was conspicuous in his avoidance of the Australians, either militarily or socially.

"In my own case, a few days after this directive...my I Corps was assigned to the Australian First Army under General Sir John Lavarak. General Lavarak invited me to come to luncheon at his headquarters at Toowoomba, west of Brisbane, where our meeting was very pleasant....As soon as my headquarters were established at Rockhampton, Australian staff officers began to come...to inspect my troops, just as would be done in any military organization where a corps is under an army."[10]

At the 14 September meeting with MacArthur, when told that one regiment was to go over the Kokoda Trail, Eichelberger asked: "How about the Australians. Do you think they could do this job?"

"No," replied MacArthur, "they won't fight." Eichelberger always assumed that by this he was referring to the Australian high command.

As the pages of the Australian Official History of the operations in New Guinea amply attest, the Australians smarted from the sting of these and other kindred remarks. Just how deeply they resented this attitude Eichelberger learned after the capture of Buna, when his Australian Chief of Staff, Major General Sir Frank Berryman, confided:

You must have been puzzled over certain things during the fighting at Buna. I want you to know that the jokes of the Lennon's Hotel, in which American officers have criticized to Australian girls the fighting qualities of Australian soldiers, have spread all over Australia. These things have cut us to the quick, especially as there have also been additional criticisms by high ranking American officers. The 17th [18th] Brigade is our best and was sent in at Buna with the hope it would show up the American soldiers. Whenever any Americans would do anything at Buna or Sanananda that we could criticize, these things at once were brought to General MacArthur's attention by our high command with the hope he would be hurt as we have been hurt in the past.[11]

November 24, 1942

Dearest Miss Em

The news from all over the world continues to be good. I firmly believe now that if Hitler had it to do over again he would not start any war. So that means he has passed his peak. The Japanese militarists have probably not yet decided whether they are sorry or not but I am sure the next six months will convince them that they have a bear by the tail.

November 28, 1942

Had a chance to let Clovis meet the Chief yesterday. He is certainly

a fascinating person and an inspired leader. He has so many ideas....
He looks fine, as does Dick [Sutherland]. Everyone here has been fine
to me — they seem glad to have me out here.

Will be glad to get away from the hotel and out with troops. I didn't
leave you to sit still — there is so much to be done.

**The opportunity was not long coming. The next afternoon, a quiet
and restful Sunday, MacArthur's headquarters called to alert Eichelberger and certain of his staff officers that they were to be sent to
New Guinea to take command of American troops in the Buna area.**

En Route
November 30, 1942

Dearest Miss Em

We were up late getting ready to go — had three hours sleep. Now Clovis and I are floating along with Eddie Edwards[12] and some others. It
is beautiful.... In spite of the number of rides I have had in past years,
I never get used to the beauty of the clouds as one looks down....

There will be a gap in my letters *but* I shall send one when opportunity offers. You may be sure that I shall always be with you in my
thoughts.... As I think of all the years we have been together, I know
you must realize how my admiration, respect and love have increased....
My love to you always, Sweetheart, and everything that goes with it....

I cannot get another sheet of paper without wakening Clovis.

**Upon arrival at Port Moresby, Eichelberger reported at once to
MacArthur. The story of this dramatic meeting has been told elsewhere.[13] "Bob," said General MacArthur in a grim voice, "I'm putting you in command at Buna. Relieve Harding [Maj. Gen. Edwin
F. Harding, commanding the Thirty-second Division]. I am sending
you in, Bob, and I want you to remove all officers who won't fight.
Relieve regimental and battalion commanders; if necessary, put sergeants in charge of battalions and corporals in charge of companies
— anyone who will fight. Time is of the essence; the Japs may land reinforcements any night....**

"I want you to take Buna, or not come back alive."[14]

**The first time MacArthur saw Eichelberger after the campaign
was over he remarked that he had received similar orders in World
War I from General Charles P. Summerall and had hated him ever
since. Eichelberger replied, "Well, I don't hate you, General."**

**Eichelberger never told publicly "just how vehement MacArthur
was against Harding that afternoon ... when he ordered me to relieve
him. It was no casual order.... 'Send him back to America, Bob, or
I'll do it for you.' That he meant it that afternoon there is no question.**

I did not know that day...what would have happened if I had disobeyed General MacArthur's directive....He was an angry and harassed man. In telling me...that for the first time in his life he had heard of American troops throwing away their arms and running from the enemy strains a bit at the facts because American troops have run in the face of the enemy many times in history (shades of Bull Run)! At that time I did not realize General MacArthur was being gloated over by the Australian High Command who had been criticized in turn by him previously."[15]

Notes

1. Eichelberger, Memo Taken from an Old Notebook Found in a Suitcase, dictated 2 December 1957. "This memo was initialed by Chief of Staff, Clovis E. Byers." The Marine regiment, it should be noted, was not released for amphibious operations in New Guinea because of the increased Japanese pressures on Guadalcanal. Samuel Milner, *Victory in Papua* (Washington, 1957), p. 105.

2. Robert L. Eichelberger, *Our Jungle Road to Tokyo* (New York, 1950), pp. 13–14.

3. Robert L. Eichelberger to Maj. Gen. V. L. Peterson, 19 January 1943. "Draft — letter not sent."

4. Eichelberger Dictations, 31 May, 10 June 1957; Eichelberger to Dr. Samuel Milner, 14 June 1957.

5. "The Chief" of course refers to General Douglas MacArthur, who assumed command of the Southwest Pacific Area on 18 April 1942. Although there had been frequent reports that his command would be increased significantly, requests for reinforcements were largely unsuccessful because of other priorities, a critical shortage of shipping and aircraft carriers, and the decision to make the primary effort in Europe.

6. On 8 November 1942, Allied forces landed at Casablanca and Oran in North Africa to begin OPERATION TORCH.

7. On the night of 4 November the Afrika Korps had begun the great retreat following the battle of El Alamein.

8. Probably Lt. Gen. Sir John Northcott, Chief of the General Staff since the reorganization of the Australian Army between July and September 1942.

9. Eichelberger to Miss Em, 2 September, 30 October 1942.

10. Eichelberger Dictations. 27 May 1957.

11. Eichelberger, Memo Taken from an Old Notebook; memorandum dated 28 January 1944; Dudley McCarthy, *South-west Pacific Area: First Year: Kokoda to Wau* (Canberra, 1959), pp. 176, 225, 234–235, 240, 247–248. The reference undoubtedly is to the 18th Brigade, which entered the battle on 18 December.

12. Capt. Dan K. Edwards, always a favorite with Eichelberger.

13. See Eichelberger, *Our Jungle Road to Tokyo,* pp. 20-21; Milner, *Victory in Papua,* p. 204.

14. Maj. Gen. George C. Kenney, Commander of the Allied Air Forces, was the only man present other than Eichelberger who has published an account of the conversation that took place on the veranda at MacArthur's headquarters. He makes no mention of the phrase "take Buna, or do not come back alive," but instead quotes MacArthur as saying "Now Bob, I have no illusions about your personal courage, but remember that you are no use to me — dead." According to Eichelberger, this was a passing remark by MacArthur at breakfast the following morning. See George C. Kenney, *General Kenney Reports* (New York, 1949), pp. 157–159. General Clovis Byers, who was also present, remembers vividly that MacArthur, after warning Eichelberger to take Buna "or don't come back alive," added the words, "and that goes for Clovis too." General Byers to the editor, 22 August 1968.

15. This version has been constructed from Eichelberger's Dictations dated 17 October 1953, 31 May and 10 June 1957, and 26 June 1961. Eichelberger did not quote MacArthur at length in *Jungle Road* "because I realized that he was under great stress and because General Harding was my classmate."

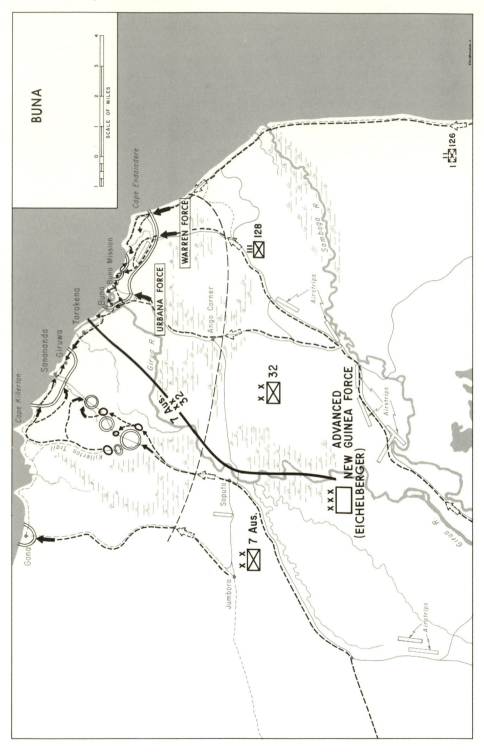

BUNA

SCALE OF MILES

0 1 2 3 4

Cape Endaiadere

WARREN FORCE

Buna Mission

Buna

URBANA FORCE

Tarakena

Giruwa

Sanananda

Cape Killerton

Killerton Trail

Gona

Giruq R.

7 AUS. 32 x 3

Ango Corner

Samboga R.

Airstrips

32
x x

Airstrips

ADVANCED
NEW GUINEA FORCE
(EICHELBERGER)
x x x

Girua R.

Soputa

7 Aus.
x x

Jumbora

Airstrips

128
III

126
I

MAP 1

CHAPTER THREE

Someone Should Fight Those Devils Off Their Feet!

The situation at Buna was serious. Inadequately trained, poorly supplied, lacking the proper weapons for jungle warfare and desperately short of artillery and engineers, the Thirty-second Division was bogged down in the pestilential swamps and tangled jungle that covered the approaches to the beachhead. Overconfident almost to the point of being cocky, the Americans had underestimated both the size of the enemy forces, which in fact numbered some 6,500 effectives instead of 1,5000-2,000 as reckoned by Allied Intelligence, and the strength of the enemy fortifications.

The latter were concentrated in three main positions, each independent, well protected on the flanks, and open to frontal assault only along narrow and heavily fortified channels. On the Allied left, the Australian Twenty-fifth Brigade had made three unsuccessful attacks since 22 November and had failed to make an appreciable dent in the Japanese defenses. In the center, the Australian Sixteenth Brigade, subsequently reinforced by two battalions of the U.S. 126th Infantry, had managed to establish roadblocks behind Japanese forward positions along the Sanananda Track but had been halted before the main lines at Sanananda.

The attempts to take Buna, on the Allied right, likewise had failed. A two-pronged assault by three battalions had been stopped cold on 19 November; the assaults were renewed against Cape Endaiadere and the New Strip the next day and again on the 21st, but despite air strikes and an artillery bombardment, all efforts on the Warren Front, as the extreme right of the line was called, were unsuccessful.

Meanwhile, in a separate action two miles to the west, known subsequently as the Urbana Front (so named after Eichelberger's home town in Ohio), one battalion of the 128th and later a battalion of the 126th that had been withdrawn from the Sanananda Front ran into a hornets' nest in The Triangle, a maze of bunkers, blockhouses and trenches of "almost impregnable strength" that defied repeated assaults.

On 30 November, combined attacks by the Urbana and Warren forces failed once again. Dead tired from the long marches and difficult terrain, weakened by short rations and fever, and crippled by heavy casualties, the men of the Thirty-second Division had reached what appeared to GHQ as the breaking point.[1]

Eichelberger's diary and letters to Miss Em during these hectic days were necessarily brief. The entry for 1 December, for example, states simply that Eichelberger reached the Thirty-second Division Command Post and assumed command at 11:00 A.M. "Reports from Mott [Urbana] Force indicated enemy counter-attack. Artillery directed to place fire on Island southwest of Buna village. Apparently attack, if any, was broken up." After the war he filled in the details.

As soon as I left the plane, I said to General Harding, in effect, "I have been ordered to relieve you but get behind me and I'll see if I can't hold you here." To this statement he made no reply. In the command post, sitting in his office, I found that he was on the telephone almost continuously. My staff was trying to get oriented so I decided to go up and see Colonel Mott [John W. Mott, Commander of Urbana Force].

Riding in a jeep with an officer and two guards, I reached Ango after luncheon and saw Brigadier Hopkins[2] walking down the trail from the direction of Soputa. He told me that he swam across the Girua River with his clothes in a waterproof bag. This meeting was entirely accidental but talking with him delayed my departure toward the front. We finally got up to a supply tent which had a telephone and I was able to talk to Colonel Mott. At that time my reaction to Mott was favorable because I had received such glowing reports from Harding.... I returned to the command post about supper time.[3]

December 2, 1942

Dearest Miss Em

A grand sleep on a real cot — rubber mattress, rubber pillow, and believe it or not, I had the light cotton blanket over me and was cool.... There is lots of noise and...laughter mixed with varied emotions.... Shuck and Eddie[4] take care of my little tent. Eddie looks fierce with a tin hat and a Tommy gun.

December 3, 1942

You would have been proud of me yesterday because I made at least 10 miles on foot through a steaming jungle and got back in condition to do my work. The noises didn't bother me, nor the smells.

Whatever I could say I must save for later. . . .

Later, Eichelberger related his experiences when he and his skeleton staff inspected the battlefront on 2 December. Sending Colonel Clarence A. Martin, his G-3, and Colonel Gordon Rogers, his G-2, to observe the fighting on Warren Front, Eichelberger, accompanied by Harding and Brigadier General Albert W. Waldron, Division Artillery Commander, made a reconnaissance of the area occupied by the Urbana Force.

Victory in Papua states that when I announced to General Harding that I wanted to go to the front . . . "he insisted on going along." The outstanding play of personalities that . . . morning in truth was the urging of General Harding that it was dangerous for me to go to the front. When I insisted, General Harding called Colonel Mott and insisted on a big guard being sent to the point on the trail where we were to leave the jeep and move into the swamp. He also insisted that a guard go with us. When I had reached the Urbana Force Command Post, about 300–400 yards from the Japanese front line at Buna Village, he tried to keep me from going forward because of the danger.[5]

Upon the conclusion of the campaign, Eichelberger explained to a friend the conditions that had prevailed his first days at Buna.

Now for a picture of what I found . . . during my preliminary inspection. The terrain occupied by our troops consisted of a number of corridors, each separated by swamps. They were facing the Japanese who held a beautifully prepared position in every sense of the word. The Japanese right flank rested on an unfordable stream, the Girua River. Their left flank rested on the ocean. The ocean was at their rear and their front was protected by several impassable swamps and streams. Every corridor was heavily protected by automatic fire. As to the physical condition of the men around Buna Village, it was pitiful. At three o'clock in the afternoon these men had had nothing to eat since the previous day and had had no hot food in ten days. Somebody had read a book about lighting fires in the presence of the enemy. They were getting two tins of C Ration per man per day or . . . about 1800 calories a day. No rice was going forward to supplement their diet. The men had no cigarettes, although there seemed to be no shortage back in the base section. It was evident that a very pallid siege was being waged. In any stalemate it was obvious that the Japanese would win, for they were living among the coconut palms along the coast on sandy soil while our men lived in the swamps.

In many places our troops were forced to build platforms on the roots of trees in order to keep out of the water. All the Japanese had to do was to wait for the fever to reduce our men to nothing or to wait for reinforcements from Rabaul. Another month and the Japanese could have come out and whipped our men with clubs.

A word as to the numbers of the two forces. It is my belief that General MacArthur never fully realized the deterioration of the strength of the three infantry regiments. Everywhere people talked glibly of battalions here and battalions there, battalions numbering well over six or seven hundred. But the actual figures ... showed that the line companies, the three rifle companies that did the fighting in all battalions, numbered about sixty-five men each. The great preponderance of strength always is found in headquarters companies and heavy weapons companies. The headquarters company, with its communications personnel and pioneer platoons, was used to carry ammunition and rations to the troops. The heavy weapons company has few people trained in scouting and patrolling and the close proximity of the opposing lines frequently makes their use impossible. On the left flank there were two such battalions, one of which had already come over the Owen Stanley Range, a feat which the Australians and Japanese had demonstrated was a most difficult one. There was no help to be expected from the right flank since ... the two forces were entirely separate. In contrast to this, the Japanese had a seashore along which they could travel and ... move troops to concentrate against any threat.... They also had truck roads. In every attack we made I am now convinced we had less men than the Japanese, although we did have a preponderance of mortar and artillery fire. However, the Japanese were dug in and had made overhead emplacements beautifully sited to cover all corridors and avenues of approach. Nothing less than 105 mm howitzers with delayed action fuses could possibly destroy any of these emplacements. We had one such weapon on the entire front. After viewing these positions I am amazed that our troops were able to carry them because one man with a machine gun could have, and did initially, stop the advance of companies.[6]

Eichelberger never forgot the sight that had greeted him at Buna.

When we arrived at the front, which was a pathway around the village, in some places not over 100 yards from the Japanese bunkers, I found conditions far worse than those responsible would have been willing to admit. There was no front line discipline of any kind. Our men were walking around and the crew of the heavy Browning at the right of our line were entirely exposed. Ration boxes could have been filled with dirt and placed around the machine gun as could overhead cover been made by placing logs from the burned-out buildings.

I was informed that the Japanese were in the tops of the palm trees and . . . forward in the jungle, to the right of the pathway, only a few yards away. Later, on December 5, I found these statements to be true. I heard the objections . . . when Colonel Gordon Rogers, my G-2, wanted to shoot the top of some of these palm trees which were supposed to have concealed Japanese snipers. "Don't fire! They won't shoot at us if we don't shoot at them."

There never was any idea of men going forward down the pathway. Five paces to the right of the path was thicket, and that was . . . where the Japanese snipers were supposed to be. As near as I could find out, nobody had gone forward five yards, ten yards, or fifty yards. It must be remembered that the Japanese were having the best of it, watching our men, listening to them talk, while we only realized vaguely that there were Japanese in the palm trees and some places forward in the jungle.

There were many soldiers at the rear, at aid stations and on the roots of trees. Undoubtedly some of these men had been sent back for a rest, and others had left the front without permission. The reasons given by Colonel Mott of all the trials and tribulations of his men before I arrived were, of course, true. A glance at the men would show what they had been through, but my orders were . . . to take Buna and I was not there to excuse myself or others. I found that the information given me at Port Moresby, that the front lines were weak and the rear areas strong, was true. Personnally, I think half the command was back there. One must re-member that 500-600 yards away from the Japanese constituted a rear area for that part of the Urbana front. . . . The engineers building air-strips or roads . . . were out of the combat picture.

I believe that 19 out of 20 combat officers would have agreed about conditions surrounding the village.[7] There were many excuses to include hunger, fatigue, fever, but . . . these were the tools I had been given to accomplish a task. When I told Colonel Mott . . . how conditions looked to me, he lost his temper, as did General Harding, who took a cigarette out of his mouth and threw it on the ground at his feet in anger. For Colonel Mott to insist that the conditions I described were not correct, and to insist in an angry manner, placed him outside the pale. For Gen-eral Harding to lose his temper at a criticism of these conditions put him out on thin ice, and particularly so when I could remember all that Gen-eral MacArthur had described about General Harding's failings and my orders to relive him. I ordered Colonel Mott to report next morning to our headquarters near Dobodura, and when they both lost their tempers a second time, I reluctantly directed that they report to Port Moresby. . .[8]

December 4, 1942

Dearest Miss Em

I am doing the work for which I have been trained and for which I left

West Point. You must just be a soldier's wife and hope for all good things. Maybe I can do the impossible. . . .

Last night I had the finest sleep I have had in years. . . . This morning I went over to return a courtesy call upon an Australian general.[9] It consisted of sitting in the tail end of a little crate,[10] but there were four or five other little crates over our heads to make us feel good. My great trouble is that I am twice as large as the lads for whom these parachutes are made. It was a very interesting day with lots of noise and not any responsibility. . . .

We have our tents in dense jungle. My mirror hangs outside on a bamboo tree. . . . I have a mosquito bar and a canvas shelter-half for our feet, . . . my rubber pillow and mattress, and I need a cotton blanket over me every night. . . . Outside of the tent I have a canvas bucket and a tin basin which stands on top of a ration box. I also have a thermos jug which someone stole from an airplane. I have a striker named Dunlop who washes my clothes for me every day, and do they need it. . . . I am about to take my daily bath which I do in a little stream about two feet deep, down by the mess tent where all the soldiers can admire.

December 5, 1942

Saturday the fifth of December will always remain with me as long as I live. I tried to do so much and while I know I accomplished some things I did not do all I had hoped for.[11] Forrest [Harding] has gone and the new Division commander who was with me was hurt, but not badly. Eddie Edwards got hurt. He was standing in front of me when it happened. One finds a lot of philosophy in life. Some want to run away and some seem to have inherited the spirit of what brother George used to call "the fighting races." . . . Eddie earned the DSO today and the bird who hurt him might have taken me had he not been standing a little in front of me. There is nothing I can tell you without hurting the feelings of the censor, I guess, although my heart is full of it.

Gordon Rogers [and Colonel] George De Graaf [I Corps Quartermaster] were also with me — they represent the height of courage and soldierly qualities.

I have made Clovis the Division Commander. Eddie Grose[12] is commanding troops where I was today although I hope to get him back as a staff officer soon. Clarence Martin is out with the boys too so my staff has many changes. . . .

As you can well imagine, I thought of you many times today, particularly as I had to spend some hours in straight walking. . . . This is of course what I was trained for, and I hope I shall conduct myself in a creditable manner. . . . You will be glad to know that I have had two good nights' sleep and that my nerves are not shot in any way, shape or form. I noticed some of the boys were having a hard time lighting a cigarette and I want you to know that my hands are steady. Of course, as you know, I am no blinking blooming 'ero.

I wish you could see some of the many types of natives. Most people don't speak to them but I always do, and I always get a very nice smile from them. On the little trip I took yesterday . . . there was a village with lots of women in it and they were working along with the men. They wear calico skirts like the men but of course stick out in front. I have decided long since that the elements of courage or courtesy are not limited to any particular race or creed. Without question, there are some very fine men who are merely savages in their native jungle. Some of the native police, with their rifles and their dignity, are fine. About fifty of them would make as fine a little private army as any man could ask for.

Merry Christmas, Sweetheart. . . .

December 6, 1942

Today has been a very quiet one. I went down to call on Junior [Edwards] who is in a hospital about six miles away. He is a very brave boy but he has had a severe operation. . . . Do not write to Mary [Edwards] yet. . . . I am afraid to write her until I know whether he will take a turn for the better or worse. . . . The injury was caused by some bozo who was not over ten feet away on my flank. He fired through Eddie's bearers and also one over my shoulder as we went back. He was later liquidated last night. . . .

I have had as an employee in my office a man named Humphries who has spent most of his life among natives. . . . He is happy as a lark out in the jungle collecting these savages. They are not far removed from cannibalism. In fact I would hate to offer any of them a bite on my arm, but they all seem to be good-natured people who would do many brave deeds if treated well.

Most of our men seem to have won their spurs and will soon gain a great deal of confidence.

December 7, 1942

I am sorry someone else cannot write to you. I want you to know that I believe I have set an example to those around me by being cheerful if nothing else. I feel keenly about your worrying over me but I know also that you would expect me to do my full duty in a situation which is no joke.

Newspaper men are beginning to swarm in so I guess they know where their bread is buttered. . . .

The trail is very bad this morning for it rained all night . . . without a stop. In fact it rains every night. A jeep does things which seem beyond the bounds of possibility. It is the great invention of this war.

Junior [Edwards] was bombed out of his tent ward and bomb craters were all around it. He is cheerful . . . a grand brave boy. Am moving the hospital tonight as the cross only means a target to those devils — 21 bombers, some at low level. . . . Where I tent is safe and usually I shall get a good sleep.

December 8, 1942

This morning early I went down to help put Junior on a plane. In the morning sunlight the "Chattanooga Choo Choo" headed into the purple mountains bearing as brave a boy as I have ever seen. When I think of all the miles that soldiers and native bearers carried him and the awful miles on impossible trails that he rode on top of a jeep, it seems impossible that he could have survived, and yet the last I saw of him was a smile and a salute.

The boys tell me . . . that most of the planes that bombed that field hospital were knocked down yesterday afternoon on the way home. As I dictate, firing has broken out over near the airstrip . . . but I think it is our planes driving off enemy planes.

I carefully refrain from telling you anything which could be a military secret. Such little personal notations as I have given you may be peculiar to most of the fighting now. I am so glad that the planes that shot into that hospital were intercepted.

This morning I received two pints of Bourbon from across the mountains. . . . Yesterday, a newspaper man sent me a lot of tea and about ten cartons of cigarettes which I shall give to the boys when I see them.

December 10, 1942

Last night I went over to spend the night with a neighboring Australian general. It is a long way around on foot but a short jump by air. One sits in a crate with a funny looking machine gun, looking for possible palsy-walsies to come down out of the skies. The mountains on the one side are beautiful and on the other the sea seems so close, but physically speaking I know it is some distance away yet. . . . The task ahead of us is not an easy one and I shall be delighted when it is over.

We talked last night until midnight. At ten we received a grand broadcast from London which was clear as a bell, so now I feel more or less up on the news, which I have been missing for over a week. They had a number of things to eat which I have not been getting, such as cheese, jam . . . syrup for their rice and canned milk. . . . The general had a fine English batman who laid out my toilet articles every five minutes and lined them up from right to left. I had a big cup of hot water for shaving and the general has a pump which takes water from a bucket and puts it into a tin can overhead, so I had a shower. . . . What you would call almost all the luxuries of home.

I could stay here a year and never spend a five-cent piece. As one officer said, "I have a new car back in the States that I would gladly trade for an orange."

December 11, 1942

I shall be moving around tomorrow. Tonight I am the proud possessor of six limes, collected by Eddie Grose in some village, and a two-handed Japanese sword.... We had canned apple sauce and grape juice. Auchincloss [Lt. Col. S. S. Auchincloss, Eichelberger's signal officer] found some sweet corn in a deserted village and we also had some taro root, which tasted something like turnip.

My clothes are being washed in a nearby stream. I rather favor my thin khaki but they will not let me wear it up forward. Things seem to go slowly but I must be patient.

I know how interested you are in all I am doing and I want to tell you as much as I can without bothering the censor.... At times we get a lot of activity. Crates are flying through the air and if it is overcast we do not know whether they are ours or some of our friends. Occasionally we get lots of noise, but I think the other fellow gets more than we do.

The rain has been pouring down and it looks as though somebody had turned a fire hose on us. I am trying to have a bamboo floor made for me. Some cannibals are making it, and I have paid them more than liberally by giving them a couple of ... safety pins. ...

Clovis is doubling in brass as a commanding general and also as chief of staff.[13] As always, he is full of energy and good cheer. One needs a lot of that where we are. His courage, of course, is what you would expect.... One finds courage in peculiar places. ...

It rained so hard that we decided to move, but cannot get away today. There is an inch of water in my tent.... The two cannibals are building a little bamboo walk out to the main trail through camp. When we move it will be to a coconut grove that is better drained. 27 little pals have been flying around for about 2 hours this afternoon — I don't like them much.

December 13, 1942

I don't remember if I told you but while I was at the bombed hospital, personally supervising the evacuation of the patients, a call was received for certain medicines. I took them back myself. ...

Left this morning with Bill [Col. Frank S. Bowen, assistant G-3] in a jeep — the trails were horrible after the rains. Beyond belief, but Bill got through farther than anyone has been able to go for some time. Then about 6 hours through swamps over the tops of my shoes — mud to my knees. A young major gave out and had to be put in a hospital.

Went through to the sea, and then fired in both directions where our little pals are. The Tommy gun I used had come out from under a dead Jap.

This is the hardest day I have ever had, but after my striker had pulled off my muddy clothes and I had had a bath and something to eat I can now go to sleep with good grace.... Don't worry about me — if that day wouldn't knock me out nothing would.

Eichelberger could not, of course, provide Miss Em with a detailed picture of his activities since assuming command in the Buna area. In the abortive attack on Buna Village on 5 December, he and his staff "took active part in the assault, pushing and leading troops forward, and in general operating as troop leaders."[14] The failure to carry the Japanese positions led to the decision to attempt no more "all-out frontal assaults" on Warren Front until the arrival of Australian reinforcements and tanks, but patrols continued their aggressive probing of Japanese lines. Meanwhile, the front-line units were being reorganized and reinforced, the flow of supplies was steadily increasing, and Urbana Force continued to hammer away at Buna Village, which was evacuated and occupied by the Americans on 14 December.[15]

The conditions of the fighting thus far are graphically described by Eichelberger in a letter he wrote to Major General Horace H. Fuller, who commanded the Forty-first Division which was still training in Australia.

December 14, 1942

When you arrive up in this jungle you will find rising up in front of you, to haunt you, the spectre of all those things you have failed to teach your men. You read about snipers in trees, but it became near at hand to me when I saw Eddie Edwards shot from a distance of only ten feet, hours after American troops had passed that very spot.... They roll grenades down out of trees. These are not high palm trees, but low bushy trees.

You have a village with its rear on the ocean and its flanks protected by tidal streams about three hundred yards across, and dense jungle on the land side. How do you propose to take that village? That is Buna.

Our men are now climbing trees and becoming snipers. Our men creep forward at night.... A battalion of the 126th Infantry, serving under the Australians, was held up by what was reported to be one machine gun. Naturally, General MacArthur felt very badly about his soldiers. It turned out to be an area heavily defended and that is ... Sanananda. The area is about one thousand yards deep and three hundred yards across, full of trees. How would you take that out? Our battalion was ordered to advance in a column of platoons, first platoon firing Tommy guns from the hip, second platoon throwing grenades, and was stopped by 25% losses. The Australians tried it and they had even greater losses. Now they are trying to whip the Japanese by the attrition method, and two of our companies are astride the track between this Japanese position and Sanananda. These two companies have been attacked from both directions.

These are some of the actual situations I have seen. You can figure out any number of combinations and I would so train my troops, because just as sure as night follows day you are going to be up against it some day. You will find that you must follow the chain of command. Develop sergeants and corporals that will really take charge of their men. Many of the bravest . . . leaders will be shot in the early days. Our troops have been in the line at least three weeks. . . .

I found units scrambled like eggs. A platoon of a certain battalion of a particular regiment might be serving next to a platoon of a different regiment, or perhaps the men were just intermingled. Men threw away their packs with food and ammunition, within two miles of the enemy, and the natives are now wearing our uniforms. . . . Study this situation, so that you will either cut your packs down to a minimum or leave them behind under guard. The man that has an unusual sized foot had better have two pairs of shoes with him in his pack. Be sure they carry vitamins and quinine and disinfectant. . . . Vitamins may win a victory.

These ideas I give you because I have been able to get near enough to a village to throw a rock into it and yet have not been able to capture it. Maybe you can think up ways to do it. . . . Their mortars seem to be very ineffective. In this mud they must hit you on the head to hurt you. Their grenades are not much. They fire some rather heavy caliber bullets of the tracer type, such as the one that struck Edwards. You could put your two thumbs into the wound.

The crowd here in the tent send you their best. Rogers, Bowen and Byers heard me dictate this and all subscribe to it emphatically.[16]

December 14, 1942

Dearest Miss Em

The village of Buna . . . was occupied this morning. I have written to you how I walked there through the swamp yesterday to urge further advance. . . . The walk . . . would have killed a horse. . . .

(later)

Among the souvenirs I seem to have . . . are a Japanese flag . . . and a native drum. Outside my tent now, the four cannibals have built a native shack with benches inside where the boys can meet and propound their words of wisdom.

Tonight I expect to open a bottle of liquor in celebration of the cap-

Tonight I expect to open a bottle of liquor in celebration of the capture of Buna. It all is not so easy because there is a lot more to take. Buna is just a village, and there are a lot of other fortified places yet to fall. Tidal streams run here and there and these make operations difficult.

I am enclosing a copy of a message sent to me by the Chief — a letter earlier in the day congratulated me on my courage and leadership. . . . The success this A.M. I hope will cheer him up. He deserves it.

SECRET

December 13, 1942

Dear Bob:

Time is fleeting and our dangers increase with its passage. However admirable individual acts of courage may be; however important administrative functions may seem; however splendid and electrical your presence has proven, remember that your mission is to take Buna. All other things are mere subsidiary to this. No alchemy is going to produce this for you; it can only be done in battle and sooner or later this battle must be engaged. Hasten your preparations and when you are ready — strike, for as I have said, time is working desperately against us.

Cordially,
(signed) MacArthur
Douglas MacArthur

December 15, 1942

Dearest Miss Em

Last night we celebrated the capture of our little village. . . . I hope when this war is over they won't sing about me that little song that goes:

Oh the general got the Croix de Guerre,
Parlez-vous,
The general got the Croix de Guerre,
Parlez-vous.
The general got the Croix de Guerre
But the S.O.B. wasn't even there,
Hinky-dinky, parlez-vous.

I am glad to state that my Chic Sale installation,[17] which has been made out of ration boxes, is quite an improvement over nothing at all. The cannibals have put on a thatch roof and walls today. . . . We have to keep an eye on the cannibal for fear he will take off with the soap. I would rather he took the clothes. . . .

Went forward today but returned early. Covered with mud from head to feet but I had a grand time shooting a lot of weapons for fun.[18]

Had a grand letter from the Big Chief.

December 16, 1942

Here it is, another rainy day. . . . It does little to raise our spirits, but I'm sure it will take a lot more than any rain to do them much damage.

A little later today I have to make a brief talk to some of our boys, and on thinking over the matter have decided I am eventually destined to become an inspirational speaker of the Billy Sunday type. It seems as though I am always having to speak my piece to one group or other....

Clovis was hurt yesterday....I am the sole remaining gentleman of my high sounding title. Three have left since my arrival here.... [19]

(later)

It cleared off nicely today and Bill Bowen drove me on the most horrible jeep ride I have ever taken. Miles of corduroy road, but the chance I had to walk out on the sands of the beautiful seacoast was worth it. Today we had a real success and I feel good over it. This is not an easy job I have although I find myself as always surrounded by friendly faces who want to do their very best.

December 18, 1942

I am remaining at home today on the telephone. There has been lots of noise from all directions and of many different kinds....Just for the moment things are not going so well, so I will cheer myself up by writing to you....

I am still the great mystery man of Australia, but I think most people know I am here.

December 19, 1942

Last night was clear and beautiful, and our little palsy-walsies were around in the distance dropping Christmas presents...but with no effect....Things have quieted down now and those little palsy-walsies who are left alive in Papua are wending their weary way through the swamps back toward safety.

This has been a very interesting time with many disappointments, ending however in one of the grandest days I have ever had when I stood in Buna Mission [Village] and watched American boys go to town on the enemy pillboxes. Billy Bowen's lower lip was long enough to step on that day because he always has a duck fit if I get close to any bullets.

One thing would be very interesting to you. We had captured a pesky triangle, after a lot of trouble, which blocked the trails into our left flank and caused us to walk weary miles through the swamps. The first day it was open I left the jeep up the trail, which was not yet able to be used. To my surprise, I found Eddie Grose looking the bunkers over. I was anxious to talk to him, and we were walking along on our way to his command post when a sniper opened up on me because I was dressed in ordinary khaki on that day. It was very evident that the fire was coming from a large tree about seventy-five yards away. We dropped into some nearby shell holes and poured everything we had into the tree, for about fifteen minutes. Later, Eddie Grose personally went to the tree . . . and found four dead Japanese under it.

This has been a very funny little war, but I feel it has been extremely important and was fought with a viciousness beyond imagination. I hope I shall be going back home soon.

December 21, 1942

At present I am in no danger, and if my number had been up it would certainly have shown up the day Eddie was wounded. Some of the boys who were some distance away from me said he created an ammunition shortage trying to get me. The only one I noticed was the tracer bullet which went over my shoulder. With Clovis away I cannot get up forward and you needn't be worried from that angle.

(later)

I try to make my letters . . . as interesting as possible because I know you are hungry for news, but at the same time I must try not to get into that great field which comes under the term of military information. I do feel I am living through a very historic period. How it will turn out or whether any of it will go down to my credit I do not know. . . . While I want to do my duty I would rather see you than have all the honors that the world could give me heaped upon my shoulders. You may be sure there is nobody up in front of me that will scare me to death, nor have I lost my sense of humor. . . . For a large amount of profanity which at times is forced upon me I know the Lord will forgive me.

(later)

Today I had luncheon with my Australian General friend [Herring] who is now not so very far away. The change of diet and scenery did me good. Coming back, I loaded my jeep up with a lot of our soldiers who were tugging their heavy burdens up a trail. They are always very appealing to me, even when I realize that some are very brave and some need a lot of leading.

December 22, 1942

It is getting mighty close to Christmas and I am thinking about you this morning as I cogitate on life in general and my problems in particular. Our little palsy-walsies are hard to kill because they keep plenty of cover over their noggins. Therefore, while we make commendable progress, perhaps, it is nevertheless slow. . . .

This afternoon I talked to a group of lads who were without cigarettes and whose clothes permitted various portions of their anatomies to stick out. They need a good sleep and some new clothes, cigarettes, etc. This they will get, and the Red Cross is giving everyone a Christmas present.

My bunch of bananas has become very popular. All visitors eye it with a certain gleam in their glance.... Three more days until Christmas. I have never pictured myself as a pal of a bunch of ex-cannibals but they grin at me as though I was their best friend.

This has been a good day.

December 23, 1942

I have noticed often that you speak of not having ever seen my name mentioned and yet you see mention of [General George H.] Patton and others whose every move is recorded in the press. I do not believe there is anything to say except that since you are a young lady of a keen mind I should think you would have figured this out by now.

Things are moving along, but of course it takes time to dig these little rats out of their holes.

December 26, 1942

You'll never know how I have missed you this Christmas season. Fortunately, we were busy night and day for the last three days, so by concentrating on our job here we managed to pass the holiday without feeling too low. As always is my luck, I am surrounded by a staff who are most friendly, and they do everything they can to make my life here if not pleasant at least bearable.

The men are getting to know me now and I get a lot of greetings. I particularly like to talk to those who are going to meet our palsy-walsies for the first time. I can usually get them laughing.

And then there is the American cemetery with its line of crosses, and I choke every time I pass it.

December 27, 1942

This is no easy life but I am trying to keep my sense of humor.

December 29, 1942

The last three days have been extremely hard ones, and when I realize how much leg work I've done and how much ground I've covered, I really feel proud of myself. My waistline is slowly diminishing, but outside of that I can notice no other effect. So far the exertions of this new job have done me nothing but good. Dick Sutherland is here with us again and of course is of considerable help.

December 30, 1942

Dick [Sutherland] left today — he is a queer duck but he is plenty hard.

Took a member of my staff who had come up for a one day visit to the front and he was hurt the same day as Gordon Rogers.[20] The latter ... had a hole through both legs but he hobbled up to me and wanted to continue. A little doctor was running around him with a pair of scissors trying to cut his pant legs away. What a man! He thought it a great joke.

December 31, 1942

There has been a lot of reason the last few days for me to feel a little low.[21] I suppose it's a little bit of frustration that I'm suffering, for our job has reached a critical stage and I'm anxious to wind it up. Consequently each little delay, and there have been many, seems the more irritating. Too many are willing to take the counsel of their fears to the exclusion of all else. However, I don't doubt I'll live through it.

Bill Bowen has been away for some time — he is tired out, as is Eddie Grose, but doing a grand job. He howls like an Indian if I get anywhere where there is the slightest chance of getting hurt. He will turn me into a coward if he keeps on.

January 1, 1943

Here it is the first of another year, and I was so busy last night I didn't even have the chance to take a drink of Scotch to the occasion.

I have a feeling the end is not far away, and while it represents just a beginning of the big task which must be done, still it is a beginning, and as I start out today I feel much encouraged and hope that by tonight we will really have the Jap's tail in a crack. . . . I sure am anxious to step on it.

January 2, 1943

At last, victory, and the little village in which I stood will have its name broadcast throughout the world tomorrow. It was a week or ten days of bitter disappointments in which the hands of nearly everyone seemed turned against me, but I had to pound on.

To see those boys with their bellies out of the mud and their eyes in the sun, closing in unafraid on prepared positions, made me choke, and then I spent a moment looking over the American cemetery which my orders of necessity have filled from nothing. Not large, perhaps, but you can understand.

There were black natives and Korean coolies, naked as jaybirds, who were glad to get out, and little palsy-walsies who had no intention of surrendering. One must admire them in a way.

January 4, 1943

I had my first quiet day for a long time yesterday, which even included a nap in the afternoon. . . . The two good nights of sleep that I have had have done wonders for me. There were many nights when I came bouncing back in a jeep away after dark, after many hours struggling through swamps. Many times, too, things were not going so well. But now Eddie Grose is mopping up the boys who were hiding in the trees, so temporarily my troubles are over.

January 5, 1943

A very high ranking Australian officer[22]...has been here for tea.... I asked if he had heard what the plans were for me and he said that after we finished this job down the line[23] I would be taken back to the mainland. If true, this will suit me fine. How long this next job will take I do not know. The other was much longer than one could have anticipated. The defenses of our little palsy-walsies were a nightmare, both the ones they had built and the ones nature had given them.

By this time, you must know that things were all messed up when I was sent for so suddenly. There is nothing much more that I can add. But, Sweetheart, I can still laugh and...at night I sleep right well in spite of iguanas and strange night noises.

January 6, 1943

Today I made an inspection trip to show my Australian boss where the fighting had taken place. He was very much impressed.... Letters came today from Clovis and others congratulating me on the successful termination of things at my front. I have, however, heard nothing from certain people although a number of days have gone by. This puzzles me, but not as much as it might.

[Maj. Gen.] Horace Fuller [commanding the Forty-first Division] is here and...he mentioned Forrest Harding. I was very sorry the way that turned out but there was nothing else I could do.

My curiosity is satisfied about certain things now. I now know who my friends are. When I was sent here, I was told by the one who should know [Gen. MacArthur] that conditions were desperate and...things ...would be done for me if I were successful....I didn't expect much, but a good many days have passed and as yet I have not received a "thank you, dog" and I do not expect to receive any. On one day I stood so close to the Japanese trenches that I could have tossed a coin into them, with all hell breaking around me, and my feelings now are about what you would expect. Outside of this, I am fine. Our enemies play true to form and fight to the death. I am surrounded by many warm friends, and those who are not friendly just must not count.

The congratulatory message from MacArthur was written 8 January and read in part as follows: "I have been waiting to personally congratulate you on the success that has been achieved. As soon as Fuller takes hold, I want you to return to the mainland. There are many important things with reference to rehabilitation and training that will necessitate your immediate effort. The 32nd Division should be evacuated as soon as permissible so that it can be rejuvenated. I am so glad that you were not injured in the fighting. I always feared that your incessant exposure might result fatally.

"With a hearty slap on the back."

January 9, 1943

Dearest Miss Em

I am enclosing as much of a letter received today from the Big Chief as I can send you without violating censorship regulations. This letter and the news of our little victory of yesterday afternoon, after my visit to the front,[24] gives me an entirely different picture of things, for the moment.

As I get the picture, the time I will return to the mainland will be dependent on the arrival of certain troops, [Forty-first Division] and that is not in the immediate future. I believe, however, that I shall be out of here in a couple of weeks, or three at the most.

I think the things I miss more than anything else in the eating line are the uncooked breakfast cereals with heavy cream. I have been quite lucky in getting some papaya, but only because my old friend Mr. Humphries is in control of a bunch of cannibals who search the deserted villages.... I gave him employment when the seat was about to come out of his trousers. These things are usually forgotten.

January 10, 1943

The boys tell me that last night the San Francisco radio carried word of what troops are here and that I have been in command.... The Big Chief ... returned to the mainland and he evidently released the information after his arrival.... Someday you will see a map of that area and you will know what a nightmare it was for our men. They lived in the swamps while the Japanese lived on the seacoast where they could bathe in salt water and could be cool and well.

It is Sunday morning and I feel more at peace than I have at any time since I arrived here. Most of my Sundays seem to be very full and Christmas Eve and Christmas were nightmares, as was New Year's Eve. I certainly had my share of ups and downs before the victory finally came, for I had to try many things and some of them failed.

A touch of victory has done wonders for everybody, or at least everybody on this side of the mountains.... I have not heard anything from the other side of the mountains except ... letters from many friends on the mainland.

The Japanese make a grand enemy, and I was pleased to see some today who had passed on to their reward. They never disappoint me for they are very brave. From other angles, though, although you know I would never shirk my duty, I would be very pleased to see you again and then go on to other work of a combat nature if it were available.

I shall try to keep my sense of humor with the idea that my good fate will return me to where you are waiting . . . at home. I always remember I am a very lucky person.

January 11, 1943

[The enclosed picture] . . . was taken deep in the heart of a jungle within a few hundred yards of the firing line and, if I don't mistake my gesture, I was probably saying to Eddie Grose, "Everything you say is true, Eddie, but by God you have got to attack." I must say for Eddie, he has been decorated by me twice and recommended by me another time for further decorations. He is a very conservative soldier and I am not.

I am shifting up a file in the echelon of command and will take over everything this side of the mountains, either American or otherwise.[25] So far as I know, the Big Chief, Dick [Sutherland] and the rest of them have all gone home from the command post across the mountains.

We still have quite a job to do here yet. How much it is hard to say, because if one looks into a jungle one does not know whether there are five monkeys there or a hundred.

It rained eight inches here last night. When one considers that this did not fall on cement roads but . . . onto muddy trails which were already vile, it is easy for you to conceive what our trails are like now. My little stream . . . is a young river. . . . This is the rainy season, however, and we must expect conditions to be difficult.

January 12, 1943

There are so many things that occur every day which will interest you. . . . Leavenworth problems on a small or larger scale but in which the pay-off comes in the snap of the . . . little .25 caliber Jap bullet.

January 13, 1943

The day promises to be clear and if we can get through I expect to fly over to visit one of my Australian friends. This will be another of those flights in a tiny little crate, but bumpy though it may be it is still to be preferred to riding in a jeep over roads that have been wrecked by the rains. That is truly the hardest work one can do around these parts right now.

Today was to have been moving day, and I had intended to move over to the camp of my Australian friends since I am to command both forces in this area. However, . . . we will have to be governed by the condition of the trails.

Our victory is almost complete and I understand we will return "home" as soon as the fighting stops. . . . Long before this reaches you (probably tomorrow or the next day), you will hear of the fall of Sanananda — the last Japanese holding in Papua. I am, as you know, in command of the *Allied Forces* north of the Owen Stanley Range. In the Buna area, I was the senior Allied commander and was in direct command, with my grand colleague, Herring, an Australian, in command north of the mountains.... I was *always* the senior American commander north of the mountains, if you get what I mean....[26] You are right when you say that you didn't realize that anyone as high ranking as I am would be so far forward, but I had to almost throw them over my shoulder and carry them in. The Japs smacked me down a few times but I always sailed in for the next round.

Blamey, when he looked over that horrible place, said that a miracle had been performed.

January 14, 1943

As I look back on... last night's letter, [it]... sounds a bit gloomy. As you know, during my early weeks here I made everything out to be perfectly wonderful, and in many ways my picture was a correct one. The personal side of any job is the interesting one and maybe the unhappy one. These things one cannot put in a letter.

I do not want you under any conditions to imagine me as being unhappy, for I have too much to do and... to think about to indulge in many personal thoughts.

One must be satisfied in a large degree in the knowledge of duty well performed. One would have a hard time convincing the many who were here, including my staff and numerous newspaper men, that I failed in any way....[27] There were a very few visitors that came to us from across the mountains but their visits were brief.

I expect to go down to live in my new Australian command post as soon as Clovis gets here. I hate to move out of my camp here because it is very simple, with the stream right next to my tent, etc. My desk is a mass of pictures of you and your letters have accumulated a lot and I haven't the heart to tear them up. It looks as though I must retain my tent here in order to keep my plunder.... You know that if I started out on the desert with a handkerchief, a week later I would have an automobile load of stuff.

I understand, unofficially, that I am to get a DSC — at least the boys cannot sing after the war that I "wasn't there" as they did about the general's *Croix de Guerre* after World War I. Don't you worry about publicity or ribbons or anything else — I have looked my death in the face too many times in the last month to care whether some office boy on the other side of the mountain gets a ribbon. If I could see you that would be all I would want, and I wouldn't care a damn for the publicity or a chest full of ribbons. If I could get away from the Southwest Pacific area to some place where I could know that my enemies were all in front of me, that would be some satisfaction.... The Australians seem to like me a lot — I haven't worried about them or about other things much, either.

January 16, 1943

We are now installed with our Australian friends. In some ways I do not like it as well as the other place, but it is nearer the scene of activities and consequently I can keep in closer touch with what goes on.

There is no little stream here for me to bathe in, but I do have the refinement of a hand-power shower bath instead. It is quite simple in operation, consisting of merely a shower head connected by a hose to a little hand pump which draws water from a big bucket. This ... Australian gadget ... is just an indication of the thoroughness with which they go into this war matter. Their installations all seem quite elaborate when compared to ours, which may or may not be an advantage.

Today is a happy one ... for Clovis arrived from over the mountain. ... You can imagine ... how happy I am to have him back with me again.

Our job here is coming along surprisingly well and the progress the last two days has been much faster than I had hoped for. My luck continues and our little friends obligingly removed one of our worst headaches, and in so doing not only forced themselves to relinquish many of their tools but also permitted us to liquidate a large number of them.[28] In addition to this, we find our own situation correspondingly improved. However, I am not letting myself forget for a moment that this is just transitory and that our job is still before us, with its many difficulties.

Various developments in the last day or so make it highly possible that within the next two weeks we will be back "home" on the mainland.... I will certainly welcome ... those big breakfasts....

January 17, 1943

From the standpoint of our little palsy-walsies, I want to assure you that in my present job I am in no personal danger whatsoever, for I stay back at the headquarters rather than go to the front as I did in the first weeks of the fighting here. Things are going well ... but it is hard to determine whether our little friends are weak or whether they are just drawing back a bit preparatory to a repetition of what we had when I first came here. In other words, it has been announced to the world that we have a mopping up job to do, but maybe our little pals don't know that that is all it amounts to.

Have tried to do my best and I think you can be proud of what I have done no matter what anyone may say. The dead Japs speak for themselves, and those who were so jittery the day I crossed the mountains can now relax and figure how they could have done it better.

January 18, 1943

Tonight we celebrated.... We had some cold limeade.... We had good cause to celebrate, too, for today one of our most annoying stumbling blocks was eliminated.

January 21, 1943

As you doubtless can see by the papers today, our job is pretty well wound up. Herring laughs when they talk about how sick the Nips are, because they seem able to pull a trigger and their sickness is not readily apparent to the lads out in front of them. However we rather hope to have things wound up very quickly now.

January 23, 1943

Last night was clear and we are now enjoying the second perfect sunny day in succession. You can imagine how welcome this is to everyone here.... Our job is practically over in this area and the fine weather is permitting our boys to prepare themselves adequate shelter for the rains we know must come....

Today Clovis and I will go forward to look over the scene of the recent operations. All activities have now ceased with the exception of a few "mopping up" operations, and the only dangers we will encounter are those of getting very tired from the long walks involved.

January 24, 1943

You can imagine how pleased we are at the prospect of leaving, particularly since we have the right to consider that the job has been well done. I think I am very fortunate in having made good friends among the Australians, with whom I have enjoyed mutual understanding.[29]

And so, the campaign for Papua comes to an end and soon we shall be thinking back upon it wondering whether I could have done better. At any rate, there is nothing for Hirohito to broadcast out of Tokyo.

Notes

1. Samuel Milner, *Victory in Papua* (Washington, 1957), pp. 125–195 passim.

2. Brig. R. N. L. Hopkins, chief staff officer of Lt. Gen. Edmund F. Herring, Commander, Advance New Guinea Force. "It must be remembered that when MacArthur went to the South Pacific, it was with the agreement that the Australians would command the ground forces. Therefore, I fought at Buna as commander of that sector under the Advance New Guinea Commander. Later during the final fighting for the Sanananda Sector, I was in command of the Advance New Guinea Forces myself, which was a joint Australian-American command." Eichelberger Dictations, 29 May 1961.

3. Eichelberger Dictations, 28 June 1957.

4. Sgt. Clyde Shuck, Eichelberger's secretary, and Capt. Edwards.

5. Eichelberger Dictations, 24 June 1957.

6. Eichelberger to Maj. Gen. V. L. Peterson, 19 January 1943. This letter was never sent.

7. Col. Rogers reported similar conditions on the Warren Front. Robert L. Eichelberger, *Our Jungle Road to Tokyo,* (New York, 1950), p. 25; Milner, *Victory in Papua,* pp. 210–211.

8. Eichelberger Dictations, 31 May, 24 June 1957.

9. Gen. Herring, Commander, Advance New Guinea Force, whose headquarters were at Popondetta. Herring had visited Eichelberger the previous morning to confer about the situation on both fronts. Eichelberger Diary, 3, 4 December 1942.

10. Probably an Australian Wirraway.

11. The attack of Warren Force "had failed all along the line. . . . As Col. Martin put it in a phone call . . . that night: 'We have hit them and bounced off.' On Urbana Front, where Eichelberger intervened personally, progress was made against the position at Buna Village and one platoon broke through to the beach to isolate the village." Milner, *Victory in Papua,* pp. 241–245.

12. Col. John E. Grose, at this time commanding the 127th Infantry, which was moving up to support Urbana Force.

13. Gen. Byers assumed command of the Thirty-second Division when Gen. Waldron was wounded on 5 December.

14. Eichelberger Diary, 5 December 1942.

15. Milner, *Victory in Papua,* pp. 145–252.

16. Eichelberger to Maj. Gen. Horace Fuller, 14 December 1942.

17. For the benefit of younger readers, Chic Sale immortalized the outhouse.

18. Eichelberger's daily letters to Sutherland place this — and other incidents — in a more proper perspective: "I have been away today on the right flank. . . . I found these boys acting as if they were conducting a siege, out in the grass telling tall stories about the Japanese being fifty yards away, and the tales were not based on exact knowledge. I had a regimental pep talk all along the line and have ordered that they go in and kill those devils or get killed. The point I want to emphasize is that they did not know whether there were one or one hundred Japanese in front of them. . . . On one part of the line I was told that if I fired I would get shot. I fired and fired plenty and nobody has answered me yet. I then went through the swamp to a beautiful raised emplacement for a 37 mm gun. Again, I was told that I would draw fire so I fired into some of their bunkers and nobody answered. . . . I intend to put all the fight into this crowd that they will take and then add some more." Eichelberger to Sutherland, 14 December 1942.

19. Gen. Byers was shot in the right hand by a Japanese sniper, leaving Eichelberger the only American general left in action. From the hospital at Dobodura, Byers wrote the following to Miss Em: "Your Bobby had conducted himself as few officers in our Army have ever done. Without his knowledge I sent a letter to General MacArthur containing affidavits from a number of officers as to his conduct. I am taking the liberty of suggesting the Medal of Honor. . . . I wish you could see the inspiration he is to these men as he goes around. . . ." Clovis Byers to Mrs. Eichelberger, 17 December 1942. For additional details on the recommendation for the Medal of Honor, see chapter 4.

20. Col. Gordon Rogers was wounded twice the afternoon of 28 December in an abortive attack upon Buna Mission.

21. By this time organized resistance had pretty much collapsed in the Old Strip, which Warren Force had taken by 28 December, but the follow-up attacks against Giropa Point had been repulsed on the 29th. When Eichelberger wrote this letter, Warren Force was poised to resume the attack. The attacks of Urbana Force against Buna Mission had failed on 28 December; the next day one company pushed its way forward to the coast and dug in, and on the 30th Eichelberger confided to Sutherland: "If I don't get Buna Mission today I am surer than hell going to reorganize tomorrow, for my men have been battered day after day since before Christmas." Eichelberger to Sutherland, 30 December 1942.

22. Gen. Sir Thomas Blamey, then Commander, New Guinea Force.

23. This undoubtedly is a reference to the reduction of the Japanese beachhead at Sanananda.

24. Tarakena Village, a Japanese stronghold on the coast between Buna Village and the Sanananda Front, was taken by two companies of the 127th Infantry on the evening of 8 January. Eichelberger reported to MacArthur: "Now that the men are living where the Japanese lived, they look entirely different. The swamp rats who lived in the water now

have their place in the sun and I even heard some singing yesterday for the first time."
Quoted in Milner, *Victory in Papua*, p. 337.

25. As a result of the conference with Gen. Herring the morning of 11 January, Eichelberger was named to command Advance New Guinea Force, comprising the Thirty-second U.S. Division and the Seventh Australian Division. Herring had taken command of the New Guinea Forces, with his headquarters at Port Moresby, and MacArthur and Blamey and the high command returned to Australia.

26. This is a guarded reference to the fact that MacArthur never was at Buna during the campaign. See chapter 4.

27. In this connection it seems appropriate to include a letter from Capt. Dan K. Edwards, who was recuperating from wounds received on Urbana Front, on 5 December: "Those of us who were with you in the front lines during the first days have no doubt ... that your personal leadership was the decisive factor. Whatever the present newspaper accounts may be, someday the permanent record will contain the story of how you were sent at the eleventh hour to salvage an impossible situation without any assistance, except your own intelligence and your own force of character.... While I was with you I was convinced that if the troops under your command did not go into Buna, you would unhesitatingly go in there alone. And I still think that that is probably what you would have done." Edwards to Eichelberger, 11 January 1943.

28. By 14 January, the Japanese had evacuated their southernmost roadblock on the road from Soputa to Sanananda, thus clearing the way for a general advance against the last remaining Japanese positions.

29. Sir E. F. Herring gave expression to this friendship in his congratulatory message of 27 January 1943: "Returned this morning from our old stamping ground. I can't tell you ... how much I feel I owe you for all you did to help me and the show generally during those rotten tiresome weeks before Buna fell. Your coming was like a very pure breath of fresh air and you blew away a great deal of the impurities that were stopping us getting on with the job.... Your attitude and that of your staff was such that I believe we had real cooperation in the battle and one united effort. How much this meant to me personally I think you know and how much it meant to an ultimate victory can't be over-estimated.

"There is no need for me to tell you how much you did personally to make success possible and for the rest of my life I will continue to rejoice at the capture of Buna Mission by 127th Infantry, largely because of the joy it brought you. It was a fitting climax that I should hand over to you command of the Corps and that you should bring off such a glorious victory as Sanananda really was...."

CHAPTER FOUR

Caught Between Acts

During the months following Buna, Eichelberger worked hard to rehabilitate and train his command and to perfect amphibious techniques. "We have learned a lot of lessons and some of them should prove valuable in the future," he informed Miss Em soon after his return to Australia. "As I sit here I can look at that picture of our Corregidor prisoners that was published in Life and can feel a little better about it." Several weeks later he wrote assuringly: "Am in a fine frame of mind, and I know that soon the unpleasant sides of the Papuan campaign will be lost in admiration for the green soldiers who did so much."[1]

Like every other successful American combat leader, Eichelberger had learned to appreciate the special qualities — and the unique problems — of the fighting men he had led in battle. When the Germans broke through the American lines at Kasserine Pass in Tunisia late in February, Eichelberger was prompted to comment: "Knowing how hard it is to push green troops up against veterans, I am not as surprised as some may have been. My great trouble out here was that no one would admit there was any differentiation between green troops and veteran troops until after their arrival at the front, and everyone did not come to the front.[2]

"I was impressed during the Buna campaign with the fact that so many men took counsel of their fears or perhaps in self-pity thought of the troubles they were having and seemed to forget that the enemy also had troubles....General Grant's old statement that the victory goes to the one who can put the last foot forward is one that I never forgot for a minute."[3]

Eichelberger did forget, apparently, what had happened to Grant after his first major victory, the capture of Fort Donelson. While the governing facts were different, his feelings were much the same as those that nearly drove Grant out of the Army in the spring of 1862.

In his Memoirs Grant revealed how the victory at Donelson brought recognition, but also a feeling of hurt disappointment. His commanding officer, Major General Henry W. Halleck, had not been at all generous in his praise and in the ensuing months had even placed obstacles in Grant's path. "The news . . . caused great delight all over the North. . . . My chief, who was in St. Louis, telegraphed his congratulations to General Hunter in Kansas for . . . sending reinforcements so rapidly. To Washington he telegraphed that the victory was due to General C. F. Smith [a subordinate]. 'Promote him,' he said, 'and the whole country will applaud.'" Grant's name was included in a formal order thanking the military and naval forces for the victory, but he received no other recognition whatever from Halleck. Later, when Grant had been relieved temporarily for his alleged disobedience of orders resulting from a breakdown in communications, Halleck sent him a copy of his dispatch to Washington "entirely exonerating me." What Grant did not discover until later was that Halleck's reports had caused the trouble in the first place.[4]

Eichelberger made similar complaints against his Chief. MacArthur's failure to visit and therefore fully to appreciate conditions at the front, the casual attitude at GHQ toward the difficult if unspectacular (and unnewsworthy) "mopping up" operations, Eichelberger's over-exposure to the public (as well as to Japanese riflemen), the obstacles placed by MacArthur to professional recognition and advancement, and the insertion of an army commander over his head all contributed to the self-pity that can be detected in many of his letters throughout 1943. To Miss Em he usually was guarded in his language and occasionally downright deceptive in concealing the extent of his frustration and disappointments, for while he wished to convey as complete and true a picture as possible of the conditions he faced, at the same time he needed her cheerful support to bolster his own spirits. "I know you will keep your sense of humor, and laugh — any other course is just self-punishment. Laughter makes one's problems unreal — I found that out years ago when I was serving with Malin."[5]

But two documents, one of them never intended to see the light of day, reveal some of the reasons why Eichelberger had grown disgruntled and disillusioned. Three days before the end of the Papuan campaign he wrote, but never sent, a letter to a personal friend in the War Department. And in October, during a brief visit with Miss Em in San Francisco, he left a lengthy memorandum in his bank deposit box that casts further light upon his relationships with GHQ during the Buna campaign.

January 19, 1943

Dear Pete,[6]

After the victory [at Buna] I heard nothing from GHQ for over a week. Then came a very nice letter from General MacArthur stating he was returning to the mainland and he had hoped to congratulate me in person. I now learn that all the advanced Command Post of GHQ, which has been living at Moresby, either has returned to the mainland with him or will shortly do so. I am at a loss to understand a situation where I, the senior American commander, had not been informed of the contemplated change nor informed as to my future role. Indications are that upon the arrival of the 41st Division, General Fuller would take over command of the area, but nothing from anybody in authority. I believe General MacArthur's letter was written as a result of General Blamey's visit to this headquarters and his inspection of the late battlefields. Sutherland visited here twice during the latter stages of the fighting. The first time, he arrived with what he said was a directive from General MacArthur to act as my chief of staff in securing a successful and speedy conclusion of the fight if he, General Sutherland, thought it advisable. I took him to the front and allowed him to see conditions as they were. The next day the situation was desperate and I suggested he be sent to the left flank as my representative, but he suggested it would be better if he returned to the other side of the mountain where he could make his report to General MacArthur. No one else on the GHQ staff has visited this front since the conclusion of the fighting in order to see at first hand the difficulties our troops were up against.

The American troops consisted of three depleted fever-ridden regiments that have had no replacements. They were below strength before they ever sailed from Australia. They have taken a total of over 2100 battle casualties.[7] The losses are enormous, but it was inevitable. I had a victory to gain and if necessary losses had to be taken. Of course, losses are always far too large among troops that have had no real training. All the sins of poorly trained troops came to the front during this campaign. One soldier told me that in twenty months of service he had had only one night problem, and asked how he could be expected to be proficient in night patrolling against the Japanese under these conditions. I had warned Generals MacArthur and Sutherland, before these regiments of the 32d came up here, that they were not prepared to fight the Japanese on equal terms and that after my preliminary inspection in Australia I could only give them barely satisfactory in combat efficiency. This was based not only on my personal observation and inspection but on reports from my staff, the members of which had observed all forms of divisions and all states of training back home. However, both vigorously denied the truth of my estimate. . . .

When I saw General MacArthur in Moresby he told me I was to capture Buna or lose my life, but that if I succeeded my name would be announced as being in Australia and that I would be a very prominent figure in the United States. Mind you . . . up until a radio broadcast the other night, my whereabouts have been successfully concealed. When one faces death as many times as I have in the last month and has seen a favorite aide shot at a distance of about ten feet, a distinguished general officer wounded in the shoulder while attempting to lead men into battle, and a very close personal friend, as well as chief of staff, evacuated because of wounds, one gets a bit detached on the subject of publicity. The fighting part of the job, I like. It is the other side of it that has been my difficult problem. The fact remains that I shall continue to be subjected to this steady and studied discourtesy by the Chief of Staff of the SWPA who in most people's eyes, and certainly in his own, represents General MacArthur. . . .

I am now in command of the Allied Forces charged with the reduction of Sanananda. This is really funny because on the same radio which announced my being designated as receiving the DSC . . . came the announcement that the campaign in New Guinea had reached a successful conclusion and that only mopping up operations remained in the Sanananda area. . . . But let me point out that this "mopping up" has held up the 7th Australian Division for two months. . . . Everyone feels that the Sanananda campaign is going to be every bit as difficult, if not more so, than the Buna campaign. The terrain is similar except that the Japanese are entrenched further from the coast and there are only narrow corridors or trails along which our troops can advance. The pillboxes and entrenchments have been steadily improved for the two months that the 7th Australian Division have faced them. The inference of course is that when the Sanananda campaign is concluded it was of such unimportance that the high command did not need to give it its personal attention, whereas if it fails I have been in command of an unsuccessful venture and will return under a cloud.

. . . In the many days of fighting the Japanese on a shoestring, there was never a time when they could not have come boiling out on any one of our flanks, in superior numbers, and have destroyed our forces. . . .

Perhaps I tell you these things because you might hear that another field where fighting offers is open. Maybe I tell you . . . because I want one friend to have a full picture should the question ever arise.

You know I shall do everything in my power to fulfill my mission here and retain the good will of all my associates, but I must be honest and admit a fear that there may be an open break, hence this long epistle.

October 22, 1943

Memorandum for Emmalina:

Before leaving you to go back into the fog of censorship, I would like to leave you some notes on the peculiar happenings in the Southwest Pacific Area. . . .

In giving me the mission of crushing the Japs at Buna it must be remembered that the American troops (only infantry then present) consisted of 128th Infantry and about 2/3 of the 126th Infantry (the rest of the latter were under Aussie command on the Sanananda trail). The 127th Infantry did not begin to come in until the middle of December. . . . These fever-ridden troops who had been on part rations for a long time had not been trained by me and the plan of campaign . . . was not mine. The troops had been roughly handled by the Japs and the situation as stated to me by General MacArthur (this was true) was desperate.

In his letter to me of December 13 . . . as well as when giving me my mission, General MacArthur pointed out that "time was of the essence," "that our dangers increased hour by hour," etc. In this he was right to a large extent — one great danger was that the malaria mosquito would lick us if the Japs didn't since our men were living in the swamps. There was also some danger of Jap reinforcement by water. Our losses . . . were heavy. 2500 battle casualties are many when our total infantry was only three times 2500 — 7500 (approximately). This is not counting the Aussie Brigade and tanks, which also lost heavily. I tell you this to show you how unfair it was to publish to the world in the communique . . . that our losses were small because time was no object. Our losses *in proportion* by bullets would have been much higher if the malaria mosquito hadn't removed so many from the field of battle . . . and therefore from danger by bullets. I believe that of the men who actually carried rifles and fought on the firing lines that about one-half were killed or wounded.

After Buna fell on 2 January I heard nothing from General MacArthur of any kind until I received his letter of about the 8th of January . . . telling me that *he* was returning to the mainland and speaking of my incessant exposure. In this connection, General Herring informed me that he had asked General MacArthur to call me off from leading troops personally or I would be killed and that he said "I want him to die if he doesn't get into Buna." The Aussie high command knew this.

General MacArthur announced his return to Australia by saying that there was nothing left in Papua but some "mopping up" at Sanananda. This was just an excuse to get home as at that time there was no indication of any crackup of the Japs at Sanananda. In fact, after he went home, the attack with tanks and the best we had at Sanananda including the fresh 163d Infantry . . . made on 12 January 1943 failed to gain

but a few yards.... General Herring was left in command in New
Guinea. He said, in effect ... that it was still a 2 or 3 month job. He was
furious and said that he and I were the goats — later he said that he
would go to Moresby and assume command and that I would get this
job to do. ...

By great good luck I had the Japs killed by the 22nd of January and
the fighting was over. If General MacArthur had known we could do
it, he would have waited to celebrate a great victory. We received *no*
information from GHQ that showed the Japs were in desperate straits
(no G-2 information to that effect). After the 12 January 1943 attack
failed ... General Vasey of the 7th Aussie Division, in an estimate of
the situation presented to me as his corps commander, showed that he
couldn't lick the Japs and that he knew no solution. Brigadier Wooten
... also told me that he couldn't crack the Japs.

When I asked ... if MacArthur knew that the Aussies had put me in
command at Sanananda, he didn't answer.

These things indicate how the great hero went home without seeing
Buna before, during or after the fight while permitting press articles
from his GHQ to say that he was leading his troops in battle. MacArthur ... just stayed over at Moresby 40 minutes away and walked the
floor. I know this to be a fact.

He didn't prove much help — his offices had wonderful aerial photographs of Buna taken early in December which gave the details of
the Jap positions. These appeared in a later report but, in spite of our
many requests, did not reach us during the fighting. Our aerial maps
were on a small scale and I had to patrol to get the information available
in these maps. In this, good men lost their lives.

His knowledge of details was so faulty that his directives to me, e.g.,
a letter of December 24th spoke of attacking "by regiments, not companies, by thousands, not hundreds" indicated that he knew nothing
of the jungle and how one fights there — that he had no detailed knowledge of how our forces were divided into many corridors by swamps.[8]

The general impression that MacArthur had been present at the front
at Buna always rankled Eichelberger. "While I am on that subject,"
he recalled after the war, "I want to tell of something that happened
much later. After we were in Japan some time, John J. McCloy,
Assistant Secretary of War, and Dr. Douglas S. Freeman, the historian, came to Japan.... Dr. Freeman said that he had come in the
interest of writing a book under the title, *MacArthur and His Generals.* He then added, 'But there is one thing I have not been able to
find out in spite of my conversations and that is, just when did General MacArthur move his headquarters to Buna?'

"I tried to dodge the question by saying that at times the water was waist deep and was no place for a theater commander, but in the end he held to the question, and while Mr. McCloy's eyes twinkled, I had to say that General MacArthur's headquarters never did come to Buna. . . .

"One must not think that General MacArthur did not realize what was going on. One time he said to me, 'Bob, those were great days when you and I were fighting at Buna, weren't they?' — and laughed.

"This was a warning not to disclose that he never went to Buna."[9]

Eichelberger also took warning from the widespread publicity that greeted him when he stepped out from under the shadows of the jungle. "When the newspapermen turned loose on me after my name was released," he explained, "my name appeared in headlines over the world and my photograph was seen in many prominent magazines. . . . When these articles began to come back from the States in such magazines as Life and Saturday Evening Post,[10] General MacArthur sent for me. . . . He said, 'Do you realize I could reduce you to the grade of colonel tomorrow and send you home?'"

Remembering Dwight D. Eisenhower's story of how he had alienated MacArthur in the Philippines in the early 1930s "because some writer had written an article praising me," Eichelberger responded: "Of course you could."

MacArthur replied, "Well, I won't do it." But the incident taught Eichelberger to fear a certain kind of publicity more than anything else. "I would rather have you slip a rattlesnake in my pocket," he confided to a friend in the Bureau of Public Relations, "than to have you give me any publicity." And to his brother, shortly before the end of the war, he confessed: "I am naturally worried before any article appears about me because . . . I went through many unhappy months because of the publicity that came out about me after Buna. I paid through the nose for every line of it. . . . While I realize that publicity is the thing that brings one in the eyes of the people, it also may prove more dangerous than a Japanese bullet. If I had received too much publicity I would not be here anymore than some European glamour boys are here."

Eventually Eichelberger came to realize "that General MacArthur, in speaking of me to someone from the States, would speak very highly of me. It wasn't a question of what he thought about me but he didn't intend to have any figures rise up between him and his place in history."[11] At the time, however, he was hurt and resentful over the "ungenerous" attitude of his chief. "If he had been perhaps a bit more appreciative or if I had been handled with more understanding while I was in the midst of that fighting, I would perhaps feel differently."[12]

Nor did Eichelberger feel that he had been "exactly covered

with honors." "He did give me a DSC along with some other American and Australian officers, some of whom had not been in combat. My citation was worded exactly like the others and the principal expression, 'for precise execution of operations,' speaks for itself."[13] Satisfied with his record as a fighting commander, Eichelberger would have preferred a citation for conduct "under fire."

This was more than a matter of inner satisfaction: medals, citations, and ribbons are a part of an officer's record and therefore influence the chances for promotion. "When I look at members of my staff with all their new ribbons I feel very proud of them," Eichelberger wrote soon after his return to Australia, "and also I am glad I did not wait until the war was over to give them some belated recognition which I was in a position to give them immediately."[14]

MacArthur obviously did not share this view. When Colonel Gordon Rogers of I Corps staff left for Washington with two bullet holes, four decorations, and "a whole lot of prestige," he took with him a number of certificates to support the recommendation of the Medal of Honor for Eichelberger. Eichelberger's affection for Mac-Arthur did not increase when he learned "that the War Department was all set to approve it, but that it was disapproved by radio by my Chief."[15]

The situation was further complicated by the establishment in February 1943 of the U.S. Sixth Army and the arrival of its commander, Lieutenant General Walter Krueger. This was in no way intended as an affront to Eichelberger, although it did dim considerably his prospects for future employment or advancement, since forthcoming operations were not of sufficient dimension to involve an entire army corps. MacArthur had known Krueger in the old days and he wanted an army staff to relieve his own headquarters of some of the burden. Above all he wanted a general with sufficient seniority to outrank the Australians. This motive became evident a few days later when MacArthur gave the Sixth Army the name "Alamo Force." As a special task force, the Sixth Army now could operate directly under GHQ free of any Australian control.[16]

Eichelberger understood and accepted the reasons why another senior officer was being sent into the area; indeed his initial reaction was that the arrival of Krueger and his staff, many of whom were old friends, would "help matters." Besides, his old chief, General Malin Craig, had written assuringly, "I believe you will find Krueger a good man. He is fearless, tireless and reasonably human."[17]

February 10, 1943

Dear Miss Em,

Walter Krueger and [Brig. Gen.] George [Honnen, Krueger's Chief of Staff] had dinner with us last night. They were in their best form. Walter said the Big Chief said magnificent things about me, and perhaps I will be better off now with a buffer. He was most friendly in every way and really quite amusing.

February 18, 1943

Today I talked many hours with Walter Krueger.... His friendship is very real. My problems will be much more simple.

March 22, 1943

I know you and others have wondered about Walter, and I shall try to explain it as I see it, but with all kindness:

Long before I came out here, a lot of rank was given out before there were any troops at the time to warrant so much promotion. When I arrived I was the Junior Corps Commander[18] and, in spite of a lifetime in the Army, did not have the combat experience of which our friends here are proud (in most cases, justly so). Many moves were made, or rather hopes were extended, leading to an American Command, but by the time I went forward there were all kinds of grades of rank south of the mountains. After Buna fell, where I was under Herring ... the next week was spent, as I now know, by my boss in getting Walter, since he is very senior except for Blamey.... At Sanananda I was in command north of the mountains but that was after Walter had been asked for. I there had an interallied corps.

Whether Walter's rank will help solve the problem only time can tell — it might and it might not. It reminds me of the poker games in Shanghai ... where the cuspidor was put on the center of the table because no one dared look away to spit.

Our allies have been grand to me and ... they have not hesitated to express themselves. I like them and I can see both sides of these things.

April 11, 1943

I realize ... that you feel there is something I should do.... Ever since I have been in the Army there have been officers who have fought with those around them for what they called a "principle." In some cases it was necessary, but many of the fights came from lack of tact or perhaps a wee bit of insubordination. I did not come out here for any personal aggrandizement.... We are too near the end of our service to have separated for any reason than a desire for combat service.

I can see why it was felt necessary to play down on what was done because to over-emphasize "round one" might have meant there would be no "round two." Our Chief has appeared very appreciative to me when he has seen me and I know he has in his conversations with others.

May 3, 1943

We returned home when round one was over. There are a good many factors that go into round two and it may be quite some little time before it starts. Certainly to a gal as bright as you are, who reads the papers, I would say that you will be able to tell about as soon as anyone. ... You will be able to watch the build-up by reading good magazines ... and then will be able to tell just about what is to happen.... Read the papers and become your own strategist. Weigh what must be done before other things can be done.

On May 15, in a conversation with MacArthur, Eichelberger was told that the War Department had requested his services to command the First Army, which was still in the United States. "I wouldn't stand in your way," MacArthur assured Eichelberger and his chief of staff, "although I believe you would rather stay here and fight."

"If it were put up to me," Eichelberger retorted, "my answer might depend on whether I seemed slated to be Mayor of Rockhampton for the rest of the war."[19] To Miss Em, however, he confessed his inner feelings: "Boy, it would be hard to discourage me from taking it if offered.... Everyone here seems very friendly and I think a lot of them believe I won't be here long.... Doesn't hurt to hope."[20]

Hope lingered until late August.

August 10, 1943

Dear Miss Em,

Personally I think I have a good chance for that job and I sincerely hope so. First and always, because I want to see and be with you, and secondly, because I will have nothing but a training job here unless a forlorn hope comes up, and I am not anxious to be any Sir Launcelot for anyone around these parts. I shall do my duty towards my country and risk my life if necessary at least as far forward as anyone will go, but I shall not do it with quite the same elan or enthusiasm as I had last winter.

August 26, 1943

Hear ... that an announcement on Hughie's job was due out today making Grunert the Commanding General, First Army.... Am so sorry for you, Dear. Keep the old chin up and pray for a break....

That is hard to take but I won't let it get me down unless it gets you down. So much is to be done and *I must* keep myself in good condition.[21]

On his next visit with the Big Chief, Eichelberger learned what had gone wrong. There had been two requests to release Eichelberger to command an army elsewhere — the First Army and later the Ninth, which subsequently went to Lieutenant General William H. Simpson. "I couldn't admit that I could spare your services, Bob."

"How unfair," Eichelberger contended, and especially "when one considers that he brought General Krueger out to be an army commander and that I had been placed to a large extent out of the picture."[22]

This was the sore point — the failure of a proud and sensitive man to draw another combat assignment for more than a year after his convincing victory in Papua. His letters in the months after Buna reveal an attitude that fluctuated between the stoic and the forlorn. MacArthur's unwillingness to release him for tempting opportunities elsewhere would have produced disappointment under any circumstances, but to do so when it appeared that he was slated to spend the rest of his days in the SWPA on the shelf is what evoked the bitterness that occasionally crept into the daily letters to Miss Em, despite his determination to remain cheerful. "If the war ... brings me no further honors," he wrote even before learning that he was being considered for an army command, "I have still had my share. I am too near the top to not get knocked around a bit by those who may follow the law of the wolf pack, but that has always been customary in all wars and all armies."[23]

The letters to Miss Em during these long, uncertain months also suggest something of the inevitable "play of personalities" in which he seemed to be caught. Here too his historical perspective was of help. "One must remember that this may happen any place and usually does. ... If I had gone to Africa as originally planned I might have been among those who did not get ashore, or I might have been in the position of the corps commander who was relieved the other day."[24]

In these letters the word "play" quickly took on another meaning. In addition to MacArthur's well-known flair for the dramatic, he had also a role to play in the SWPA theater. "We all think that our Chief has a very sincere affection for me, but he will, in the future, be a queer combination of a Sarah Bernhardt dominating the stage and, at the same time, fighting off — as he sees it — a great mass of personal enemies, both foreign and domestic, who have no connection with our natural enemy, the Japanese."[25]

So the Big Chief, for the benefit of the censor, soon was identified in the letters as "Sarah," for there were times when his performances almost matched those of the great French actress.

May 5, 1943

Dearest Miss Em,

I could be in far worse places than I am. It is true that I have not a lot to do unless I go make Bill Gill[26] unhappy by sitting on his neck. But at least that is not my fault. One must realize that the enemy often makes our plans for us. His strength may determine what you can or cannot do. . . . I realize that Washington has heard about me in part from a man whom it was necessary for me to relieve, and from a man who is the greatest "I" man I have ever met.

May 25, 1943

This morning I have been talking with an officer from McNair's[27] office. I am amazed at how little they know back home of the true picture. Some day they will know what we went through.

May 30, 1943

Generally speaking, I think I am in a better position with the Chief than I was earlier (say February), because he realizes what I went through better. His attitude is a very friendly one. Walter [Krueger] is friendly, but I think wants to get some of that which I had in December and January if opportunity offers. If so, I may miss something for a period and that may or may not be a break, depending on Lady Luck. The future is in the laps of the gods. They all have me marked as a fighter (I believe), and want to use me when the time arises. Then too I realize that the mosquito by a bite or two might change the whole picture — all this leads up to my desire to be as happy as possible. To have no more nights like in February when I couldn't sleep and spent my days feeling sorry for myself.

Asked the Big Chief what he thinks of Forrest's job[28] — he didn't know whether it was aimed at him or at me but thought at both. An amazing thing when one remembers what I had to do.

May 31, 1943

Walter is here today. . . . Presumedly he should be happy but doesn't seem to be nearly as much as I am. . . . It is evident that things get under his skin. He is getting a little of the same reaction that I had before he came.[29]

June 2, 1943

One must develop a hide like a rhinoceros, or rather I think one must develop the habit of happiness. Through life I have seen so many people unhappy under conditions when others under the same circumstances are very happy.

June 13, 1943

We must . . . insofar as we can, develop the habit of happiness. A few good laughs I find with my staff grow like a snowball rolling down hill. If I am ever worried or sour I find my staff reflects my moods, so I try always to act as though I am cheerful and often I find myself happy on that account. . . . You would be astonished at some of the things I could tell you about the play of personalities.

I went to see the Chief and he talked for 1½ hours on many subjects. It looks as though he is being short changed again in the tools he is to use. While this is a matter of some months in the future, it shows that he is not going to be given much. . . .

My Chief talked of the Republican nomination for next year — I can see that he expects to get it and I sort of think so too.[30] Maybe he could run a good race.

July 15, 1943

I had about an hour and a half with the Chief last night in which he covered everything that happened on his recent trip and his observations on world conditions. . . . The Chief was in fine fettle and was most entertaining. He could charge admission when he is going good, and I would be glad to pay.[31]

July 28, 1943

I have not seen Walter for a long time. He left without telling me where he was going and, although anyone from [Sgt. Thaddeus] Dombrowski [Eichelberger's orderly] up can give me all the details of what is going on, I have never been told anything by him. The Big Chief keeps me well oriented. This attitude on the part of Walter is not aimed at me but is peculiar to him. As the Chinaman said, it makes those around him "very unhappy."

July 29, 1943

Mussolini and the war in Sicily are our main topics of conversation — really I think it has been fine. Maybe the war over there will look better and wind up in a year or so. . . .

Over here the war is not progressing by leaps and bounds. . . . I know nothing that you cannot read in *Time* and in your papers. . . . The little Jap doesn't fold up as he is supposed to do, but I hope that Lady Luck will fly up for those kids. According to the papers, the Air Corps pounds them a lot. . . .

While I realize that the Air Forces have been destroying great industrial sections in both Italy and Germany, I agree with our Chief of Staff in Washington, who has stated in the press that it will take all branches of the service to secure a victory. I don't believe anyone is so foolish as to believe that the Germans would have surrendered in Tunisia because of the bombing alone, although I must admit that air superiority is a very great factor in victory.[32]

August 4, 1943

I have not seen Walter for nearly two months. He went away without telling me where he was going or anything about it, and I feel he does not want me to share in any glory he might achieve.[33] This glory, by the way, is a long time in the future if I do not miss my guess.

I shall have plenty to keep me busy here and I do not intend to make myself unhappy over things I cannot help.... I probably have the most loyal, happy staff anyone ever had. Many of them were willing to die to put things over for me and such things come to few men.

August 10, 1943

Talked with [Maj. Gen. Charles A.] Willoughby [MacArthur's G-2] who was very interesting. He talked with the chief in Washington [Marshall] for some time. He doesn't believe that much will be done for the people out here until the number one job is over.[34] In fact, he feels also that something may and will be done to hurt the Japs but that everything possible will be done to see that the Jap is hurt and MacArthur not helped in doing it. He confirmed a lot of things I had been told before by the Chief [MacArthur] about things out here.

I talked with the Big Chief for some time. He didn't mention what has just been going on[35] so I judge he is not too well satisfied.... He talked a lot of the future — his plans are not as yet too definite, but I did gather that Walter is coming back soon and he (MacArthur) is going up soon to stay indefinitely in the same place where I had my historic talk with him (the one from which *he* led his troops last winter). Walter, I know from many sources, has had not too easy a time — rumors say he is to be the training man back here and that GHQ will do the leading (in the same old way). In things to come, my corps staff will be used back here for training and ... probably will be used to command definite things in the more or less distant future. The pattern, it seems to me, is for no prima donnas to rise from the trap drum players, and those who get results may find themselves running for mayor of some such town as the one in which I live.... I am going to have a lot more to do soon but I am not going to be any big Indian....

This letter is not written to disturb you — I want you to know how things stand. Remember that I am, when at "home," surrounded with the best food and the greatest amount of laughter in Australia.

August 14, 1943

I notice what you say about hearing over the radio that things are going according to plan. Naturally, the Japs have a tendency to slow up things because they do not surrender. Those who go into the jungle to fight them have my sympathy. They have one great advantage over me and that is that they are operating in the winter time rather than during the rainy season. Of course material help has increased rapidly, such as air and artillery.

August 15, 1943

Much to my surprise I am in the big GHQ plane again en route to the city [Brisbane].... Yesterday noon your dickeybird [Gen. Sutherland] called up and said the Chief wanted to see me. At first, I was all jazzed up thinking it was that thing we have discussed [Command of the First Army], but after questioning I found not — neither is it a trip like the one last December. He said it was something to do with a distinguished visitor.

The distinguished visitor was Mrs. Franklin D. Roosevelt, who was scheduled to arrive shortly in Australia on one of her frequent visits to American hospitals, troops, and Red Cross installations. General Eichelberger was given the task of escorting her and making the necessary arrangements, which involved meticulous planning, cheerful tact, and even touchy diplomatic problems.

The trip is described in some detail in Our Jungle Road to Tokyo, and the letters to Miss Em indicate that he learned to enjoy and respect Mrs. Roosevelt. "Her visit here was an historical event and she is undoubtedly going to be a person who will go down in history as one of the great women of her time. We are shoved up so close to events now that it is a little hard for us to know the true importance of things."36

All the same, Eichelberger drew a deep breath of relief when the trip was over. "One of the greatest dangers," he confided to Miss Em, "from the standpoint of my military service, was terminated on the departure of our visitor. There were so many ways of having things go wrong, and so many conflicting interests." And again he wrote: "I would rather be fighting the Japanese again than going through the horrors of one of these trips."37

August 15, 1943

Dearest Emmalina,

See by the papers that Munda fell — the Chief talked about that area.38 Also, about the row in his area [Salamaua]. Some are coming home and I am a bit fearful for my friend Ned [Herring] because there has been a lot of boom boom and not anyone to close in on those devils. Horace [Fuller] is back. He didn't get where it was actually going on but some of those he sent had a hard time. . . . I am not out of this picture but the time hasn't arrived to use an American of my rank yet.

August 17, 1943

This morning when I was talking to the Big Chief, Walter arrived — first time I have seen him for months. Didn't know he was back. . . . I know I am not definitely on the shelf and if I am going to stay out here I shall hope at some time to be used. Certainly it will not be any time soon as the Aussies are doing their stuff now. . . .

Never have seen the Chief as happy as he was today — you will have noticed in the papers the bypass of Vila and the landing in Vella Lavella in the Solomons. Then you will notice . . . the destruction of a lot of Jap planes on the ground near Wewak.[39] Don't blame him for being happy, and George Kenney was too.

August 21, 1943

We have just seen Walter off. He had a perfectly wonderful time. Yesterday they showed him Fuller's outfit [Forty-first Infantry Division] but today we have seen Fred Irving's [Twenty-fourth Infantry Division] as well as my own corps troops. He was very well pleased with everything but was particularly pleased with the laughs he got out of everything. . . .

The Chief and most of the rest are leaving for a long time to come. Walter has not been in action yet out here — my friend Ned has been handling that and what a headache it has been. Walter's work has been principally logistical stuff. He is a very lonely man.

September 17, 1943

Frankly I do not expect the future to bring me much opportunity for direct action such as last December. . . . As far as you are concerned I imagine you would prefer that I not close in again on our little friends. Our Chief in one of my last interviews said: "I realize now Bob that in the end some one must *fight* those Japanese — that artillery or bombing alone will not do it."

September 22, 1943

Naturally if I am to be out here I desire further combat duty. . . . This career of mine, funny as it has been, has furnished some moments of pride and lots of laughter mixed up with some bad spots here and there. . . . I can smile and laugh often in a way that makes me proud of my ability to shake things off and I intend to keep it up.

September 25, 1943

There are so many wheels within wheels that I confess things have gotten far beyond me. I guess I am too simple a soul to know what it is all about.

September 30, 1943

I saw the Chief yesterday and talked with him at some length.... Then later Bill Ritchie[40] came to have dinner.... A good many interesting points came up in talking to him. One was that he said he saw the wire in which objection was raised from over here to releasing me for some position back home....

There is a great deal of personality wrapped up in this whole thing and it is hard to get a clear picture.... Again, there enters the question of my ambitions.... These things I cannot discuss with you very well. If one were always able to talk to someone like the one with whom I served in 1918–19 [Gen. William S. Graves], it would be possible to reach decisions more easily. Over here I must be on the job in talking to anyone not of my own friends because not every one is frank.

At this point Eichelberger's thoughts turned to his forthcoming trip to the United States — not to take command of the First Army, as he had hoped, but to spend a brief leave with Miss Em in San Francisco. The ostensible purpose of this visit was to help settle the estate of Mrs. Eichelberger's mother, but he was also anxious to give her a clear and full picture of "the peculiar happenings in the SWPA." To put Miss Em's mind more at ease about the future was a necessary part of his own mental reconditioning.

Leaving Rockhampton on 6 October, Eichelberger spent a "very nice and friendly time" that evening with General Krueger, and the next day he took off for San Francisco. At Honolulu he picked up some interesting gossip from Lieutenant General Robert C. Richardson, Commanding General of the U.S. Forces in Pacific Ocean Areas. The Japanese stronghold at Rabaul was to be bypassed and the Central Pacific line of advance would cut north of New Guinea, "shutting MacArthur out." At a recent conference in Hawaii, Admirals William F. Halsey, Chester W. Nimitz, and Ernest J. King made it apparent that it was to be "their show and no one else's." MacArthur, it appeared, would not even be permitted to retake the Philippines.[41]

Notes

1. Eichelberger to Miss Em, 30 January, 24 February, 1943.

2. Ibid., 21 February 1943.

3. Ibid., 27 February 1943.

4. U.S. Grant, *Personal Memoirs of U.S. Grant* (New York, 1885), I, 316-17, 328.

5. Eichelberger to Miss Em, 25 March 1943. The reference is to the pre-war years Eichelberger spent with Gen. Malin Craig, who succeeded MacArthur in 1935. "He had a reputation as a strict disciplinarian; to me he was a wise and understanding mentor. For three years I lunched almost daily with him in his office and heard at first hand the troubles of a Chief of Staff. Gen. Craig wrote frequently to Gen. Eichelberger throughout the Pacific War. Eichelberger, *Our Jungle Road to Tokyo* (New York, 1950), p. xvii.

6. Maj. Gen. V. L. Peterson, Inspector General. At the top of the letter is written "Draft, letter not sent."

7. Milner puts the American ground casualties for the Papuan campaign at 2,848 (Samuel Milner, *Victory in Papua* £Washington, 1957., p. 370), but when this letter was written the fighting had not yet concluded.

8. "After my return from Buna . . . he had the gall to question my exposure to hostile fire in spite of the fact that he had ordered me to take Buna or not come out alive. . . . He told me . . . 'I could have led them into Buna, Bob. I replied . . . 'You may have been able to lead them, General, but you must remember that in most instances not over half a dozen men could have seen you at the time in that dense jungle.' In other words, in spite of all the reports he must have seen and my many reports to him in the form of personal letters, I think he still visualized a two-mile American front instead of little isolated high-ground projections that led towards the Japanese lines and which limited the American advance to various narrow places. . . ." Eichelberger Dictations, 11 November 1960.

9. Eichelberger Dictations, 24 September 1953, 17 February 1956.

10. Mr. Roy Larson, president of *Time* and related to Gen. Eichelberger through marriage, wrote to Miss Em in January 1943 that he had briefed his Washington bureau chief "up to date on the mysterious secrecy surrounding Bob's whereabouts and activities," and he expressed his determination "to see that he gets proper recognition for the toughest of all assignments." (Roy Larson to Miss Em, 9 January 1943.) "As far back as the issue of *Life* dated February 22, which had certain pictures of the Buna fighting, Mrs. Eichelberger pleaded with Roy with tears in her eyes *not* to say anything about me. He thought she was just a 'little teched with the heat,' but she was right." Eichelberger to Maj. Gen. Alec D. Surles, 21 October 1943.

11. Eichelberger Dictations, 9 September 1953, 28 March 1955, 27 October 1955; Eichelberger to Maj. Gen. Alec D. Surles, 21 October 1943; Eichelberger to George Eichelberger, 8 July 1945.

12. Eichelberger to Miss Em, 28 May 1943. The reverse side of this coin is seen in a letter to Miss Em dated 19 July 1943. Mentioning "a grand chap" who served as assistant to one of his staff officers, Eichelberger requested of Miss Em: "I would be glad to have you ask his wife in for a cup of tea or something. . . . At any rate . . . be sure to call her and tell her I have said nice things about her husband. These things mean a great deal to a young officer."

13. Eichelberger to Miss Em, 23 July 1943.

14. Eichelberger to Miss Em, 29 March 1943.

15. Eichelberger, Memorandum for Emmalina, 22 October 1943; Dictations, 28 March, 1955. General Eisenhower related to Eichelberger after the war how he had refused a Medal of Honor after the African campaign "because he knew of a man who had received one for sitting in a hole in the ground — meaning MacArthur."

16. See John Miller, Jr., *Cartwheel: The Reduction of Rabaul* (Washington, 1959), p. 54; David Dexter, *The New Guinea Offensives* (San Francisco: Tri-Ocean Books, Canberra, 1961), pp. 220–222. At that stage the Sixth Army comprised I Corps, an Engineer Special Brigade, a Paratroop Infantry Regiment, and an attached Marine Division.

17. Eichelberger to Miss Em, 11 January 1943; Gen. Malin Craig to Eichelberger, 26 February 1943.

18. There were at the time of Eichelberger's arrival in Australia three Australian Corps. His friend Gen. Herring, who originally was commander of the II Corps, was given command of the I Australian Corps late in September and hence was senior to Eichelberger.

19. Eichelberger, Memorandum for Emmalina, 22 October 1943; Eichelberger to Miss Em, 14 May 1943.

20. Eichelberger to Miss Em, 7 June 1943.

21. The last sentence is taken from Eichelberger's letter of 27 August 1943. Hughie was Lt. Gen. Hugh A. Drum, and his replacement was Lt. Gen. George Grunert.

22. Eichelberger, Memorandum for Emmalina, 22 October 1943; Eichelberger to Miss Em, 30 September 1943.

23. Eichelberger to Miss Em, 24 March 1943.

24. This would be Maj. Gen. Lloyd Fredendall, who was replaced by Maj. Gen. George S. Patton as commander of II Corps in Tunisia. "Was surprised to see in the paper today that George Patton has taken Fredendall's place. . . . Of course I had read about our troops being pushed back some time ago but didn't know who would be held responsible." (Eichelberger to Miss Em, 20 March 1943.) "Lloyd may not have been responsible for the tactical stuff, but the leader in the field usually is held responsible for the fighting qualities of his troops even if he is just a bit out of luck. Some leaders in World War I were pulled out after defeat although they hardly had time to meet the staff." (Ibid., 17 April 1943.)

25. Eichelberger to Col. C. L. Fenton, 20 October 1943.

26. Maj. Gen. William H. Gill had taken over command of the Thirty-second Division after the Buna campaign.

27. Lt. Gen. Leslie J. McNair commanded the Army Ground Forces.

28. Gen. Forrest Harding was placed in command of the Canal Zone and Antilles Department after being relieved at Buna.

29. The last two sentences are taken from the letter to Miss Em of 1 June 1943, and are included here because they grow out of the same conversation with Gen. Krueger.

30. In his *Reminiscences,* Gen. MacArthur claims that in 1944 he had entertained no political ambitions whatever and that he had firmly disavowed any intention to enter the presidential race (MacArthur, *Reminiscences* [New York, 1954], pp. 184-185). That the reverse was true is indicated in Eichelberger's letters at the time and in his postwar dictations. "Before the 1944 election, he talked to me a number of times about the Presidency, but would usually confine his desires by saying that if it were not for his hatred, or rather the extent to which he despised FDR, he would not want it." Eichelberger Dictations, 12 November 1953.

31. The last two sentences, which refer to the same conversation, are taken from Eichelberger's letter of 18 July 1943.

32. The last paragraph is taken from Eichelberger's letter to Miss Em of 31 July 1943.

33. When headquarters for ALAMO Force were established on 20 June, the staff involved moved from Headquarters Sixth Army, near Brisbane, to Milne Bay.

34. The number one job was the defeat of Germany and Italy in Europe, a priority first established at the Anglo-American ARCADIA Conference in early January 1942.

35. This is probably a reference to the diversionary attack by a combined Australian and American Force against Salamaua, on the Huon Gulf some 175 miles northwest of Buna.

36. Eichelberger to Miss Em, 26 September 1943.

37. Ibid., 7 September 1943, 18 September 1943.

38. Munda Point in New Georgia, a vital site for an air base in the Solomon Islands, had fallen to the XIV Corps on 5 August 1943, after twelve days of fighting. Eichelberger made a point never to mention a military operation until it had been described in the newspapers, when he then felt free to comment upon it in general terms.

39. On 17 August 1943, the Fifth Air Force began the air attack on Wewak and satellite fields to neutralize them for the coming offensive against Lae. In two days the Japanese lost 100 planes by their own count, "over 200" according to Kenney's headquarters. Miller, *Cartwheel,* p. 199.

40. Col. William Ritchie, of the Operations Division, War Department, General Staff, who was in Australia to deliver papers containing the Combined Chiefs' decision on the strategy to be followed in the Pacific war.

41. Eichelberger Diary, 8 October 1943.

CHAPTER FIVE

Our Stars Are Looking Up

Two weeks with Miss Em provided the right tonic, and when General Eichelberger departed on 25 October they were both in a better frame of mind. "Your grand attitude toward life and the way you looked are of great comfort to me now," he wrote immediately upon his return to Australia. "I hope that my visit will clear the atmosphere a bit. We know where we stand at any rate."[1]

In the intervening weeks General MacArthur's spirits had also improved, for in his diary on 28 October Eichelberger noted: "Arrived to see MacArthur and talked. He is on the top again. Marshall has backed down and he will capture Philippine Islands."

There would be more disappointments, and still another refusal by the Big Chief to release him for a high command in the Channel crossing under General Eisenhower, but the increased tempo of military operations in the southwest Pacific and the gradual build-up of men and materiel did suggest to Eichelberger and his staff that they might soon play a more active part. In February came the long-awaited call, and before the month was out Eichelberger and his immediate staff found themselves winging northward to Goodenough Island, off the northeastern tip of New Guinea, at the top of the Coral Sea. The ground was smothered by thick jungle, the shacks that until recently had housed Sixth Army Headquarters were in bad repair, and much work remained before the island was ready for use as an amphibious and jungle training area by the Twenty-fourth Division, but there was no complaint. Everyone was busy and interested and the long months, "with their many military and personal disappointments,"[2] at last were over. No one had time to think about them.

November 17, 1943

Dearest Miss Em,

This morning I drove in with Walter ... because he wanted to see the Chief. ... Walter is very friendly and I am glad to say that he expects to take my staff forward some time after Christmas. ... Of course my staff will be delighted to move over to uncomfortable surroundings because they have felt sidetracked and frustrated. Think our turn will follow some months later, but of course this is all in the realm of fancy yet as even plans are not yet made. We know we are *not* to be in the first show.

November 22, 1943

I can understand your inability to follow things too well since I get a bit bewildered myself at times. ... There are rumors there will be another organization such as I command organized out here, but whether the staff will come from the States or be picked from this vicinity is something I have not heard. ... When I came up with Walter the other day I knew the situation very well. Now that he has been called back for two days of conferences, I am not sure. ... I find it very interesting to talk to him as he comes back to Ike every few minutes. He is also interested in other well known individuals. ... I am not nearly as interested in who gets this and who gets that as I might be. If the devil himself would come along and win some victories for us I would be all for him, and their wives would have my permission to advertise themselves to the nth degree.

November 23, 1943

This morning I heard a broadcaster talking about George Patton. Unfortunately I was not in a position to rush to the radio, but I gathered he is still in command of the Seventh Army, that no enlisted man had refused to obey his commands, and that he has never been reprimanded by Ike. ... Of course a reprimand means many things to different people. In the Army it means either a formal written statement or an official bawling out orally. I have found that sometimes words are intended to deceive rather than to enlighten. ...[3]

This morning you read in the papers, as we have, about the landings in the Gilbert Islands. It will make the little Jap wonder where he is going to be hit next and will make him divide his strength in many directions.

November 25, 1943

The papers are playing up the case of my classmate George very heavily. ... I am afraid somebody is going to suggest his promotion be held up, which of course would be hard for him. ... The general reaction is that one could lose a battle and be forgiven, but one cannot hit a man in a hospital and get away with it. . . . I feel very sorry about it because I feel George is a man who can win victories and that is what I want. He certainly is a grand soldier in spite of certain well known peculiarities.[4]

November 26, 1943

Our visitor [MacArthur] came today at about nine-thirty, and in the next few hours we rode approximately a hundred miles over very rough roads, in addition to talking to quite a few people. He really put in quite a hard day. . . .

He talked on many subjects and seemed to enjoy himself. He really has fine . . . and young looking eyes. Being with him all day is not an easy job, but I certainly enjoyed talking to him. He thinks my classmate George is through because of this late publicity, and perhaps Ike also because he permitted denials to be issued before the story finally came out.

. . . He does not think that Ike will be the No. 1 boy because of this trouble about George. . . . I find this reaction on the part of two of the older gentlemen over here. George was a great fellow until he began to get a lot of publicity, and then I haven't heard anything more about what a great soldier he is. From it all, I gather he does not think George has a Chinaman's chance anymore.

He told me also that when that list for promotion came out he protested it because your friend [Eichelberger] was not on it. He received apologies and the statement that he would be placed on the next one. . . . He gave out quite a lot of praise whether due or not. . . . I don't know, lady, I don't know. I'm just a boy from the country. Things have come far, far beyond the simple little principles I used to follow when I took whatever was given to me, with regret, perhaps, but still I took it. . . .

I shall be glad when the spring nominations are over. Many things may then be clarified.

November 27, 1943

I am following the Patton case closely, I cannot believe that Ike was personally connected with those denials. If one case is known, undoubtedly all three . . . are known, so I rather look for George's name not to get by on that permanent promotion. In the meantime, however, mine is also held up.

December 2, 1943

The morning papers carry accounts of the Cairo Conference, which is now no longer a secret — nothing to indicate that Dick [Sutherland] was there, although they speak of the absence of General MacArthur.

All very interesting and very important.[5] Also, you have noticed in the papers that our destroyers have bombarded Madang.[6] This is very interesting. Keep a good map and draw your own conclusions....

December 5, 1943

You really know lots more of the news than we do because you are able to get the two best papers in the world there in New York City.... I trust you study the situation with great intelligence. One of the things you should observe very carefully in your reading is the question of Japanese air strength. As soon as that is radically reduced then things can happen, and not before.

Some of my staff who have been up with Walter for a long time[7] have returned, and the experience and knowledge of conditions they have gained will be a lot of help. In many ways I have been lucky in not having as many bosses as I used to have a year ago.

It is just a year ago today that Eddie was shot, and those things come back to me now very vividly. Whatever changes I would make if I were to do that over again, I still do not believe I could improve on my willingness to fight those people. One hears occasionally from Walter about the fact that high ranking officers should not expose themselves. There will be some astonishment when he finds he won't have much trouble that way. I found my great difficulty was in getting people to expose themselves at the right time. In other words, to get moving.

December 7, 1943

This morning I am delighted with the news ... about the success of the [Tehran] conference in Iran. I consider it the greatest victory of the war. Without that cooperation, nothing final could be accomplished. With it, we should get a victory over Germany in a reasonable amount of time. If Russia stays in there swinging we should have Germany out in a year. If Germany is given any kind of terms short of unconditional surrender, they might quit more quickly. I am of course anxious to have the entire effort put into the Pacific as soon as possible so that we can get this war over.

December 8, 1943

We are interested again this morning in the story of the conference in Cairo with the President of Turkey. If these conferences are successful, I rather imagine people will hesitate to vote against our present Commander in Chief [Roosevelt] in favor of one who has had no diplomatic experience. I doubt if there is anyone in our public life who would appeal to Mr. Stalin as much as Mr. Roosevelt.

I am trying to tell you everything I can these days because it may be later I shall not be able to write to you so freely.... I notice in the paper an interview with Halsey. Although my Chief gives out the communiques, Halsey does not mention him in his review of the fighting in the Solomons except to say that his bombers helped. Watching the communiques that come out from Colonel Knox and the Marines following every little fight, I feel a mistake was made when our hard fighting was played down over here. We were the first to make a successful offensive through Japanese prepared positions, but you cannot tell it from anything that was ever put out. Some day I would like to write about it in a very modest way as a tribute to the men who fought and died there.

December 9, 1943

It always interests me to get into a camp and see the different way the men fix themselves up. A man like Fred [Irving] will do nothing more than be clean and neat and will put all his time on training. Another place I saw yesterday morning, officers had contributed from their own pockets to the building of cement walks and had concrete floors for their tents, as well as many other comforts in their officers' clubs and messes. It is surprising what a difference that makes. In one case of a club of battalion officers, they had the finest officers' camp I have ever seen. Even the walks were lined with whitewashed stones.

December 11, 1943

I have been interested in whether or not the story about...[Patton] drawing...the pistol...has ever become publicly known....All those real tough looking pictures were fine when he was known to be solely a warrior, but they don't do him much good in view of his later publicity.

We are all very much interested in the Russian war front. If the Russkies block off that Kiev drive, while hitting the Germans in other places with a nice winter attack while the ground is frozen, it should fix things up for them.[8]

You warned me about certain person, and of course I realize his lack of friendship. When I was with you I made up my mind not to worry about those things I could not help, and I have gotten myself into a very good frame of mind. If someone else is chosen to do the fighting I shall try to make the best of it....I agree with you that your little friend[9] might want to interfere with my use, although I am not 100% sure of that.

December 12, 1943

Walter finally broke down and gave out a little interview the other day — I read it in a paper last night. He told me when I saw him last: "Do you realize that nothing goes out of GHQ except what they want?"

I appreciate Dick [Sutherland] just as much as you do, and I shall always be prepared for the worst. . . . It doesn't hurt though for me to meet things with a laugh, because it is hard to get a fellow down who has a grin on his face. . . . While you are well and reasonably happy I can get by in fine shape.

We do not know when we shall leave home — there are other things to happen (which have been delayed from time to time) before we can be called without being in the way. Whether your friend will throw a monkey wrench after he gets back I do not know, but I doubt it. The Big Chief knows that we expect to leave before long. . . . These things I tell you . . . represent my honest opinion after consultations and daily thought.

December 14, 1943

Since [Col. L. A.] Diller, who is the spokesman [and MacArthur's press-relations officer] out here, gave out the things contained in the clipping you sent me, I do not think I am violating the censorship rules when I say that Diller's account in this case is quite correct. While there may be approximately three times as many soldiers here as there were when I came, we still have only enough for what Diller calls the "strategic defense." If that is the role which the War Department desires my Chief to have, then we have enough. If he is to go on to bigger things then he needs more combat units. Naturally if one gets more combat units one needs more boats . . . and naturally these have to be divided up between Italy, Central Pacific, etc. I think I understand the feelings of all concerned.

Gris[10] was fine but full of trouble. I imagine everyone has lots of trouble. . . . He states, with reference to high ranking officers, that we are like the monkey — "The higher up the pole we go the more of a certain portion of our anatomy we show."

(later)

I am beginning to see that what my Chief called the "repercussions" against Ike may be true. . . . It is also reported that Georgie is in Cairo with his staff, and it may be they will give him a job there. I have a lot of sympathy for Ike for it could be he did not want to admit the truth of these things. It is too bad some public relations officer did not come forward to take the blame.

December 18, 1943

This morning we are reading . . . about the landing at Arawe. Naturally we have been waiting for this news for some time, and it is a relief to know that all went through successfully, although of course the press reports indicate that we did not get off Scot-free. There is no more difficult operation in the military than the landing on a hostile shore under fire.

December 23, 1943

Yesterday we had quite a day. Shortly after we arrived from camp we were called to the secraphone. A friend of mine[11] (and I have several) told me that the day before yesterday a request came in for me to go to the United Kingdom to command an army. It was turned down by my Chief out here who stated that because of my combat experience I was needed here. The War Department offered him Jimmy Collins in my place. I realize that Ike must have asked for me and that it must have had the approval of the Secretary of War, the President and the Acting Chief of Staff. I am not sure that GCM was back in Washington when the request was sent. . . . The question that now arises is whether they will take me in spite of the turndown. If they do there will be no waiting, for I realize the British commanders have been chosen and there already has been a lot of wonder because the American officers have not gone over. . . . Bradley is already there. I can see why, if a man like Montgomery . . . is to be there, that they would want American officers who have had some fighting experience and . . . if one eliminates Clark[12] and Patton it does not leave many in the higher brackets. I also have, I believe, a reputation for being able to get along with people. . . . We figure if anything is going to be done it will be done within forty-eight hours. . . . Again, I do not intend to let myself get down over this thing. My ambition is to be alive and well and to get back to you some day. . . .

You can imagine the excitement around here. . . . I think the War Department will again give in, as they have done before, and not send me, and this in spite of the seriousness of the detail and its importance. While I realize it would be an advance for me, I do not minimize the difficulties involved of which history has few equals.

December 24, 1943

Of course the big question is whether or not I get that army in England. If it were anyone else in command they would take me without question, since Ike has evidently asked for me and it must have been OKed by everyone in Washington. They have always deferred to my Chief on such things, while not giving him all he wants in others, so the decision will probably be to take someone else. . . .

I have made the rounds of all the officers to wish all the soldiers and officers a Merry Christmas. It seems so different from my Christmas of last year when I was struggling up that jungle trail. . . . Whatever comes out of this, I do not want to get discouraged, because nothing could be much worse than it was a year ago. . . . Maybe Lady Luck or the Lord may be looking after you (and me) again. . . . That Channel crossing is a desperate venture and while I would go into it . . . with eagerness, nevertheless I may be fortunate if I do not get it. That is the way you must be thinking of it. . . .

I think Clovis, Clyde, and Eddie are even more anxious than I am to get away. The two aides are young and they are not apt to consider the many pitfalls that lie ahead. In many ways, though, I am just as much of a kid as they are.

December 29, 1943

I have definitely given up hope of getting that other job. My disappointment is keen. . . . I am grateful to Ike who evidently kept his word to me that he would try to get me to serve with him. Naturally, Clovis and the aides are about as disappointed as I am, and there is nothing I can do about it. I cannot even complain. . . . Of course you realize, as I do, that in the words of the Bard of Avon, "That was the unkindest cut of all." . . . I could have kept this from you . . . but we have always been very frank with one another and it will give you the complete picture.

The line-up under Ike looks good to me. It has evidently been hard for them to find any leaders who have a war reputation. I have thought of Gris [Griswold]. It is too bad they did not offer him to my Chief because certainly they could not have complained about his seniority.

The papers have been full of the Gloucester landing.[13] The first accounts that came out did not "pay it much mind" and bore down on the sinking of the *Scharnhorst*. . . . If they would just sink the *Tirpitz* and the *Gneisenau* we would be able to transfer lots of boats out of that theater.

December 30, 1943

The Gloucester landing apparently went through in fine shape. I have seen nothing official . . . but I rather expect we will receive a call in the next few days for at least an advance section to leave. The ease with which that operation went through was encouraging, although of course there are certain things which are not going out to the public.

While I believe I am to be used in the future, I always have felt that those who have done you wrong are always glad to do it again. If I thought that having kept me from commanding three armies, as well as the Medal of Honor, would be all that would be done to me, I would feel better. Some time I want to write about it.

January 1, 1944

This year will settle the presidential ambitions of some and we can get on with the war without having so many clashing interests involved.

January 2, 1944

You speak of wondering about the Chief — he is where he was when I saw him on December first of last year. From there he can jump over to say hello to Walter who is probably near Finschhafen, although I have not been so informed. I predict the year will bring more and more acts as June approaches.

Read an article by Hanson Baldwin in *Foreign Affairs* for July called "America at War." In speaking of the Bismarck Sea fight he said: "In March our fliers under General Douglas MacArthur attacked and *claimed* to have destroyed an enemy convoy of 22 ships in the Bismarck Sea." At the foot of the page in small print: "There is some doubt as to the accuracy of these claims. Possibly all or nearly all of the convoy was destroyed but perhaps it was not so large as publicly reported." The Aussies orally had many doubts on the subject. The Big Chief told me: "Halsey claimed to have killed 40,000 in one convoy so I guess I can claim to have killed 15,000."

January 4, 1944

The radio has just announced the landing at Saidor. As you have seen, the forces going ashore are comparatively small, but even then I think they are larger than the Jap garrisons by a long shot. I imagine the Japanese have plenty of troops in their perimeter [inner defenses] but the difficulty of supplying them necessitates small garrisons at any outer point. Our Navy and planes ... dominate all nearby waters. Just as we have imitated the Germans in the bombing of cities, we now imitate the Japanese in the way they bypassed the British on the Malay Peninsula. One must admit it is good strategy to land where they are not and then prevent the supplying of garrisons which have been bypassed. Of course one can only do this provided there is air superiority as well as control of the sea lanes.

Certainly the situation out here has improved immeasurably in the last year. This is in the large part due to the fact that we have many more troops.

(later)

We have been very much interested in the Saidor landing. If I could tell you some of the things I hear it would astound you, but I know that a fellow like my old G-3 can muddle along with anything that is given him. He is really a grand soldier. You have doubtless seen in the papers that Martin is commanding that show.[14]

The Japanese have lost many ships and this makes their supply problem very difficult. I imagine most of the interceptions of barges which are reported to be Jap reinforcements are provisions coming in. At any rate, the New Year opened with the Japanese in a not too favorable position on their outer perimeter. Their inner perimeter has not been scratched yet.

January 7, 1944

The fact that our planning group has been delayed makes the staff, who have become very sensitive, feel that we are again going to be left out of things. The delay in the departure of some of Fred's boys [Twenty-fourth Division], however, coupled with my knowledge of the number of groups that must now be supplied over water by small boats, makes me think that the delay is due to normal supply problems. At any rate I hesitate to believe that until I hear from Walter that I am being shelved again. I realize that Walter with his enormous staff is perfectly capable of handling these small groups that make these landings directly without passing the job through a corps, but I still will not believe there is anything ulterior until I have further reason to so think. There are going to be so many changes this year due to nominations, etc., that I feel my best bet is to keep in good health and spirits. Anything else would be absolutely foolish. From a strictly military standpoint, if anyone wants to leave me here that is perfectly justified.

Rather an interesting thing, so I understand, took place in a movie theater here a few days ago. When the movie starts they show the King [George VI] and others on the screen. When a certain person's face was shown there was booing by our soldiers. I am a bit surprised at this because the victories that have been obtained should bring . . . some popularity. Of course the fact that other theaters have sent the wounded people home and that there has been a rather strong policy out here about soldiers going home, might make a difference. For example, it would have been nice if numbers of the 32d Division which fought at Buna . . . could have gone home as did many of the Marines, both officers and men. On the other hand, there are good arguments why such a policy should be adopted. The question of whether or not veterans should be retained for use in battle is one in which there are good arguments on each side with, I believe, the retention having the better of the argument.

I am being very frank with you . . . and I feel that this is a compliment to you and to your intelligence. Last night I talked with Fred Irving for some time about things and he agrees with me that the best bet is to keep sweet and . . . in fine physical condition.

Just reached the office and I found a letter from Walter dated 3 January which states in part: "The men of the planning team from your headquarters will probably be deferred for some time because of a switch in plans. However, the men will not be too long delayed." Otherwise, the letter was also very cordial. So you see I was right and the gloomy ones wrong.

January 13, 1944

We all wonder what has happened to Georgie. . . . He is certainly through in the Mediterranean theater and I do not believe they would try to use him in the British theater. He has always been a great exhibitionist since his cadet days, and I rather doubt if he has a profound knowledge of the use of large bodies of troops. However, he has many of the elements of leadership. Clovis, who has served with him a number of times, insists that the men do not like him. Apparently his superiors do. Walter liked him a lot in the early days out here but became a little lukewarm when George became such a well known figure. This was prior to the slapping incidents. I try to keep my mind free to appreciate those who may bring us victory. Whatever agents we may use I would like to see them successful, and I want to give them credit mentally for everything they do. Victory is the thing that counts. I have seen those who impressed me as being willing to have local defeats come to our arms rather than to have a certain person achieve fame as a victor. In no sense should this be a personal war, although I realize that a certain amount of ambition and feeling enter into these things from the top to the bottom. You have doubtless noticed from out here a release of information about people which would have been unthinkable a year ago. I have always thought we should build up more publicity on our men and their achievements and incidentally on our officers. The Marines have this down to a science. A funny sidelight on this is the attitude of my friend Clarence [Martin] who at one time was our G-3. When he was to command a task force, which was subsequently called off, he was told that a certain number of newspaper men would join him. He protested ... saying that he could not take care of them. On the other hand, [Maj. Gen. William H.] Rupertus [Commander, First Marine Division], so I am told, took all that were allotted to him and stated he was willing to take more.

January 17, 1944

In our little morning paper we have seen that Kenney is in Washington. You can see how little we hear up here. I have not been down to the city[15] now for a month and a half. I may go soon as I have an excuse to watch some amphibious training. According to the letters we get from Walter's staff, they are working on the plans which we will in turn work on and when they have progressed to the proper point our planning group will be sent for.

One never knows what goes on. For example, I have no idea what sort of efficiency reports I am getting, although I believe that Walter will do quite well by me.[16]

January 18, 1944

Sandy Barr of our G-4 Section got back from the north where he served on the Arawe task force....[17] He tells some tall stories which never came out in the communiques. For example, some of the green boys still take off when the shooting starts unless they are carefully watched. Some officers still spend their entire time in a dugout and never see what the men are doing. Jap planes still come over and destroy planes on the ground, without one finding it out in the communiques.

We are personally anxious to get away but I know we will get our tummies full of it when we once get there. In one thing we are fortunate, and that is that the hot and rainy season is passing day by day.

January 19, 1944

The morning papers tell about the appointment of Omar Bradley. I realize I missed the opportunity for that job or something equally attractive, and of course as you know I am full of brotherly love or something of that sort.[18]

January 20, 1944

I am . . . enclosing an editorial from the local paper which brings out a point which has been very noticeable to me here. I have never seen an Englishman or an Aussie who was not strongly for the reelection of FDR. This is very understandable and it is very evident they do not want my Chief or anybody else to beat him out.

January 21, 1944

We are still being delayed in our departure. I think it means there will be another show before the one we are expected to take part in. Of course, as you realize, there are few landing operations large enough to be given to me as a personal commander. Most task forces are built around a regiment of infantry and are not suitable jobs for a lieutenant general. In fact, the famous Japanese landing at Milne Bay a year and a half ago was built around a single battalion.

January 22, 1944

The news in the morning paper about Leningrad[19] was very welcome although I have been stating at the house for some weeks that the Germans must have been drawing back rapidly from that area. It was very evident there would be no object in leaving that salient pushed out into north Russia when the Germans were getting out in central and southern Russia. The whole Russian venture has been a lucky one for us. . . . What a mistake Hitler made!

January 24, 1944

I am serving in a peculiar theater but, on the surface, I have been getting a command commensurate with my rank. The troops that will fight, such as those at Saidor, have been trained in a large measure by my staff, and we can take pride in what they may do. While I have received very unusual treatment, we have agreed not to worry about that and I intend to do my darnedest to live up to that.

Sarah has always had a lot of admirers who have not known her well at all. Someone told Clovis of seeing her getting off a small boat early in the war. He watched her from above, dragging herself up the stairs and then suddenly at the top getting ready for her audience and strutting ashore.... You are right about the question of her veracity. She prides herself on being cute or smooth or subtle or whatever one would call it. Thinking others liars, it is easy to excuse a matching cuteness in herself....

January 26, 1944

Bill Bowen said he just heard over the radio from San Francisco that the Big Chief had spent his 64th birthday with the veterans of the Papuan campaign and had his luncheon with their commander....

On arrival, I took him into the jungle where we were set up and he at once told me he wanted to speak to me alone and went to my tent with me. He said he wanted to talk and explain the situation. He is certainly a wonderful person and was looking very handsome. He brought me up to date on everything that is going on.... *Said his place of greater power had been assured two days before, that Halsey comes under him, ... etc. Big conference now on in Hawaii.*[20]

After lunch I drove him in my jeep through the camp and then we started back [in the sedan] for the plane, which was then thirty-five miles away. Whenever we passed any place where the soldiers were turned out, I put him in the jeep and drove down through them so they could see him. There was quite a battery of photographers, so if you see some pictures of me driving him in a jeep don't be surprised....

It was a really pleasant time. It was my Chief's birthday and I feel highly honored he should visit me on such an occasion. There should be some grand photographs to send to you. By the way, if you see my fingers crossed ... you will know I did not rely entirely on that St. Christopher's medal for protection....[21]

I know now when it is contemplated to use me.... He hinted at armies out here — maybe I might get one some time — who knows. Who knows. ... Hope you get a good laugh out of this letter.[22]

January 28, 1944.

Edwin [McArthur],[23] in talking to the man of the same name, said that he was told that he had read the article in the *American Mercury* and that he had never read such lies and misstatements, but that there was always a thread of truth which prevented his answering it. It was given as a type of the cross it was necessary for him to bear. He said that he received a surprising, frank and critical talk full of statistics, etc., which kept him awake that night. What a life, and I thought I had troubles of my own.

January 29, 1944

Famous statements of famous people: "They are afraid of me, Bob, because they know I will fight them in the newspapers."

January 30, 1944

Edwin [McArthur] told me that he heard on perfect authority (Sid Huff, etc.), that Doc Morehouse will *not* return because of certain interviews he gave out back home — was relieved. The one interview I saw repeated over here intimated that his chief did not want to be President but wanted to capture the Philippine Islands. I can see why it would not be desired to let it be known that the Presidency is *not* wanted since it would discourage certain supporters. . . . Naturally he doesn't want to say he wants to be President and he doesn't want to say he doesn't. . . .

We all like Doc. . . . He probably knows a lot which might be dangerous and I wonder how it was ever decided to relieve him.[24]

February 4, 1944

We have been very much interested in the radio and news reports which indicate a very successful operation in the Marshall Islands.[25] . . . If they really want the Japanese fleet to come out and fight, I think they have overplayed the radio propaganda about the size of our fleet. The Japanese have no more desire to commit hari-kari on our doorstep than we would have under similar circumstances. Of course, every success that the fleet may have makes it a wee bit more difficult for my Great Chief to play a leading part. If he is successful while the fleet [sic] are having a difficult time, then maybe he will get the added power which will lead to great victories. . . . I think it would be a good thing to have him in charge of the entire Pacific, but of course . . . some do not agree with me. Personally, I would gang up with anybody who would give us victories.

February 6, 1944
6:45 A.M.

Clovis phoned yesterday [from Brisbane] that he was having a very successful time seeing friends and finding out what was going on. Bill [Bowen] too was going to town getting news. Walter was due at 4:00 P.M. yesterday afternoon and would be there several days at a conference. My boys had found out that new things were growing out of (I suspect) the successes which you have been reading about in another theater.[26] Maybe certain things that my Great Chief was expecting to do may now be done by someone else and he may be able to do some things which he had planned to do later.[27] By the happy tone of Clovis' voice, I knew that our stars are looking up. He had seen my fraternity brother [Willoughby][28] who was very good to him. . . . Last night he was to be out with some of Walter's boys. I suspect we will go forward before too long. . . .

Just now I have talked with Clovis. . . . While I had to use code talk . . . to get information, I did get a lot. Asked him if we were to be used and he said yes, very much so. The plans he had heard were not yet known to Walter, but I knew of course that if they sent for him that it meant a change or speeding up or something. When some other theater has successes it changes things a bit for my Chief. . . . Am glad that Clovis was there just at this time or we would be consumed with curiosity.

I realize that you will have mixed emotions about our going anyplace away from here, but it has been a pretty long pull for my staff, who, for better or worse, are anxious to get into . . . "combat zone." As you know, only a few of them were at Buna and they have been very patient and very loyal. I have a grand staff. While it is true I have lost a few, we have also taken on a few bright young chaps from Fred Irving's outfit. Up to date only one officer has asked to go home under that rotation policy[29] and he is over age for his rank and has already been notified he has no chance for promotion in spite of the fact that he is a good man.

February 7, 1944

Don't worry or try to imagine things. Nothing will be the same as a year ago. Better weather, better food, better equipment, and more of every-thing . . . and I shall probably not see or hear a Jap.

February 9, 1944

A telephone call indicates Walter will not get here until tomorrow. . . . In the meantime however I have received orders by phone to send cer-tain of my key or planning men on ahead of me. I still don't know when I shall leave and will not know until I have talked with Walter. . . . My day of departure from here will not have anything to do with the actual date I will be used. Naturally Fred Irving and Horace [Fuller] have ants in their pants and some of my boys do also.

February 10, 1944

Walter arrived. . . . There is little I can say to you except . . . that I am satisfied and as happy as I shall ever be away from you. . . . I have been getting an earful of information and discussion which will be very valu-able to me.

February 11, 1944

Today we were up for an early breakfast after talking late last night. Then Walter and I went to the office and talked until ten o'clock when we went out to Fred's outfit and spent the rest of the day with him. We saw a lot of training. Then we came back to the house and ... I talked with Walter and Clovis until nearly midnight.... Walter is a very interesting talker and knows much of the world. Clovis and I even listened tonight with the greatest of interest when he was telling about the fighting on the Sanananda trail ... which I had commanded.... I always find when I am thrown with him very closely that it really amounts to hard work.[30]

February 17, 1944

I am still laughing about your letter which came yesterday in which you thought that I had been fooled when I saw your friend Sarah the last time. You know she is no favorite of mine. When I saw her she impressed me with the fact that she would not look at me. I am not going to change my mind about her until the day I retire.

Clovis heard today that George Kenney is sending me a Fortress in the middle of the week so that I can take myself, aides and my ponderous baggage without too great a discomfort....

February 23, 1944
4:05 A.M.

It isn't nearly time for me to be up ... but here I am awake and excited like a kid. Nearly everything has gone out to the plane....

(later)

While ... I cannot tell you about the nice ride I had today in any detail, I want you to know I had a grand trip. I enjoy flying in nice weather and we made eleven hundred miles in a little over five hours....

I don't believe I have described the place where I live. This is a two room building.... The roof is the best type of native palm.... The uprights, however, are of seasoned lumber. The house is well off the ground. Inside this frame is a complete, screened house.... The walls and partitions are like you would find in any warm weather house.... This particular one was built for ... [MacArthur]. Near the house I have a screened Chic Sale and I share a shower bath with Clovis who has a house exactly like mine, next door.

February 26, 1944

Outside I see an Aussie sergeant lined up with about thirty-five natives. He is making them show their tools and then he checks the tools out at night by making them hold them overhead again. They are all dressed either in some discarded American shorts or in a piece of trade calico wrapped around their middle in the form of a short skirt. Most of them have long bushy hair and about half of them have used some kind of peroxide to make their hair red. They look older than they really are. They tell me some of the best boys are only thirteen. None of them have shoes and none have a rag above the waist. Some of the colors are very bright. Dick McCreight tells me that en route to a shower bath in a pair of striped maroon shorts, he almost started a riot among the natives. They were all full of envy. The sergeant is able to put them through a perfectly tremendous amount of work. At one time our home was a very dank jungle, wet and dark, but they have cut a swath about a hundred yards wide around the camp. They have also cut down many trees. . . . As a consequence this is going to be a very bright place.

March 2, 1944

This morning I awakened and found an order from Walter to go up to see him. . . . near Finschhafen and I am taking off as soon as I can throw a few things in a suitcase. . . . While I am there I shall probably write you innocuous notes which I can put in the regular mail, but you will understand and then I will catch up when I get back. . . . We heard over the radio last night . . . that a landing has been made in the Admiralty Islands.

March 3, 1944

I had a beautiful ride yesterday of some hundreds of miles, including a chance to circle over some scenes I know well. . . . I had been told that I wouldn't recognize old scenes but until the day I am ninety I could still locate myself within yards. The path where Eddie was shot is now a road but I would recognize it — the old strip is now covered with buildings instead of Kunai grass, but there it was and the streams over which we fought and Maggot Beach and all. . . . My host talked until nearly 1:00 A.M. last night. . . .

March 4, 1944

My host pulled out yesterday without saying goodbye while I was at a conference — he has troubles of his own — hope he gets back this morning so that I can pull out.

They do say that someone went ashore from a cruiser recently and that two small boats followed his boat. One had photographers and one had a gun firing tracer bullets past the leading boat so that in the photographs the tracers will look like enemy bullets. This comes from Navy sources (high) and may not be true. If true, they certainly put things over on my Grand Chief.

I hope you find my letters interesting — naturally I shall violate no secrets . . . but I want you to get a laugh or two and also to get some idea of the type of life I lead.

March 6, 1944

Walter said a couple of times: "I do not get any of the glory — just the responsibility." I believe he feels some of the things which grated on you in the winter of 1942–43.

March 7, 1944

You say that when one area makes a claim, a "bigger and better" one comes out within 24 hours. When I was with Walter things were nip and tuck at first in the fighting at a certain place[31] at the same time that stories about 3,000 dead Japs were being heard on the radio — at that time our boy up there was yelling for help, but look over the clippings now.

March 8, 1944

I must be with Walter on the 11th....I thought we had things tentatively settled to do certain things, but now there must be a change, and an important one, because Clovis and a lot of my staff were called for a preliminary meeting while I shall go to a more important one. We are quite busy, but you needn't worry about me....I shall have plenty of company when I go and not be on another shoestring.

March 13, 1944

I wish you could see some of the beauty of this place....When I first came over here...we planned to walk over the Owen Stanleys by various trails. One of the river valleys which we planned to follow hits the ocean at a place over which we passed yesterday. It wasn't much like I had visualized it — much more rugged. The Japs were along that coast a year and a half ago and now they seem far away. Really, our Great Chief has done fine with what he has had.

March 15, 1944

They say that the old town in which I lived for so long [Rockhampton] is not so happy now as some British Tommies have moved in....I think that is one town that is more friendly toward the Americans than any other place in Australia. Our relations as a whole were very fine. ...Our discipline was not perfect, but it was better than in any other place out here....

While I miss our beautiful home, I am enough of a kid to enjoy camp life, and if I must be away from you I would rather be out in the open this way.

March 20, 1944

I told you in my letter of yesterday that Clovis had gone to the scene of my jungle debut, and this morning at three o'clock came a telegram saying that...Admiral [Barbey][32]...was very anxious for me to come over this afternoon. Therefore, I shall go...because I feel that Clovis has probably committed me to some extent. It will mean I will miss a number of people who are coming here to see me today.

When Clovis' telegram came ... Clyde [Shuck] answered it saying that I would go, and I am glad he made the decision because I would have been very doubtful about it.[33] I think all these boys realize I will stand back of them if they make an honest decision based on the facts as they know them.

March 23, 1944

Just at this time if I could have an army in Europe or anywhere else, that might mean something, but I don't believe that I would find a training army at home as interesting as a corps in an active theater. This does not mean I have changed my mind for a minute about many things. ... but from a *military* standpoint I guess I am more happy than I have been at any time since I declared the battle of Sanananda officially at an end. The long months with their many military and personal disappointments . . . do not affect me now because for one thing I haven't time to think about them.

March 25, 1944

My mind turns away from past disappointments, ambitions and self-pity. I only want to do my duty, to gain victory, and to get back to my Doll where we can laugh and enjoy home life again. There is no low morale here — lots of hard work but plenty of good cheer. Was surprised when I went to bed at 11:00 last night to hear so much singing in the Command Post — just people singing while going to bed. Mostly soldiers, I guess. . . .

In spite of the rain we just had San Francisco on the radio as clear as a bell. . . . Clyde says the best music comes from Radio Tokyo. I listened to one of their news broadcasts and it is comparatively conservative. Being directed at white listeners I guess they try not to let it sound foolish, although of course they present an improper picture.

March 26, 1944

We went to church this morning George De Graaf, Clovis and I stood together and you could have heard us sing the hymns for a mile. Just like a lot of bulls in a pasture.

March 27, 1944

My new boat ... ran up here today. As soon as we went aboard, it put to sea. It is painted battleship gray and ... is 104 feet long. . . . It has a rather small deck in front and then a pilothouse with flying bridge enclosed in canvas on top. . . . The crew's and officers' quarters are underneath the pilothouse and forward deck. The galley is large enough to cook for about twenty. . . .

I liked all the crew, which numbers thirteen at present. I shall have to add a couple of gunners at least, and maybe another radio man.... There is quite a large living cabin [that]...I am going to have...fixed up as an office so if I ever want to live on it I can do so....I shall have *Miss Em* painted on [it] as soon as possible....The Captain is convinced that he has the best crew and the best boat in the world, so that's a very healthy situation.... It sort of made me laugh to see the way they wanted to help me up and down their ladders, because I can climb like a mountain goat.

March 29, 1944

This has been a very nice day throughout.... I went aboard the new boat. ...We at once put to sea and I cannot tell you how beautiful it was. To me, a jungle is a hateful, nasty place, but when seen from the sea at a distance of a mile it really has some glamor. A coconut grove seen from the sea or air is very pretty....

I am always hoping that you will not be bitter towards Sarah — or anyone. Am far too busy to even think about her.... My one great ambition is to get home to you in good health and with laughter in my heart rather than hatred or bitterness.... War is a hard game. Lots of boomboom around in training — last thing last night was artillery fire and the first thing this morning.

March 31, 1944

The "America at War" annual of the *Army and Navy Journal* has articles by high ranking officers at home and abroad — many of them, but nothing from our theater. They asked me for an article, and may have asked others, but it was decided best for me not to write anything.

April 3, 1944

A letter came from Woody today saying that he had been put in command of a different corps and was living in a rather fancy billet.... A letter from Hugh Cort also came in, but written a day later, said that Woody had been ordered home and had left. After praising him very highly, he said "I feel very much adrift tonight for after two years of close association I have lost my boss. Today he left for home. Through no fault of his own, either of commission or omission, he fell afoul of a policy and had his heart broken."[34]

April 4, 1944

Your friend [Sutherland] arrived about eight o'clock and stayed until two. I must say it was a very interesting visit as I asked him a thousand questions about conditions at home, conferences he had been in at Cairo and other places. He seemed very glad indeed to enlighten me on these things and I feel much more up to date. I have never seen your friend so friendly. . . . It was very evident that he was not seeking information from me.

April 5, 1944

I know the leopard [Sutherland] doesn't change his spots but I would rather have the leopard reasonably friendly than hiding in the jungle ready to leap out at me. I think the leopard is well fed, pleased with himself, and not trying to get me.

April 7, 1944

I cannot look around . . . and realize the life that revolves around me and still feel that I am not a vital part of what is going on. . . . My great ambition when my part of this war is over is to be back with you — whether I am a big Indian or not is very minor providing you will think that I have done my best and that my best has been vital to the war effort in this portion of the world. . . . No one here feels bitter — everyone is busy. I imagine Bill [Bowen], for example, is working 16 hours a day. I can get him at his office as late as midnight. My aides are the ones who really live the life of Riley although I keep them quite busy.

You must understand there is no unhappiness here.

April 8, 1944

If there should ever come a gap in my letters of any great length, after I have given you warning, then you will have to follow the papers. You can tell where I am.

April 16, 1944

Clyde has left me and I shall not see him for a while — not until we reach the far shore and meet in a new Command Post. . . . Eddie, Dombrowski, Clovis and Bill will be here for dinner and breakfast along with me — then we are off on a pickleboat [a destroyer]. Should fare well on that pickleboat because there will be [Admiral] Barbey with me and he will get service — there just won't be any room though — that will be the trouble. Would prefer to ride on the *Miss Em.* . . .

We are sort of packed up and cleaned up. . . . George DeGraaf, Clovis and I went to the little chapel this morning — I have gone every Sunday since I have been here.

And so the weeks have passed and I come to the place where I can hope to do my duty to my country in the finest possible way. No easy task, but I shall hope to come out without getting my nose punched. It must be hard for Walter to see me go into it — he may and will be around as an observer for a day or two but in the end my status will be what officers all long for — high command in critical places.

Certainly at such a time there is no room for bitterness because young men die at my call and that is too important a time for self-pity or self-ishness. I want to do my job and hope they will say "Well done." . . . This is a soldier's pride and joy no matter how difficult.

April 17, 1944

This is the day that the gap starts. . . . Spike[35] is getting up in the next room. He told me last night that Sarah speaks very highly of me. He was told by my distinguished Chief: "If Bob gets away with this I am going to do something handsome for him."

Ain't that sumpin!

Notes

1. Eichelberger to Miss Em, 1, 2 November 1943.

2. Ibid., 23 March 1944.

3. This refers to the celebrated slapping incident that occurred in August 1943, when General Patton slapped a patient in a corps evacuation hospital in Sicily. The man was shell-shocked; Patton maintained that he was a coward.

4. This passage is composed from two letters to Miss Em dated 25 November 1943. The entry in Eichelberger's diary for 26 November puts it in even harsher terms. MacArthur "thinks Geo. Patton will be remembered for 100 years as the man who struck a soldier; said he was washed up and that it would prevent Ike Eisenhower from being Chief of Staff. Said there was a crooked streak in Ike and George Catlett Marshall which would show up in a long war."

5. The Cairo (SEXTANT) Conference was a meeting attended by President Roosevelt, Prime Minister Churchill, and Generalissimo Chiang Kai-shek to discuss plans for an Allied cross-channel invasion of Europe, possible new operations in the Mediterranean, and the strategy to be followed in the Far East. At the time of this letter the principals had just completed their historic meeting with the Russians at Tehran. See Maurice Matloff, *The War Department: Strategic Planning for Coalition Warfare 1943-44* (Washington, 1959), pp. 347–387.

6. Madang, an important Japanese base on the north coast of New Guinea and west of the Huon Peninsula, was a threat to any future operations on New Britain and essential to the control of Vitiaz Strait, which any seaborne invasion of western New Guinea would have to utilize.

7. At this time ALAMO Headquarters was still situated on Goodenough Island, where it had been located since the move from Milne Bay on 21 October 1943. Sixth Army Headquarters remained at Camp Columbia near Brisbane until 2 February 1944, when it joined ALAMO Headquarters at Finschhafen, on the southeast corner of the Huon Peninsula. ALAMO headquarters had moved to Finschhafen on 24 December 1943. John Miller, *Cartwheel; The Reduction of Raboul* (Washington, 1959) p. 276 n.; Gen. Walter Krueger, *From Down Under to Nippon: The Story of Sixth Army in World War II* (Washington, 1953), p. 29.

8. This is what ultimately happened. The Russian attack against the southern flank of the Fourth Panzer Army occurred on Christmas Eve, and two weeks later a two-pronged offensive was successfully thrown against the German Sixth Army. The Germans retreated in February.

9. "Your little friend," or "your Leavenworth friend," is the code name for General Sutherland, MacArthur's Chief of Staff. After the war Eichelberger wrote: "Sutherland . . . wanted my three stars until he obtained that rank and [he later] wanted command of the Eighth Army when it was organized. Nothing remarkable about Sutherland — he was a natural climber trying to advance his own interests at the expense of the other fellow. He told me personally with great pride of how he had managed to get rid of Eisenhower

and become MacArthur's Chief of Staff.... Sutherland was a smoothie and I had to be something of one myself in dealing with him." Eichelberger Dictations, 31 August 1959.

10. Maj. Gen. Oscar W. Grisworld commanded the XIV Corps, which had been activated on Guadalcanal on 2 January 1943. He led the forces that captured Munda on 5 August 1943.

11. Lt. Col. S. S. Auchincloss, who had served at Buna as Eichelberger's signal officer, is identified in the Eichelberger Diary, 22 December 1943.

12. Lt. Gen. Mark W. Clark, then commanding the U.S. Fifth Army in Italy. Patton was still under a cloud.

13. The First Marine Division began the main invasion of New Britain at Cape Gloucester on 26 December 1943. This last sentence comes from the letter dated 28 December 1943.

14. The 126th Regimental Combat Team of the Thirty-second Division, commanded by Brig. Gen. Clarence A. Martin, constituted the main element in the assault on Saidor on 2 January 1944.

15. Sixth Army Headquarters at Brisbane.

16. This later became a sore point and influenced Eichelberger's feelings about Gen. Krueger. "Krueger's failure to make out a proper efficiency report for me during the 14 months I served under him allowed him to say nothing good or nothing bad about me. It showed over a long period of time his determination not to help me in any way improve my standing before the powers that be in Washington. Of those things I did not know until I looked at my efficiency reports in Washington." Eichelberger Dictations, 31 August 1959.

17. Arawe, on the southwest coast of New Britain, was invaded 15 December 1943 and secured on 16 January 1944. Originally intended for use as an airstrip and PT base, neither the Arawe Peninsula nor Cape Gloucester, which was seized during a subsequent phase of the same operation, proved to be of major strategic importance in reducing Rabaul.

18. "I resented these facts because there is a great difference between commanding a corps of 50,000 or 65,000 men and an army of from one-half to one million men. It would be equivalent to the refusal of a chairman of a board refusing to permit a vice president to be promoted to president of a big corporation. I doubt if history will show another case where an officer deliberately held down a subordinate. My own feeling was that part of his satisfaction was in saying no to George Catlett Marshall and Dwight Eisenhower." Eichelberger Dictations, 28 March 1955.

19. This refers to the converging attacks by two Russian Army Groups against the German Eighteenth Army in the Leningrad Sector on 15 January 1944.

20. The passage in italics is taken from the Eichelberger Diary, 26 January 1944, and is inserted here to give some point to the vague reference to "the situation." In order to minimize the quotations in footnotes this practice will be followed whenever the diary casts additional light on matters that could not be explained to Miss Em at the time. The "big conference" in Pearl Harbor, 23–28 January, is described in George C. Kenney, *General Kenney Reports: A Personal History of the Pacific War* (New York, 1949), pp. 346–349.

21. "I was engaged outside of Rockhampton in Australia in a Command Post Exercise. With the I Corps Headquarters completely established following an assumed landing on a beach, and the division headquarters set up some miles further in the jungle and wired in, the number of troops was assumed. Then a wire came from Brisbane saying that General MacArthur would fly in that day and wanted me to continue whatever work I might be doing. I had forgotton this was his birthday, which was a real *faux pas*. He found us in the jungle when I had sent the car to bring him to us, dressed in jungle clothes, making a very realistic scene. Photographers took pictures showing him riding with me in a jeep . . . and standing in front of our jungle tents and so forth. We were directed to send all negatives to his headquarters and he selected the ones which were not to be destroyed. A number of these were sent to all the papers in the United States under such captions as, "General MacArthur at the Front with Gen. Eichelberger in New Guinea." Eichelberger Dictations, 24 September 1953.

22. "If I use some expressions of praise which puzzle you, I may do that to present a certain picture if a stranger should read it." Eichelberger to Miss Em, 4 February 1944.

23. Edwin McArthur was a musician who was doing "a splendid job" entertaining the

troops. "This passage illustrates the frankness with which Gen. MacArthur talked to all who were permitted to see him." Gen. Clovis E. Byers to the editor, 2 July 1968.

24. Col. Sid Huff, one of MacArthur's aides, subsequently wrote *My Fifteen Years with General MacArthur* (New York, 1964). "A good line on MacArthur's desire to be President arose when General MacArthur's medical aide, Major Morehouse, went back to the United States to see his sick mother.... Asked by a newspaperman if MacArthur desired to go to the White House, he answered to this effect, 'No, he is a soldier and desires to march on to Tokyo.' Although Morehouse was a grand chap and had been with MacArthur since Corregidor, he was summarily bundled out of that office and connection with MacArthur was severed. "Eichelberger Dictations, 12 November 1953.

25. The Marshalls were invaded at Kwajalein on 31 January 1944.

26. This would probably be the wrap-up of operations on Kwajalein Atoll in the Central Pacific by 4 February 1944.

27. Because of the prompt seizure of the Admiralties, MacArthur on 5 March urged the joint Chiefs of Staff to bypass Hansa Bay, his next objective and the subject of the conferences just concluded at Finschhafen, in favor of a direct jump to Hollandia. Robert Ross Smith, *The Approach to the Philippines* (Washington, 1953), p. 9.

28. Maj. Gen. Charles A. Willoughby, MacArthur's G-2, Maj. Gen. George Decker, Krueger's Chief of Staff, Gen. Byers, and Gen. Eichelberger all were members of Phi Gamma Delta national social fraternity.

29. "As you have read ... there will be a rotation policy started for the relief of a certain number of men and officers to go back home after a certain number of months of foreign service. I don't believe there will be many [to] apply from my own little group at this time." Eichelberger to Miss Em, 3 February 1944.

30. This last sentence is taken from Eichelberger's letter to Miss Em dated 12 February 1944.

31. Probably Los Negros in the Admiralties, where a fierce Japanese counterattack occurred on the night of 3 March 1944.

32. Rear Admiral Daniel E. Barbey, commander of the VII Amphibious Force, Seventh Fleet, was slated to command Task Force 77 in the forthcoming Hollandia Operation. In his story of the Amphibious Force, he described Eichelberger as "an able officer with a warm personality ... well liked by the press and not averse to friendly publicity." "Because of his outspoken, critical, and sometimes belligerent manner, he had not endeared himself to the top command in the Southwest Pacific. But now he was back on combat duty again and I enjoyed our close association." Barbey also observed: "There was no place in the Southwest Pacific for two glamorous officers." Daniel E. Barbey, *MacArthur's Amphibious Navy: Seventh Amphibious Force Operations 1943-1945* (Annapolis, 1969), pp. 27, 170.

33. The reason for Gen. Eichelberger's reluctance to visit Adm. Barbey is suggested in the entry in his diary for 4 March 1944, when he was still at Finschhafen. "Krueger arrived before lunch.... General Eichelberger invited by Barbey to stop off at Buna. General Krueger advised General Eichelberger not to go there at this time."

34. Maj. Gen. Roscoe Barnett Woodruff, in command of the VII Corps, was one of two corps commanders sent back from England on the ground that neither had experienced combat command in the war and both Eisenhower and Bradley were reluctant to entrust the D-Day assault to anyone who lacked this experience. Omar N. Bradley, *A Soldier's Story* (New York, 1951), p. 227. Col. Hugh Cort had been Woodruff's chief of staff. Woodruff was so anxious to fight that he willingly stepped down to command of a division, and he led the Twenty-fourth Division with distinction throughout the later campaign in eastern Mindanao. See chapter 13.

35. "Spike" was the nickname of Frazier Hunt, a journalist and well-known war correspondent who had recently arrived in the Southwest Pacific area. For a flattering portrait of the Big Chief, see Frazier Hunt, *MacArthur and the War against Japan* (New York, 1944).

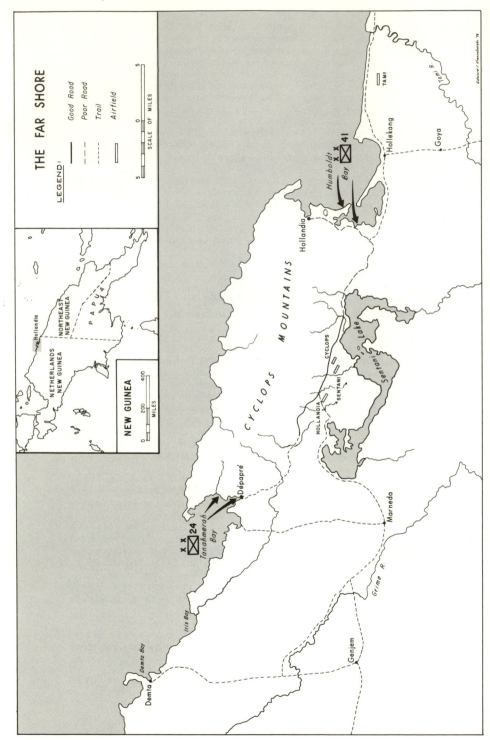

MAP 2

CHAPTER SIX

The Far Shore

"The gap" mentioned so frequently in the letters to Miss Em referred to the time Eichelberger must spend aboard ship as RECKLESS Task Force steamed a slow thousand miles to Hollandia. The unexpected success in the Marshalls had made it possible to accelerate operations both in the Southwest Pacific and the Central Pacific areas, but it was the landings in the Admiralty Islands — which grew out of what originally was to have been a "reconnaissance in force" — a month ahead of schedule that encouraged MacArthur to start thinking about bypassing Hansa Bay and seizing Hollandia. Such a move would cut off Japanese ground troops at Hansa Bay, Madang, and Wewak, and at the same time provide the Allies with a vital staging area and air base for further operations in western New Guinea. If successful, it would be the most significant step taken thus far on the return march to the Philippines. Approval of the Joint Chiefs was won on 12 March 1944, and D-Day was later set for 22 April.

The different units comprising RECKLESS Task Force, some 37,527 combat troops and 18,183 service troops, embarked from the main staging areas at Goodenough Island and Finschhafen. The convoys from these and other assembly points in New Guinea left the Finschhafen area on 18 April and headed north, toward the Admiralty Islands, in order to deceive the Japanese as to their destination. On 20 April the convoys, well protected by the fighting ships of Task Force 58, steamed westward from the Admiralties, arriving at the landing areas early on the morning of the 22d. "Chances for local surprise seemed excellent."[1]

April 17, 1944

Dearest Emmalina,

Well here we are on a ship and I shall try to tell you all I can without violating the censors' rules — there is no question of secrecy involved because long before you get this letter you will have read about all the things that we now ponder on.

We sailed at 11:30 and passed many beautiful island scenes — mountains, coconut groves, etc. I am living with Fred Irving in one of the two upper deck cabins.

April 18, 1944

Everything all dark as far as I can see so I have come in to write to you and then go to bed.

The boat is a bit narrow and is rocking a bit — imagine it would jump around a lot in a real rough sea.

It has been heavily overcast and raining since early this morning — just as well, I guess, because no one can see us from above.

The question arises whether to sleep in our clothes or go to bed right. I am really going to bed because I cannot, or rather do not want to, arrive at the far shore all tired out — we will be in here a number of days and we might as well get rested up.

April 19, 1944

It is moderately overcast this morning but not raining. I don't like it at night because the deck is so dark that one cannot find those to whom one would wish to talk. Inside it is hot ... with portholes closed. Friendly planes flying around give one a good feeling. Our sister service does a fine job and a friendly one — no inefficiency there.

Today has been much like yesterday — I did get a fine nap ... and then joined some of the crowd on what I would call the flying bridge, way up above everything. There we sat in the cool breeze. ... I had to wear my raincoat to keep warm. Read part of the time on *A Tree Grows in Brooklyn*. ... Most of the time we just watched the islands — speculated on friendly planes, etc. ...

A while ago we passed lights that looked like Coney Island — just your old friend Palmer's happy home.[2] Would have liked to have seen him.

One of the newspaper men who doesn't know me asked me if I were worried — I told him: 'No, that I didn't worry over things which I cannot help.' I do not lie awake when I get in bed. There is of course no play of personalities or detailed work for me on here.

April 20, 1944

Today is beautiful and covered with friendly vessels — you will read about this in the papers. . . . Big powwow in here all morning. . . . Don't worry about me and expect the best all the time. . . . We are well and we do not worry in advance.

Right after dinner I went up on the flying bridge with Fred and Clovis to watch the beautiful sunset and the fading lights on a most interesting scene. We wondered what you gals would think if you could have seen us there all alone. Later others came and for the last hour the Admiral, Spike and I have been settling the war all over again. . . . Was quite busy all day but I am not going to do anything tomorrow but loaf, read, and write to you. If I were a hero in fiction I would say 'The die is cast,' or some other darn fool thing. As it is, we remark about the fine meals, look over to where Walter is riding alone or perhaps Sarah (temporary visitors) and then talk about everything under the sun, especially about how much we like the ship.

April 21, 1944

My old friend is about a mile away and my rather reticent friend about 15 miles ahead. Guess they will not stay long.

Spike is hearing lots of things that are a bit different from what he has heard recently. He is a bright, alert chap and is enjoying life. . . .

We are not sorry for ourselves — nor are we too happy. Just right. . . . Wouldn't change it for that channel show.

Beautiful day. . . . Everything looks peaceful and no evidence that our little brown palsy-walsies know we are out here on their side of the fence. . . .

The very fact that this vast movement is going westward will make history — I wonder how great a surprise it will be at home. I am fully aware of my responsibilities and that it is no simple war game that I am engaged in. I can only hope that the Air and Navy bump off a lot of them, because that is where I take up the fight — just where they must leave off.

April 22, 1944

Up at 3:00 A.M. These Navy boys take no chances. Dressed slowly and reluctantly. Went down to the ward room where I had two ham sandwiches, one jelly sandwich, one cheese sandwich, one glass of water, one glass of tomato juice, and two cups of coffee. Spike was in bed. . . . In getting up, with that sunburned face, he looked like a washerwoman out on a spree.

I think I am to have breakfast at 5:30 and the boom boom starts at six. Hope it is a surprise. Fred is ready to go ashore, but I will hang back. Next reincarnation I want to join the Navy. Good coffee, no dirt and no bugs. . . . Really, I admire them very much — no question in my mind of their efficiency.

The boys out on deck report a light rain. I shall go up later to see what I can see, but I shall probably stay on here tonight. Make one trip ashore today.

7:00 P.M. Lots of boom boom — interest — disappointments regarding terrain perhaps — gratitude that there were few casualties. All these things you will read in the paper. Met with Walter and my Great Chief and Barbey on a ship of somewhat greater grandeur. The Chief brought me two chocolate ice creams and did I like them.

Went ashore with them all. Guess they saw plenty of sand and mud and heat and swamp and jungle. Big Chief told me that if this goes over he will make another army and make me an army commander. I shook hands with him[3] and thanked him. And so it goes, Darling.... We are lucky....

The Americans were indeed fortunate. Plans called for two landings — two regimental combat teams from Irving's Twenty-fourth Infantry Division at Tanahmerah Bay, and two regimental combat teams of the Forty-first Division at Humboldt Bay, on the other side of the Cyclops Mountains and some forty miles to the east. Eichelberger accompanied the force at Tanahmerah Bay, which was to have been the main thrust.

These landings were unopposed, but because one of the beaches proved to be narrow and isolated by an impassable swamp while access to the other was seriously impeded by coral barrier reefs, Eichelberger and his division commander, Irving, were confronted with a serious logistical problem. For a time the difficulty of moving supplies, rather than any effective opposition from the Japanese, threatened the drive of the Twenty-fourth upon the airfields of Lake Sentani plain.

Consequently, the weight of the attack was shifted to Humboldt Bay, where Fuller's troops landed without incident and pushed rapidly inland. Four days after the initial landings, advance units of the Twenty-fourth and Forty-first Divisions met near Hollandia Drome and completed the pincers movement. This ended the major tactical phase of the operation, although mopping-up operations would continue for some time.

Eichelberger's main responsibility now was to develop Hollandia into an elaborate staging area and airbase from which Allied aircraft could "dominate most Japanese airdromes in western New Guinea... fly reconnaissance and bombing missions against the western Carolines... and provide support for subsequent landing operations along the north coast of New Guinea."[4]

April 23, 1944

Dearest Emmalina,

I didn't get to start another letter last night — two conferences that lasted until after midnight. Then call to quarters early this morning as daylight approached. Have been ashore twice this morning — once I took Spike and Frank Prist.⁵ The last I saw of them they were starting up a jungle trail with Fred.

Things are going fine.... Our route was such that our arrival was a complete surprise. They were hiding out in the forest to escape bombing when the doughboys arrived. While we are not out of the woods, we are a long way on the road to victory. Had expected more Japs and a bitter fight. What a lucky break!

The second time I went ashore I went with Walter — the tide was out and we had to transfer to a 'buffalo' that can crawl over coral niggerheads. Walter was fine — very happy and very appreciative. He left today — the Big Chief last night. Because of the swamps here, which make access almost impossible, I am shifting my Command Post to the other side [Humboldt Bay] where Horace is. May have a hard time finding my things in all that mess....

You would be proud of our officers to see the intelligent way they go to it.

A terrific squall came up when I was...going ashore with the Big Chief. He certainly could take it — didn't perspire a bit while I was wet from head to foot. Am delighted over the way things have gone — expected a terrible row and will doubtless get some yet, but not like we expected. Must get a nap — more later.

9:30 P.M. After dinner there was a beautiful sunset and we were sitting with Barbey on deck admiring it when an alarm came. Seconds later we were in motion getting out of there. What efficiency. I like those Navy guys. Little palsy-walsies dropping things. Of course I feel very gratified about things so far — my decision to move from here is a good one I believe. I would have been on a mountain side out off from everything.

April 24, 1944

Good night's sleep. Horace and Fred doing well but latter having terrain troubles. We are leaving in a few minutes for other side.... My little palsy-walsies made a lot of fire and smoke over there last night....

There are not nearly as many of the little so-and-so's as I had been led to expect, so the desperate conditions do not exist at the moment. We not only got surprise, which let us overrun their positions, but there are only about one-third what we had expected.

A week ago if I could have anticipated conditions as good as they are today I would have been very happy....I am as safe as one can be anywhere here: not like Buna at all — don't expect to get in any personal fights. The Japs are quite broken.

April 25, 1944

Big day yesterday — a little palsy-walsy made a jackpot with one nickel and started a grand fire.[6] It has set us back a bit but not for long. Fred is going like a house afire and Horace also.... Fred walked 17 miles yesterday and brought home a lot of bacon — what a boy he is!

April 26, 1944

About eight this morning I came ashore to find Clyde in the jeep and Ventura in a command car ready to carry our luggage up to the Command Post. We are set up in a plantation in which are coconuts, bananas, kapok and cacao trees. The bananas seem to have been all eaten by the late occupants of this area. One thing which has impressed me all day has been the tremendous amount of materiel spread all around on both sides of the road, the lightness of the construction by our pals, and the wonderful defensive positions every place which they have failed to utilize.... Tactically ... we have continued success and our troops have taken the airdromes in accordance with our mission....

Nearly every house has a great quantity of preserved fish, maggoty rice, American and English canned goods.... I suppose some of these little Japs are back in the hills and will be coming back in this area seeking food from their old homes. Others are plenty dead ... and others have taken out to the northwest.

The Jap prisoners, the Sikh[s] ... who were captured at Singapore, are all very interesting.... We have recovered ... a great number of white missionaries.... In addition to these there are a lot of Japs who have been living around here and raised native families. I would like to have somebody tell me what to do with those people.

The first night in camp was a pleasure — a lot of recruit sentinels conducted a war all night. It sounded like the battle of Gettysburg.

April 27, 1944

Today I have had a day which reminds me of December of 1942. It included two rides in a buffalo, miles in jeep, and a long walk over a mountain. At one point Horace and I connected up with Fred.... We then inspected that area you have been reading about.[7] Captured things are everywhere....

Fred looks fine in spite of the tremendous walks he has taken. In fact, he looks better than any of his staff. Horace of course is old like I am and looks a bit on the nervous side.

There are many destroyed enemy planes, gasoline dumps, etc. It all makes a very interesting sight but I never have felt so confident of victory as I have in the last week. I am even beginning to be an optimist in feeling that another year and a half will end it.

April 28, 1944

One of the funny sights I saw yesterday was a soldier with a tin cup transferring gasoline from a Jap 50-gallon drum to a Jap truck he was about to use....

Today was very interesting.... You will read in the papers about the different missionaries that we have repatriated. There are about a hundred of them including fifteen Americans. Three of the latter are nuns. These people have been prisoners for a long time and were perfectly delighted to be released. There was a missionary named Braun with his wife. The latter of course has been through a lot. I was so sorry I had not taken her some fruit juices and things.

One Catholic priest, who has a grand face in spite of all he has been through, was cooking for the Japanese in a little camp on the bay when our ships came in and started firing. He did not expect to get out alive. The German missionaries and their wives seemed happy at their treatment by us and said the Japanese treated them worse than they did the Americans.

Bill Bowen went over to look at an air strip today and brought back a couple of prisoners. From all descriptions they are not nearly as anxious to fight as they were a year ago and that is the best sign we have had here.

I have a local guard composed of Clyde, Dan, Ventura, Dombrowski, and two... other sergeants.... We realize that the woods are full of palsy-walsies wandering around loose who have been driven away from their food, which is plentiful in this area. The night before last we were all kept awake by a trigger-happy guard which I relieved the next day. Last night my local guard planned that if firing broke out they would gather round my tent armed with bolos and knives.... In this I would look to Ventura to be prominent, for he has found a real Philippine bolo left by some Jap.... I have not yet found what I am supposed to do, but take it I should lie on the ground and shiver. As you can well imagine, we will not let anyone fire within the perimeter or we would all be in danger.... I am plenty safe, particularly with Ventura out there.

April 30

Today I have received... a Jap photographic book which I will have to turn in as it contains pictures taken on Corregidor and in Manila by the Japanese. It shows Ned King and Skinny Wainwright,[8] also army nurses and other things of interest.

Horace Fuller came in today and thinks he has discovered the new

Command Post location for us. It is on a hillside looking over the lake, which is a very beautiful spot. The house was built by . . . an American explorer who was here for some time. While nothing very fine, it has a hardwood floor and walls and the best thing of all is a breeze which blows down the lake and off the mountains constantly.

This morning I sent some soap, tooth brush . . . and other little things to Mrs. Braun, the wife of the medical missionary who was repatriated from the Japanese. I only saw her for a moment, but she seemed such a brave figure as she was carried on a stretcher to the hospital. They are all leaving tonight and, fortunately, good medical attention is available on the boat since it was provided in expectancy of heavy casualties, which we did not have.

We are still plugging along here. There are some tactical things going on . . . but nothing major. My problems for a short time now will be those of supply and construction.

May 1, 1944

Today has been another unusual day but quite a pleasant one. We first went . . . to a great Jap storage place. There is everything there from beer and saki to enormous quantities of quinine and atabrine. Many of the things are really wonderful. Their use of rubber wrappings for medicines, and their method of carrying liquid vitamins in small bottles without breakage seemed very unusual to me.

Our great trouble has been to keep the soldiers from sticking bayonets through valuable things while looking for loot. We put a heavy guard on down there. When I arrived, the native canoes were going out loaded with everything from canned crab meat, coffee, saki, etc. I made four boats I found there unload everything they had and sent them away without any loot. I have just looked at a cartoon in *Colliers* for February 12, showing a couple of Germans running from some American soldiers and throwing their clothes off behind them. They are saying that they had heard Americans were great souvenir hunters. My thought is that if the enemy would only arm themselves with picture postcards and phony money to throw over their shoulders that they could always escape. Even Dombrowski is wearing a pair of Japanese breeches and a Jap shirt. I do not blame him because they are much cooler than our own.

One thing I bought home today is an aluminum tube which has inside it a bottle of iodine. In many of this type of gadget they are away ahead of us, but when it comes to big equipment such as graders, bulldozers, and things for building airfields, they are still in their infancy. Today is only D plus 9, but our planes passed over in a continuous stream. Everything seems to be going along all right.

May 2, 1944

Be sure to let me know all about the way things broke in the States. I wonder whether interest in other theaters was so great that they did not have any interest in our going to Dutch New Guinea. Certainly it was a grand move for our Chief to make and of course the responsibility was solely his. If we had gone half as far, as was originally planned, we would probably have had a terrific fight.

May 3, 1944

It seemed to me I had lots of conferences yesterday. . . . [Col. Clyde D.] G-3 for Walter Eddleman, states he understands another army is to be organized here at some future date. He called it a "training army," so there is something in the wind. There will be plenty of divisions out here to warrant it. . . . It was his opinion I would be in command of this area in a year. This sounds like a pipe dream.

It was very interesting to me yesterday when I heard that my Grand Chief had announced he was not a candidate for the Presidency.

Things are going along very well. Personally I think we have made remarkable strides. I do not know just what the visitors from GHQ think because they do not see this thing perhaps from the standpoint of the fellow who has to do it. At any rate, we have already exceeded my wildest dreams. The surprise, which was complete, enabled us to get a quick tactical victory and the Japanese who are in the hills are only partially armed. The greatest battles being fought are the ones engaged in by our own troops who are staging forward to the dromes. Every night they engage in a heavy battle here. They think they are firing at Japs but really every bird or bullfrog gets a volley. Our own guards around our immediate camp never fire a shot, and the engineers work all night getting gravel for the road. At the same time, this terrific fighting is going on by the recruits who are temporarily camped around here. Sixteen Japs surrendered to a truck last night — what a change. . . . These are not like the Japs I fought in Papua.

May 4, 1944

Today we . . . traveled . . . to Tanahmerah Bay . . . on the *Miss Em*. We had a very beautiful trip of about forty miles each way. The mountains were beautiful and the sea was blue as indigo. This may have been a Jap sea a little while ago but it certainly is not now. It was a scene of commendable activity both in the air and on the water.

When I arrived on the other side I went ashore to see Fred Irving, who is having a lot of trouble on account of mud. The most interesting thing there was a great group of Jap prisoners. One part of a company had captured thirty-five. They have been in the hills since our arrival and were rather miserable looking specimens. Some were young and some fairly old. We also saw some Filipinos who have been repatriated by our troops. They look quite well.

I have sent you some of this Jap invasion currency, which was at Hollandia in bales. In addition, there were literally tons of those little aluminum coins. George De Graaf came along today and saw a soldier selling them to sailors. He was getting a dollar each for the paper bills and was selling the coins for three for a dollar. He also sold a pair of Jap shoes for twenty dollars. George had a pocketful of the stuff and he gave it away to the sailors and took the rest...from the soldier and gave that to the sailors too. This game of souvenir hunting is quite a problem.

May 6, 1944

Today has been a very interesting day. I started out on the *Miss Em* to visit a little air strip which lies outside the harbor. It had been built originally by the Japs but they had not done much of a job.... Coming home we passed what must have been the inhabitants of a village who were probably returning to their home — everything from old men and women to babies. There must have been 150 of them...all of them giving some kind of a salute to express their friendship. They were armed with spears and bows and arrows, so they really are quite primitive.... In characteristic fashion the Yanks were handing out some rations which they had no business to give away. Except for some rather unusual wood carvings...they appear to have no form of visible culture.

May 7, 1944

Every day I realize more and more how lucky we were that the Japanese were completely surprised, for I never have seen a place more easily defensible. It would seem impossible for an attacking force to capture this place if the enemy would fight. So I think again that I am lucky.

A lot of my thoughts are put on getting boats unloaded and getting this road in shape so it will carry heavy traffic to the dromes.

I see a nice big moon coming up, so I imagine it will not be many minutes before I hear people yelling "Lights outs!" and then a siren will blow and we will have to sit around in the dark. The Japs have not done much, just enough to be a nuisance.

May 8, 1944

Another truckload of prisoners came in today. They were all quite sick and to me seem quite pitiful, although I am aware of their many cruelties and the fact that so many of our men, when captured by them, have been killed. Today, the first thing that happened when the Japs reached here was that a doctor started working on them immediately. I think they suffer from malaria, exhaustion, dysentery and other ailments.[9]

May 9, 1944

Most of my worries now are logistical. A great fleet of ships will come in and the slogan is to get the stuff out "immediately if not sooner." Insofar as fighting is concerned, it is confined to patrol actions in many different directions. As a matter of fact, I am beginning to get doubtful whether it pays to send people out to kill these little Japs or capture them. A truckload which came in here yesterday were so puny and sick looking that I believe they would have been unable to walk in another week. It looks as though the great effort which Hirohito made in the direction of Australia, and particularly in the Solomons and New Guinea, has all gone sour. Many thousands of them are dying along trails and in the mountains. They are without food, proper clothing, medicines, etc. . . .

To look at the map one would think the Japs could walk from Wewak to Hollandia in a short time, but over mountain trails it is slow work and many never make it. In past months the Japanese have had barges and these have been destroyed or driven away.[10]

I never get over being grateful to General MacArthur for making the decision to come up so far, because I am sure if we had gone half way only, to Hansa Bay, we would have had a desperate fight. A few more jumps like this and we will reach paydirt.

May 10, 1944

Yesterday afternoon I went up to the new Command Post and I must say I was pleasantly surprised. It has about nine rooms and the hardwood floors are what one would call Early American (wide boards). The . . . windows have real glass in them. The verandah across the front is approximately eighty feet long. . . . The view from there is directly down the lake and out over the mountains.

The lake must be fifteen miles long and the mountains are perhaps 7700 feet high. Yesterday they were a deep blue and very beautiful.

There are various flowers and bushes around the house . . . and quite a few lime trees with limes growing on them. There are a couple of boat houses. . . . We are going to put up a number of guest houses and the natives are building some native-type houses for officers. . . .

The MP guard we have had there have captured ten Japanese in the last few days, and I don't imagine that any that are left would put up much of a fight. The natives are ready to turn them in, just as they turned over our aviators to the Japanese when they bailed out. At least they report the location of the Japs.

May 14, 1944

Yesterday afternoon it was very interesting to see the natives who were working on our camp going home to their villages, which are miles away, out on the water. The breeze was behind them and they all had big palm leaves in their canoes which they used for sails, and you would be surprised by the speed they made. . . . It hardly seems possible in this peaceful spot that such things were going on a short time ago.

My great work has been getting heavy Air Corps equipment forward over this little road as well as heavy ack-ack. The Japs built the road for their light trucks. The hot, sunny weather we have been getting has been a Godsend and in another two weeks the road will really be two-way.

We have done wonderful things to the dromes — the Japs would never recognize them. As soon as they are in complete operation we will not have any more of these alerts. Our Air Corps really does a wonderful job. Here they had destroyed about everything the Japs had, and we are only sorry they did not leave some of the gasoline dumps.

This morning Bill [Bowen] and I took off up the lake to the dromes, about a ten-mile ride to where Fred Irving met me in a jeep. You would have been interested to see Bill and me sitting in the flatbottomed boat with the powerful outboard motor. We had two folding iron chairs and sat there like kings looking out over the lake. The water was smooth and the lake was beautiful. It is one of the most beautiful places on which I have ever lived, until one gets on shore in the dust or rain. . . .

Ack-ack has just started and we are going to have another red alert.

May 15, 1944

This morning we had a very nice ceremony for Fred Irving in quite a beautiful setting. . . . I gave him the Silver Star, which is the only thing I can give except the Purple Heart, the Soldier's Medal and the Bronze Star. Of course I could have recommended him for other things, which probably would be held up interminably. . . .

As far as I am concerned it is perhaps better that I receive little publicity, but I am glad to have the Army know I was in command of this expedition. While not large by Russian standards, it was certainly much larger than our expedition to Cuba in 1898 and much more complicated.

May 16, 1944

I have just watched the guards going out for the protection of our Command Post. There are still some Japs in the hills here but I think they are rapidly falling on their faces.

There goes the three ack-ack shots which announce a red alert. All over the camp the boys are yelling "lights out." The three shots are repeated in all directions with all caliber guns, and it is very difficult to tell whether bombs are dropping or guns are firing.

The Japs could get a landfall if they were to come in and they haven't many opportunities left, but I imagine all that will happen will be that a snooper will get in and at the worst he will drop half a dozen bombs. Up here on the lake we would not offer a profitable target for anyone, and I feel we are perfectly safe. The Japs who lived in this house had an enormous air-raid shelter, but it would never occur to us to use it. It is beautiful out over the lake right now and it is hard to realize we are still the furthest point of advance.

May 17, 1944

Message from Walter: "I am highly pleased that Air Force require-ments for _____ have been met on time." This referred to getting the dromes fixed up, roads, gas, etc., so an attack could be pulled off this morning. . . . I thought they had brought in plenty of gas by air but at midnight night before last I found it necessary to stop everything to rush gas to the dromes. My problems are many but interesting. Got up early to have breakfast with Clovis and then see him off. . . . He rides this morning over this new landing. I gave him permission because I knew I shouldn't risk it myself.

(later)

It is three o'clock and I have been sitting around waiting for Clovis to get back from his ride over Wakde where . . . a successful attack took place today. All the news coming in appears good, and particularly that given in a telephone message from Clovis.[11]

Clovis is full of enthusiasm about the big time he had today. He was able to fly in a fast plane and see everything that went on from the air. It certainly was an experience. I would like very much to do that, but I know I could not explain it to those in higher authority.

May 19, 1944

Yesterday we went to a demonstration of a Jap machine-gun with Fred Irving. Then a naval officer came along as my guest and spent the night. . . . An Australian officer who had been out in the hills for two months came to talk to me and after that, until almost midnight, there was an unceasing flow of visitors. . . . The great trouble is that when I go away the papers pile up and then when night comes I cannot work on them because we are blacked out so much.

May 20, 1944

Most of my work now consists of seeing how many boats I can get un-loaded, how much gasoline I can get over a road which could hardly be termed a road, and how many rations I can get distributed. With it all, I think we are doing quite well.

May 21, 1944

Last night and this morning for the first time we had no red alerts, so we were able to work right through to bedtime, and I was not disturbed in the night except when a lizard got on Sergeant Manturi's face. Then there was a lot of yelling which included such calls as "I see you. Who are you anyhow?" My bodyguard . . . slept right through that racket, so you can see how much help they would be to me.

Across the arm of the lake there is a little place called Koejaboe, which is just a little spot on the map, but past it go the trucks all through the night. In the evening the Japanese come down and shoot at the trucks, but up to date have not hurt anyone. Apparently the Japs who live near the food dumps get along very well, but those who have tried to escape to the westward have had a very difficult time, as the work of walking over the jungle trails is very grueling.

It has not rained now for a week and during that time things have looked up a lot. Before very long SOS [U.S. Army Services of Supply] will take over the unloading of ships and I will not have that to worry about. In the meantime, we have been doing a good job. With our limited facilities, we are unloading lots more tonnage per man than is being done in the rear areas.

At Wakde, they ran into some hard-fighting Japs who decided to die in place, but it is all cleaned up nicely now.

May 22, 1944

Carl Dockler came in a little while ago with a little Jap prisoner who was picked up several days ago. He is about nineteen and says he is a civilian who worked with the Japanese forces as orderly to a vice admiral. His story was very interesting for it showed that our landing here was completely unexpected and caught the Japanese here entirely unprepared. The old admiral went off into the mountains with others but probably couldn't last so he sent the others on ahead. The boy walked over the mountains to Tanahmerah and it took him twenty-six days . . . which makes me more convinced than ever that the Japs who fled from this area will probably die on the trails. The youngster made roughly about a mile a day and he was in good physical condition when he started. Like so many others, he has no desire to go back to Japan after the war for he feels his parents will not want him because he was captured.

May 24, 1944

This has been quite a day. After breakfast Clovis and I went up to the strips to meet Walter. . . . We had a beautiful ride down the lake to our Command Post here, but Walter apparently does not like the water and I don't think he had a good time.

In addition to everything else today, a singer shows up and asked me to come to his performance tonight. The fact that we were up very late last night and that I hold my staff conferences at night means nothing to him. I tried to beg off but I could see I was hurting his feelings so I guess I will have to go for a while.

The following message was sent voluntarily by the Air Corps Commander here to his chief: PERSONAL FOR GENERAL WHITEHEAD AND COLONEL COOPER. ENTIRE I CORPS WORKING FOR AIR FORCES. THEIR COOPERATION AND ASSISTANCE MAKES THIS OPERATION POSSIBLE. EVERY REQUEST MET EVEN TO COMPLETE DETRIMENT OF LAND FORCE UNITS THIS AREA WITHIN PHYSICAL LIMITATIONS OF RESOURCES OF ENTIRE AREA.

We certainly have been doing everything possible to help him. The Jap air strips were nothing but cow pastures when we took them over.

May 27, 1944

I have not seen Walter since the first day he came here. As you have noticed in the papers there was another landing today[12] and he has been here for that purpose. I shall go to see him tomorrow.

We are all sitting around waiting for the second front now and hoping everything comes out all right. The news about Italy was great. We were very fortunate to have gotten out of that.[13] I hope that now they do not start bragging about how good they were for we certainly were worried for a long, long time.

May 28, 1944

This has been quite a day. This morning I went down to call on Walter, who is living on a beach. After three hours of that I was exhausted, but we stayed for lunch. When I got home I received an unsigned message from an unknown boat saying "Big boy will land at Pim at five o'clock and wants to go to I Corps." I figured out it was probably General Lumsden and went down to meet him. Then I realized Walter was grieving because Lumsden had not called on him when he passed through his other home the other day. Therefore, I took him across the harbor in the J-boat and we arrived there just as Walter was taking a bath. However, he came forth and invited us to dinner.

About eight o'clock we ... started for home, by jeep to the bay and then across in the J-boat to Pim. As we got off the boat onto the newly made dock I was walking ahead of the general. I happened to look around and saw he had disappeared, and when I went back to look I found him struggling around in the water. He had just gone through a hole in the dock.[14]

Today I got word to start building an advance Command Post for

GHQ. That means our engineers won't be able to get my road in good shape.

May 29, 1944

You make some laughing comments about publicity. It is a decided buildup, of course, as you can well understand, and the central control committee puts the publicity where they feel it will do the most good. In our operation, the second place the newspaper people went was to Walter, who wanted his organization to have the publicity they have not been receiving. They told me all about that, so when I talked to them I told them I was glad to have Walter's outfit get the publicity. Even so, I do not think they got very much and . . . I do not believe my outfit got much. That is all right. There are so many things going on in the world that the interest of the people in any one area is limited.

Tonight Walter called me and said he had a vacancy for second in command of a division for Clovis, and asked me to give him a reply by tomorrow noon. . . . Clovis has decided he doesn't want that job so it will be necessary for me to explain that diplomatically to Walter tomorrow.[15]

May 30, 1944

I feel that I am now safe with reference to a critical strip I have been building. At any rate, I shall turn all that over to the SOS in a few days.

You have doubtless read all about Biak Island. My classmate [Fuller] is there and I don't believe he is having an easy time. . . . Things are not always just exactly as they seem.[16]

June 1, 1944

I do not know what Walter thinks about this publicity. Someone said there is a picture of me in *Life*. It is hard to push these newspaper men around. I treat them with courtesy but have never asked anything of them except once in a while to take a letter down to Charlie[17] for me. . . . I agree with you that nobody is trying to give anyone else any publicity around here. Naturally the great central organization is built around the great central figure, and Walter's organization is built around him. One of the two is not particularly newsworthy and therefore has not received very much.

After lunch I talked with Frank Kluckhorn for a long time. He was trying to get a message out on a sea action he had seen. I was able to do this for him. He gave me a lot of inside history of the newspaper fraternity. Apparently Walter's crowd are not popular with them. They have no organization for handling newspaper people and yet they hope to get favorable publicity. . . . He said Ike would run the Army after this war like Pershing did after the other war, providing he does not stub his toe, and that the men around him would be the fair-haired boys. He said I would not know him now as he was very puffed up.

June 4, 1944

Walter has been here so he could be close to Biak.... That show ... has not been an easy one. Eventually there will be an advanced Command Post for GHQ and also Walter will put his Command Post here.... In the meantime I trust that the time is growing closer when we may move on to more exciting places. Already we feel we are in a rear area as Biak is three hundred miles beyond us. We have not even had an air alarm for a week, and we used to have three or four every night.

June 6, 1944

The radios tonight are ringing with the announcement of the invasion of France. You can imagine how interested we have been. Of course, of even greater interest to us is the situation immediately around us, which is not as simple as it looks. We can only pray that all goes well on that channel crossing, because if victory comes it will only be a matter of time until the Japanese are forced to fold up.

June 7, 1944

This morning I had a very interesting time talking to a Japanese air officer who was taken prisoner the other day. He said he has been an athlete all his life and that was the reason he got through, but it took him thirty days to cover the last forty miles before he was captured. I asked him what he thought would happen to the Japanese forces in New Guinea, and he said that they have no place to go and "whether they go north, south, east or west, they are cut off."

Clovis has applied for a leave of absence for three weeks.... He falls well within the policy and I see no reason why it should not be granted. I find that quite a few of the boys are ready to go home and stay home. ...I imagine after they have been there a while they will be sorry they did not go to the Philippines. Of course there is nothing I can do or say about a change of station back home now. There are no more jobs commensurate with my rank and I would be putting myself in the position of being a quitter if I would seek a change. If I find they want to use me, I shall be glad, and I feel I can do a little to hasten the time when we will all come home.

June 8, 1944

Today has been very unusual for me. This morning I made a rather delayed visit to see Walter, who ... has been here to watch the show Horace is putting on at Biak. He expected to be here only a short time but, of necessity, he had to stay longer. Horace has had a bit of a time and I don't mean maybe. We had a grand talk....

When I got back to the inner bay I found Colonel Brickley there, who wanted me to visit a hospital ship in the harbor which had a lot of wounded from Biak. I did this and really felt glad, because they seemed so happy to see me and talk with me.

I have intentionally not talked of the statement made by my Chief . . . that a new army is going to be formed. One office at GHQ congratulated me on the honors which are coming to me. I have heard that my Chief asked that an army staff be sent out here, but not an army commander. Otherwise, I have heard nothing.

You spoke of the fire started by our little brown palsy-walsies. It really was a jackpot and took about everything I had except my shirt. It lasted for a week and held up things terribly. All done by one bird.

June 9, 1944

You were puzzled because nothing was said about me in the Aitape article. I had nothing to do with it. . . . Doe[18] landed there with a force built around one of Horace Fuller's outfits and under [Sixth] army command. . . . Aitape is about a hundred miles to the east of here. . . .

When I had my talk with the Commander in Chief on the *Nashville* on D-day at Tanahmerah, he suggested I take a force at once and go to Wakde. In view of the fact that we did not know then for sure that the Japanese were licked, for the reactions of the first few hours may not be the final ones, I was largely instrumental in talking him out of it. When we had fixed up the airfields, Jens [Doe] went with his outfit from Aitape to Wakde. Later Horace left for Biak with Jens back under him. That is the whole history. As I see things now, based on the best dope obtainable, there will be nothing more for us until about a year from the time I last saw you [October]. Others may do this and that from time to time, but unless things go wrong I shall probably follow that pattern.

Horace had a pretty hard time for a while and Walter told me he had considered sending me in there to help. However, that is no longer necessary.

June 11, 1944

I have been getting lots of rest since I signed off my SOS work. From now on, though, I am going to begin to get out and inspect troops.

The great problem that we had at our last station was the preparation of plans, the drawing up of orders, the determination of what troops would land where and in what wave. . . . The number of units is perfectly tremendous. Even such things as malaria-control and malaria-survey units. The engineers are always a very important part of any move of this type for they must build the roads and build them in a hurry, and also must fix up air strips or build new ones.

June 13, 1944

Walter . . . is still here hoping that Horace will finish up his job on Biak. He has already been fighting for over half a month, and I know from experience that that is a long time.

All these recent movements have put my Chief in a fine strategic position and I do not doubt he will capitalize on it. So if I were you I would keep a close watch on the situation and follow it with a good map.

June 14, 1944

About five o'clock this afternoon Walter sent for me on an emergency telephone call. He said when I got there that he wanted me to go up and take command at Biak, and leave tomorrow morning. The whole situation reminds me quite a bit of the one of the 1st of December '42; in other words, things have not gone well. As a consequence my office, which is also my bedroom, is chock-full of talking people and Dombrowski is trying to pack my clothes. . . . I realized . . . that there has been a delay there. It is principally terrain, but the Jap units were well-rested combat troops who have fought back hard.

I have authority, of course, to relieve Horace, but I shall hate to do that if I can avoid it. We are going in very light in a couple of navy cats with, I understand, suitable air cover. Being a soldier, I am glad to go and it is something of a compliment that they reach out and get me again when things are running crosswise.

This letter will have to convey all the thousand and one things which I cannot say. You will understand, however, I am sure. . . . Be a good old Doll and do not worry. I shall have a larger force to start with — I think about half my age in thousands. While not large like the one I brought in here, it will be no puny force to be kicked around by anyone.

The hours are flying by and I should be in bed.

Notes

1. Robert Ross Smith, *The Approach to the Philippines* (Washington, 1953), pp. 51–53.

2. Maj. Gen. Innis Palmer Swift, commanding the First Cavalry Division, was in charge of the occupation force for the Admiralty Islands, the rendezvous point for the RECKLESS Task Force.

3. MacArthur's word, Gen. Clovis Byers claims, was always good as long as he would shake hands on it. If he refused to shake hands, then one never could be sure. On several occasions Eichelberger would reach for MacArthur's hand after a verbal commitment with the words, "Shake on it, General." Sometimes, Gen. Byers recalls, MacArthur would shake — once in a while he would draw back. Notes of an interview with Gen. Clovis E. Byers, 17 May 1965.

4. Smith, *Approach to the Philippines*, p. 13.

5. Frank Prist, an Acme photographer, had been at Buna. He was later killed on Leyte.

6. On the night of 23–24 April, a solitary Japanese plane dropped a bomb on an old Japanese ammunition dump and the spreading fires touched off an American gasoline dump and other equipment accumulated on the beach in Humboldt Bay. Over 60 percent of the rations and ammunition landed on the first two days, the equivalent of 11 LST loads of supplies, were lost, thus creating a critical logistical problem. Smith, *Approach to the Philippines*, pp. 78–79.

7. Sentani, Cyclops, and Hollandia airdromes. Eichelberger Diary, 27 April 1944.

8. Maj. Gen. Edward P. King, Jr., commanded the Luzon Force during the last days

before the surrender; Lt. Gen. Jonathan M. Wainwright was the ranking American army officer in the Philippines after MacArthur's departure for Australia.

9. After the war Eichelberger elaborated upon his remarks on Japanese prisoners captured at Hollandia. "Some of them were starving and were captured along the trail bypassing Hollandia. Some were captured in and around our area who were hiding out in jungle and were coming down at night to steal from the almost countless piles of supplies which we had captured. . . . We found photographs of heads being cut off by Japanese. . . . Yet when I captured these men, I gave orders for them to be furnished from our great captured stores. . . . They ate Japanese food . . . cooked in Japanese utensils and were clothed well from captured Japanese uniforms. There was a Japanese doctor whom I captured and kept in the camp for a long time while various prisoners were sent to Australia. One peculiar thing happened, and that was that a number of Japanese came out of the jungle and turned themselves in. This is almost unbelievable when one remembers the almost fatalistic attitude towards the prisoners' status. Most Japanese said they would rather be dead than captured. . . .

"In view of the Japanese fatalism towards death, one would imagine that very little information would be secured from Japanese prisoners, but I found we did get some very valuable military intelligence. Because the Japanese would never be willing to admit that any soldier would ever be captured alive, they had been very poorly instructed about how to conduct themselves when captured.

"On the other hand, *I have never heard of a live infantryman captured by the Japanese from Milne Bay and Buna to the Philippines who came out of it alive.* . . . When I asked . . . an officer prisoner . . . how he accounted for the terrible way the Japanese treated the American prisoners, he explained that Japanese military considered a prisoner to be in disgrace and that they felt they were even doing a man a kindness to kill him. . . . I did not fall for this 'kindness' talk. The Japanese military were cruel.

"At Hollandia, I walked around inside the prison enclosure. The prisoners were comparatively cheerful looking and well nourished. They must have been very surprised at their humane treatment, but somehow I could not bring myself to imitate the Japanese. . . . I remember one badly wounded Japanese naval officer prisoner. . . . I told one of the men to give him a drink of water, but I have never seen such hatred blaze out of anyone's eyes as when he looked at me." Eichelberger Dictations, 25 August 1955; 24 February 1961.

10. Japanese casualty figures at Hollandia are staggering. Of the 7,000 men who had escaped the pincers movement at Hollandia and assembled at Genjem village, about fifteen miles west of Lake Sentani, "the Japanese themselves estimated that only 7 percent survived to reach the Sarmi area." Fewer than 1,000 of the approximately 11,000 stationed at Hollandia at the time of the landings "could have survived the war." By comparison, American losses were trifling — 124 killed, 1,057 wounded, and 28 missing in the first six weeks. Smith, *Approach to the Philippines,* pp. 83, 101–102.

11. The reference here is to seizure of Wakde Island, which was to be the next airbase site after Hollandia, by the 163d Regimental Combat Team of the Forty-first Division, Brig. Gen. Jens A. Doe commanding. The landings on this day were at Arare, on the New Guinea coast, to cover the main assault, which was to take place on Wakde the following day. The landings at Arare, a native settlement, were unopposed. There was some fighting on Wakde but by 20 May the island was declared secure. The airstrip was operational on the following day. Smith, *Approach to the Philippines,* pp. 206–231 passim.

12. On 27 May the Forty-first Division, minus the 163d Regimental Combat Team that had seized Wakde the previous week, landed on Biak Island, 180 miles to the northwest. Biak was of major strategic importance both to the SWPA and the CPA theaters because of its airfields.

13. This probably refers to the success of Operation BUFFALO on 23 May 1944, when Allied Forces broke out of the Anzio beachhead to join the Fifth Army advancing northward.

14. In *Our Jungle Road to Tokyo* (New York, 1950), Eichelberger states (p. 121) that Gen. Herbert Lumsden, who was Churchill's representative to MacArthur, actually fell in a brand new latrine that had not yet been covered over.

15. Gen. Byers explained his decision to Miss Em: "In the past everyone has known Bob to be an outstanding administrator, and more recently even Walter has acknowledged

his prowess as a courageous and skillful leader of troops, but this most recent task is a supply one of extreme difficulty. Bob's intelligent curiosity has enabled him to reach the bottom of the complexities of the problem and the results are nothing short of remarkable. . . .

"There have been some difficult moments, particularly during the last seventy-two hours. We have been at loss to know the reason for them. I think they are brought about because Walter has heard a rumor that a new army staff has been requested . . . for this area . . . and that Bob will get the call. I think Walter feels these last days were finishing lessons in order that Bob might know how to act as an army commander.

"Walter ended this difficult period by asking Bob to release me to become the infantry brigadier for Sibert's division. Bob said he knew that I realized how he felt and he would say nothing for fear of influencing me. I have never been happier in my service than I have these last two years . . . and Bob has furnished many opportunities which seldom fall to the lot of the average army officer. . . . Bob told Walter of my decision and his blunt retort was, 'Napoleon once said the reason so few officers succeeded was that they did not recognize opportunity when it knocked.' The question of opportunity is a matter of personal opinion. . . . I'm sure 99% of the officers in this theater agree with me." Byers to Miss Em, 30 May 1944. For corroborative evidence of this last statement, see Harold Riegelman, *Caves of Biak* (New York, 1955), p. 165.

16. On 27 May 1944, Task Force HURRICANE, consisting largely of the Forty-first Division minus the 163d Regimental Combat Team, landed on Biak. The Japanese counterattacked the next day, driving back the 162d Infantry before it could seize the airfields, and Gen. Fuller felt compelled to call for reinforcements.

17. Frequently Eichelberger used to send his letters to Miss Em through Gen. Willoughby's office.

18. Brig. Gen. Jens A. Doe, Assistant Division Commander, Forty-first Division.

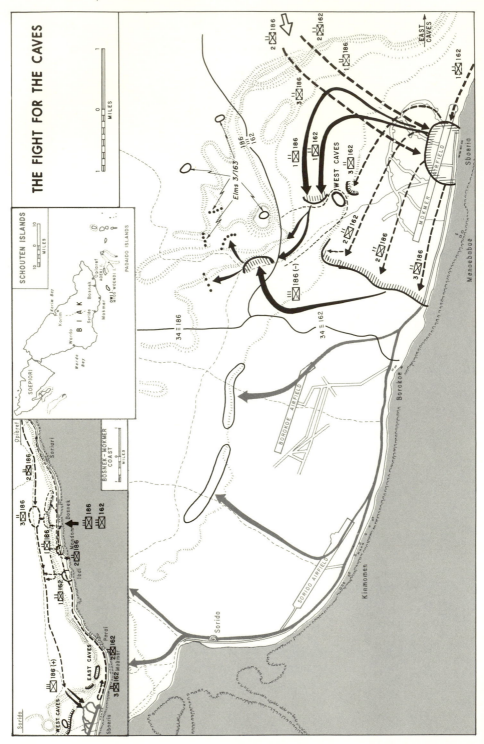

THE FIGHT FOR THE CAVES

MAP 3

CHAPTER SEVEN

"This Fight Is a Witch"

Biak, one of the Schouten Island group, is located just south of the equator, some 300 miles west of Hollandia and less than 1,000 miles from the Philippines. Seizure of this island and its three airstrips would provide additional air support for the invasion of the Marianas, which was scheduled to begin with the attack on Saipan on 15 June 1944. And to the Japanese, gearing themselves for a naval showdown with the United States Fleet, which they anticipated would take place either off the Marianas or near Geelvink Bay, Biak was equally important as a base for planes because of the heavy loss of aircraft carriers in recent operations.

After Hollandia, the next step in the westward advance to the Philippines was to have been directed at the Wakde-Sarmi area, which was roughly halfway between Hollandia and Biak. Indeed, the surprisingly light resistance to the landings at Hollandia had even encouraged MacArthur to consider an immediate advance.

"This was at a time," Eichelberger later recalled, "when I did not know whether there were Japanese regular regiments at Hollandia. At a conference on the cruiser Nashville on the afternoon of 22 April, I raised strong objections. My objections, without the support of General Krueger or Admiral Barbey, who remained silent, were based on the fact that our ships were combat loaded for the Hollandia operation. We were in no sense prepared, after a partial unloading on the Hollandia beaches, to go at once to Toem [Wakde] Sarmi. The surprising thing is that General MacArthur would not have in his mind a clear picture of the supply situation which would in itself prevent the quick advance of plans."[1]

Subsequent delays caused by the supply congestion at Hollandia and the need to wait for higher tides in the invasion area forced a reexamination of the entire operation, and when aerial photographs of the coast around Sarmi indicated that ground conditions in this part of New Guinea "were not suited to airdromes adequate for heavy bomber operations," MacArthur decided to cancel the Sarmi phase of the operation in favor of a prompt movement against Biak.[2]

The revised plan called for the 163d Regimental Combat Team to make the initial landings in the Wakde operation on 17 May, with the rest of the Forty-first Division, reinforced by artillery, antiaircraft, tank, and engineer units, to land near the airdromes on the southern coast of Biak on 27 May. Although most of the troops came from I Corps, and HURRICANE Task Force was commanded by General Horace Fuller, one of Eichelberger's subordinates, the planning for the seizure of Biak was done by the staff of Krueger's ALAMO Force. At the time Eichelberger was summoned to Krueger's headquarters, he "had received no information of the progress of the fighting at Biak. . . . General Byers and I were old hands at this game and particularly remembered the time we were ordered to Buna with no warning of any kind. . . . Working as we were at Hollandia, we received absolutely no reports from Sixth Army or GHQ about how things were going at Biak. This would seem unbelievable, that a force in the field wouldn't be kept informed about what was going on in adjacent combat units, but it was a fact and it was typical, even into Japan. . . .[3]

"When we reached General Krueger's headquarters, we found him sheltered in bright flood lights in his tropical home. . . . He said things had been going wrong at Biak and . . . were more or less at a standstill with the Japanese on a cliff a mile or so away from the airfields and dominating the fields by their fire and preventing any planes from landing. Krueger wanted me to fly in there . . . the next morning at daybreak . . . to take command. He said he had notified General Fuller that I was on the way. . . . I asked him whether we were to return to Hollandia and he said, 'We never draw backwards,' or words to that effect."[4]

Fuller had indeed been having his troubles. Although he had achieved a complete tactical surprise on Z-day, the first wave had hit the beach, or rather a mangrove swamp, some 3,000 yards west of the intended location because of strong westflowing currents and poor visibility. The remaining elements of the 186th Infantry had been landed at the planned location, and by noon this regiment had firmly established its beachhead.

But the 162d Regiment, which was given the task of pushing westward from the beachhead along the cramped coastal corridor to seize the airdromes, was soon halted by Japanese mortar and machine-gun fire from the caves in the coral ridges that dominated the southern shore of the island. Two battalions did manage to get as far as Parai, over halfway to Mokmer Drome, when they had to dig in for the night.

The advance was resumed the next day. The Third Battalion, in the lead, encountered little enemy resistance until it reached a road junction several hundred yards from the Mokmer Drome. Here a furious Japanese counterattack drove back the Third Battalion, and the rest of the 162d Regiment was unable to outflank the Japanese on the ridges above. On 29 May, the Japanese threw three strong counterattacks against the 162d, driving it still further eastward to a new perimeter at Ibdi. By this time Fuller had already called for reinforcements, and the 163d Regimental Combat Team at Wakde was promptly ordered to Biak.

The 163d arrived on 31 May and relieved the 186th, which was then freed to participate in the fight for Mokmer Drome. On 1 June, the 186th, joined the following day by the Second Battalion of the 162d, began its outflanking movement over the inland plateau to clear the high ground north of Mokmer Drome, which was reached on 7 June. But the Japanese stronghold in the West Caves, which might have been taken in reverse by this movement, had been neglected in the drive for the airfield, and Japanese troops, securely lodged in the Ibdi Pocket and the East Caves, held up a coordinated movement by the other two battalions of the 162d along the beach until 10 June.

For the next four days Fuller's troops fought to clear the airstrips and eject the Japanese from their admirable defensive positions in the cliffs and caves on the high ground to the north. Meanwhile, Krueger, with a deadline to meet and under pressure from MacArthur, kept prodding Fuller to speed up the operation. After officers of his own staff reported from the battlefield that the stalled attacks could succeed if renewed by strong, aggressive action, and Fuller had requested still another infantry regiment to meet the threat of Japanese reinforcements on Biak, Krueger decided to have I Corps assume direction of the Task Force, leaving Fuller to devote all of his energies "to the tactical handling of his division."[5]

June 16, 1944

Dearest Miss Em,

We were off yesterday morning about 8:30 in two Navy Catalinas. The trip in the thirty-eight-foot boats down the lake to the planes was a very beautiful one. . . . I sat in the copilot's seat a large part of the time. Eight smaller planes circled us all the way up. I was glad to fly over Wakde because I have heard so much about it.

We landed first on a lagoon, expecting to get a boat from there to the shore, but there was no boat; so we took off again and came down on the open sea in a rain squall. I thought surely the bottom was coming out of the [flying] boat because I never felt such a banging. It was a real adventure for us all.

An LCM, which is a steel landing craft about forty feet long, came out to get us. It was jumping up and down and the plane was too, and the passing of our baggage ... took a long time. We had to come out on the slippery snout in the rain.... The pilot ... who was helping pass things, including the men, along, fell in the water, but was a good swimmer. We finally came ashore and Ken Sweany,[6] who occupies the same position to Horace that Clovis does to me, met us with jeeps. They had just heard we were coming. Horace, in that short time, had already submitted a letter asking for relief from his division and requesting his retirement. He says he does not intend to serve under a certain man again if he has to submit his resignation every half hour by wire.... He cried when he recalled that it was thirty-nine years ago yesterday since we entered the military academy together.

Clovis and I are living in a tent vacated by Horace. It has a wooden floor and wooden sides made of Japanese lumber. The floor is about five feet below the level of the ground and there are sand bags all around the top.... The pyramidal tent stands up high with the walls held out by poles, so it is really quite large.... My bed is well below the ground level....

They don't sleep much around here at night apparently, as the little palsy-walsies don't like Americans very much. It rained most of last night so we were not disturbed until about three o'clock. Then Clovis, Ken, Horace and I spent an hour in a dugout. I finally had to give up and go to bed.

[Today] Clovis and I left early and went by fast sixty-six-foot boat to the nearby island where we have a new airstrip rapidly nearing completion.[7] We then took off in turn and went over the water to Mokmer Drome which is still within long-range small arms fire from the Japanese.... Then we drove up to the front because I found that we could get quite close. We walked up to the top of the hill to an observation post and there found a tank fight nearby in progress which was very interesting. The Japs were shooting with heavy mortars and I was a bit afraid that they might not have the correct deflection so we moved on.

At one o'clock we were back at Mokmer Drome where we found two cubs, so we both took off for Owi Drome, from which we had started early in the morning. The Japs fired a few farewell shots at Clovis to express their dislike for him.... Horace is leaving tomorrow, and I feel very sorry for him.

You can see what an interesting day we had. Thanks to the Piper cub and the fast boat, we were able to see a lot without any great fatigue.

To do that on foot and by jeep would have been quite a problem. We seem to have our little pals pushed back a bit and I am hopeful of cleaning them up in the not too distant future.

June 17, 1944

We were lucky last night because it rained and none of our little pals came to see us. There was, however, a big gun back of my tent that fired all night, sometimes at half-hour intervals, sometimes at ten-second intervals. It is designed to keep our little pals awake and it succeeds in keeping me awake too. I have directed that the battery commander be fastened onto one of the shells as a fitting punishment for all this loss of sleep. [Brig. Gen.] Horace Harding [artillery officer for I Corps] cannot see anything funny in my suggestion. Word came about Horace Fuller last night. As he had requested he will go home soon. That was bound to happen.

This place is as ugly as our old place was pretty. It is true that we are on the water and in the moonlight it will be pretty, but the coral reef goes out about a quarter of a mile so there is no place to swim nor have boats come up. . . .

Clovis and I are going by small, fast boat to a nearby island [Owi] where an airstrip is rapidly nearing completion. I shall be glad when we get our planes in our own front yard. They will help me capture the other dromes for which we are fighting. They probably expect me to do this in a day, but this fight is a witch — if you will pardon the paraphrase. The many coral cliffs leading away from this narrow coastal shelf have innumerable caves in which our little friends are willing to die.

You will wonder how I am. I look . . . and feel about the same. Mr. Mills [a general staff warrant officer] says that I look different because, having a hard job to do, my eyes are brighter and I look more alive with the determination to do it. I must say that I enjoyed the sights and sounds of the battleground yesterday, although I did not go up on the front line. I was anxious to talk with the men and I did get a chance to talk to some of them, but there is no reason for me to go up to the front unless I can see something. Up there it is very thick.

It is funny how easy it is to get to sleep when one should get up. I must have dropped off five times in five minutes this morning while talking to Clovis, who was shaving. That shows how enlivening his conversation is. The first night I was here Clovis complained because he would try to read me a long G-2 report and get a snore in the middle of it. I claim that it is a fine indication that the report wasn't worth much. . . . As always, Dombrowski fixes me up fine. I am really very comfortable, but I am afraid that our meals leave something to be desired.

This is the toughest terrain I have yet seen to fight in except at Buna. We are living in a coconut grove which is very nice, right on the water.

The interior is a series of coral cliffs with numerous natural caves. It has been and will continue to be a tough fight.

June 18, 1944

This morning Shuck and the rear echelon arrived and before I had my breakfast I looked out and Ventura was sitting in my command car outside my tent. Of course there is a tremendous confusion as Horace's old headquarters had to move out so that mine could come in. Fortunately, I have been able to keep my sunken tent.

Horace [Fuller] has already left to get aboard a destroyer which will leave tonight. I shall go down in a little while to say my official good-byes. . . . I feel very sad about Horace and I know he feels terribly about leaving his division. There was one thing he was determined about, though, and that was he would not serve another day under Walter under any conditions. He told me that on D-day at Hollandia my Big Chief had promised to give him a corps, so that will not make him feel good. I tried to get him to reconsider his decision but he would not do so. Any man who requests relief of course puts himself out on a limb.

Jens [Doe] will temporarily take over that outfit. Whether I will recommend him for permanent command will depend on how quickly he cleans out these little devils. . . .

Up at the front I have a grand airfield ready to use, but there is just enough fire on it to make the air corps unwilling to use it. . . . I was delighted yesterday afternoon when I found that the new airstrip on the island just opposite me was in good enough shape so that fifteen of our planes, which were running out of gasoline because they could not get through a storm, were able to make emergency landings and save their lives. I feel they didn't believe me when I told them how fine that strip was getting to be. Being on an island, it is of course safe from the Japanese while the Mokmer strip . . . is just near enough to the Japanese that they can drop an occasional shot on it. I landed on it yesterday and I would not hesitate to land on it at any time under the present conditions.

We are going to take a crack at the Japanese tomorrow and of course every day thereafter. Today has been a day of rest and of reorganization. Also, more troops are being moved forward. I think by tomorrow night the Japanese will be in a much worse position tactically than they are today.

We have not heard much in the last few days about the situation in Europe or other places, although I understand Japanese territory has been bombed by B-29s. . . .

June 19, 1944

I want to start this before the time comes for me to go up forward where I shall watch Doe's men make an attack.

I wish you could see this place now, for all of our headquarters sections have set up their tents so that the area is a maze of tents, tent ropes, vehicles of all kinds, slit trenches, and bomb shelters. No Jap could ever penetrate here at night unless he had eyes like a cat. This area is definitely too small for our needs....

(later)

When we were about halfway to the front this morning I permitted an MP to block us off because a Jap with a machine gun about a thousand yards away was firing at the road. It made me so angry because I was headed for the front, where it was incomparably more dangerous. I walked around the danger area and bummed a ride on the other side. Jack Sverdrup[8] was with me. We joined Jens [Doe] who reported the fighting was going well.

Jack and I, with Eddie and some other boys, then went in a jeep to Mokmer Drome and over the trail we captured three days ago, and then down through the area which was captured this morning. There were a lot of dead Japanese around and some few live ones, so we were escorted by a couple of tanks. Our attack this morning came in on him from the front, both flanks, and now we are across his rear, so I guess that particular bunch of Japs will no longer threaten Mokmer Drome. One of the most interesting sights were four big six-inch guns on the ridge above Mokmer Drome. It is a good thing our troops did not try to land near there. It was probably one of these that shot a hole in an American destroyer.

All in all it was a grand day. Tomorrow, Jenna[9] attacks with a fresh regiment to the westward, and I expect to get the other two dromes before nightfall.... I just radioed Walter what happened today and I know that he will be very happy.... You should have seen Ventura when he was driving me over that jungle trail with dead Japs and sniping. His eyes were rolling around, but he tried to look nonchalant. This will be a terrible place to clean up — Jap trash every place....

[In a subsequent letter to Miss Em, Eichelberger went into somewhat greater detail about his own activities during his first days at Biak.]

I arrived on Thursday and on Saturday I was on top of a ridge having pointed out to me where the Americans were supposed to be. I had left Jens and Clovis down below some distance as I did not want anything again to happen such as happened to Waldron [at Buna]. There were some tanks below me and the Japanese were putting down a lot of 90 mm howitzer fire on them. Every ridge, including the one I was on, that was supposed to have Americans on it, turned out to be covered with Japanese. There were also some Japanese on the other side of the tanks about a hundred yards away. I therefore concluded they did not know where they were and the situation was very obscure. I therefore ordered a day of rest [18 June] and reorganization so everybody could find out what they were doing. I then placed one battalion on the Japanese left rear, and two battalions to cut across their rear from the right. This attack took place on Monday [19 June] and it broke their backs. Jens tried to talk me out of doing it.... I realize I will get no credit for that fight but . . . at one time I planned every major move they made. On June 21, according to a prisoner, the colonel of the Japanese regiment had a ceremony and burned the regimental colors.[10]

June 20, 1944

Last night was really a celebration because we had a distinct victory yesterday.... Last night was wonderful too because we had a red alert and I just stayed in bed. . . . As I was drifting off to sleep I wondered what you would think if you could see the shadows of the two men who walk round and round my tent with fixed bayonets all night. Of course it is not the same men throughout the night. One walks about ten feet behind the other. That is the kind of country in which I live.

We have been fortunate since I have been here that there have been no bad bombing raids. That I think is principally due to bad weather, but I do not know what kept them from coming last night. Of course our air . . . has been cracking down on them.

There is some kind of a gun, about a 75 mm, that fires at us at a certain hour every night. We do not know exactly where it is but think it is in one of these caves in the cliff. I would certainly be glad to locate it.

I understand that Tokyo Rose, who talks over Radio Tokyo, reported that we were about to be driven into the sea.

Clyde, Eddie, Sverdrup and I went up to watch Bill Jenna's attack. He captured two airstrips and one of them should be a knockout. We had lunch a couple of miles beyond the second airstrip. Right underneath where we were eating they located two Japanese in a cave by the water. They threw a grenade at them and it was thrown back out and burst outside. Then they tossed a phosphorus smoke grenade which must have made them very sick. Then, because no one could think of what to do next, they tossed in some TNT. Eddie finally went down to take a look and he said it was an awful sight, with a little bit of Japanese every place. . . .

The fire fight on the other front did not go too well,[11] for although the Japanese had been driven back yesterday they still are putting up a vicious fight. I noticed the old tendency which I found in Papua for our troops to get very sorry for themselves and to forget what a hard time the Japanese are having. As a matter of fact, I imagine they get fifty rounds of artillery and twenty-five rounds of mortar fire for every one we get from them.

When I came back tonight I found a couple of ships lying off the jetty, so I realize I am going to have some more supply problems.

Sverdrup is off for Brisbane tomorrow and I think he has had a fine time. He is a very brave chap and a fine engineer. He has walked over the Owen Stanley Range more times than any white man, with possibly the exceptions of old New Guineaites who lived there.

June 21, 1944

Last night we had another calm night without any bombing. This morning I am going down to look at some unloading while Clovis goes up to the front. We have a boat down here with fresh food straight from San Francisco. I do not imagine, however, there is any fresh beef aboard.

10:00

I have just been down ... to where we plan to put our new Command Post. It is the best place we have seen here, right on the water with a certain amount of sandy beach and with the road up above on a low cliff. There is a native village there ... built out on the water on pilings. This will be burned, and after a little cleaning up ... we will have a fine place. There is a big cave that the Japanese fixed up, which is apparently quite elaborate. It will do for a bomb shelter. . . . The trouble is that for the present it is in the wrong direction, away from the fighting, but once the fighting is reasonably over I shall be glad to go there, for it will be away from the planes. The view from there, out over the islands, is fine.

There is nothing new now except that I am anxious to inject a little punch into our fighting as I think I detect a tendency to wait around for the artillery to do it. That does not always work out.

(later)

Noon reports from Jens were to the effect that the enemy's fighting qualities were deteriorating. Our patrols have gone another mile or more without getting opposition that amounts to anything. I hope it means that the little yellow so-and-so's are going to try to escape. Jenna is just to the south of the main trail which goes to the north coast, and it will be along this trail that they will try to get out. I think I will have him block the trail at once, although I hate to do so, for if they really want to get away it might be easier to let them go. The PT boats stationed here go around the island every night and ought to be able to prevent any barge movement. They did catch some coming in about the 15th, but I think the Japs will begin soon to wish they had not tried to reinforce this place.

134 / Dear Miss Em

Maybe the Lord will forgive me for all the profanity I used yesterday. I cussed them all out from Jens Doe to Billy Bowen.

The most aggravating thing I have is the fact that they have different types of guns up in caves on cliffs that remind me of the Palisades on the Hudson. They pop in and out of these, fire and then run back, and the terrain makes it almost impossible to find them. Bill Bowen flew in a cub all over the area today and located one big cave which I think we can wipe out. They fired at him some and I think I will present him with a Silver Star, particularly as he has done this a number of times at Hollandia as well as here.

The Jap rifle which I brought back from the front the other day was very rusty and dirty. Dombrowski took it apart and oiled it up and it looks fine now.... The usual Jap rifle has a very long barrel. It is a .25 caliber with a very high velocity bullet, almost like an old-time squirrel rifle. The one I have is shorter by about a foot.

We have fighter planes tonight on our new drome which we built on an island in less than a week. Fighters are also due on Mokmer, but I have not heard any reports of their arrival. They seem to be afraid the Japs will come in during the night and destroy the planes. Cargo planes also arrived over on the island today in great quantities. One of the two strips we captured yesterday will be a wonder as it has no commanding ground around it and it will be fine for bombers.

June 22, 1944

Today Clyde, Eddie, Sturgis, who is engineer for Walter, Jimmy Collins[12] and I went up to the front. I promised Sam Sturgis I would show him some sights today and I certainly did. We drove forward in a jeep over the same ground I covered several days ago accompanied by a couple of tanks. When we reached the 186th Infantry we found that they had had a fight a little while before in which they had killed over a hundred Japanese. There was no doubt about the Japanese for they were right there, piled up right against the fox holes of the little perimeter. There must have been fifty bodies within a radius of a hundred yards. All of them were well equipped and armed, well fed infantry soldiers. Many of them died with grenades in their hands. One of our boys continued to fire a .50 caliber machine gun until one Japanese was killed right beside him and another fell over the gun. It makes my task just that much more easy. The funny part of it is that the enemy attacked over the ground I covered the other day, from the direction of our lines rather than from his. The area from which the attacks were made was one in which we have been mopping up for several days. They have come out of caves.

I take my hat off to our boys for their bravery.

Later we went back and watched a couple of tanks trying to clear some Japanese out of a cave. The little Japs were holding out all right until they put in five hundred pounds of TNT and that ended that particular fight....

On my return tonight I found a telegram from Walter stating that he is anxious to reconstitute the Corps at Hollandia as soon as I feel the situation is sufficiently clarified here to turn over to Jens Doe. I hope this means I can get away in about two weeks.

I suppose Walter will tell me he has heard of some soldier who did not have a shirt on. At any rate, I don't have to listen to his stories of the Louisiana maneuvers.

Tonight I have gotten word that the sump where I watched them fighting this morning is entirely taken. It is a series of depressions with interlocking caves. I have a feeling that the Japanese soldiers who made that brave attack at daybreak this morning were part of the garrison of the sump.... I feel personally that we have come a long way in the week I have been here and if I must pat myself on the back I feel the way we had been fighting the Japanese would have ended in a victory for them or the fight would not have been over until next Christmas. They [the Americans] were using little nibbling attacks that would not have gotten any place.

We feel OK tonight, but I do think that the boys needed a kick in the pants and I had to give it to them.

June 23, 1944

This afternoon I went up to the front again and watched a lot of mortar firing at a bunch of Japanese in a cave, got thoroughly rained on a couple of times and then got out to look at the three caves which constituted the so-called "sump." These are depressions about seventy-five feet deep with interlocking caves. The Japanese were hard to lick in there. There must have been 200 dead Japs in a small area, and what a sight and what a smell. There are some Japanese around in the hills yet and we are still mopping them up, but I think our victory is about official.

We have a bunch of Japanese located in a deep cave in the cliffs that overlook our line of communication, and some bombers are going to drop thousand-pound bombs on them tomorrow. They invited me to look at it from a Piper cub but I do not believe I will do that. We had a red alert this afternoon but the planes went by about thirty miles away.... Our pursuit planes are looking for them. We have real air protection here now so I do not look for any trouble in the daytime ... or at night either, for we have a lot of anti-aircraft. By the time I get back to Lake Sentani, air bombing there will be only a memory.

Clovis and all the officers think I have done well here. At least they can see no possible criticism. I think I have done fine, thanks to profanity, flattery, offers of rewards, threats, and Lady Luck.

June 24, 1944

At noon we went out on a 66-foot boat where we had lunch and watched some bombing by twelve of our planes, using thousand-pound bombs. They were trying to put one of these bombs down in a deep cave from which the Japanese had been shooting at us. I am not sure they succeeded but they came very near to it.

For a long time the Japanese have talked about the so-called "west caves" in their documents and, although we have not taken many prisoners, we finally got one who said he had lived in the west caves. Today we sent him out with a guard and he went to those in the sump. He said that six hundred men lived in them at one time. It is not a bad place at that, for they were entirely safe from aerial bombing. That is the place I have been describing and which I watched the tanks shooting into.

Personally, I shall be glad to get out of here. . . .

The news from Europe is at least not discouraging, and fine news comes in from the Central Pacific. The Jap fleet didn't get destroyed but apparently it was slapped around a bit.[13]

June 25, 1944

At the present time we have this war licked. There are still many Japanese scattered around in caves and they have the capability of sneaking through our lines and killing people. Up to date, however, none of our planes have been damaged and they are flying off our fields.

Today one of our cubs flew over the caves where we put thousand-pound bombs yesterday and the Japanese were shooting at the pilot.

This morning I sent a telegram to Walter saying I thought the situation was such that I could now return with my staff to Hollandia, turning over command to Jens.

Spencer Akin, who is signal officer at GHQ, arrived today. . . . Tonight at dinner Akin said that he knew I was going back to Hollandia, and when I asked him if he had ever seen my beautiful command post there he said, "How do you think it would do for an Army command post?" So I asked, "What's happened to the Army they were going to bring in here?" He told me the advance elements of the staff are about to live by the new Sixth Army Command Post in Hollandia. I then said, "Do you know who the Army commander is going to be?"

His answer to that was, "Don't you?"

I told him all I knew about it was what General MacArthur had told me on D-day at Hollandia and also various rumors thereafter. . . . He said there was no question in his mind but he did not want to be quoted.

The new army is to be the Eighth Army. Even with all this, I am not at all certain that I will get it. . . . I do not know what kind of an army this is to be but I doubt if General MacArthur would agree to giving me an army that was to be used in the rear areas, so if I am to get one I imagine it will be an active one. I understand that Walter does not like the idea of a new army.

It is my understanding that GHQ monitors all radiograms going to the Sixth Army so that General MacArthur has had the privilege of reading my breezy wires to Walter.[14]

June 26, 1944

Last night we were kept awake by red alerts and a tremendous amount of artillery firing from nearby. The Japanese got in on the airstrips three times ... twice with bombers and once by strafing. They caused no damage but wounded three men. We are six or eight miles from the airstrip so the chances of their coming down here is not very large.

This morning I started out in an L5, which is a sort of overgrown cub with a Stinson motor instead of the small Continental motor. I landed at the airstrip, where Clyde met me with the jeep. We then went forward to some of the caves in the sump, or what the Japanese called the west caves. I found they have regular native houses in there, with palm roofs to keep off the drippings from the interior of the caves. They also had dining room tables, kitchens, radios and weapons of all kinds. I imagine they used these caves as protection against bombing but lived outdoors normally.

We then went to the front where I inspected a six-inch naval gun which had been captured and five three-inch guns which were real beauties. These were dual purpose guns.

Except for isolated pockets, we have them driven out of this area now and in another week the mopping up will be completed. There are no indications of any counter-attacks in force. If you look at your map you will realize what a powerful weapon our Great Chief will have for use in wiping out the Japanese fields. The Jap is being hit at so many places that he will have to spread his sunshine very thinly.

It is interesting to me to go into the jungle and see how the soldiers live. Every company has an individual little perimeter in which they dig in each night. They clear a field of fire in the jungles and it reminds me of the stories I have read of the Indian days out West.

June 27, 1944

When the troops landed here they captured quite a stock of Japanese beer. A guard was put over it and today I have had it issued to the men, starting with the infantry. I understand there will be enough for every man to get at least one bottle....

The Japanese here were well disciplined, fine soldiers and they had many weapons, from 20 mm rapid-fire guns to three-inch, five-inch, and six-inch guns. Again, I think I have been very lucky.

June 28, 1944

This has been quite a day. Jimmy Frink[15] came in with a great bunch of people from GHQ and the city, in his Flying Fortress. . . . Then we went to the sump, which was a bloody sight, and continued from there to the regiment against which the Japanese made that suicidal attack several days ago. Just before we got there, a Japanese on the trail blew himself to pieces with a grenade, and that was a sight for the city boys. I am glad he did it to himself instead of throwing it at us. . . .

In coming back from Mokmer in a jeep Clovis and I noticed how many of the native families were coming in out of the bush. Children, old women, young men and old men were all there. That means to me that we have won the fight. In fact I think there will be nothing but little skirmishes from now on.

I really think I have done a good job. . . . I realize that nobody is getting much publicity but I am very pleased to have it that way. If I can get an army out of this mess I shall be very fortunate because it will mean a definite standing in our army, since I will have gained it in combat.

June 29, 1944

We were up at six this morning and . . . at ten we took off in a microscopic plane . . . to fly over three hundred miles of water with storms in every direction. We hit Tanahmerah Bay just in time to be entirely shut in and we went round and round looking for a place to get out. Finally we found a break through the mountains and came in. . . .

Walter evidently took a trip to Wakde today for he is arriving at the airfield at three-thirty and I shall meet him at Nefaar. . . . At the present time I have no command as Fred Irving has not yet been relieved of command of the task force.

I am very glad to be back here. The vile water up there was pretty hard to take . . . and I am afraid of an epidemic because there are so many latrines and dead Japanese around. The coral soil is very porous and . . . the water will soon be contaminated. They are moving all Biak natives to another island.

June 30, 1944

As I lie here on the bed, while Clyde uses the only chair in the room, I can see a big lizard playing around in the lemon tree. The only other activity I can see is Dombrowski trying to get a kerosene ice box started.

The boat with the rest of our staff is leaving [Biak] this morning and will be in here tomorrow. When it gets here we will have our staff together for the first time since April 17. The rear echelon stayed a long time at Goodenough and while en route to Biak they were stopped here.

When I talked to Walter yesterday, he was very agitated about Fuller.

He thinks Fuller quit because a task force commander was put over him, but that was not the reason. He really objected strenuously to the messages he was getting from Walter.

Here, perhaps Eichelberger's later reactions should be noted. In mid-July Colonel Bernard A. Tormey of the GHQ Staff told Eichelberger "that the Big Chief was stirring Walter up a bit about Horace's work, and that is why Horace was being hazed a bit. Tormey said that they were worried because advances that were scheduled did not take place despite the fact that losses were very small."[16] General Byers recalls that when he went ashore at Biak, Fuller met him with the comment that his thirty-fifth anniversary of his graduation from West Point was a terrible time to be relieved. Byers hastened to explain that this was not why they had been sent: the operation was being expanded into a Corps Operation and reinforcements from the Thirty-second Division were on the way. Fuller then declared that he had already asked to be relieved because he could not stand any more insulting letters and messages. Byers asked permission to wire General George Decker, Sixth Army Chief of Staff and an old personal friend, to return Fuller's letter of resignation unopened, but this Fuller would not agree to do.[17]

"General Fuller," Eichelberger wrote after the war, "was unfortunate in that he met a regular regiment of Japanese infantry and there he brought down upon his devoted head the censure of his army commander . . . far, far away in Finschhafen. Perhaps that army commander would have seen affairs differently if he had risked the long flight to Biak. Sometimes a commanding general far, far in the rear, who watches the numerous pins on a map, cannot get the feel of the battlefield and the problems of the commanders.

"General Fuller's great error was in throwing boat loads of artillery ammunition at areas that might or might not be occupied by Japanese. Noise would not frighten the Japanese, although it might canalize some of their movements.

"Incidentally, part of the slowness at Biak, in my opinion, was caused by the fact that General Fuller had not gone to the front, and General Doe, the Assistant Task Force Commander, although well forward, was living on the seashore and not keeping in direct touch by personal observation with the fighting only a mile away. . ."[18]

[June 30, 1944 (continued)]
Except for one visitor who stopped for two hours and another who went to Biak and stayed overnight, both of them before I got there, nobody from Walter's staff except Sam Sturgis came to visit me. Sturgis stayed several days and saw a lot.

I was away from here just two weeks to a day. In that time I was able to break up what might have become a stalemate. By throwing three battalions across the enemy's rear I broke their hearts. On June 21, they burned the regimental colors and launched a number of suicidal attacks on which they took tremendous losses.

We have been wondering a great deal about why your old friend [Krueger] did not mention the fact that he had heard I am to get that army. I realize Walter has a lot on his mind right now and maybe after things clear a bit he will be a little more courteous.[19]

The impression I get is that the Sixth Army staff take a very poor view of General MacArthur's desire to have an Eighth Army. Walter acts as though he had been spanked. Yesterday...he got on the boat and never spoke a word after the original greeting until he reached here, about a forty-minute ride. Then, as we came ashore and Clovis went down to salute him, he said, "I congratulate you on the fine job you have done." Then as he got in the jeep to leave, he again made the same statement....His chief of staff, George Decker, told Clovis this morning that they are all proud of the wonderful job we have done. George is a very nice chap. I feel that from the top down they are very jealous of this new army, but if there must be one they would have no objection to me getting it.... In the meantime, I must keep my sense of humor, which is not as easy as it sounds.

4:30 P.M.

I went down to thank a bunch of the air corps men who have supported us so well.... When we got back to the boat at Nefaar, I found Fred Irving with several officers of the Eighth Army staff.... The Chief of Staff, named Shoe [Brig. Gen. Robert O. Shoe],...said there are eighteen officers and eighteen enlisted men of the Eighth Army down there. The rest of them are to come by boat. I asked who was to command them and he said, "You are." When I asked him how he knew he said General MacArthur had told him.... Clovis seems a bit agitated that Walter had not mentioned it to me, but one must not expect too much of life.

July 1, 1944

Clovis got away this morning early for the city....[20] I hope he has a fine time at home because he has worked hard and deserves a vacation. ... It is going to be lonely without Clovis for he is one of the few to whom I am able to talk who can really analyze and size up things....

I can realize that neither Walter nor his staff want another army to be formed out here, but I do not feel that this is being done in any way as a favor to me but is because the Chief wants to command two armies instead of one. I realize I am going to have a hard time for the next couple of months until that staff gets out here and the decision is made.

Perhaps when I see the Big Chief he will iron it out.... In many ways I realize I may lose out by all this. For example, the advance to the north, when it comes, would probably have been given to me as a corps commander. I doubt if I get any further crumbs as a corps commander.

Don't think I am not cheerful, but I realize that insofar as this new army is concerned, I can expect no friendship and little courtesy until such time as the cleavage may be made.

July 3, 1944

This morning I went to church like a good little boy and now I am going to take my Sunday afternoon nap. In the meantime, I inspected all the camp, cussed everybody out and made a general nuisance of myself.

Eddie Grose wants to be transferred out of the Inspector General Department and I know he wants me to recommend him for command of an infantry regiment. This I cannot do, for while he has many fine qualities, he has a terrible time making up his mind.

July 4, 1944

The general attitude of Walter toward me seems to be worse than the mere fact that he heard I was to be given the Eighth Army would cause. It does not seem reasonable he would be so discourteous merely on that account because he knows that somebody is going to get it and therefore perhaps he would prefer to have me. If he had the impression however that the Big Chief might use me to steal a lot of his thunder, then he would feel a bit broken up.... I am just waiting to see what is going to happen. Certainly I do not intend to let anybody get my goat....

July 5, 1944

Thinking things over, I have a feeling that Walter knows more than one would suspect and that he may be worried about some possible leading part I may take in future operations. I think he stands very high with the Big Chief and I feel he has done very fine work. His disposition has grown more and more sour and his head is perhaps a bit larger. He may, like so many, become a walking bundle of pomposity.

As I have said before, however, there is something in this picture which has hurt Walter a lot or he would not have been so discourteous. I do not know what it is. He must have known something about this army coming here. I have heard nothing from him since that first day and although he gave me a grudging word of congratulations I did not think he acted very nicely.

July 6, 1944

Today I spent almost the entire day with Walter. I had not seen him for a week and received a call that he wanted to come by and talk to me. I went down to Pim to meet him and brought him up here.

Walter was just as nice as pie today. Butter wouldn't melt in his mouth. I think he was really a bit worried about Fuller. I told him General MacArthur had promised Fuller to make him a corps commander and that was one reason I felt very sorry about the whole thing. I also told him that certain messages Horace had received was one reason for his anger.

Walter did not mention anything about the Eighth Army, but several times he asked me what division commander I would select for a corps commander if I were doing it.

The sunset tonight was beautiful and I am only sorry that you could not share it. I have written Clovis once but I shall be writing him again in the very near future.... He will be intensely interested in all that is going on.

Notes

1. Eichelberger Dictations, 17 February 1956. Since Eichelberger here speaks from memory, it is only fair to see how the other principals recall the incident. Krueger apparently also opposed MacArthur's suggestion to attack Wakde immediately, although he is described by Admiral Barbey as being "noncommittal." "A date prior to 12 May would not do," Krueger wrote after the war, "for the success of the operations depended in part upon the major engineer and air force elements due to arrive at Hollandia on that same date...." Walter Krueger, *From Down Under to Nippon* (Washington, D.C., 1953), p. 18. Barbey later admitted: "I was all for it and told him [MacArthur] that our preliminary planning had already been done...but General Eichelberger was vehemently opposed to the idea. He pointed out that our initial success did not mean we would not run into heavy fighting later and that it would be dangerous to take on another operation before this one was further along. Eichelberger still had bloody memoirs of the Japanese combat capabilities in the Buna campaign.... As he was to learn later, however, their capabilities had greatly deteriorated since those hard-fought days." Daniel E. Barbey, *MacArthur's Amphibious Navy: Seventh Amphibious Force Operations, 1943-1945* (Annapolis, 1969), p. 173.

2. Robert Ross Smith, *The Approach to the Philippines* (Washington, 1953), pp. 210–211.

3. But see p. 143.

4. Eichelberger Dictations, 29 July 1957, 29 May 1961.

5. Krueger, *From Down Under to Nippon,* p. 101.

6. Col. Kenneth S. Sweany, chief of staff, Forty-first Division.

7. Owi Island, which lies off southeastern Biak, was seized on 2 June. Construction on the airstrip was commenced on 9 June. Smith, *Approach to the Philippines,* p. 341.

8. Brig. Gen. Leif Sverdrup, Airdrome Engineer from GHQ.

9. Col. William W. Jenna commanded the Thirty-fourth Infantry (Twenty-fourth Division), which was attached to the Forty-first Division on Biak.

10. Eichelberger to Miss Em, 3, 5 July 1944.

11. "Arriving back at Doe's Command Post I found that the 41st had not been doing much up the valley above Mokmer Drome. Only 2 batts of the 186th fighting there. Bawled everyone out there and hope for better luck tomorrow." Eichelberger Diary, 20 June 1944.

12. Col. Sam Sturgis, engineer officer of the Sixth Army; Col. James Collins, artillery officer of I Corps.

13. The reference is to the battle of the Philippine Sea, where carrier planes tangled with Japanese carrier planes over the Marianas on 19 June and destroyed over 400 enemy aircraft with but trifling losses. On 20 June, U.S. Navy planes attacked a strong Japanese naval force west of Saipan and sank two carriers and three other ships, severely damaging eleven others. "It was the last classic carrier battle to be fought and was a clear-cut, decisive victory for the Americans." Donald Macintyre, *The Battle for the Pacific* (New York, 1966), p. 180.

14. If true, then it is only fair to point out that certain of the staff of I Corps were playing the same game. When it became apparent to Eichelberger and Byers that the Forty-first Division was in trouble at Biak and that the signs all pointed to the inevitable intervention at the Corps level, they grew concerned that their summons would come — as it had at Buna — without any advance warning. Byers therefore ordered his signal officer to intercept the messages between GHQ and Sixth Army in order to win as much time as possible for making plans in the event they were sent to Biak. "We caught the dickens from Spencer Akin, GHQ Chief Signal Officer, for intercepting messages . . . but I refused to stop because this was the only way we could keep aware of the trouble on Biak." Although Krueger and MacArthur had been considering the idea for several weeks, the first intimation that Eichelberger had directly from Krueger came at dinner on 14 June. Already, because of the intercepted messages, the staff of I Corps had begun to make the necessary plans, which in large measure explains how Eichelberger was able so quickly, as Akin remarked during his visit to Biak, to "go after the Japanese in your usual manner." Interview with Gen. Clovis E. Byers, 17 May 1965; Byers to the editor, 2 July 1968.

15. Maj. Gen. James L. Frink, Commanding General, United States Army Services of Supply.

16. Eichelberger to Miss Em, 17 July 1944.

17. Interview with Gen. Clovis Byers, 17 May 1965.

18. Eichelberger Dictations, 29 July 1957, 29 May 1961.

19. This passage comes from a second letter dated 30 June 1944, and is included here because of its contents.

20. Gen. Byers at this time took the leave he was granted prior to being sent to Biak.

CHAPTER EIGHT

A New Command

In one of his letters to Miss Em explaining what had happened on Biak, General Eichelberger compared the circumstances that threw him into the battle with those in December 1942: "Things were going badly," and "my call was a hurry-up one to go at once. On the other hand, my tools were far better this time."[1]

There was another significant difference. Whereas he had emerged from the jungle in Papua to find the Sixth Army inserted between his command and GHQ, he now found himself embarrassed by rumors that he was to command the newly activated Eighth Army. While the signs increasingly pointed to his elevation to this new command, the lack of any official notification prevented him from raising his hopes again, as he had the year previous; the uncertainty also contributed to his uneasy relations with General Krueger and made it awkward and sometimes difficult to prepare adequately for the arrival of the new staff.

Fortunately, as Eichelberger soon was to discover, the Eighth Army Headquarters consisted, "almost intact, of the experienced Second Army Staff built up by Lieutenant General Ben Lear and Lieutenant General Lloyd R. Fredendall during three years of training in the States."[2] All that remained was to pry General Byers and Colonel Bowen away from I Corps and the new staff was ready for its test. What role exactly the Eighth Army might play in the coming campaign for the Philippines, however, was something that at this point the Big Chief himself probably was not in a position to determine.

In contrast to the months after Buna, now there was activity with a purpose. There was a purpose, too, in Eichelberger's comment to

144

Miss Em: "Sorry to learn that our dignified Mr. Chips has had his fleas removed. Now he will have time to brood over being a dog. Nothing better to keep his mind occupied than fleas. "[3]

July 11, 1944

Dearest Miss Em,
Sunday morning when I was out with Fred Irving going down the lake to inspect a company we began to laugh when we realized that my chief worries now are whether I will get an army to command or whether it would be better for me to retain command of my corps. A few years ago I did not believe I would ever be in a position to expect such things.... My principal desire is to keep my sense of humor and my ideas of the relative importance of things. I do not expect much thanks and will probably get very little, but I have had the friendship of many officers and men which I value. Above all, though, I want you to be cheerful....

July 16, 1944

I am just looking across the lake, as I dictate, at a great big Jap barge which was rehabilitated and which brings the natives down to work. I don't imagine the Japs ever thought our soldiers could fix that barge or they would have burned it.

I understand when the Japanese left our house the day we landed they went down the lake in native canoes and landed on the south shore from which point they could walk. Those are the type that got away. Our record here now is approximately 4300 killed or captured. There were of course thousands more who died along the trails and that is still going on. Personally I do not anticipate any serious troubles from Japanese attacks by that group that has been bypassed. You have read ...about fighting at such places as Aitape, but when you think about the trouble they would have in trying to drag a field piece along a jungle trail, or ammunition or food or the thousand and one things which make up an army, you will imagine how poorly equipped they would be.

While our Chief may have some faults he is really quite a person, a great strategist....[4]

July 19, 1944

This morning I talked with Decker, who is chief of staff to Walter. He says that Walter has missed me and he asked me to go down to see him. I told him that when I got back from the last operation Walter, in response to my inquiry, intimated he would be too busy to see me. At any rate, I shall go down to see him tomorrow.

July 20, 1944

This morning I went down to see Walter.... I brought Shoe, who is Chief of Staff of the Eighth, back here with me to spend the night. I asked Walter about the Eighth Army and first he said he couldn't discuss it but later went on and discussed it in great detail. He was in a fine humor.

I don't propose to make myself unhappy over conditions around here. The thing I like best has been the active service against the Japanese but even though I have enjoyed it, I realize it is dangerous physically and risky on the reputation. It is only necessary to fail once in that game and after that you will be the only one that will think I'm a great soldier.

Let me know what the people back home think about the second front.

July 21, 1944

Shoe was here . . . and I find him a very attractive person and doubtless an efficient one.... I told him that if I were able to put it over, that I would try to get Clovis in his place if I get that command; that this action was not taken because of him but because I felt that I owed that to Clovis because of his long and faithful and devoted service to me. I also warned him that if I did not put this over right away, I would continue to try to do so in the future, but that barring that, I would enjoy serving with him. Furthermore, I told him that if he were relieved on account of Clovis, I would try to get command duty for him, which is really what he would like to have.

I never get over being homesick for my Doll — sometimes it hurts. Maybe right now it is made worse by the fact that I would like so much to talk with you and cannot do it. . . . Your old friend's [Krueger's] pattern is well defined — he always wanted to keep everything in his own hands, especially with reference to me, and has succeeded fairly well. When we have been permitted to do a job though we have done a good one *and everyone realizes it.* Naturally he is not enthusiastic over a new unit of the same kind as his own, and that is understandable. He realizes now that I will not go around him anymore if he is not courteous and I think he will try to be friendly. Calls me "Bob," etc. However, when I see him in the Army and Navy Club in future years I shall not use him as a pet.

He hinted in his *roundabout* way that he either had or would recommend me for an award. I cannot always tell what he is talking about, but after I get away and think it over in the light of past actions I can figure him out fairly well.

July 22, 1944

I was interested in your remark about most officers not wanting to come out here. The officers who were here today[5] say all the officers at home want to go to other theaters because there is more publicity there. I have gotten beyond any thought of that.... If I can get an army and do well with it ... I will have no complaint about my part in the war. I only trust I can do whatever is given to me in a way that will be helpful to Uncle Sam. I sometimes think that the latter gentleman is not considered as often as he might be.

July 23, 1944

The radio news about the landings in Guam must have interested you. Hope they do not get the losses we did at Saipan because ... they were about as heavy as in the first few weeks of the Channel crossing in Normandy. Losses mostly come in the small units that are doing the fighting, and that hurts.[6]

July 24, 1944

The latest information, although not yet written as an order, is that the new staff will be established here on its arrival. That means a lot of construction even though temporary, and I would like to have something in writing that would permit us to get busy. Apparently the GHQ staff has been informed that I am to get that new outfit....

No job is an unmixed blessing; they all have their drawbacks. When the time actually comes, I shall hate to leave the Corps and I shall be sorry to have it get into any kind of action without me. My ways may be peculiar but I do get along with those lads, particularly when we are in an active operation.

I do not propose to worry about the details ... until I have something definite. The Chief of Staff of the new unit ... tells me that it is a good staff.

I am not going to be vitally concerned about who is going to run this Army after this war is over. Most of the people with whom I serve out here will be on the retired list and probably will be writing books. Maybe I will write one myself. I threatened to do that after the last war and I am sorry I did not do so when I consider what poor ones came out of that Russian venture....

As I look back over a long life, I realize how lucky I have been in certain periods of my service. In recent years, however, I have run more into the clash of personalities such as I found when I was secretary of the General Staff. That perhaps is unavoidable. I have found so often that the men with whom I have associated have been far more personally ambitious than I have been. As you know, I have never wanted to play all the instruments in the band.... I have never gained more than a moderate pleasure out of those things which might pass for success.

July 25, 1944

When you read of things happening, don't worry about me being in them because you are bright enough to know that when I get a new army staff that has never been in the tropics, I am going to have to get it settled for quite a long time before they are able to function in combat. They can get plenty of practice by handling such places as this, Wakde, Biak and other places forward where the fighting has been stabilized. ... They are not giving out the designation of units any more or the names of the commanders. That is a perfectly reasonable military precaution.

July 26, 1944

No orders have arrived about the Eighth Army and Walter says he has received no official news.... Under these circumstances there is nothing I can do to get ready for them and yet Walter's Command Post is not yet complete after two months of work. It takes time to prepare for such a large staff as that for it includes 218 officers and seven hundred men. That does not include such units as signal battalions and other attachments....

I have been tremendously interested in the revolt and purge in the German army. I am sorry it did not succeed, because it would have meant peace over there in a very short time. Certainly the morale of the German army must be getting much lower due to the fact that defeat stares them in the face.[7]

The situation out here is favorable, as you can see by the press reports.... Certain losses that have been announced ... occur principally in the fighting platoons of whatever branch may be doing the fighting. Therefore, heavy losses have a tendency to slow one up while there is no reorganization and rehabilitation. This happened ... after Buna but in that particular case we were slowed up by malaria more than by battle losses. Malaria is no longer considered a hazard if the soldiers have good atabrine discipline....

Off in the distance I can hear Radio Tokyo broadcasting. Nobody ever pays any attention to anything except the music part of it.

July 29, 1944

By this time you know all about the fighting at Biak. I was just as glad that my name was left out of that operation because I can assure you that I am not seeking any publicity just at this time. The impressions I get now are that Walter was being needled himself and he was laying it on Horace partly for that reason. The job wasn't being very well handled and the situation was very confused when I got there. (Horace and his G-3 had never been to the front.) As soon as I could find out by personal observation what was going on, I made a decision that resulted in the defeat of the Japanese, and that was to put three battalions across their rear.

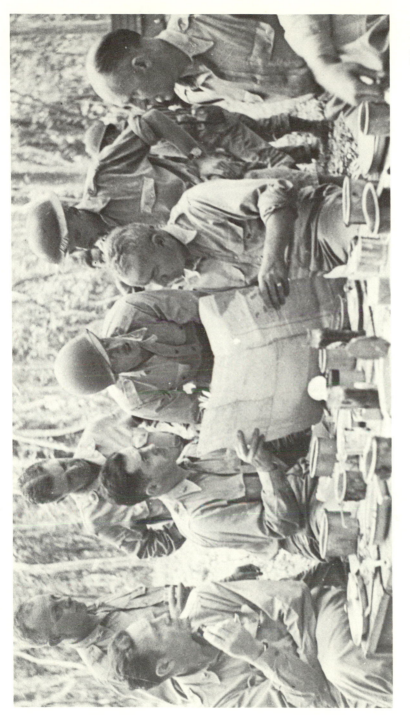

U.S. Army

General Eichelberger and staff on a rubber plantation about a hundred miles from Port Moresby at the start of the march over the Kapa Kapa trail by the 126th Infantry (p. 26).

Thurs 3 Dec ~~Hutsroby~~

Dearest Miss Em –

You would have been proud of me yesterday because I made at least 10 miles on foot through a steaming jungle and got bad in condition to do my work.

The noises didn't bother me nor the smells.

Whatever I could say I must save for later but this is just a message of my love to you and my hopes that you will keep cool.

Am going to save a souvenir or two for you.

Eddie Edwards makes a fine jeep driver and as a native gun bearer and watch dog he is OK.

My love to everyone & best wishes to all for Christmas

As for you Darling – Words just fail me

I love you
Bob

Egebuy you me a grand hunting knife yesterday

Reproduction of a letter to Miss Em written during a battle.
Date: 3 December 1942.

Buna: The approach.
George Strock-LIFE Magazine
©Time Inc.

George Strock-LIFE Magazine ©Time Inc.
General Eichelberger scanning the Buna mission
during the fighting about 27 December 1942 (p. 49).

Buna. "At last, victory."
George Strock-LIFE Magazin
©*Time Inc.*

George Strock-LIFE Magazine ©*Time Inc.*
Buna: "the American cemetery which my orders of necessity
have filled from nothing. . . ."

U.S. Army Signal Corps

A soldier's reward. Lt. Gen. Walter Krueger presents Eichelberger with
the Legion of Merit for outstanding work in organizing the
Seventy-seventh Division in the United States.

Associated Press, World Wide Photo

A fighting general celebrates birthday at the front (p. 90).

U.S. Army

Eichelberger and native:
"I was ready to run if he
showed that hungry look."

U.S. Signal Corps

En route to the far shore. Deck cargo and troops of the Forty-first
Division on LST prior to embarkation near Finschhafen, New Guinea.

U.S. Signal Corps

Beach landing. Forty-first Division, near Aitape, New Guinea. The steady stream of men and supplies poured onto the beachhead in every landing.

U.S. Signal Corps

Pushing inland. Infantry of the Forty-first Division penetrating the
jungle at the edge of White Beach, Hollandia.

U.S. Army

Biak. Eichelberger chats with the men of the 186th Infantry
after the Japanese attack on 22 June (p. 134).

U.S. Army

"I have been thinking how faulty the guerrilla reports were." A skeptical
Eichelberger views map with Filipino guerrillas about eighteen miles
south of Manila, 4 February 1945 (p. 209).

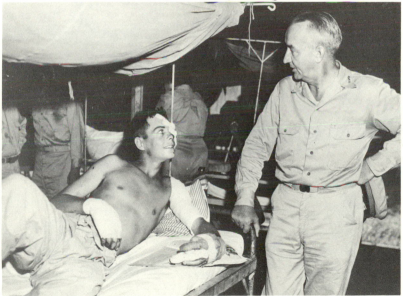

U.S. Signal Corps

Eichelberger visits the wounded of the Seventy-seventh Division (p. 189).

U.S. Signal Corps

"The Amphibious Eighth." Eichelberger goes ashore at Parang, Mindanao, 17 April 1945. With him are "Billy" Bowen, G-3; Clovis Byers, Chief of Staff; General Sibert, Commanding General, X Corps; Clyde Schuck, aide-de-camp; and Dick Bergholtz, a war correspondent.

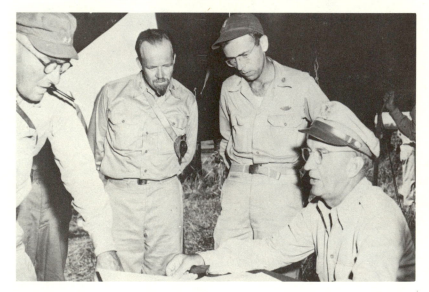

U.S. Signal Corps

Malabang airstrip, Mindanao, 26 April 1945. Left to right are General Sibert, Colonel Fertig, Dick Bergholtz, and Eichelberger. A message has just arrived from General Woodruff that he was about to occupy Digos and would move at once on Davao City (p. 259).

International News

The end of the road. Eichelberger and MacArthur shortly after "Sarah"
landed at Atsugi airfield, Japan, 30 August 1945 (p. 307).

Yesterday I had luncheon with your old friend [Krueger] and he was good as pie. He intimated that he had recommended me for the command of this new unit and dropped the pretense that the whole matter was just a rumor. He authorized me to go ahead and find a place for the corps to go so that the new unit can go in this location. It will be impossible to get things ready properly. If materials were at hand and we had every priority we would still have a hard job. . . . The new command will cover a tremendous territory in some of which fighting, although possibly of a minor nature, will be going on.

July 30, 1944

Today . . . I have had a number of conferences in an endeavor to hurry up the fixing up of camp. A report received this morning indicated that the staff will arrive ten days sooner than had been originally scheduled. In the meantime, there is nobody except Shoe who is officially responsible and he is serving under Walter. Walter acts as though he considers it more or less as an illegitimate child and as though he would like to strangle it or put it in a sack. It is really a big organization. I understand in the immediate staff there are about 250 officers and 700 men.

These are going to be unusual days ahead because I expect to leave the corps for which I have a deep affection and also because I doubt if anybody is going to rally behind this new crowd of mine. They are, however, a very experienced staff and I will . . . put them up against anything that the Big Chief wants.

In many ways I have felt that our staff here has been the best staff in these parts. It has certainly been the happiest staff. Of course, we have lost a good many key men in the last two years.

I didn't tell you the other day I had a joke with Walter about how the war in Germany would soon be over so that Georgie Patton with his two pearl-handled pistols could come over here and show Walter how to liquidate the Japanese.

August 2, 1944

Walter went through here this morning. . . . Every time Walter comes . . . we pass the word down for the boys to put on their shirts. We also call off the handball games and all other forms of sport.

Nothing more has been heard about when the Eighth Army will be formed. . . . I don't believe that Sarah has ever considered anything but giving me the army. A lot of my own staff have thought I would be allowed to keep the corps until after the next fight, but that of course has been wishful thinking.

August 3, 1944

Last night I heard a radio report had announced that Walter will get a very high Dutch decoration for being the conqueror of Hollandia.

Of course there are many people in the chain of command who deserve credit and particularly our Big Chief, who took the responsibility for coming so far. The one who commands a landing has his chin stuck way out and it is only necessary to fall once to fall by the wayside.

I wrote to Horace [Fuller] last night as I feel very sorry for him. He had never had any trouble and, as a matter of fact, he was what you would call "a fair-haired boy" with Walter and the Big Chief. I know General MacArthur was sincere when he told him he was going to give him a corps and, as a matter of fact, he would have gotten this one.

Walter yesterday ... was very pleasant. I rather imagine he will be from now on. I think he probably had a great deal pressing him before I went up there and finally gave in to the recommendation of his staff that I be sent. . . . I got darned little thanks for it and no mention was made of my presence. . . .

I have not lost my feeling that Uncle Sam should be the one big figure in the picture. For many years I have been a student of my fellow man and as I get older I realize how ruthless some people get in their later lives in quests for glory, high command, publicity, etc. The Shadow of Uncle Sam often seems very dim. . . . Now my feeling is that I would like to fight the Japanese as often as possible, but I realize, too, that in most operations one must be more afraid of the man behind than the enemy in front. I believe our Big Chief has a keen appreciation of individuals. I think he likes me and I think in many ways he admires me. Except that he will never depart from his chosen pattern, I feel that he wishes me well in all things. I wish I were as sure of your old friend [Krueger].

August 11, 1944

The news from Europe is most gratifying. For a while it looked as though that movement might bog down, but the Americans have certainly made fast time in the last two weeks. . . . You must remember that even the Russian Army must move in spurts. Advances are made, then consolidated, supplies are brought up, troops prepared and then a new drive starts. Railroads must be repaired because the old statement that an army moves on its belly is certainly true. Certainly the Brittany drive has been brillant even though there has been little apparent opposition. To have three ports — St. Nazaire, Brest, and Cherbourg — will be a wonderful thing and certainly will discourage our enemies.[8]

Bradley will be a big figure in our military history, and I know he deserves to be. He is a grand soldier.

August 16, 1944

For the last hour and a half I have been wandering through this camp looking at the new buildings. If we can only hold our engineers for a little while we shall have a lot. I think that ten office buildings are already up.

Dick [Sutherland]... said that Walter had promised that he would do everything to help us. We were glad to hear this because the help up to date has not been particularly noticeable.... Of course I realize that one must get out and forage, and it looks to me as though the new unit has officers that will be plenty tough.

I will admit that your old friend didn't do himself exactly proud in his attitude towards me. Sometime I imagine he will regret it a bit. I was particularly impressed with his attitude when I came back from that last operation. Even if one admits the Big Chief's simile that "a thoroughbred race horse must be willing to have a bit and spur used in coming down the home stretch," I still remember that after victory they usually put a horseshoe of flowers around his neck and give him an extra feed of oats.

I had to laugh today when I read another letter from Freddie Barrows[9] out at Leavenworth. He is always trying to get me to write an article for his *Military Review* on jungle fighting or some kindred subject and I cannot explain to him why I want to be a shrinking violet without saying too much.

We were delighted to hear about the landing in Southern France[10] and I hope the German resistance there will be quite weak. I had rather expected it. There are few good German troops down there.... Without knowing, I would say that there must be a great call for Germans in East Prussia for the defense of the homeland rather than the defense of France. People, after all, are only human.

August 21, 1944

Orders came through yesterday relieving me from command of the First Corps and assigning me to USAFFE Miscellaneous Group. I was directed, however, to remain on my present station, and the 18 officers and 18 men of the Eighth Army were directed to report to me for duty. ... Bill Bowen was also directed to report to me and I know that is to fill the one weak spot in the Eighth Army staff. Nothing was said about Clovis and there is nothing I can do about it for the moment, except that I now intend to write to General MacArthur and thank him and in that mention how glad I was to hear from Clovis that he (General MacArthur) had spoken to Clovis about his accompanying me in my new command.

I am going down this morning to pay my respects to General Krueger. Since yesterday, I have not been under his command. Palmer[11] gets the First Corps and I am going to make a farewell talk to them later on in the morning.... We all think that Palmer will be a good selection for the Corps. After all, he is a good soldier.

Bob Hope, Jerry Colonna, Frances Langford[12] and quite a few others arrive here today and young Graham invited me to stay at the Big House with him, Hope and Colonna while the others are to be distributed around the hilltop. Last night it sounded good, but this afternoon I am going to back out because I want to get things ready for Palmer and push the construction here. In other words, I do not want my first two or three days with the Eighth Army to be taken up with laughing at Bob Hope, even though it would be a lot of fun. Then, too, I know those people start their parties after they have given the shows for the enlisted men, and judging from the ones we had for Gary Cooper they will last till . . . 3:00 o'clock in the morning.

August 22, 1944

It was very hard for me to make my farewell talk to the Corps yesterday. Most of them have been very fine. In many cases I have been able to get them steady promotion and in some cases awards and decorations. The reputation of the Corps has always been very high and I think they were sorry to see me sign off.

HEADQUARTERS EIGHTH ARMY
UNITED STATES ARMY
Office of the Commanding General

August 24, 1944

Dearest Miss Em:

Last night I found that another one of those big headquarters is moving up and will be located on a beautiful ridge which I can see from my front veranda. This makes it unanimous that they are headed this way and I do not think there will be much left back in the city but a small rear echelon. It convinces me that victory is in sight and that the boys do not want to get caught down on the mainland. . . . The news from France is wonderful today and I am beginning to think that it will not be so long until I see you.

I do not know what the other headquarters are going to be able to get but I am convinced that this crowd of key men from the Eighth Army can hold their own against any crowd. Buildings have gone up like mushrooms.

August 27, 1944

Last night I heard by chance that Judith Anderson, the great actress, and a troupe would give a performance in a nearby camp. We went over . . . and it turned out to be by far the best thing that has been given. In fact, there has been nothing that would even run second to it. The male pianist played everything from Tschaikowski to swing; a girl violinist was pretty and very accomplished; a singer who sang; and an Italian girl who was also easy to look at furnished the naughty songs. Judith Anderson herself and a Naval officer who formerly worked with her on Broadway gave parts of *Macbeth* and she also gave some other recitations. The soldiers reacted ten times better than they did to the Bob Hope show.

I am still waiting to hear from the Big Chief about Clovis.

Eichelberger was waiting to hear from the Big Chief about other matters as well. Rumors of the top-level conference that had been held at Pearl Harbor the last week in July were now circulating at Hollandia, and, as commander-designate of the Eighth Army, Eichelberger was most anxious to discover to what extent the strategic plan for the Southwest Pacific would be altered as a result. In June the Joint Chiefs of Staff had raised the question of accelerating the tempo of the Pacific campaign and perhaps even bypassing the Philippines. MacArthur and Admiral Chester W. Nimitz, Commander in Chief of the Pacific Ocean area, both contended that their logistic resources were already strained to the limit and would therefore not permit any advance of target dates for scheduled operations. MacArthur especially was adamant that the Philippines be liberated for political as well as "purely military considerations." President Franklin D. Roosevelt made a surprise visit to Hawaii to confer with MacArthur, Minitz, and other top commanders. "During August the Army and the Navy planners sought to marshal their forces — the former in behalf of the Philippines and the latter for Formosa."[13]

August 29, 1944

Dearest Miss Em,

Bill Gruber[14] has a lot to tell me about that conference.... He said that Nellie[15] told him that he is very unhappy. It is evident that he is getting pushed around by experts and that is, of course, what would have happened to us had they been able to eliminate our Chief. Apropos of that, Clovis said that when he went through Tarawa on the way that there were great Navy signs describing what each boat did. A Marine officer complained bitterly... "Our Marines up in the cemetery must have committed suicide." I have heard a story that Howling Mad Smith the Marine[16] tried to keep Nellie from inspecting some of his troops on a certain island. These troops had fought under the operational control of Smith but Nellie has certain responsibilities such as administration and training. Bill said that Nellie was not in on those conferences at all.

I see that references have been made in various releases since that conference that my Chief is to go to the Philippines. He won out again because I understand that one of the results was to be a directive to him that the Philippines would be bypassed. I am anxious to talk to the Chief when he comes up here.

September 6, 1944

From what I get from many sources, I believe that the intention had been to drop Sarah from any further consideration. Before she returned home, however, she had won out and that is one reason why this outfit [Eighth Army] can still be organized.

September 8, 1944

Clovis has received an order to be Chief of Staff of the unit. Bill Bowen is still on the same status as I am in that he belongs to the USAFFE Miscellaneous Group with orders to report to me for duty. Bill has made a grand reputation for himself as a planner and presentation man.

When Walter comes through here to take one of my boats he is always moving fast and hasn't a minute to stop. He reminds me of Nellie Richardson, who would spend ten minutes getting to my office, using a very slow step, and then at the door almost break into a run to impress me with his dash and force.

September 9, 1944

The meetings at Nellie's place (Nellie was not invited) . . . could not be described perhaps as being as friendly as a bunch of bugs in a rug. It was a last attempt to stop Sarah's career in place and if Sarah had not won out it would have been unpleasant for me. When I see Sarah I shall probably get the whole story.

September 10, 1944

Clovis and I arrived at the airfield about an hour before the Big Chief's plane came in. He was very cordial and said he would be down to see me. . . . Big Chief looked fine this morning and I shall drop Jean [Mrs. MacArthur] a note to tell her about it. I hope he likes his new home.

My orders to command 8th Army were issued on the 7th of September and reached me yesterday.

September 12, 1944

Yesterday afternoon I came back with the whole story right out of the horse's mouth. I know now all about Cousin Frank [FDR], Horace [Harding], Nellie and Pa.[17] The humorous side and the serious, no one else could have done so well in view of the galaxy of stars in the picture. It was one of the most interesting talks I have yet had and I have dictated it in substance as a matter of interest both to you and to me.

Memorandum of Interview with General MacArthur

I opened the conversation by saying, "General, since I last saw you you have had a visit with your cousin Frank." He said, "Yes, the _____." He said, "The meeting was purely political[18] but he followed the protocol very carefully by always keeping me on his right. One of the results of the meeting was to be the information given to me that the Philippines were to be bypassed.[19] I told him that the history of the war might justify the abandonment of the Philippines to the Japanese at the beginning of the war but neither history nor present public opinion would justify the abandonment of the Philippines at this time. I talked to him for six hours and the Navy remained mute. Pa Watson said he had never seen the President so affected. The next day when the Navy came, however, they had been able to communicate with Washington and were prepared to argue. I told the President he could never justify releasing a bunch of Chinese in Formosa and abandoning a lot of Filipinos in Luzon. We had been thrown out of Luzon at the point of a bayonet and we should regain our prestige by throwing the Japanese out at the point of a bayonet. At the present time, however, all I have won out on is the agreement that we will go up to and including Leyte. The question of whether or not the route will be by Luzon or Formosa has not yet been settled in Washington.[20] I have sent Marshall[21] to present my case there. From the Philippines we can cut the Japanese lines to the Dutch Indies just as well as we can do it from Formosa."

British Attitude

He said, "Recently I have received a wire from Mr. Churchill backing up my attitude almost 100% in refusing to let the British occupy Dutch islands."[22] I said that I did not believe the American public would countenance the British taking over any of the Dutch islands any more than they were willing after the last war to countenance the taking of Shantung by the Japanese. General MacArthur agreed with this.

President Roosevelt

He said he was amazed at the poor physical condition of the President. "When he was animated he looked familiar, but otherwise his jaw sagged down and he looked to be in very poor physical condition. At no time did he stand up as he used to do with the use of leg braces. He was carried every place he went. He will not live through another term if he is reelected." General MacArthur said he had asked the President, while driving to Schofield Barracks, what chances he thought Dewey had. "I felt I could do this as I knew him very well in the past." He answered that he had not had time to think of politics. "I threw back my head and laughed. He looked at me and then broke into a laugh himself and said, 'If the war in Germany ends before election, I will not be reelected.'"

Pa Watson

General MacArthur told me Pa Watson had come to him and said, "Are you for us or against us?" and "I answered, Pa, I always try to do the right thing," and Pa said, "I knew you were for us." Pa then said, "What do you want after the war, to be Governor General of the Philippines?" "I said, Pa, that job was cut out ten years ago." He then said, "How about Secretary of War?" "I said, Pa, why not drop that until after the war is over, and he said, 'That is right. That's what we will do.'"

General Fuller

"General Harding, when he came back, struck out at everybody connected with his downfall. But in the case of Fuller there was nothing I have seen so fine as the manner of his passing. He had good things to say about you [Eichelberger] and Doe and had no complaints except to say he could not see eye to eye with General Krueger.... He may have had a trembling jaw, but he stood straight like a soldier and walked out of the room. It was not until I told him I had given him the DSM that he broke down. I have put him at the head of the Pacific Strategy Board, which will be a good thing for him. He is a grand soldier."

When I said that if General MacArthur ever wanted to give Fuller command duty again I would be glad to have him he said "If he receives anything it will have to be a Corps and that would be a special case that would have to be settled in the future. It would not be probable."

Central Pacific

"The Central Pacific authorities asked that they be given 200,000 of my troops, and that is a sign of weakness. It is the first that I knew they did not consider they had enough troops."

He said, "Richardson is an unhappy man. He lives like a prince with fine cars and a fine home, but he has no authority. He is a fine, courteous gentleman, so the Navy have him licked. They have beaten him so many times there is nothing more he can do. He has a very small place in the picture."

He said that the Filipinos in Honolulu "... gave him a much finer reception than they did the President and that FDR did not like that."

September 13, 1944

Dearest Emmalina:

Everybody over here thinks the war will wind up before too long, and then they wander further on in their thoughts and try to visualize what will happen over here. Many of the heroes of France, some equipped with pearl-handled pistols, will probably want to come and join us. On the other hand, there may be a lot of men who had been here a long time who will want to go home, too. This will be particularly true since many have served out here for a long time. Even the heroes of Brisbane and Sydney will feel themselves particularly deserving. The Big Chief... said that the question of morale would be one of my most difficult problems after the fall of Germany.... I believe that the divisions that have just come over will be more cheerful than those which have been here a long time.

In our talks, we are orienting the staff in things that have gone on in the past so that they will have a clear understanding of the conditions which we have met. Sometimes I think that combat has been my easiest problem.

September 24, 1944

We are beginning to get down to work now and I think the officers will be glad to be busy.

Notes

1. Eichelberger to Miss Em, 29 July 1944.
2. Eighth Army Historical Section, *The Amphibious Eighth* (N.p., n.d.), p. 20.
3. Eichelberger to Miss Em, 27 September 1944.
4. This last statement is taken from Eichelberger's letter to Miss Em dated 13 July 1944.
5. Eichelberger's Diary mentions the visit of two engineer officers from the Eighth Army Staff, Gen. Irving and one of his battalion commanders.
6. At Saipan (15 June–9 July 1944) the American forces lost 14,111 killed and wounded, or about 20 percent of the total strength engaged.
7. On 20 July 1944, a group of army officers including a former chief of the German General Staff, Colonel General Ludwig Beck, and a grandnephew of Helmuth von Moltke, the architect of the victories over Austria and France in 1870, attempted unsuccessfully to kill Hitler.
8. A portion of this passage comes from a letter dated 9 June and is inserted here because of its contents.
9. Colonel Frederick M. Barrows, Editor, *Military Review*.
10. On 15 August, after two weeks of air and naval bombardment, the U.S. Seventh Army, accompanied by units from the French First Army and U.S. Paratroopers, landed on the French Mediterranean coast. Operation DRAGOON succeeded with slight casualties.
11. Maj. Gen. Innis Palmer Swift, who had commanded the First Cavalry Division, was named by Krueger to command I Corps.
12. To those of the present generation these popular entertainers need no introduction, but those who may read these letters in the future may not be aware of the fact that Hope and his popular colleagues devoted many weeks each year to entertaining American troops and servicemen in remote corners of the world during World War II, the Korean War, and the struggle in Vietnam.
13. Maurice Matloff, *Strategic Planning for Coalition Warfare 1943–1944* (Washington, 1959), p. 485.
14. Brig. Gen. William R. Gruber was the new Twenty-fourth Division Artillery officer.
15. Lt. Gen. Robert C. Richardson, Jr., Commander in Chief, Pacific Ocean Areas, who

since August 1943 had also been placed in charge of administration and training of ground and air forces in the Central Pacific.

16. Maj. Gen. Holland M. Smith commanded the Northern troops and Landing; Force at Saipan and in the Marianas. See p. 187.

17. Maj. Gen. Edwin M. Watson, Roosevelt's military aide.

18. This statement would seem to contradict Courtney Whitney, who asserted that he had "never heard MacArthur associate himself with the viewpoint that it was more political than strategical." Courtney Whitney, *MacArthur, His Rendezvous with History* (New York, 1956), p. 126.

19. This was MacArthur's interpretation. According to Professor Morison, the real reason for the trip was Roosevelt's desire to "exchange ideas with the senior Army and Navy commanders in the Pacific, and if possible to reach an agreement." MacArthur had previously asked permission to come to Washington to plead his case for reconquering the Philippines. Samuel Eliot Morison, *Leyte: June 1944-January 1945*, vol. 12, *History of United States Naval Operations in World War II* (Boston, 1958), p. 8.

20. The debate over Luzon and Formosa as the next step after the seizure of Leyte continued throughout September and finally resulted in a Joint Chiefs' directive, dated 3 October 1944, that Formosa would be bypassed in favor of Luzon. See Robert Ross Smith, *Triumph in the Philippines* (Washington, 1963,) pp. 3-17 passim.

21. Maj. Gen. Richard J. Marshall, MacArthur's deputy of chief of staff, was in Washington "on official business" at the time. Ibid., p. 15.

22. "He meant permanent occupancy." Eichelberger.

CHAPTER NINE

No Time to Brood

The next few weeks were dominated by conferences, speeches, and meetings with the commanders and staffs of the various units as they arrived and were absorbed into Eighth Army. There were also lengthy inspection tours of the new command, which at this time comprised some 200,000 troops scattered all the way from Australia to Morotai Island off the western tip of New Guinea — "at least the distance from New York to San Francisco."[1] This was possible because, to oversee his troops, Eichelberger was now the proud possessor of a B-17 Flying Fortress. A veteran of seventy-four missions, with eleven enemy aircraft and eight ships to her credit, the Miss Em had been remodeled to serve as a flying command post. With these new and wide-reaching duties Eichelberger obviously had accumulated enough "fleas" to keep his mind occupied.

There were, of course, many frustrations. "We are just in that stage where no one knows a great deal," he wrote several weeks after assuming command. "Everybody wants to do things but there are many intangibles. Sometimes it looks as though we might be here for a long time and then again it looks as though our time will be comparatively short. I haven't seen Sarah for a long time."[2]

Nor did he see much of Krueger, who "seemed to be taking the attitude of pulling the wings off a fly."[3] "I think he is so afraid that somebody might be strong enough to threaten his retirement that he is on the alert every minute," he explained to Miss Em. "His attitude towards me . . . is a strange mixture of vanity and defensive attitude. . . . I have not seen him for a long time and probably shall see him very seldom in the future. That would apply also if I should see him back home after the war. I don't believe I could see him because of the natural loss of eyesight which an old man like myself would have."[4]

Early in October the Joint Chiefs of Staff had finally directed MacArthur to follow up the seizure of Leyte, which was scheduled to begin on 20 October, with the occupation of Luzon. MacArthur had won out in his fight with the Navy, which encouraged Eichelberger to write: "Things are moving. While at times I feel that I am not going to take as prominent a part as I would like to, at other times I feel like I will get my tummy full before it is over." "The future opens up some interesting possibilities."[5]

If his own role in the campaigns that were still in the planning stage remained uncomfortably uncertain, the months immediately ahead did provide excellent schooling for his new staff. Until 15 November the task of Eighth Army was to consolidate, train, and inspect its new units as well as to supervise the organization, equipment, and training of those earmarked for the upcoming invasion of Leyte by Sixth Army. It was anticipated that by mid-November the Eighth Army would move up to Leyte and that by 15 December it would assume control of the Samar-Leyte-Mindoro area. Then, while engaged in mopping up and consolidating these areas, it would also assume responsibilities for staging, equipping, and training divisions destined for other future operations.[6]

The tempo of things had indeed "been moved up."

September 26, 1944

Dearest Emmalina,

About Thursday I am going to start out on my travels to see some of the new units which are just now coming under our command. Within the next few days I will have my old outfit under me.... It looks as though the place I live in will be way back in the rear before long but of course that won't prevent me from going forward a lot to inspect my units.

October 15, 1944

About next Tuesday I expect to go to the forward points where I have troops. This will include of course the last place which has been captured as well as all stations back to and including Biak.

As you can well imagine, Walter's group [Sixth Army staff] has had much more experience in planning pick and shovel work than my own. On the other hand, Clovis, Bill [Bowen] and I have had more experience in actual fighting than any of them, and my staff I believe is a better staff and certainly not so nervous. Having come freshly from home they are not haunted with the desire for rotation and other things which come up after officers have been out here 18 months. I shall be up close on Walter's heels always, but there will come a time when my mission will be entirely different from his and it is not beyond the bounds of possibility that I shall be included in the final show.

October 18, 1944

[Yesterday] I was rushed until bedtime and then just fell into bed. We had a grand ride ... and only took 2 hours and 10 minutes in spite of the fact that we flew over the scenes of our fun in June. ... Old scenes brought back memories of sounds and smells and excitement.

The waist guns are out, loaded, and the gunners are sitting on them. Not much chance of a Jap plane but always a slight chance of a snooper. ... There are a lot of P-38's hiding up in the clouds. There is no doubt about who has air superiority in this area.

October 19, 1944

We had a fine day at Morotai yesterday. ... We were due to leave there at 2:15 but didn't get away until after 3:00 because a stream of planes were returning from a mission. These places grow up like mushrooms and are a mass of planes. Then the war shifts to the north and like Hollandia the strips become deserted.

There are still Japs in Noemfoor and Morotai but they are sad looking and have little fight left in them. Mac[7] has a bunch of [Japanese] prisoners which he uses for labor. ... I walked many miles today and some through sand (Clovis estimates 9 or 10 miles). It always interests me to see how well a good outfit can fix itself up in a jungle so far from home. And then the white crosses of the cemetery with those lads in there who have reached the end of the road.

October 20, 1944

While returning [from Biak] we heard the broadcast of the landing at Leyte. Of course we had been waiting for this and I am glad everything went so well. Unless the plans change I shall be up there myself within a month and take over in the Visayas. What happens after that will be subject to change without notice.

October 21, 1944

You are right about the fighting still going on at Morotai. There are still Japs left at Aitape, Wakde, Sarmi, Biak, Noemfoor and Morotai. All these places are held by units under my command.

I was amazed in the changes since I left Biak ... the wide roads, docks, the condition of the airstrips and the large camps in the area which was still jungle and full of stray Japs when I left. Of course the coral lends itself to the construction of good roads. In a lot of that area all that was necessary was to bulldoze through the jungle and then scrape off a wide road with a high crown.... Those coral cliffs looked even worse than I had remembered them.

October 22, 1944

You have heard over the radio of course the announcement of the landing at Leyte and the size of the convoy.... The boys at GHQ complain that they are not getting any information in from Walter. I would like to send him a few telegrams.

We expect to begin the movement of the first elements of my staff before very long as I am to handle the cleaning up in the Visayas and possibly help Walter later on if he needs it.... I understand the actual date of my taking over will be about a month after the original landing.

October 25, 1944

Charlie has just been giving me the first reports of a great sea fight off Leyte.... Maybe the Japs believed their own reports that they had sunk 11 heavy carriers, etc. Hope we make good in that fight. It is a time for prayer.[8]

October 26, 1944

Naturally I am very interested and want to know what happened yesterday off Leyte. Apparently we had a victory and undoubtedly some Jap battle ships have been sunk. You are probably getting as much information as I am but of course a communique does not always tell the entire story.

October 27, 1944

Am very interested in the Leyte fleet action and wonder how this Jap fleet got down there undetected. At any rate we will get the details later and it was a victory.

October 28, 1944

Yesterday morning we had a grand trip on our plane. We were in the air at seven and in three hours we had reached our destination. I am always amazed at the amount of water and jungle one can pass over in that time. Among other places, I was intensely interested in seeing Hansa Bay, Madang and Saidor, particularly Hansa Bay. To look down on that little curve and realize that is where we were going to land, in face of fire from many directions, makes me more happy than ever that my Chief was courageous enough to jump all the way to my present home.

October 29, 1944

Your remarks about the history of this war interest me because there is an old saying that "history is just a misstatement of facts agreed upon."

October 31, 1944

There were a number of boys back from Leyte with whom I talked. . . . Things have gone well from a land standpoint and the Lord looked after us in that big fleet action. Apparently . . . Kincaid did a grand job in the Surigao Strait where the Jap fleet was badly defeated. Admiral Halsey was about to go to town on a big Jap fleet off northeastern Luzon when he got word that a big Jap fleet had come through the San Bernardino Strait without being detected and were off Leyte Gulf. There was nothing there but a few small carriers and several destroyers, but they went right into combat and bluffed the Japanese out of what might have been a great victory. I suppose long after we are gone they will still be squabbling over who was responsible for letting them come through the Straits undetected because that fleet had been observed for two days out in the Sibuyan Sea. However, all is well that turns out well. We did have a victory although I would have been happy to have it even more decisive.

November 4, 1944

I haven't been able to make up my mind whether one has the hardest time out here or in France. Certainly there are no chateaux in which to live here and my future homes for some time will be quite crude. I also imagine that I shall have some hard fighting ahead. I am not sure that the boys that fought over here are going to let the boys that fought in France outtalk them. It will probably be a standoff.

November 5, 1944

I see by the news radio that General MacArthur had a .50 caliber bullet strike a wall a foot from his head. We are all hoping that nothing happens to him because it would be a severe blow to the strategy of this area. I can imagine that it would be quite a fight among those who are willing to step into his shoes.

There are so many visiting feather merchants that I can hardly get to the table. . . . We have about the best food and most attractive camp so I can see why they should wish to remain here, but nevertheless I get tired of looking at them and like my own mess where I can cuss to my heart's content.

I notice over the radio today that some high ranking admiral in a press interview has sunk the Japanese Navy almost in its entirety. I wish they would cut out that super optimism and then some other admiral will not be surprised when some other Japanese fleet shows up later. The Japanese do the same thing. They brag of how they have sunk the American fleet and then some other admiral gets the hell knocked out of him.

November 7, 1944

Yesterday Admiral Wilkinson,[9] who has returned from the Leyte operation, came to lunch.... I take it the boys have been having a pretty hard time there. The reports indicate a succession of bombing raids at night.... The announcements from that particular place by... [MacArthur] have proved to be a bit dangerous. Knowing what boat he was on they were able to attack that type of boat and they did sink a sister ship, largely through a suicidal attack.[10] Later, when he was in a certain town and it was announced, they knew approximately what house he would be in. We are very anxious that nothing happen to him, as I do not want to serve under a sister service or under your old friend.

I was interested in the following quotation from a letter written by Chink Hall.[11] "I also wish to state that from a business standpoint I don't believe either I or any of my staff members have ever accomplished as much in such a little time. This of course was due to the co-operation of your staff officers and their willingness to say yes or no quickly." I think that under Clovis the staff is working very well and I have no doubt that we shall be successful when we get into combat.

November 10, 1044

Yesterday afternoon Clovis and I went up [to GHQ] to see Dick [Sutherland], who was making a quick trip to my future home.... I had expected to take command up there about a week from Sunday, but it may be put off for a few days as everything has been put back a wee bit. The Japs seem to be objecting to being shoved into the water.... However, they must be killed someplace along the line and it might as well be one place as another.

November 11, 1944

I am enclosing a clipping from a paper with a New York headline which ... was the first indication I had had that conditions [at Leyte] were so serious, although later I was forced to lose hours of sleep last night because of this question. If it were possible to send your friend Walter a typical telegram such as he was accustomed to send anybody so... unfortunate as to serve under him, the message would read... "I am very disappointed at your slow progress which threatens to delay future operations." I am sure that Bill Gill or Horace would gladly sign such a message.

November 12, 1944

Jack Turcott[12] has just left.... He told me many things about Leyte. ...He said he thought Walter was very unhappy because there were a lot of raids and things were not going too well. He said the last time he had seen Walter he saw him in a fox hole wearing a tin hat, with poncho and underwear....

Jack emphasized several times that the Big Chief sits around under bright electric lights during these many air raids in the biggest house in town, he having previously announced to the world the town in which he was living [Tacloban].¹³ Of course I think the broadcast was made under the assumption there would be little fighting. Usually there is very little firing while the big ships are just off shore waiting to pour in a hail of bullets. The firing breaks out later — the Japs . . . are throwing in a lot of reinforcements. The big fleet is up off Luzon and is not helping in the Visayas now except to try to knock out planes in Luzon which might fly to Leyte. . . .

The question of whether or not I shall leave here Thursday will depend on whether or not the time of my taking over command on the 20th has been put off. In view of the fact that the battle on Leyte has developed into a major operation I feel they will hesitate to relieve Walter on the 20th. However, I do feel that they will give a certain definite time which I rather think will be around December 1. I imagine all future operations will be set back a bit.

We do not minimize the hard work that lies ahead. Plans are being made which will take me a long distance, but of course these may be subject to change if the status of my Chief changes following the election. Insofar as I know, I stand in well with the Navy, however, and it may be possible they will continue to use me.

November 14, 1944

[Lt. Col. Lawrence Moore] Cosgrave, the Canadian Military Attache [to Australia], left this morning after what I know was a very interesting trip for him. Being around us he gets enough information to write up notes on jungle warfare which will keep him in good with his War Department. . . .

Yesterday morning Clovis and I went up to GHQ and had lunch with Dick, who is just back from Leyte. . . . As you have read in your papers the Japs have been able to rush in a great lot of reinforcements. Why this has been true after the many recent victories that have been announced in the air and on the water, I am unable to state. The fact remains that they have run in a number of convoys into a bay that is only about thirty miles from our Command Post and according to your radio news they now have about 45,000 troops. Nobody knows better than I do how hard it is to whip 45,000 Japs who are ready to die in place. I don't think for a minute that these Japs are fully equipped and I doubt the numbers a bit. But it is evident that they have enough there to give an awful fight.

November 15, 1944

I see in the morning radio news that the Japs are supposed to have five divisions on Leyte. I think the term "elements of" would be better. They are not miracle men and if they run things in the middle of the night it doesn't mean they can unload heavy equipment without proper facilities. I am a bit surprised that arrangements were not made with our Navy to knock off any convoys coming in.

November 16, 1944

My friend Charlie [Willoughby] is getting away tonight for Leyte to stay, and over the phone he had some very caustic remarks to make about the failure to wipe out the Japanese air around Leyte because reinforcements have come in within about thirty miles of our airstrip.

While I have had no details, the situation right now is about as follows: We have expected a very quick clean-up of the Japs on Leyte since originally they were only expected to have one division.[14] As a consequence I was to take over on the 20th with the view of cleaning out the Visayas and going on to other missions which have already been planned. In the meantime, Walter could go on another mission in which I was not included except in a small extent in case he got into difficulty. Recent events have probably produced a respect for the Japanese fighting ability and it would not surprise me if Walter were given practically all the available forces for use in the fairly near future. . . . These are just thoughts that go through my mind and are not necessarily based on fact. Time alone will tell and I must admit that I do not know the true situation up there. We have received some very frank and illuminating reports from some of our staff who went in with Walter, but just what the Big Chief may be thinking about as he walks up and down his office is something I do not know. I imagine many things pass through his mind.

November 17, 1944

George Kenny . . . [was] down to dinner last night. . . . George is full of reasons why those Jap convoys got into Ormoc. One of the reasons is what he calls the slowness of the doughboys in their attempts to get there. Charlie [Willoughby], on the other hand, thinks that George offered to take over too soon the protection of that area and that Halsey should have been allowed to remain a few more days with his heavy carriers to knock out those air fields.

I think our standing among the pick and shovel boys is very high. . . . The power behind the throne of course in the last analysis is the "Old Man" himself and he will probably decide things in no uncertain language. One would say that the present situation would delay things but that is counting without taking into consideration a very proud man with a lot of force who has his own ideas. When I get up there I am going to see Fred[15] and I imagine his boys are a bit tired, because three or four weeks on the ground in the rainy season is no job for a boy even without any enemy.

I expect to get away on Monday [20 November].... After I get up there I shall probably not be able to write very frankly to you because my knowledge then will be more exact than it is now. I can only give you a general picture now, which you can use in filling in my future letters.... While my part in the coming big show[16] ... may be a comparatively small one, I would not be surprised if I should end up in it in a big way, either in total command or as a supporting commander, because after all there is only the health of one man between me and that responsibility.... If I never kill another Jap I still can sit out there in Biltmore[17] with you in the morning and admit to myself that I have had an interesting part in operations such as we could never have anticipated in the old days.

November 19, 1944

One must admit that success in serving one's country must in most cases come from inner satisfaction.... If my success is going to depend upon the amount of publicity that one or two older gentlemen give me then I am not liable to be very successful.... Don't ever let those two rather elderly egotists get your mind off bigger things. Things seem to work out quite well in the end.

(later)

We have successfully completed our first Eighth Army show which was the capture of the Mapia Islands.[18] We think we killed them all and they only number 149. We lost twelve killed and a few wounded because one of the Buffalos landed right in front of some machine guns. ... We heard this morning that a successful landing had been completed on Asia Island, which is even nearer Morotai than the Mapia group.

(later)

We are off tomorrow.... This is just an extra word to say goodbye and to tell you how much I love you.

Was interested in the radio commentator who stated that the "rose-tinted communiques" were not quite true. I have told you the difference of opinion — Charlie [Willoughby] who said that a terrible mistake had been made in sending Halsey and his heavy carriers away because George [Kenney] said he could handle things, and George, who said that the Navy couldn't do it so he took over. Charlie says that the 5th Air Force is a bunch of Hollywood artists who are brave individual fighters and can put on a strike if given lots of time but who cannot take out sudden targets. At any rate the Japs with poor air cover landed a number of convoys only 30 miles away and have created a lot of trouble. The airfields up there do not seem to be very good especially with reference to hard standings for dispersals.... From Palmer [Swift]

I get the idea that the day raids are kept down but that the Japs come over many times every night to strafe and drop bombs. . . .

I expect to take over from Walter a few days after I get up there — then he will get ready for another big show. We had all thought that things would be delayed due to the landings at Ormoc Bay, but I understand that the Big Chief insists that all proceed on schedule. Therefore they are going to see some fireworks, because the Jap apparently is going to make quite a battlefield of the Philippine Islands. Maybe he will make his show down there. Of course the [U.S.] troops that are fighting on Leyte are the ones I was going to use to clean out the Visayas — they are naturally going to emerge a bit tired no matter if the fighting there ended tomorrow — which it won't.

My future use will depend on the Jap — on how many troops are left to give to me — my health and other things. Naturally I cannot go about my job until shipping is available and practically all of that will depend on the next big show.

I am interested in what you say about Sarah — I would hate to see her start something that she cannot finish. She only needs to make one misstep and I hope she will not let her pride induce her to go too far.

Palmer says that my Big Chief is the most nonchalant man there — he won't take counsel of his fears. . . . Walter is "your old friend," and I shall so identify him when I do not call him Walter. . . . You will understand that I cannot be frank when I get up there so I am trying to give you all the picture possible . . . before I go. . . .

We expect to stop a night . . . at Noemfoor so that we can get the plane through Palau and then into Leyte early in the morning.

November 21, 1944

. . . We are off on the last lap. If you get this you will know that we arrived OK.

Was surprised at the fortifications in concrete and steel that the Japs had here [at Palau]. They must have worked for many years. This is the first time I have seen anything as elaborate and can see why the marines had trouble. The Japs are still in certain tunnels equipped with steel doors which go down into the cliffs. The island is mostly flat and small.

We expect to run into a bit of weather before we get in, and a lot of Nips possibly. No job for a boy but all one needs is a bit of luck. . . . The various guns are limbering up — it was a funny feeling when the two tail guns fired. The side guns are firing now — my crew are old timers and should give a good account of themselves.

November 21, 1944
In the Philippines

We came in roughly about ten o'clock. . . . Fred Irving . . . met us at the field. There was plenty of transportation and we started off . . . for Fred's new headquarters.

I was amazed to find that our next door neighbor at West Point and the man who served as my number two man in the spring of 1942 have changed places.[19]

I feel terribly about Fred although I must say that he didn't shed a tear. I have not had a chance to investigate conditions but I imagine that his outfit slowed down a bit as time went on. He told me that he received many compliments in the early days.

I shall go up to see the Big Chief tomorrow morning.

November 22, 1944

It rained all night but I didn't hear it. In fact I didn't see Hedy Lamar (in some new film called "Heavenly Bodies") last night, either. I was there but . . . shortly after I arrived there was a red alert and they turned the lights out and . . . I went to sleep.

When I awakened this morning it was about 5:30. I got up, took my calisthenics and then shaved in hot water. . . . I also had hot coffee. Then I looked around camp a bit and inspected other officers' messes to see if they are getting good food. They had just started to serve fresh eggs and hot cakes.

About 9:00 Clovis and I are going out in a duck to a fast crash boat which will take us down to call on the Big Chief. It would take at least two and one half hours by jeep to get to where the Big Chief lives, so you can see that the roads are not good. All bridges are one way and of course that creates jams.

A lot of American planes have gone by but I don't see how they have found their way in here as the weather is right down on the water.

(later)

This has been a very interesting day. . . . This morning of course I went up to try and pay my respects to the Big Chief. I had not been able to make an appointment with him because the telephone doesn't seem to work here. . . . Clovis and I started out in a duck, which as you know runs like a truck into the water and then goes bobbing along like a boat. Then we came alongside a 63-foot boat which gave us a fine ride for fifteen miles up to the dock. . . . Knowles, my new aide, had the jeep at the dock and we drove through horrible muddy streets to the very nice home in which the Big Chief lives. Unfortunately, when we got there we found that he had a lot of war correspondents from the Central Pacific signed up for luncheon and we therefore made an appointment for 1:30 and went down to see Mr. [Sergio] Osmeña [President of the Philippines]. While there we had an earthquake. . . . Then we went up and had luncheon with the Headquarters Commandant of GHQ. . . .

We had a grand talk with the Big Chief and we discussed everything from the Army football team to past and future operations. He is full of ideas for my use but of course these things may be prevented by the various objections that staff officers always raise. . . . As always [MacArthur] was very pleasant. . . .

The traffic and the mud on the streets defies description. . . . The rainy season has definitely started here. I wish we had Ormoc because the dry season is on there.

Mr. Osmeña has invited me to a pig dinner in his home town when we get there. That is Cebu City. You will recall that that is the home of the ten-year-old virgin about which Army officers have been singing since the Spanish American War.

It was very pretty as we left the dock in that fine boat. It had its four .50 caliber machine guns on two mounts all ready for use. There were low clouds and frequent air alerts but I have yet to see my first Japanese plane on this trip. . . . You can imagine what a sight it was as we went through the harbor and by the airstrip. Then out into the ocean with its storms in every direction. We can always tell when we are approaching our home by an old Spanish fort on a hill. It must have been considered hard to capture in the old days. Now grass is growing out of the roof in memory of the glory of Spain which has departed.

November 23, 1944

While we were talking before supper we heard a tremendous racket over the horizon. Just some of the little palsy-walsies sending out a welcoming committee. . . . The alerts come all day and all night. We are so far away from everything that we do nothing more than turn out our lights. Certainly we do not constitute a profitable target for anyone as we are just a little camp hidden in some palm trees. . . .

This morning . . . I went to see your old friend Walter, who looks quite well . . . [and] was very friendly. . . . You know how sympathetic I am and my tears dripped off my chin when I listened to excuses such as I would not have been allowed to make myself some time ago. I think back about my old commander of World War I when I say that nobody is going to hand me an unwiped baby and make me think it is a wiped one. I will take and try to perform any job that is given to me, but I will do it with my eyes wide open. . . .

It seems that our little palsy-walsy is a tough bird. I have been preaching that for a long time but some people seem to be just finding it out. It is one thing to sit hundreds of miles away and settle things on a map but it is different when one gets out in the rain and mud. Of course I don't mean by this that everybody gets out into the rain and mud if you get what I mean. Most people even when near the enemy just stay in and solve a map problem.

November 24, 1944

Last night I went to bed at ten o'clock and I do not believe there were over ten minutes that I did not have to sit in the dark and read ... by flashlight. Just as soon as the alerts go on somebody pulls the central switch.

There has been a regular Fourth of July going on since breakfast time. ... We are just far enough away so that we can see the bursts and hear the reports but ... the ack-ack does not fall on us. This applies to the ships and installations on both sides....

I asked your old friend [Krueger] when he wanted to turn over to me and he was very indefinite. I am not at all anxious, as they have a bear by the tail and I would be glad to have him settle some of his own troubles. I could not congratulate him because I did not know whether to praise or weep.

(later)

We are getting very blasé and the howling of sirens and the popping of guns does not even take us to the veranda unless it gets very heavy. Our front yard, the ocean, is a scene of never-ending activity. A boat is lying just off-shore and other boats are going by constantly. Planes pass overhead but they are not always our planes.

Tokyo Rose said over the radio that they were going to give us a good time on Thanksgiving [23 November] and from what I hear, things were very interesting, but today has been a much more active day. I am personally glad I am not down in Tacloban where I might be kept awake at all hours.... I wish the Big Chief would move up here near where we are.

November 25, 1944

Last night Fred [Irving] was up for a meeting and it was one of the few beautiful moonlight nights that they have had here.... Overcast rainy clouds are the rule....

We were busy this morning working up some data for the Big Chief. ... When we arrived at GHQ ... the General invited me to eat with him. ... He asked me to present the data to Dick [Sutherland] and Steve [Chamberlin],[20] which I did, and I really believe I have a wee bit of Daniel Webster and Patrick Henry in me, because Clovis and Bill [Bowen] said that I put over everything that I have been thinking about the last month.

November 27, 1944

Yesterday was an extremely interesting day as I was at a conference with the Big Chief all day. This was most interesting to me and the people there were an extremely interesting group, most of whom I have known before. In some ways I was not made very happy over decisions because I see no place for myself in what one might call the big show. Of course we have our immediate job coming up here and the battle for Leyte itself is not any job for a boy. I have not yet taken over but when I do we will have to go at them with hammer and tongs. I hope when I do that nobody insults my intelligence by making the task an illegitimate child known as "mopping up." The only difference between a big fight and mopping up is that when victory is obtained nobody can call it that. It is just as difficult and the bullets go by just as fast.[21]

I had luncheon with the Big Chief sitting next to Kincaid so it developed into sort of a three-cornered conversation with the Big Chief. Three times around lunch time tremendous barrages were put up against hostile planes. The noise was terrific but the Big Chief went right on talking. The only chance I had to take a look I could see hundreds of bursts and a couple of Lightnings.

Last night was magnificent. Up until I went to bed about 11:00 o'clock there was never a period that the red alerts were not on. Fortunately, I have my office fixed up for blackouts so that I can continue to read. One silver plane came by in the moonlight with hundreds of bursts around it.... Later it went on down to Tacloban and I have never seen a more beautiful sight than the tracers going up.

November 29, 1944

At 9:30 this morning Clovis and I boarded our duck... and rode out to the crash boat.... I always enjoy the trip on the crash boat. It is very comfortable. There are easy chairs on the deck and if it is not raining we can sit there and see the boats, planes and everything with a grandstand seat. When we reached the dock... we bummed a ride in a passing jeep and went up to GHQ....

Bill [Bowen] spent a large part of the day with Eddie,[22] who told him that he and your pal [Krueger] hated to turn such a mess over to me. He stated in effect, "The higher-ups keep asking for results without taking into consideration the conditions." Bill said he got a good laugh out of this when he remembered the statements such as "I demand the impossible and get it." Believe me when I tell you that I am going to be busy and I mean plenty.

This battle of Leyte is going to be a witch.... The other islands in the Visayas are not far distant and they run in convoys from time to time. Sometimes by boat and sometimes by barge. However, I am a lucky cuss... so I shall capitalize on any break they make.

Not having been in on the inter-conferences, I do not know why our pals of the sister service have not cleaned out that bay [Ormoc] from time to time.[23] Bill said that Eddie was not very happy but that he refrained from saying "I told you so." This was particularly true when Eddie said in effect, "I do not see why you have not been leap-frogging with us." We had always blamed Eddie for trying to hog things, but maybe it was someone else.[24]

November 30, 1944

About ten o'clock your old friend came over and talked for about an hour ... and a half.... [Krueger] looks well but I believe he feels badly that he has not been able to finish things up here.

The date ... of my taking over the battle of Leyte is not definitely set due mainly to minor changes in plans from day to day.... In the meantime, my men are out getting acquainted with conditions. The big difficulty is getting proper signal communications such as telephone and raido so that all units, front and rear, are connected up properly.... We have lots of reading to do and I am making Clyde [Shuck] and Knowles become geographical experts so that if I want to locate a spot they can tell me.

Tomorrow morning I am going to get up in the dark and leave here early for a trip over to the north shore. It will be an all day ride over muddy roads by jeep. I could do it more easily by cub or by crash boat. ... However, there is only one way to find out what conditions really are, and that is to see them for yourself. I shall take ... a jeep full of MP's with carbines. While there is practically no danger there is no use in taking any chances with some Jap that might infiltrate.

December 2, 1944

Clovis and Bill went down to talk to the big boys today and it seems that they are going to try and let your palsy-walsy [Krueger] finish the job he started provided he doesn't take too long. They do not want to hurt his feelings.... It has been necessary to set things back a wee bit anyway so this fits in with the plans all right. It will mean, however, that I may sit around here until almost Christmas with nothing to do except keep in touch with the situation.

December 5, 1944

We were up at 4:30 this morning, had breakfast at five and had actually been taken out by duck to the crash boat ... before six o'clock. We had a beautiful trip which lasted about four hours to Carigara Bay. ... When we went aboard ... the moon was shining and we could see the great dipper as we started off. Then a little later the sun came up. I would like to be able to describe the many views and types of boats that we saw as we went along but I suppose that is a military secret, even though of course well known to the Japs. I think I could say without giving anything away that at one time a bunch of PT boats went by us ... going about 45 miles an hour and it was a beautiful sight. They were in column.

It was the most beautiful day we have yet had. It was perfectly clear going over and I was very interested while going through the Straits in passing so many Filipinos with their outriggered canoes and biancas which are almost like Chinese junks.

Going in we passed a school of whales, some of which were very close to our boat. They stayed with us for a long time. We tried shooting at them with a pistol but I must say that I missed by about a hundred yards.

As soon as I could get ashore I went up to see my friend Bill [Gill]. . . . After some conversation some of us went forward by jeep to where that fighting has been going on so long. I saw and talked to many whom I had known in the early fighting in Papua. It all seems so familiar now; the smells and the dead Japs, the mud and with it all the cheerful soldiers, many of whom have been out now for forty days. They have been getting good food. . . . Of course the question of supply is always a nightmare. The worst part is the attempts to keep the roads open, to keep the ammunition going forward and to bring the wounded and sick back.

While out there I ran into my old friend Monk Meyer[25] leading an outfit forward and I walked beside him for a while telling him about the Army-Navy game.

December 6, 1944

I am glad I went yesterday because I think I am the only one faintly approaching my rank who has had a first-hand look at the soldiers in action. It is good to know that they are so cheerful right on the ground where the fighting is going on. I can tell in about ten minutes whether the troops are all in mentally or not, and those boys out there certainly expect to lick these Japs and I think they will do so.

December 8, 1944

It is over three years since Pearl Harbor and it will soon be three years since we left West Point. I have a feeling that Japan will quit within another year. This will be partly due to the terrific pounding which the cities will receive and partly because I think Honest Joe [Stalin] will push down into Manchuria.

Don't worry about me because I am sleeping like a horse, eat like one and even give a lot of horse laughs from time to time.

(later)

Last night ... to our surprise we didn't have a single red alert throughout the movie. The Japs were too busy yesterday. A convoy headed this way was attacked and completely eliminated and that after all is the easiest way to kill them.[26] Then my old outfit of 1942 made a successful landing.[27] It looks to me now as though the number of Japanese on Leyte is a lot less than we had thought, so it will not be long before they call this thing "mopping up" and turn it over to me. ... The situation here ... has decidedly improved with the sinking of that big convoy. ...

Fred Irving is coming down to have luncheon with me. I feel sorry for him sitting down the beach with a small staff and nothing to do. I shall give him a job when he comes under me the day after Christmas. Look for a lot of thanks being offered up to the Lord about the 25th, and thanks for a victory which will then be concluded. The next day no Japs will officially exist.

December 10, 1944

I wish I could tell you my views on things here but ... you are able to draw better conclusions than most people even here on the ground. You can tell from the communiques what troops we are using ... and ... the number of Japanese who are supposed to have been killed. You know my views on this subject. For example, certain convoys are supposed to have been sunk. The question always arises whether or not they had already unloaded their troops. The other day I thought we caught one en route but it turned out that it had already shed its troops.

As you can well imagine, troops are being used that I had expected to use on future operations, so the whole picture has changed quite a bit. I shall do what I am ordered to do but I do not feel as near a volunteer as I have many times in the past. ... From now on ... I am asking no favors of anyone.

I imagine this whole situation is being turned over and over in a certain person's mind — he is very nice to me, almost affectionate in his manner. He knows I will fight and that is more than he knows about some of the Command Post leaders who solve it as a map problem.

December 12, 1944

Your friend Charlie [Willoughby] has built up a picture that everything comes easy with very small losses. To explain this great delay it was necessary to build up a picture not only of enormous losses but of enormous Japanese reinforcements. Now they are beginning to change the picture rapidly. The 45,000 Japs are rapidly being killed off on paper so that about the day I take over, or in other words Christmas day, it can be announced that the battle is over and that the Japanese are practically all killed. Then it will be turned over to me to mop up what remains. It looks as though two more bunches of Jap reinforcements have come in lately. However, I have never thought that the total was anything like I have seen indicated in the papers. I imagine right now the Japanese number not less than 15,000 and not more than 18,000.[28] These are probably well equipped with rifles and machine guns.

At 9:15 this morning Clovis and I, with Art Thayer, left by fast crash boat for GHQ. . . . The Big Chief told me how disappointed he has been that the troops have not moved faster. I told him that there were certain viewpoints which I thought were dangerous for us. One I call the Empress Augusta-Bay viewpoint,[29] which is when large bodies of troops get into a perimeter and allow an inferior number of Japs to wander around outside. That went on for a year at Bougainville. Another viewpoint is one I call the Nassau-Bay–Salamaua viewpoint.[30] That is "not to have your infantry advance but just to kill the enemy by shell fire." I told him that if the Lae operation hadn't come along they would still be fighting below Salamaua. Then the corollary is what I would call "pinned down by fire." That is when your troops will stop if two or 1,000 Japs are firing at them and then announce that they have been "pinned down by fire."

Steve [Chamberlin] and Dick [Sutherland] are both worried by slow progress. . . . Sarah . . . is not so keen about your old friend any more. In fact she is disappointed in him and has so informed me.

Will try not to say anything that the Censor wouldn't like.

In his diary, General Eichelberger reported his conversation with General MacArthur in greater detail. In a passage that was unusual both in length and content, since most entries contained only the essential facts to document his activities for the day, Eichelberger recorded: "I talked with Big Chief who explained dissatisfaction with Walter and stated he might have to relieve him. Said he had held him on over-age and expected him to be a driver. He said he wasn't worried about Leyte but was worried about conduct [of] troops on future operations if actions here were indicative. I told him the fundamental error was made last summer when so many things were given to the 6th Army that they could not do anything well. He said he wanted me to become a Stonewall Jackson or a Patton and lead many small landing forces in from South just as the Japs had. Very cordial and when I left he yelled at me to come back often. I stayed to have luncheon with him and talked football. Walter was there . . . and tried to act real jolly without much success. . . . Saw Steve Chamberlin who hoped I would come there often as he feels Kenney gives Chief wrong picture. Big Chief stated 32d never had been any good and that he was very disappointed over slow progress of 77th and 7th. He said Walter states these units have had

fine records and are doing well. He says Walter makes many excuses. . . ."

December 15, 1944

Bill Chickering [*Time* correspondent] was here for dinner last night. . . . He received a very frank discussion from me which I think he appreciated although he probably found my viewpoint a bit different. I am enclosing a song written by Bill which we sang last night with great gusto.

By Bill Chickering. Tune is "Bless Them All."

> There's a convoy now leaving Luzon
> Headed for old Ormoc Bay.
> Its decks are all covered with regiments of Japs.
> The skies are all filled with their Oscars and Haps.
> We are saying hello to them all
> As into our fox holes we crawl.
> The Navy don't mind them, the Air Corps can't find
>   them,
> So who gives a damn, land them all.
>
> Land them all, land them all,
> Their social success will be small.
> They'll get no attention
> Except for slight mention
> In G2's report of it all.
>
> There are transports now leaving Cebu,
> Heading for Tanauan Drome.
> Filled with explosives and parachute troops
> And other varieties of Nipponcompoops.
> And we're saying hello to them all
> As out of the heavens they fall.
> We've plenty of rifles to cope with whole skyfulls
> So Geronimo Nip, drop them all.
>
> Drop them all, drop them all,
> Their number turned out to be small.
> But spare your derision
> They'll keep one division
> Holding them off 'til next fall.

I still expect to take over here on the 26th. In the meantime I sent Chink Hall back to Morotai to clean up that mess. The Japs, according to the press, have started to take a new interest in it.

December 16, 1944

I have just read the figures of [Japanese] casualties given in a radio report out of San Francisco which are perfectly enormous.... However I must admit that nobody can give even an approximation in tangled country. I never presumed to count dead what a man wouldn't put his foot on.

You have doubtless read... about the small landing made by the man who was football coach at Kemper when we were there.[31] Apparently he had no trouble except from suicide planes which are our greatest pain in the neck. You will hear more about these things later....

Fred Irving spent two nights with me. He has made quite a point of asking Clovis and me to come down to his camp tonight for dinner.... Apparently Walter is going to be there and he is very anxious to have me there to keep him from being embarrassed....

In spite of the figures given out, there are still many to be killed off before the Island can be turned over to me as a "mopping up" job. Bill [Gill] has made little progress since he arrived and my old outfit [Seventy-seventh Division] has been quite a disappointment. The landing was a bold thing and skillfully conceived. Somebody then took counsel of his fears and failed to move fast. They have not gone far since landing and I see no immediate prospects of wiping out that remaining 16 miles before we take over. The Japs can then still back up to the west shore and offer quite a problem since supply is very easy for them from one angle. The numerous surrounding islands are close enough so that their barges can move over during the night and return before dawn.

December 17, 1944

I hope you will remain calm and not become too serious about things out here. I have tried to let you know how I am getting along, but I must say that I still think that I may be lucky to be a bit on the outside of certain things — like the Irishman praying on the raft who said, "This is no job for a boy."

Today I had to laugh when I read some messages sent to the man who coached football at Kemper. They brought back so many memories of last spring.

You can look for me to arrive back home with a big grin on my face and then I shall sit down and devote myself to writing my views on my fellow man.[32]

December 18, 1944

Today... Clovis and I left... in the "Miss Em" [the boat] to pick up Mr. Osmeña and several of his staff. It was a beautiful trip down and I wish I could describe just how interesting it was and the different types of vessels... we went past.... We made a perfect three-point landing up against a small dock through a bunch of boats and Mr. Osmeña, with General Valdez, Captain Madrigal, his aide, and Bonner Fellers came aboard promptly.

Bonner Fellers was very interesting and I was sorry he did not return on the boat with us because I wanted to talk to him some more. He said, among other things, that the Big Chief and your old friend [Sutherland] had a row and he did not believe that the latter would last long . . . [and] that your palsy-walsy [Krueger] was in bad, and that if a group of armies were ever organized over here he wouldn't get it.

In fact he indicated to Clovis that *I* would get the golden spurs. This of course is pure hooey and I laughed but I have been fooled before. Bonner says that he feels that *he* is on the way out too. His job, in charge of civil affairs, has been given to a Manila lawyer for whom he does not have a very high regard. He says his trouble has been that he has been very frank with the Big Chief when he was asked to give his opinion, in contradistinction to certain others whom he feels tell the Big Chief what they feel he wants to hear.

I don't believe any of these things . . . are going to happen. The Big Chief doesn't like to hurt people, therefore I think he will hang on to his present staff, including Bonner. . . . From the things he told me I know he doesn't like what your old palsy-walsy has been doing but he would hate to hurt him unless it became much more evident that he hasn't the ability to lead men in a desperate situation.

Your old palsy-walsy talked to me the other night when I went to Fred's dinner about the possibility that I may be made an Army Group commander. I laughed at that, because I knew what he really meant was that he was hoping *he* would get it. If he wants something badly he always starts out by denying that he wants it.

Progress is being made in the Ormoc Valley so I guess they will be able to announce a victory on Christmas. That will leave us lots to do.

December 20, 1944

Clovis, Bill Bowen and I went up to GHQ this morning where I was held up a bit before the Big Chief could see me. I finally saw him about eleven and we talked on many subjects.[33] As always he was very pleasant but he has grounds for new fears that things will be taken out of his hands after the next operation. He is the only one who carries the Army banner and the only one who has the prestige, power and courage to do it. If he drops out, things . . . will be run by that lad who used to raise dogs where we lived ten years ago. As far as I know he has never heard a bullet shot by an enemy.

Recent developments on Mindoro . . . and the recent advance of those troops with whom I served in the spring of 1942 have raised your old palsy-walsy's prestige a bit, but he has had his honeymoon.

You would be surprised at the great friendship with which we are greeted by everyone up there at GHQ. Without exception they are all happy to see us and that is of course a gratifying atmosphere in which to work. It may also be an indication of things to come.

December 21, 1944

If your palsy-walsy should be put in command of an Army Group I will have a very hard decision to make, because I feel about it just as Horace Fuller did. He was deliberately discourteous to me on a number of occasions and I would be forced to decide whether it would be to my best interests to run the chance of being humiliated or to ask the Big Chief if he did not feel that I have done my share of the fighting in this war. . . . I do not think that any superior necessarily knows the true character of those who work under him. With some delay he [Krueger] has won his first fight and it will be put out as a great victory.

December 23, 1944

I am very much worried about the German drive into Belgium.[34] I hope they are able to stop it promptly. If the Germans throw everything they have into that fight and lose, maybe it will be a great advantage.

December 24, 1944
Christmas Eve

The long road lies ahead, but it is not so long as it was. I shall be alert to decide when I shall be justified in going home. For example, *if* our Big Chief, after victory, comes to the end of his work and his troops are given to the Central Pacific, then I would feel that I could sign off with pleasure.

Christmas Day

We are all saying that we want to be home next Christmas, and I know we are all sincere in that. Certainly after I have gone through another year of this I can conscientiously leave it to some of the younger boys. By another year the Japanese should be in a bad way, but whether they will give up that soon I do not know.

Yesterday morning . . . I dropped off . . . to see Walter. I think some people are just cuckoo — he explained to me that his troops had fought the great fight against the worst conditions that American troops have ever fought under, etc., etc. . . . Clovis said he had never been as proud of me. I wasn't going to have the Big Chief say that I failed to listen to your old palsy-walsy before taking over.

Take over tomorrow and am ready to go. Will have to push the remaining Japs off the island — personally I think they will leave by small boats for some of the nearby Islands, but most people don't think so.

At any rate I think two weeks more will do it, especially if this grand weather keeps up.

When Walter leaves here I shall have lots of things to do, particularly if things do not progress too fast with him and Sarah. We have been making plans for future possibilities.

Notes

1. Eichelberger to Miss Em, 21 October 1944.
2. Ibid., 4 October 1944.
3. This observation was communicated by General R. B. Woodruff in a chat on 11 October 1944.
4. Eichelberger to Miss Em, 11 October 1944.
5. Ibid., 7, 8 October 1944.
6. Col. F. S. Bowen, Jr., Memorandum to Commanding General, Eighth Army, 12 October 1944; Historical Section, Eighth U.S. Army, *The Amphibious Eighth* (N.p., n.d.), p. 20.
7. Brig. Gen. Hanford MacNider took over command of the task force and the 158th Regimental Combat Team on Noemfoor Island on 6 September and came under Eighth Army Command on 9 October. Noemfoor had been invaded on 2 July; on 31 August the operation had been officially declared over. Robert Ross Smith, *The Approach to the Philippines* (Washington, 1953), p. 424.
8. It would appear that Eichelberger is referring to two separate actions. The extravagant Japanese claims of having sunk eleven carriers (later inflated to nineteen), two battleships, and three cruisers grew out of the Formosa air battles of 11–16 October, when land-based planes had made repeated attacks against Task Force 38. If Eichelberger did not know officially that only two American ships had in fact been damaged, certainly Admiral Halsey's message to Admiral Nimitz, which had been released on 19 October, to the effect that the "sunken" ships had been "salvaged" and were "retiring at high speed toward the enemy" would have raised healthy skepticism about the accuracy of the Japanese figures.

The battle that was raging at the time Eichelberger wrote this letter was the greatest naval battle in history, and here he did have cause to worry. In a desperate effort to destroy the American shipping and amphibious forces in Leyte Gulf, the Japanese had employed three naval forces, one to lure the main U.S. battle fleet away to the north while the Southern Group negotiated Surigao Strait south of Leyte and the Central Group approached from the San Bernadino Strait separating the islands of Luzon and Samar.

The Southern Group was practically annihilated by Admiral Thomas C. Kincaid's Seventh Fleet on the night of the 24th, but the Central Group, although it had suffered serious damage from U.S. air strikes on 25 October, managed to slip through the San Bernadino Strait undetected, while Halsey's Third Fleet, which contained all of the attack carriers and the new battleships, was preparing to strike the decoy force some three hundred miles to the north. Only a few slow, vulnerable, and lightly armed escort carriers stood between the Central Group and the exposed Leyte beaches. But thanks to the heroic actions of these and the accompanying destroyers, to "our successful smoke screen, our torpedo counterattack — and the definite partiality of Almighty God," the Central Force failed to capitalize upon this extraordinary opportunity; and by the time it had turned about the Japanese fleet had been largely destroyed.

9. Vice Admiral Theodore S. Wilkinson commanded the Southern Attack Force (Task Force 79) in the Leyte landings.
10. This probably refers to the cruiser *Honolulu*, which was severely damaged by a Japanese torpedo plane attack on the day of the landings, 20 October 1944.
11. Maj. Gen. Charles P. Hall commanded the XI Corps.
12. Jack Turcott was a war correspondent.

13. By the time this letter was written the Japanese had already sent four convoys carrying reinforcements to Leyte, and a fifth was probably en route from Manila. All told, these and four subsequent convoys landed some 45,000 troops and 10,000 tons of materiel, but since 80 percent of the ships sent were sunk en route — or so the Japanese later claimed — many of the soldiers had to swim and wade ashore and their equipment was lost. M. Hamlin Cannon, *Leyte: The Return to the Philippines* (Washington, 1954), pp. 101–102.

14. This would not include garrison and service troops, which Sixth Army G-2 estimated in September would raise the strength of Japanese forces on Leyte to over 21,000 troops. Ibid., p. 22.

15. Maj. Gen. Frederick A. Irving, commanding the Twenty-fourth Division, X Corps.

16. "There are two schools of thought in consideration of an attack on a large island called we shall say 'X.' One is that one army should command everything and the other is that two armies should go in if separated by the enemy in the center."

17. A comfortable and prestigious residential section near Asheville, N.C. General and Mrs. Eichelberger lived in Biltmore Forest at the time of his death.

18. On 15 November the Eighth Army, with elements of the Thirty-first Division, assaulted the Mapia Islands 160 nautical miles northeast of Sansapor. Little opposition was encountered and the operation was successfully concluded on 20 November. The islands then served as sites for radar stations.

19. This refers to the fact that on 17 November Maj. Gen. Roscoe B. Woodruff replaced Maj. Gen. Frederick A. Irving as commander of the Twenty-fourth Division. Irving was given command of the Leyte Garrison Force, "which would hold the island upon completion of the operation." Krueger, *From Down Under to Nippon* (Washington, 1953) p. 176.

20. Maj. Gen. Stephen J. Chamberlin, MacArthur's G-3.

21. See pp. 62, 63-64.

22. Probably Maj. Gen. Clyde D. Eddleman, Gen. Bowen's counterpart (G-3) in the Sixth Army.

23. According to Professor Morison, Task Force 38 was too busy "to keep a cork in the Camotes Sea bottleneck," and the Army Air Forces on Leyte were needed for support of the ground troops. This left the task to the destroyers, and it was not until the evening of 27 November that the mines had been removed from the narrow passages through the reefs so that four destroyers could attack enemy shipping and shore installations in Ormoc Bay. Samuel Eliot Morison, *Leyte: June 1944-January 1945*, vol. 12, *History of U.S. Naval Operations in World War II* (Boston, 1958), pp. 368–369.

24. See p. 305.

25. Lt. Col. C. R. Meyer, commanding a battalion of the 127th Infantry, Thirty-second Division. General Byers recalls the incident vividly. After listening most of the night before to the Army-Navy game, Gen. Eichelberger turned to him and said: "Clovis, who, of all the people we know here, would be the most happy to get a play-by-play account of the game?" Byers answered without any hesitation "Monk Meyer," a standout player at the Military Academy only a few years before. The next day they visited the Thirty-second Division in the Ormoc Valley, and despite protests from the division commander, Gen. Gill, that he would be taking unnecessary chances, Eichelberger insisted on visiting the front lines just to tell Meyer about the game. While narrating such details as he could remember, the cluster of officers was spotted and shelled by Japanese artillery, but Eichelberger refused to leave until he had completed his "replay" of the game. When he finally withdrew, it was much to the relief of all concerned. Notes of an interview with Gen. Byers, 17 May 1965.

26. Only 400 naval landing troops, of a reinforced infantry regiment, one artillery battalion, and a special naval landing force actually reached their destination on Leyte on the night of 7 December. The remainder were landed on San Isidro Peninsula, to the north, where they were isolated from the Japanese garrison on Leyte. Morison, *Leyte,* pp. 386-387.

27. The reference here is to the Seventy-seventh Infantry Division, which Eichelberger commanded briefly when it was first activated in March 1942. On the morning of 7 December the Seventy-seventh had landed at Deposito, in Ormoc Bay, and immediately began the advance inland.

28. Estimates of the Japanese strength on Leyte at any given time still vary. On 26 December, Sixth Army estimated that 5,000 Japanese remained on Leyte and Samar; Eighth Army estimates for the same date gave 25,000 Japanese on Leyte. A Japanese source states that Japanese strength on Leyte about this time approximated 11,000. Cannon, *Leyte,* p. 367; *Report of the Commanding General Eighth U.S. Army on the Leyte-Samar Operation,* p. 3; Saburo Hayashi, *Kogun: The Japanese Army in he Pacific War* (Quantico, Va., 1959), p. 126. Stanley L. Falk puts the number at 15,000. *Decision at Leyte* (New York, 1966), p. 301.

29. This refers to the landing of the Third and Ninth Marine Corps Divisions on Bougainville on 1 November 1943.

30. Australian and U.S. forces landed in Nassau Bay on 30 June 1943.

31. Originally scheduled for 5 December, the landings at Mindoro were postponed by MacArthur because of supply problems and lack of necessary air support. The landings occurred on 15 December 1944, under the command of Brig. Gen. William C. Dunckel. This operation of the Western Visayan Task Force was the responsibility of Sixth Army and it served as a stepping stone to the next major invasion — Luzon.

32. This last sentence is borrowed from the previous letter.

33. According to Eichelberger's Diary, MacArthur was "no longer critical of W [Krueger]." He "estimates 170,000 Jap casualties." (Six days later the Sixth Army officially estimated Japanese casualties as 56,263 killed and 389 captured. Cannon, *Leyte,* p. 367. After the war General Tomochika, Deputy Chief of Staff of the Japanese 35th Army, estimated that by 17 March 1945, some 48,790 Japanese had been killed on Leyte. Ibid., p. 368.) MacArthur "told me he had been directed to plan to relieve all but five Divisions and a lot of his supply troops and ships to Central Pacific by July 1. He said he wrote GCM [General Marshall] saying that he would not do it. I told him he was the only one who would have the prestige and courage to fight for the Army. . . . Everybody thinks battle of Leyte is about over. Big Chief estimates not over 5,000 Jap troops. . . ."

34. This is not the first reference to the Battle of the Bulge, which began on 16 December 1944, when a quarter of a million of Germany's best soldiers achieved a stunning tactical and strategical surprise and punctured the weakly held American lines in the Ardennes.

CHAPTER TEN

The Unwiped Baby

Leyte reminded General Eichelberger of Buna and Sanananda. Once again mopping up, as it was called, proved an inadequate and misleading term for a dirty and unrewarding kind of war. While General MacArthur contended that all organized resistance had come to an end, the wary and tired infantry who stalked the remaining enemy through rain, mud, and dense jungles took a different view of the operations to clear the island of remaining Japanese. "It was bitter, exhausting, rugged fighting — physically, the most terrible we were ever to know."[1] It did not make the task any easier when public attention followed the Sixth Army to Luzon: the existence of the Eighth Army had not yet even been announced.

Uncertain of his future, anxious to demonstrate the capacity of his army for independent operations, and still smoldering over his recent relations with General Krueger, Eichelberger kept a watchful eye on the campaign for Luzon. For the present he had other responsibilities, chief among which was to stage and supply units engaged elsewhere in the Philippines and also to reequip and load the XXIV Corps for approaching operations in Okinawa. This was "probably the greatest job my staff has done in this war," he later explained to Miss Em. "It was a task to try the patience of a saint and it was one performed most ably by my staff with Clovis at the wheel. It is the reverse of combat but of tremendous importance, and it was that work which made our first big hit with the GHQ staff."[2]

December 26, 1944

Dearest Emmalina,
This is the day after Christmas and I am personally glad that the holi-

day is over. I was homesick and in an endeavor to have a decent Christmas we managed to get our hours all jumbled up so that not very much work was done. . . .

At midnight . . . I took over the command of the troops on Leyte. After the movie last night I talked to your old palsy-walsy who offered to do everything he could to help us. I think he was trying to tell me also that the fighting was all over, although there are some thousands of Japs yet to kill. It is true that the main resistance has been cut and that was done in a large measure by the 77th Division. The Japs of course have had no easy time. They probably never had any great amount of supplies at any time and their problem of distribution has been worse than ours because we were able to use small boats on water for a large part of our supply and the main roads have been in our possession.

From now on I will be very busy and I shall have to apportion my time with intelligence.

2:30 P.M.

Clovis and I are on the "Miss Em" enroute to a conference (at GHQ). . . .

Joe Swing came in to see me this morning. . . . Joe tells some very interesting stories. In one case he sent his assistant G-3 to accompany a unit that was making an attack. This officer was with the assault units all day and only saw two dead Japs. The next day the reports indicated 240 dead ones. In another case he saw a hospital reported to have a thousand dead Japs in it. He said he could only count between 50 and 60. However, there may have been some dead ones which nobody counted. I wouldn't know, being a little boy from the country. . . . [3]

We are going to try and push the remaining Japs up against the sea coast and wipe them out. How many there are of course nobody knows. Joe said way back in the mountains there are hundreds of Japs very much alive and full of fight. They are cut off and without any supply lines, although there are lots of native gardens up there. Joe stayed for luncheon . . . before he went back. I am going to try and get around to see them all as soon as possible in view of the fact that I am now in command. Every day I shall try to go someplace.

at home 9:10 P.M.

The meeting was very interesting. I sat on the left of the man with whom I served in 1935 and Nellie's boss[4] sat on his right. . . . I liked the way Nellie's boss [Nimitz] handled himself. I think he is honest and that is something.[5]

December 27, 1944

You can see what a big victory has been announced and indeed it has been a victory. The Japs have had their successes too. With certain losses (not the announced ones) they have delayed operations and have forced us to use troops which will not now be fresh for future operations. Of course some of these troops do not belong to us but were loaned by the POA and will go back to them.[6] They will need rest, rehabilitation and reequipment. Some of this they will get only in part. If Ike didn't need so much then the matter of replacements would be no problem. If things were as easy as has been announced in the communiques, then we would have nothing to worry about....

We will have various things to do even where we lived in 1920,[7] but whether we will ever be announced I do not know. Eddie [Eddleman] told Clovis yesterday that he couldn't understand why they didn't leap-frog instead of using his outfit [Sixth Army] exclusively — that they had had more than they could do.... I do not know why the Eighth [Army] hasn't been announced. The best explanation I can think of is that *two armies* would indicate more tools than it is desired to admit.

8:00 P.M.

In your letters you sometimes seem to think that I have been deceived by certain people. Sometimes I will say so-and-so is such a wonderful person, and if you know that he has been "pulling my wings off"... you may be sure that I am being sarcastic. Sometimes I like to give the censor a bit of uplift in case he should read my letter. I do from time to time say that so-and-so was extremely friendly, but that is to indicate a passing attitude, not necessarily that I believe he is a real friend.

I am inclined to think now that your palsy-walsy at one time was in danger of being relieved by me, but since this has now been called the most wonderful victory in history of course he is more or less on top again. I even think that when someone [MacArthur] yelled to me "Come back and see me often" within the hearing of another person [Krueger], that he was trying to put the screws on that person. There is one person out here ... that I will never trust until the day he dies [Sutherland]. Sometimes he is very friendly and in fact during recent months he has seemed to be quite so.

Yesterday I told you what I think about the losses. You may be sure of one thing, that it is beyond the power of any man to count the dead in 75 miles of jungle. It is also beyond the power of any man to make leaders who are not doing particularly well keep from exaggerating the enemy's losses. There is no proof for or against any statement. Complete control of news permits the development of any picture desired.

December 28, 1944

We have just finished our usual morning conference in which the principal staff officers turn over the picture of the day.

I find a great many things to read. Last night I did not finish until twelve o'clock....

Fred [Irving] has been invited to come down to our early morning conferences.... Within the next day or so I shall call Dick [Sutherland] and ask him if he is going to assign Fred. I do not really need him and in fact it will be quite a problem to decide what to do with him, but on the other hand I think it would be good for Fred to be with me.

December 29, 1944

Today has been very interesting and I shall describe it in some detail.... Along about noon I got a telephone call that Dick [Sutherland] wanted to come down to see me by boat, ... and a little later I got a call that Nellie [Richardson] had left GHQ and would be here about one o'clock also. They arrived within a minute of one another. Dick had come to discuss Fred and his staff with me. He wanted to settle the status of Fred and his staff (the latter all from POA) before Nellie had a chance to talk with Big Chief. The pick and shovel boys had wanted to split up Fred's staff, giving a few to me. Dick said that in order to combat Nellie's desire to take them back to POA he should tell the Big Chief that I could use them all. I think now that I am going to get the whole works. I do not know how I am going to use them but I shall find some way later. ... I am inclined to make him [Fred] Deputy Commander or what might be called Area Commander of the rear areas, which will include Leyte after we get all the Japs killed.... Dick has spoken many times very highly of Fred, and since he has volunteered this change, which is rather unusual of him, I believe he really means it.

Nellie was in fine fettle.... He had a lot to say about the lack of friendship between the man for whom I worked in 1935 [MacArthur] and certain others of a sister service. He agrees with me that our Chief is the number one strategist of our Army. One of the favorite knocks that one hears according to him is that he is not brave. Of course that is pure tommyrot because I think he is as brave as any man in the Army, if not more so. I think the big trouble is that my Chief is willing to fight for the Army and for himself and the other people want to fight for their own interests, therefore there is a natural clash. Nellie agrees with me that our Chief should be given the overall Army command out here.

Rich told me he has had a very hard time in POA. He said recently he had a conference with the joint chiefs of staff in Washington and had advocated that the Big Chief be given overall command of the Army troops, and Admiral King put in a very caustic remark against it.... He said he was very much opposed to have Army troops serve again under Marine command. He said he had a board of officers investigate trouble between Howlin' Mad Smith and Ralph Smith[8] and that he had told Nimitz that if he ever attempted to put Army troops under H. M. Smith again he would release [the] report.... H. M. Smith had no knowledge of terrible conditions in front of 27th Division.[9]

The one editorial from the *Tribune* which you sent concerning certain communiques is a very scathing one. I do not know who prepares them but I have heard people say things right here about what you read in the editorial. We all deplore fairy tales while we applaud successes that come from a great strategic mind.

December 30, 1944

I realize that ... you are wondering how I am being treated. In talking to ... correspondents last night I realize that there are bigger questions: (1) Will there be bloody revolutions throughout the world after the war such as we now see starting in Greece? ... (2) Will there be any such thing as life insurance if this war goes on much longer? Will money be worth anything or will inflation be necessary? (3) Some wondered whether the 11,000,000 who have been in the war, with their families, will dominate our political life and stand with their feet in the treasury door for the next hundred years. When I think of these things I do not feel that it is very important whether I get three stars or four ... or a red and white ribbon. ... I realize that I have been mixed up in the vanities and ambitions of men and some of these are no chickens. I left West Point with high ideals and with the feeling that I was willing to die for my country if it were necessary. I do not want to live a life of hatred. ...

Not all the things that affect me are aimed at me. For example, the failure to announce the Eighth Army is *probably not* aimed at me. A certain person [MacArthur] has always presented the picture of the poor little boy who has done a lot with a very little. He may not want to admit in a communique that he *now* has two armies to do it with. ... Steve[10] does not give us much encouragement about any major use of our unit. He is supply minded and he does not want to complicate the supply system as he sees it. I believe he would feel the same way if I had the other unit. I know it is nothing personal as far as he is concerned. He seems to think that anything that may come in the future will be a pushover (no one that I know agrees with him) and that may influence him.[11]

While there is one person whom we knew at Leavenworth [Sutherland] whom I do not trust, I think he is perfectly willing to be friendly to me when it is to his best interests. Therefore, when he is evidently trying to be friendly we feel that we should meet him half way. We know he is the type that will cheerfully cut our throats if it will present him any advantage. There are certain people, however, whom we feel he really dislikes and ... he does not dislike me. He is just untrustworthy. ...

I cannot and must not let anything get me down. Fighting, responsibilities, the queer actions of certain people towards me must all be taken in stride. ...

We all feel that the way ahead is long and uncertain. ... If your palsy-walsy stubs his toe — and he might — we may be drawn into a different situation. In any case there are plans for us for various operations so we will be doing our little part. Unlike your palsy-walsy I do not think it is necessary for me to catch all the cats. I am perfectly willing to let somebody else do a bit of it.

After a long conference this morning I went up to see Joe Swing. . . . I am very favorably impressed with his outfit [Eleventh Airborne].

New Year's Eve, 1944

We are still getting quite a lot of action. I think there were something like 1,700 Japs killed yesterday. Today the 77th captured six .75 mm guns and had one of our Sherman tanks knocked out. . . . We take over Mindoro at midnight tonight. The great trouble up there is in trying to get supplies to Bill.[12]

January 1, 1945

This has been an interesting day. Early this morning I left for Valencia to hold the decoration ceremony for the 77th Division. . . . I pinned on over a hundred decorations and talked to each man. Then we went to the hospital where I talked to the wounded. . . . I have seen enough eyes of wounded men light up to know that I am still remembered by that old crowd.

Some people think that it is dangerous to ride in a Cub but I do not have that feeling. To get out there by road I would have to ride two days in a jeep with the chance of being sniped at, . . . overturning . . . or being hit by a passing truck.

Tomorrow I think I shall go up to see the Big Chief because if I do not do so then I may not get the chance to see him for a long while.

January 2, 1945

This is another beautiful day after a very noisy night. We had everything from planes, bombs, ack-ack and even an earthquake to keep us amused. . . .

I had a rather nice talk with the Big Chief. . . . He told me of various plans he had for me. . . . *MacArthur again emphasized his desire that I land in South Luzon at a number of points and push on to Manila in spite of all obstacles. He told me that the Navy felt that they were unable to furnish minesweepers and other things but I must overcome all obstacles and push in every man I can get. I told him he must stand in back of me and force the Navy and his own staff — who are none too sympathetic to this question — to give me certain necessary things which I must have. He said he did not think the M-1 operation (Mike I — plan for the Invasion of Lingayen Gulf) would be an easy one since the Japs were shifting all their strength up into the valley. I told him I was sorry that he was going up on the first convoy but he did not seem to think much of the danger involved. He was very cordial and asked me to come up to see him in about S (day) plus 4.*[13] Many of the boys ... think things are going to be a pushover. . . .

The Big Chief thinks that Ike's reputation as well as Bradley's will be dimmed quite a bit because of this German penetration. . . .[14] As I have read the terrible things that have happened to the First Army, I have thought that I may have been lucky not to be in command of it. . . . The German advance is only comparable to their advance in 1918 when they overran Gough's British 5th Army. I would have been very much in a cloud. . . .

January 4, 1945

This afternoon I returned from Mindoro. . . . I was very busy all day yesterday until night, and then we sat around in the dark until bedtime because the Jappies were flying over the house. It was one of the noisiest nights I have ever heard but yet I managed to sleep through most of it because I was very tired. . . . I could lie in bed and watch the ack-ack people shooting at the Japs over the house. . . . The Japs seem to enjoy it. They kept it up all night and had three planes shot down.

After some delay yesterday ... we took off in a B-25. You would be surprised how rapidly one passes over Leyte, then by the north end of Cebu with Negros lying a bit to the south in the distance, and then right by the north end of Panay. . . . Coming back this morning there were some storms around so we swung back over Panay, running over Jap territory for about 75 miles at high speed just over the tops of the trees. We certainly saw many rare sights.

As you will read in the papers, we have made several additional landings in Mindoro during the last few days, including the taking over of another big island near Luzon.[15] If I had the ships I think I could take over all the Visayas now without much trouble, and I hope to be able to do so before too long. The Japs put a lot of their strength into Leyte so I do not think any of the Visayan garrisons are large.

January 5, 1945

Yesterday when Commander Davis gave me that lunch he presented me with a bottle of Japanese liquor, so I had one of our Japanese interpreters ... read the label and tell me what the contents might be. He said the bottle contained whiskey with the strength of forty percent alcohol, and the instructions that this whiskey was to be used by Navy pilots after they got in the plane. I have heard that the Japanese are liable to jazz themselves up when going into combat. In fact, not long ago some paratroopers dropped on one of our airfields, burned up a plane, and then danced around it as though they were drunk. I guess

they were.[16] You can remember that the Japanese can take very little hard
liquor. I can remember so often in Japan and Siberia how drunk they
would get on a little sake, which is really rice wine of the strength of
twelve percent. We have often thought that their suicide ground attacks in which they attack en masse across the open have been induced
to a large extent by liquor.

Clovis tells me that we killed over 900 Japanese yesterday, or perhaps it was the day before. The only place I have taken over in which
they did not call off the campaign before I took command was on Mindoro, but we have killed more Japanese here since I have taken over
than were killed on Morotai, Sansapor and Noemfoor put together.

They all tell me that the breakthrough in Belgium has been stopped
and if so I am delighted. I do not doubt that our casualties were severe
and the German communiques may be correct. Certainly any troops in
the path of that advance were badly mauled.

January 6, 1945

We are gradually rounding up the remaining Japs on Leyte.... Without doubt many of them have escaped in sailboats and canoes because,
as you can see from your maps, there are many adjacent islands out of
which they can stage. Of course the guerrillas can handle a good many
of them. I would rather have them get out than stay in the mountains
and make a nuisance of themselves. They staged a little attack on Ormoc
yesterday morning.... A few hundred armed Japs living off civilian
gardens could make a lot of trouble for months to come. Japs are still
being killed at Biak although I left there over six months ago, and there
has been more fighting going on at Morotai recently than they have ever
had before.

January 8, 1945

This theater has been the victim of overoptimism almost as much as
the European theater. They may accuse my Chief of overoptimism in
his immediate communiques, but he is not a man to underestimate the
difficulties that lie ahead. The real optimism, such as the statements
you have read in the press, "The Japanese fleet has been destroyed,"
has been given out by visiting firemen who have gone back home. If you
listen to some of the people you would think that the Japanese have
neither planes nor a navy....

With reference to the failure to announce this unit, I ask you whether
you would expect during the fighting that took place here an announcement that two armies were on this island at one time. My Big Chief is too
bright to pick the wrong time and I certainly think he was correct in
that. He has enough people out after him with a ball bat and unless he
has at least one more big victory the dogs of war will still be on his back.

No matter what anyone can say about his peculiarities, he is the Army's big hope. I would hate to have Howlin' Mad Smith of the Marines commanding an Army of American troops. I have no prejudice against the Navy. In fact, to the contrary: I admire a great many of the admirals very highly. I know what a big job they have been up against. Nevertheless, I do not want our regular Army reduced to the status of the regular Army of Australia, which is about the all-time low in military history....

There was a victory obtained here and the Japs have been eliminated. Of course some of the figures are astronomical but nevertheless that is the way our history will stand up. The things about a victory which do not appear in addition to our battle casualties, which usually are correct, are (1) sick casualties, (2) loss or wearing out of equipment, and (3) battle fatigue. You can imagine how the average man who spends two months out in the line on short rations will feel.

January 9, 1945

We figure that we have killed over 5,000 Japs since we started mopping up on the 26th, and I think our Japs are real ones. In addition, a lot of them have escaped by small boats to the north and some to Cebu. Besides this we have several thousand still with us. I hope they either die or leave me alone.

January 10, 1945

By this time you have read the press releases about Lingayen.[17] It must have been a great sight in that gulf. Before they left here it used to be a wonderful sight when I would go down in the "Miss Em" by the boats. ... The Japanese fought them quite hard on the way in but without breaking up the formation.... We have landed with little trouble and are on our way. Personally I would like to see the Big Chief get a speedy victory because God knows we need one in this world today, and the people are feeling low over the Western Front. Then I would like to see him be given command of all the army troops in the Pacific. He is lucky in addition to having a very fine strategic mind. It takes a lot of courage to do what he did, and in order to get there he has had to quietly bring pressure on a good many people.

Although I didn't land in Lingayen you can imagine the immense amount of work and responsibility that has been thrown on us in connection with the equipping, staging, resupply and so many other things that present problems which are never ending.... Fortunately I have a fine staff.

January 11, 1945

The latest news from Lingayen indicates continued advances against small resistance. It looks as though the Japanese have allowed our troops to get ashore and to get all that artillery settled. It has been my experience that the Japanese use their artillery very poorly, and we should be able to blast them out of any position they try to hold in force. There are no caves between Lingayen and Manila to hide in, and I have a feeling that they will not try to hold Manila too long. They may even go into Bataan as we did, but that will be a losing battle.

Bill's[18] big gripe is that practically no high ranking officer came to see him and therefore they could not know the conditions under which he was fighting. There are always good arguments why high ranking officers should stay back in the rear. There never has been any doubt in my mind that when he goes forward there is some tangible good accomplished.

January 12, 1945

I have been interested in the press dispatches from London. . . . They are worried over there that a major offensive is possible over here. I think they believe that the Big Chief has recently been sent a large number of troops, but this is not so. He did fall heir to certain troops when the South Pacific broke up[19] and he did use here . . . a Corps from the Central Pacific (now called Pacific Ocean Area). In certain ways we have received lots of things out here, but in other ways we are not in the same class with either Europe or the POA. We could use a lot of the major landing craft of which I saw photographs following the landing in Normandy.

Clovis is working like a beaver. For example, you wouldn't think that the question of supply of Mindoro would be any problem. But it is, and that is one of our responsibilities. You have read . . . about the enormous number of ships engaged in the Lingayen landing. While these ships were at sea, and since the landing, the Nips lost all interest in Mindoro, but there was a time when we had difficulty keeping anything afloat there.[20] We have had to improvise ways and means of getting certain types of things there which became nonexistent. For example, right now there have been very few planes in the air due to this baby typhoon. Therefore, we shall have to sneak some boats through without waiting for a real convoy.

3:30 P.M.

We are getting very little news on the Lingayen operation. . . . No one is particularly concerned in sending us anything but rather terse reports. . . . I have been intending to go up to Lingayen to see the Big Chief but I do not like to go until the fight has adopted a bit more of a pattern. I do not believe that developments have been such as to warrant any very strong views one way or the other. All that I have heard from the press reports is that we had gotten ashore without much trouble and that we have not yet met heavy opposition. My news, however, is at least thirty hours behind time.

Chink Hall is back and I think they have pretty well cleaned things out at Morotai. We feel also that we have things well under control here.... Reports indicate something like 15,000 Japanese have been wiped out since we started "mopping up." ... This is in addition to what got away. This would indicate that either the numbers here were much greater than we thought or that the numbers reported killed prior to Christmas were given a bit too large. Reports indicate that a lot of Japs got away in canoes and sailboats.

It would be to the interests of the Japs if they would all go to Luzon now, and I have a feeling that they will try to do so.[21] It would make the task of cleaning them out that much more easy. I think I could take a regiment now and clear out big islands like Panay if we were able to spare the tonnage.

January 13, 1945

My chief worries for a while will be logistical. We must get these units in fine shape for future operations wherever that may be, and we shall probably have to do it with the minimum amount of tools.

Clovis came back [from GHQ] tonight some hours after I did and he said that he felt ... we were treated better than we had ever been. Things that your palsy-walsy tried to get for his own use up there were taken away from him, and things that we asked for were given to us. *I do not feel that we are getting enough engineers for M-7 (invasion of Zambales coast) but I was pleased to get a Company of the 1st Cavalry tanks.*[22] We have, I believe, demonstrated to everybody that we can handle this new unit very nicely. The reason your palsy-walsy got away with so much was because my unit was organized so late that it was not in on any of the planning.... Before long ... I will be in on a whole lot more than you will want me to take part in....

You must have realized that every theater has its troubles. I have heard from so many people about the unhappiness in Africa. Many a throat has been cut in this war, although I do not believe there have been as many as when Eli Helmick was wielding the knife back in World War I.... I cannot give myself the pleasure of disliking your old palsy-walsy to the extent that I really brood about him. Hatred is a pure luxury and I try to avoid it as much as possible. That is especially true of a person with my temperament. For example, we were talking about that big windbag ... that did my 30th Infantry dirt down at Camp Ord in 1940. I still despise him.... I fear me much that that is going to be true in my feelings towards your palsy-walsy. For some reason I do not feel that way towards the man for whom I worked in 1935 [MacArthur]. At least not nearly to such a great extent. He is a queer genius but he has given the American people results. He has had courage and he is one of the few who still has the courage and prestige to fight for the American Army. He certainly has many funny sides which would appeal to your feminine mind.

January 13, 1945

Insofar as I can, I keep a placid frame of mind towards certain individuals.... We do not feel that there is any direct objection to me as an individual from the Big Chief. In fact, I believe that I have his high regard. He does not intend, however, that any other actor shall walk on the stage and receive any applause if he can help it. He will not change and I think he will probably get worse as he gets older.... The big thing is that the Big Chief has been getting victories, and for that reason I would be for him no matter if he had horns and a tail. As a matter of fact, although quite a peculiar individual, he has many of the qualities that make for greatness.

Your palsy-walsy is a different type. If everything is going well with him he can be very gracious, but he also has in a large degree the meaner traits of his race.... Most of his despicable actions towards me were based on his feeling that I might get his job away from him or that my army might overshadow his. Your Leavenworth friend is ... bright and efficient and meaner than hell. At the present time he has no reason to feel anything towards me except to be rather friendly insofar as it is possible for him to be so.

Make no mistake, these things are going on in other theaters. I don't think for a minute that I have had anything like the hard time that Brett had out here, or Barnes....[23] I have been interested in the press reports about the reaction against Ike in England. I hope they don't put that little beret-wearing bird [Field Marshal the Viscount Montgomery] in command of our troops.

I feel that in a large measure the reasons this [Eighth] Army has not been used in the recent offensive are: (1) it was organized very late and (2) Steve Chamberlin felt that it was much more simple for him to operate with a group that he has been working with for a long time. He felt that the other unit was much more accustomed to working with all elements and that it understood the very complicated work involved in an amphibious landing more than a new unit could. On the other hand, Steve is essentially honest and he has fought your old palsy-walsy when he has felt they were trying to put something over on my unit. I know all these people very well.

January 16, 1945

I still cannot make up my mind whether the Japanese are being stupid or rather bright at Lingayen. According to the press reports there has been little or no fighting. We kill more Japs here every day than they have killed since they landed. In fact, yesterday the Jappies launched a full-scale attack with about a battalion in one place here. It was well organized and accompanied with plenty of heavy mortar fire. We still have some work to do before we get rid of them.

The overall picture from over here is a very fine one. The Big Chief was given a fair amount of combat units but he has always lacked shipping and service units. The necessity of having so many of our supplies come from Australia caused a large proportion of our troops to be held in the rear areas. It was necessary to construct a series of bases and these were built up. Then they gradually began to fade out of the picture. For example, Milne Bay is now way back and yet I know its warehouses must be full of things and I know there are many thousands of troops still there. I do not know if this could have been helped or not. If we had unlimited shipping, of course, the Big Chief could send back and bring a lot of that stuff forward. The easiest thing is to send block-loaded ships out of San Francisco.[24] These contain a little of everything and require no handling until they arrive at the point of destination. For a long time it was necessary to unload ships in Australia, cart the stuff into warehouses and then reload ships to come north. We have had a very successful movement back to the Philippines. It has not been easy and it has been very costly for the Japs. In American lives the cost has been cheap. If the Big Chief had not had the courage to take chances this campaign for the Philippines would have ended a thousand miles before it started. Certainly not further than Hollandia.

January 17, 1945

The situation up north still remains very strange. There has been very light fighting and few casualties on either side. They do not even seem to have many Japs up there.... The troops that tried to advance towards Baguio met opposition, but little or no opposition has been met down the valley. Most people thought the Japs would fight in the valley, get licked because of our tremendous artillery power, and then our advances to Manila would be easy. It is a bit hard to make out where all that Japanese force may be now....[25]

I expect to take a run up to see the Big Chief within the next three or four days.... We are busy re-equipping and rehabilitating troops, some of which will be returned to POA, some to be used by me and some to be used by your palsy-walsy. There is an SOS base here but we have been given the responsibility to see that these things are done properly. These things we are able to do because I have a fine staff and I do not have to use a lead pencil myself.

We hope that our operations here are drawing to an end. The ones on Mindoro are not worrying me any. At one time we were short of supplies there but we were lucky enough to get a convoy through in a hurry via a short route.

January 18, 1945

Charlie [Willoughby] came up on my boat today to spend the night. He ... talked to our officers this afternoon and it was one of the most interesting things I have ever heard. He was just discussing the possibilities and locations of our little enemies and I had my whole staff assembled to hear him. Charlie has heard from your friend Sarah. She has been quite critical of your palsy-walsy since I have last heard from her.

January 19, 1945

This afternoon Steve [Chamberlin] and Admiral Fechteler arrived for a conference and we pow-wowed most of the afternoon. Steve said that your palsy-walsy wanted to get a little show away from me that I am putting on near the place where we used to live in 1920. He wanted the troops to come under him as soon as they hit the beach. He wrote to Dick [Sutherland], who referred it to Steve, and Steve told me he said "nothing doing."[26] My remark to Steve was that your old palsy-walsy wasn't able to fight [with] the troops he has now, much less to take on any more.

Fred [Irving] now has three Silver Stars and I think he feels a lot better about his being relieved.... Most of the time he only had one regiment in his advance and yet when a fresh division with three regiments in addition to part of his own division came into the line they made practically no ground in the first three weeks.

January 21, 1945

For the sake of the Army and also for the sake of Old Uncle Whiskers himself I am very anxious that my Chief remain in command after this Luzon operation clears up. To be honest, I do not relish the idea of having the Navy in command of the Army in the Pacific. If an admiral takes Tokyo with the joint overall command of the Army and Navy, it will mark the beginning of the end of the regular Army. General MacArthur is the only man I know who has the prestige and the will to fight for the Army. Certainly other prominent persons in this war are not doing it....

7:20 P.M.

This has been one of those days when everything has gone wrong and we are far from cheerful.... Tomorrow will probably look different. To be specific, we thought we were about to put on a couple of small operations. Your palsy-walsy again requested that one of them be turned over to him upon arrival on the beach in his area, and that was finally agreed to. Then the other [operation] I am going to put on I feel is about to be declared too risky. Clovis is always my Pollyanna and thinks everything is going along fine, so I am not nearly as surprised as he is. Dick was here for luncheon and Admiral Fechteler arrived about one o'clock. They were both keen about the operation but apparently Steve and his boys think it might run into trouble. Maybe it is just as well, because I intended to go in with it.[27]

January 22, 1945
8:20 A.M.
Bill [Bowen] and my other staff officers got back here at 1:00 A.M....
Apparently Bill talked them out of their fears and everything is OK
again. They found that my staff knows all the answers. They were re-
hearsed plenty before they went down.

(later)
If they do not stop me now we are going to have a lot of fun. From the
time I first saw the Big Chief up here he was interested in having me take
a few people and see what I could do in something of the nature of a fast
dash.... These things seem fantastic but with a little buildup we may
have some fun yet.... He apparently wanted me to be a Jeb Stuart. We
have built it up into a respectable force. Everyone, including the Navy
behind me. Now if they just don't call it off.[28]

January 23, 1945
Sir George [Kenney] told Clovis today that the Big Chief had served
an ultimatum on your palsy-walsy that he must be in our old home town
[Manila] by the 5th of February. If he succeeds it will be a hard pull
for me to beat him out, because I shall have a long way to go.... The
old man bawled out Sir Charles [Willoughby] for overestimating the
Japs they were to meet, and he also said to another man, "I don't see
how I have gotten as far as I have with the staff I have been surrounded
with." So you can see they all have their troubles....

I cannot possibly get into our old home town within the time limit
given your old palsy-walsy, and I doubt if the Chief would want me to
do it although on several occasions he had invited me most heartily to get
there first. We will not have the engineers or construction facilities
that would go with a completely equipped force. It should, however, be
a tremendously interesting adventure....

Part of the review yesterday up at Joe Swing's was the dropping of a
bunch of paratroopers out of Cubs. Several of them landed in the deep
water but they managed to cut themselves loose in a hurry and needed
no help. Joe has been using the Cubs a lot for dropping small groups
of paratroopers behind the Japanese and for supplying his troops up in
the jungle.

January 25, 1945
The time is approaching. This is the last letter I shall write before I
start off on a little trip with my friend [Admiral] Fechteler.... In looking for news I think you will find that when the Eighth Army does anything it is called "Our ground forces have landed," and if it is the Sixth
Army they say "elements of the Sixth Army."[29]

I shall probably go ashore, make certain decisions, and then back away for a few days and tend to other business. However, I expect we shall be quite busy for a short period of time unless your palsy-walsy by some miracle starts moving fast. I do not doubt that I am being used to stir him up.

I was down to see Sir George [Kenney] this morning. I wanted him to bring pressure on some of his boys to give me additional help. This whole show ought to be very pretty. Reports vary — one bunch of guer-rillas will give perfectly astounding figures and another bunch for the same place will indicate nothing at all.

With reference to the saying, "minor mopping up," we have now killed over 15,000 of the enemy and yet yesterday they were firing merrily at us with 75 mm guns. It is true that they never seem to be in much force in any one place and that they are getting pretty well crowded over on the west side of the island. It has been difficult for me to keep up interest of some of the units in the fight as they have been trying to relax since they were told that the fight was over. This is just plain human nature.

January 26, 1945

Another fine day — go aboard at noon tomorrow. Joe Swing will be in the boat with me. Right now I expect to stick with Fechteler until we land and until we go back, pick up reinforcements [at Mindoro]. . . . Then I shall return with Fechteler to Luzon. At that time I may stay there a while. . . . All this started out with: "Take a regiment and capture Manila if you can, Bob." Now maybe I can do it . . . [but] I believe your old palsy-walsy will get there first and with the mostest men, as Jeb Stuart[30] used to say.

January 27, 1945

The news which came in last night indicated that Fort Stotsenburg had been taken, so . . . the Jap apparently is not going to put up a serious fight for Manila unless he defends the Pampanga River at the Plaridel corridor,[31] and there is no evidence that he will do so. Therefore, the chances are that my little landing may be abortive or may even be stopped en route. . . . If the Jap doesn't put up any more fight than he has done to date, then it will be a great triumph for our Chief, whose losses have been small. Of course many will be left in those hills around Baguio and up in the Cagayan valley. To kill them off will be no small job.

I imagine the Chief will want to get busy as soon as he hits Manila and pull off some other things. His speed of strategic ideas has kept ahead of the tactical fighting. The speed of his advance down the plains in this operation has been slow, but not so slow as to bring criticism. He has had to speed your palsy-walsy, who has been cautious. . . .

The Chief wanted to be in *personal* command and apparently he has done so. From an historical standpoint it is a real triumph for him.

We have done a grand job back here and a very difficult one. Taking over when the great mass of units . . . had been designated for immediate or later movement to Lingayen, my staff has done a grand job. This has been probably the hardest job we have had out in this area from a logistical standpoint. Clovis, Bill, Tubby Burgess, G-4, and Mike Shea (Transportation Officer) have just about worked around the clock.[32] What lies ahead I do not know, but I imagine we shall have lots to do from now on until such time as a decision is made to give our Chief more jobs or to take away a large part of what he has used in getting to Manila for the use of the POA, which Nimitz commands. . . . A lot would depend on the ease with which Manila might be taken.

Notes

1. Quoted in Eichelberger, *Our Jungle Road to Tokyo* (New York, 1950), p. 182.

2. Eichelberger to Miss Em, 4 April 1945.

3. Major General Joseph M. Swing commanded the Eleventh Airborne Division. "It is evident that he takes a poor view of the enormous amount of Jap losses announced by our communiques." The unit in question was a battalion in the Ninety-sixth Division. Eichelberger Diary, 26 December 1944.

4. Admiral Chester W. Nimitz. According to Eichelberger's Diary, the M-1 (Mike I, plan for the invasion of Lingayen Gulf, on the western coast of Luzon) operation was discussed in detail. "Very interesting."

5. The last statement comes from Eichelberger's letter to Miss Em dated 27 December 1944 and is included here because of its content.

6. The Seventh, Seventy-seventh, and Ninety-sixth Infantry Divisions of the XXIV Corps participated in the Leyte campaign.

7. This is a reference to the planned subsidiary landing on Luzon to be carried out by the Eighth Army; in 1920 Eichelberger served in Manila as chief of military intelligence.

8. Maj. Gen. Ralph C. Smith was relieved of command of the Twenty-seventh Division by Maj. Gen. Holland M. Smith on 24 June 1944 for failure to advance.

9. The passage in italics comes from the Eichelberger Diary, 29 December 1944, and is included here because of its content.

10. Maj. Gen. Chamberlin, G-3 at GHQ.

11. The passage regarding Gen. Chamberlin's views is taken from Eichelberger's letter to Miss Em, 31 December 1944.

12. Brig. Gen. William C. Dunckel, commanding the Western Visayan Task Force on Mindoro.

13. The passage in italics was taken from Eichelberger's Diary, 2 January 1945.

14. In the Battle of the Bulge.

15. On 3 January, elements of the Twenty-first Infantry seized Marinduque Island.

16. This probably refers to the Japanese parachutists' attack against the Berauen Airfields, on the fringe of Leyte Valley, the night of 6–7 December. Although they caused momentary confusion and destroyed "minor fuel and supply dumps," the Japanese failed to achieve "any major objective." H. Hamlin Cannon, *Leyte: The Return to the Philippines* (Washington, 1954), p. 305.

17. On 9 January, beginning at 9:30 A.M., the XIV and Eichelberger's old I Corps landed on the shores of Lingayen Gulf, on the western side of Luzon.

18. Probably Maj. Gen. Gill, who attended a staff conference with Eichelberger the morning of 11 January. Eichelberger, Diary, 11 January 1945.

19. On 25 March 1944, the Joint Chiefs of Staff broke up the South Pacific forces and transferred the army troops, namely the Twenty-fifth, Thirty-seventh, Fortieth, Ninety-third, and Americal Divisions, together with XIV Corps Headquarters and corps troops, to MacArthur's command. Mary H. Williams, *Chronology 1941-45*, (Washington, 1960) p. 183.

20. On 3 January, Gen. Eichelberger noted in his Diary that "one Liberty only ship left in harbor undamaged. Rest either sunk or on beach."

21. The day before Gen. Eichelberger had assumed command on Leyte, Gen. Tomoyuki Yamashita, commanding the Fourteenth Area Army in the Philippines, had ordered Lt. Gen. Sosaku Suzuki, Thirty-fifth Army commander, to evacuate his forces from Leyte. During the next two months, about 1,000 Japanese made their way in small craft to Cebu. Suzuki planned to make his stand in Mindanao, where he might hope to draw off U.S. reinforcements destined for Luzon. Robert Ross Smith, *Triumph in the Philippines* (Washington, 1963), pp. 89, 586–587.

22. Passage in italics quoted from Eichelberger's Diary, 13 January 1945.

23. Both Maj. Gens. George H. Brett and Julian F. Barnes had commanded the United States Army forces in Australia in the early days of the war.

24. Block shipment: "Shipment of supplies to overseas theaters of operations, to provide balanced stocks for an average balanced force for a certain specified number of days." Frank Gaynor, ed., *The New Military and Naval Dictionary* (New York, 1951).

25. Yamashita did not oppose the landings at Lingayen Gulf because of the terrain. "Having decided to abandon the Central Plains — Manila Bay region, Yamashita concentrated his forces in three mountainous strongholds that ... the Allies could overrun only at the cost of many lives and much time." Smith, *Triumph in the Philippines*, p. 94.

26. "A conference was held about 2:30 to discuss fake landings in southern Luzon, also M-6 (Plan for invasion of Batangas and Tayabas Bays) and some phases of M-7 (invasion of Zambales coast).... I recommended to Chamberlin that the Navy be required to pull off the simulated landing at Tayabas Bay at any point they thought they could get through the minefields, providing the Big Chief still wanted to keep the Jap troops in the south.... It was decided the Navy should pull off the simulated landings the night before our landings at M-6. Chamberlin, Fechteler, and I agreed on Nasugbu and then the other behind it. I took a dim view of the ten day turn-around that the Admiral said was necessary, and recommended everything possible to be staged out of Mindoro using LCI's as much as possible.... Chamberlin told me that Walter Krueger has written to Sutherland recommending that M-7 come under him as soon as it lands.... It is evident that W. K. is trying to hog things as usual." Eichelberger Diary, 19 January 1945.

27. "Gen. Sutherland left at 1430 after advising me that I would lose command of M-7 as soon as the command echelon reached the beach.... Advised by GHQ in late afternoon that additional shipping would not be available for M-6." Eichelberger Diary, 21 January 1945.

28. "Learned at 0100 that we will retain command of M-7 until first phase line is reached and that the original plan for M-6 will be carried out. The 19th Infantry will be made available as a reserve and the 41st Div. will be available as a reinforcing unit on M-6 if it is found to be profitable." Eichelberger Diary, 22 January 1945.

29. This statement actually comes from Gen. Eichelberger's letter to Miss Em dated 24 January 1945.

30. This saying is usually attributed to Gen. Nathan Bedford Forrest.

31. This report was premature. Although there was fighting in the Fort Stotsenburg area, which lay in the western section of Clark Field, Fort Stotsenburg was not actually secured until 31 January. Walter Krueger, *From Down Under to Nippon*, (Washington, 1953), p. 241.

32. Col. H. C. Burgess, Eighth Army G-4, and Col. Mike Shea.

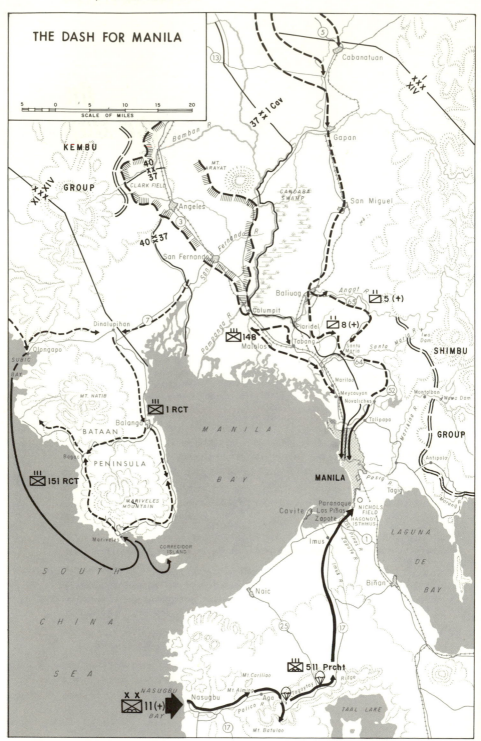

THE DASH FOR MANILA

SCALE OF MILES

MAP 4

CHAPTER ELEVEN

On the Map

By the last week in January the Sixth Army had secured its communications and had begun its final push toward Manila. The tempo, however, was too slow and deliberate to suit MacArthur, who then sought to divert the Japanese — and possibly to spur on General Krueger — by landing the Eleventh Airborne Division from the Eighth Army at Nasugbu, fifty-five miles south of Manila.

Whether MacArthur intended this to remain a reconnaissance in force, as the orders indicated, or hoped that Eichelberger on his own initiative would enter the race for Manila must remain a matter of conjecture. Some of his directives were verbal, and it is difficult to know what he had in mind. He may well have utilized the rivalry between his two army commanders to produce quick military results, for the device was as old as Napoleon and would be used again in a few months when Stalin invited Marshals Konev and Zhukov to compete in the drive for Berlin. One of Eichelberger's staff officers did confide to Miss Em a few weeks later that according to a MacArthur aide, "Sarah thoroughly appreciates Walter's green eyes and took advantage of them in the Manila operation."[1]

What is certain is that nobody in the Eighth Army was about to let this opportunity slip through their fingers. They had waited too long to ignore this opportunity once and for all to place the Eighth Army on the map — particularly when the map was Luzon.

At Sea
In the Philippines
January 28, 1945

Dearest Emmalina

Before we left the news reports all indicated that Clark Field had been occupied so I am not at all sure that the Japs are going to put up any fight for Manila.

My plans are a bit uncertain and are governed to an unusually large extent by the enemy. If he is quite thick and our movements are slow it will be necessary for me in my position to draw back after the landing to the nearest place where I can be in touch with my units. If the Japs are in very little force and we can move very rapidly, I may stay in a while. I am prepared to draw back or stay depending on conditions.

Right now my unit has two of these things on the water and the other one is bigger than this one. As small as this is, though, I understand there are over a hundred ships in the convoy. It is really a beautiful sight and the Navy certainly know their stuff. They run these shows in grand style.

We are getting grand treatment and I am really enjoying the change.

January 29, 1945

This is the morning that the Eighth Army sends a landing party ashore north of Subic Bay.... Command of that unit [XI Corps] however will pass to Walter after a couple of days.

The question of whether or not I stay ashore or go back to ... [Mindoro] will depend on conditions as I meet them. If the resistance is very light or non-existent, I think I shall stay ashore until I have discovered whether or not the Japs have pulled out of the section where we land.... I might try a fast drive to Manila.

Your palsy-walsy apparently is somewhere around Clark Field but that has been reported in the press for several days. We still do not know whether the Japanese are going to put up any resistance to the capture of Manila. In spite of guerrilla reports, air reports, etc., none of us are able to determine for example whether on landing day after tomorrow we will meet heavy resistance or no resistance. The guerrillas are liable to exaggerate greatly, and the Air Corps can seldom give reliable information about the ground troops. They can tell you that they saw no one but they cannot tell you definitely that there is no one there. They do secure wonderful photographs.

The Big Chief seems to be having a good time. Up to the time I left, Sir George had not been up there and your old Leavenworth friend was getting his teeth fixed. With a small staff the Big Chief can keep himself informed and use a big club to spur some on to greater speed.... Of course in the end everything will be sweet and lovely and your palsy-walsy will have gained a great victory. These annoyances always come up but I am very anxious that the Chief capture Manila promptly and with little loss. Then he can present his record in comparison with others.

7:00 P.M.

Almost dark.... Have been selling Joe [Swing] the idea of a rapid advance — will back him up if he gets his pants shot off.

All reports from the Subic Bay area tell of a rapid advance so I hope the Big Chief will be pleased with the 8th Army. We planned it and put it ashore. I warned Chink [Hall] to go fast and reports say he had made about 12 miles without opposition before noon of the first day.

January 30, 1945

Tomorrow morning about this time we land ourselves. This morning I had to laugh at the usual announcement over the loudspeaker.... "Sick call — all the sick, lame and lazy report to the Sickbay."

I am feeling fine and ... the boat ride has been a nice rest. We have been lucky in getting through some very narrow waters without any attacks. At times we could see land on both sides.

The weather is fine and we now have the pleasure of seeing many good old American planes flying overhead.... There are four planes right now flying over my head and circling around.... We are not expecting any air attacks but of course one never can tell with people as unpredictable as the Japs. They are just liable to pass up a good target and attack a rowboat.[2]

Joe Swing is grand to deal with. He and Fechteler both seem very glad to have me around, which makes me laugh when I think how last April Barbey went to Brisbane to keep your old palsy-walsy from riding with him....

This afternoon I talked to Joe Swing for about an hour-and-a-half.... He spent quite a long time in Africa and in the Sicily landing on a very peculiar mission.... He saw a great deal of the interplay of personalities and from what I judge we get it rather lightly out here....

I still do not know whether I shall stay ashore if I go in tomorrow. Fechteler will not leave until dark, so I can come back to approximately my present location by staying on this boat tomorrow night.

Billie [Bowen] and I are standing here now talking about what we may run into tomorrow. This is always a big gamble. One always gets surprises. For example, the PT boys at breakfast told me they were cruising in a bay where they had never drawn any fire for a long time, and then yesterday they got an awful blast from about twelve places. Fortunately, that is not ... where we are going to land.

As one travels along like this, I realize how unimportant little things can be. Things that seem important to some people, such as publicity and reputation, mean nothing at a time like this. All we will care about for a while are victories, food, health and the eventual return to our homes.[3]

January 31, 1945
8:30 A.M.

Landings going according to schedule — no opposition as far as I can tell from out here.

Do not know yet whether I shall stay ashore ... or not, but think I shall do so.

Lots of rocket bursts from our rocket ships — air strafing, bombardment, etc. Afraid they have knocked down the building I want to have. Can see Corregidor with the naked eye although it is some distance away.

9:30 A.M.

Everything is going forward very nicely so far. There is no opposition and I know Joe [Swing] will make fast time. I must make the decision after I hear from him whether to put any more troops ashore. The first landing is called a "reconnaissance in force."

I had to laugh a while ago, standing on the bridge with Fechteler, when a message came from a big boat which has just arrived outside of the harbor[4] to furnish additional protection. This admiral sent this message: "Like the June bride, I am ready and willing."

I have enjoyed it on this boat and I shall hate to leave it. We shall do our darnedest, but I realize that this is really task force "Shoestring." At any rate, I cannot go much slower than your old palsy-walsy....

The picture right now is of course very favorable. Lots of friendly planes overhead and lots of power in the harbor. After they all go back, however, there won't be so much, but I like Joe's outfit. They look like they'll fight plenty....

I am very fond of Fechteler, who is a very good egg. I find that Fechteler generally dislikes the people I dislike and likes the people I like.

7:00 P.M.

What a day. About 10 A.M. a flying boat landed near us containing a bunch of newspaper correspondents. After I talked to them for some time in a very hesitant way, one of them showed me today's release from GHQ, which states in part: "LUZON — In an amphibious operation the 38th Division and elements of the 24th Division of the XI Corps *of the 8th Army* have landed on the Zambales coast [italics added].... The surprise of the enemy was complete both strategically and tactically and the landing was accomplished without loss of man, ship or plane." They told me that [news of] the Eighth Army had been definitely released, so I told them how much I appreciated what the Navy had done and how fine I thought Swing's 11th Airborne was going to be.

Right after lunch I went ashore where about 25 officers and men of the Eighth Army staff have established an office in the schoolhouse on the plaza at Nasugbu.... I do not intend to take command. I am just around speeding things up a bit.

Due to the shallow beach, our biggest amphibious craft could not get ashore and were stopped about a hundred yards out in the water at a depth of about four feet. A lot of the stuff was unloaded into smaller boats to lighten these LST's and another attempt will be made at midnight ... to bring them in closer to the beach. We shall unload them in the moonlight and in the meantime Joe will be pressing his troops on the Japanese. In view of the fact that we cannot get our LST's unloaded before morning I have decided to stay on the boat tonight....

We have some wounded and sick in the hospital, but not many.... I talked to all the wounded men and took their names so I could write to their parents.

Sometime before morning, Joe may run into more Japs. He had already gone about seven miles and [was] moving rapidly at 5 P.M. We were very fortunate in capturing a bunch of bridges on Highway 17 before the Japs had a chance to blow them up. I saw a number of big packages of explosives which they never set off.

It is almost dark and apparently some of the Nips are getting fresh because I can see on the north end of the beach that one of our gunboats is pouring in a stream of rockets and the tracers are going across almost on a level.

February 1, 1945
5:30 A.M.

I have had a good night's sleep — when I wakened just now I looked out of the porthole in the bright moonlight and I was looking at the Southern Cross. We were steaming at high speed due east. Guess the admiral just cruised all night to avoid the moonlight in that bay.

I have been thinking how faulty the guerrilla reports were — we were expecting to find a lot of Japs and deserted towns from which the Japs had evacuated everyone. On the contrary, there were few Japs and the towns crowded with hungry civilians who will try to beg all our food and feed drinks to any soldiers who will take them.

February 2, 1945

One of my letters tonight was from Bonner Fellers.... He said that the Commander-in-Chief is very impatient and that Bonner hopes that I will get to Manila first.... The Big Chief has given me the go-go sign.

When I came ashore yesterday I went to the front immediately as far as I could get and not have a shell fall on my head. In fact, Bill was scared to death for me. I then went to Nasugbu and spent the night.... There was an awful lot of firing outside of the harbor which turned out to be some kind of Naval action. We thought at first that we were being shot at.

This morning...I went forward where the "Shoestring" task force has been attacking a very powerful Japanese position located on a narrow front between two mountains directly across the road. Thanks to plenty of air support and good artillery work, we were able to push them out this morning. I managed to get in there just as they pulled out of their command post.

I then came back to Joe Swing's Command Post where I am going to spend the night. It is on the Palico River about six miles out of Nasugbu. The furthest point I went beyond here this afternoon, however, was eleven miles, and when I turned around I was with the leading company.

Ventura drove me this afternoon and you can imagine how excited he was. I am fixed up here very nicely in a barracks which was built some years ago for the Philippine Army. If I spend...tomorrow night in Tagaytay I shall be looking into Manila, about thirty miles away, with a downhill pull on a concrete road. If I get to Tagaytay tomorrow, I am going to start for Manila the following morning. We have some self-propelled mounts which are like tanks. We obtained these from the 24th Division, but otherwise the men are mostly on foot. They had to walk up that terrific incline. Tagaytay is as high as Asheville.

As you can see, I am making a rapid dash with a very small force. We are taking big risks.

I feel that the Eighth Army is now definitely on the map.... On the other hand, you must realize that when the Eighth Army gets into combat I am going with them, and we will probably have lots of it in the future. I am not a good dugout soldier.... I never go out, though, that I do not find out things that make me glad that I have gone.

I am very keen about this 11th Airborne. They are small in number but they are willing to fight.

February 3, 1945

This has been another interesting day. At breakfast this morning I was informed that we only had one day's supply of 80 octane gasoline. This was partly due to the fact that we have had a terrific uphill pull for the motors since Tagaytay is 2000 feet above the ocean, and there is a steady rise all the way. Then some of the gasoline never got unloaded from one of our boats, which was stuck in the shallow water on the beach.

Last night they worked on what had been just about a Cub airstrip and enlarged it to 4000 feet during the night. I sent a special plea to my Air Corps friends and today they flew in a bunch of C-47's to bring in gasoline and take out the wounded. After I inspected the airfield . . . I went over to the hospital and talked to all the wounded. . . . Then I went forward. From then on it was a steady go all day. We were stopped early by the enemy at a very crooked and narrow defile. While we were waiting there I walked up on a commanding elevation and found that I was looking right down into Manila.

The guerrilla reports make me laugh. The report tonight is that Manila is being burned by the Japanese, and yet I can look right down into the town and see lights and one little fire. . . . Yesterday they told me there was a town ahead of us containing 30,000 Japs, and yet we took it before noontime today. . . .

I must admit that we have been very fortunate so far. . . . Small as our losses have been from a percentage standpoint, since I think we have only lost about a hundred wounded and killed so far, I still regret very deeply that there have been that many. . . .

A telegram from Clovis today asks permission for him to come up to see me for a conference. . . . Think Clovis just wants a bit of fun.

February 4, 1945

The battalion of artillery of the 511th Parachute Infantry just dropped out in front of here. The Infantry dropped yesterday.[5] The Big Chief was in a B-17 looking down on us, because the boys could hear him talking.

I have not been able to find out where our supporting troops are, although I have sent numerous messages to GHQ. I do not seem to be able to get an answer. When I get to see the Big Chief I am going to enter a protest. I am sitting here with my little force without any knowledge where your palsy-walsy is and what help I can expect from them when I hit the outskirts of Manila. My patrols in the night went forward 18 miles and we have armed a lot of the guerrillas to help us. It is my understanding that there are guerrillas on the hills for at least 20 miles north of here. . . . I have received no replies to any of my telegrams to GHQ including requests for a regiment of Infantry which I have been holding ready down at Mindoro. . . .

With it all I have been having a lot of fun. I am feeling in grand health and am raring to go. . . . Don't think that I am complaining. It just occurs to me though that if conditions are serious enough to warrant this little group being here, somebody should ride herd and insist that I get the proper information, and at least answers to my radiograms.

6:00 P.M.

This has been a hectic day. Early this morning I started forward and we kept running into Japanese pockets which were protected by buildings and this slowed us up. However, by two o'clock this afternoon I was in Las Pinas near Paranaque, which I believe is about seven or eight miles from the Manila Hotel. Our troops were moving forward from the rear rather slowly, so I came back here to Tagaytay to speed them up. I am going forward again tonight.

I do not know where your palsy-walsy is. He sent me a message today that a patrol of the 1st Cavalry Division had reached Grace Park ... in the northern part of Manila ... about six o'clock last night. ... We have also received a report today that the 1st Cavalry Division and the 37th Infantry were running a race for Manila and were about thirteen miles out.

I shall sleep in a jeep tonight if I sleep anyplace. ... While I kick like the dickens, I am still having a good time. I am in a terrible rush at the moment. ...

February 5, 1945

My note yesterday was a very hurried one but I did not want to break my record of getting a letter off to you each day. In order to keep you better informed, though, I will start from yesterday morning.

Early yesterday morning the troops started shuttling and trucking forward on Route 17 (concrete) so about nine o'clock I started forward myself. As we passed through the villages the guerrillas were out with flags and all the civilians were cheering us. Many gave us eggs and fruit. We did all right until we reached the town of Imus, where a bunch of Japs were in an old Spanish stone barracks which was surrounded by a stone wall. They had blown up the Highway 17 bridge so that our troops had to pass right by this barracks. Things were bogged down a bit so we jazzed it up, particularly after Joe Swing landed in a Cub on the concrete road. We finally broke away from there, however, by the use of our tanks [self-propelled mounts] and proceeded on down the road. The Japanese were not expecting us to be there and a truck ran out from a side road onto the main road. It was an old American GMC truck and had about fifteen Japs in it, all of whom were killed. The Filipinos very quickly took their clothes.

By two o'clock in the afternoon I was in Las Pinas, which ... is almost in Manila. ... Things seemed to be going a bit slow ... so I drove all the way back to Tagaytay Ridge, a distance of about thirty miles, to speed things up. ... At a quarter of seven, just as it was getting dark, we started down the road again towards Manila. ... We finally reached Paranaque, which is right near Nichols Field. ... The fires in Manila were bright enough so that we did not need a flashlight. After I went to bed we started pounding the Japanese with artillery and they began to reply. It sounded as though these shells were coming in one window and out the other. The Japs are still firing at us here today.

Just before luncheon [today] I was sitting out on that stone fence looking at the big buildings in Manila through my field glasses. A shell landed
out in the water about twenty yards from me. All it did was make a big
splash. A little before that we drove down the street towards Nichols
Field. Some fire broke out and we got out of our jeep and hid in an alley.
Then we got back in the jeep and a bofor — a 40 mm Swedish type rapid
fire gun — hit just where the jeep had been standing. It was not a direct shot because I am not that foolish. It had ricocheted off the steeple
of an old church down the street.

Clovis[6] has advised me that we are going to be very busy from now
on, although I can promise you that I shall not personally attempt these
things as I have done in this case. The Big Chief put this up to me as
a personal job, but [Col.] Joe McMicking, who is with me here, says
that nobody at GHQ except Sir Charles [Willoughby] thought I had
a chance to get any place with this small force. Joe is bogey-eyed himself.

Just as I was leaving last night to drive down here I heard that a
news release had said that the Eighth Army was knocking at the southern
approaches to the city of Manila. . . . We all hope and think that the Eighth
Army is now definitely on the map. That is what I tried to do and that
is why I am stuck out here like a sore thumb with shells breaking around
the house instead of being back on Tagaytay Ridge reading dispatches.

Right now we are being held up by some tanks and a bunch of guns
down at the Polo Club, but we are putting an air strike on them in a
few minutes. We will also pound them with lots of artillery.

Some of the things I am telling you . . . about the shelling, etc., I
would not tell you except that it will all be over before this letter reaches
you. In future operations, however, . . . I will send the other boys out to
do the work while I will take all the credit. Bill is in the next room
laughing at me. In fact I think he has been very disrespectful, but I gave
him a good working over yesterday afternoon to put him in his place.

7:00 P.M.

Clovis, Joe McMicking, Clyde and I are sitting here watching one of
those famous Manila sunsets while off in the distance to my right it looks
as though the whole city is in flames. . . . We can see and hear the various
explosions. . . . Two battalions from Fred's old outfit [Twenty-fourth
Infantry Division] arrived this morning, so we will be a little better off.
I have not heard any shelling for some time but I imagine Joe will move
up in the dark.

It seems like a dream. . . . I had long ago given up the idea that I
would have any part in the battle for Manila.

February 6, 1945

The view of Manila last night was a terrible thing as the whole part of one side of the city seemed to be on fire. Smoke and flames were going way up in the air.... Dombrowski... spent the night at the airstrip and said even there, fifty miles away, he could see the flames of Manila. What a shame it is. This is particularly true since the Filipinos are going to have their independence and it is really the destruction of a neutral city.... It was something which I shall never forget....

The steady refusal of the Sixth Army to send me any information of our friendly troops indicates to me that they are not really in town.... If your palsy-walsy were in town I am sure he would be glad to tell me, so maybe he is still further away than I am.

One of those big six-inch guns that has been firing around here all day landed in the Command Post of one of Joe's regiments. I understand there were a lot of casualties.... We are not getting off unscathed in this fight, although I do not believe our losses have been heavy from a percentage standpoint.

February 7, 1945

Bill finally got a message from Eddie Eddleman[7] that at noon on the 5th we were holding the banks of the Pasig River from near its mouth to Malacañan Palace. He said all the bridges were out and I do not believe they have been able to get across yet.... [8]

I have been out here three nights.... Our troops are fighting for final possession of Nichols Field and they are pretty well along. I have not yet heard the morning report, but we ran into a world of power, particularly ack-ack guns.... We could take Nichols Field more quickly but there are restrictions about bombing Manila and our artillery is mostly pop-guns. We have no tanks.

This house is certainly in a bad place because our artillery is firing over it and the enemy, in trying to locate our artillery, is shooting in the direction of our house. We would not have stopped here originally if we had thought we would be here any length of time. As a matter of fact, Joe Swing, in the dark on the night of the 4th, crossed one too many rivers and found himself right in the middle of the enemy. The advanced element had forgotten to leave MP's behind....

This is a fine fighting outfit and I am proud to be with them. Being a cagey old bird, I am doubtful of any reception I would receive, so I am going to get out of here as soon as I find out that your palsy-walsy's multitudinous troops have been able to get south of the Pasig River.

This afternoon the black smoke from north of the river has been drifting across the front of the town so that we have not been able to see it nearly as well.... In view of the fact that the fires have been springing up... north of the river, I am inclined to believe that your palsy-walsy is not yet in full possession of the city north of the Pasig River. He is probably running into house-to-house sniping as we are. We have had a tremendous number of concrete and stone pillboxes to knock out and we are about through the western defenses of Nichols Field. As somebody put it, our line is a thousand yards wide and seventy miles long.

February 8, 1945

I have them all stirred up and moving now. I heard today that a crossing of the Pasig River[9] has been made at one place in the city and it is possible that the Big Chief will be able to enter the city proper within the next three or four days. I have never wanted to end up in the city . . . before he arrives, for reasons which you will understand. So this morning, acting on a hunch, I sent most of my little staff to Nasugbu from where they expected to fly back to Leyte tomorrow. . . .

This afternoon . . . I received a telegram from the Big Chief saying that before long he wants to put all troops on Luzon under the Sixth Army and he is particularly anxious for me to clean out a certain area of great importance which is not on Luzon. . . . I think our coming here has definitely put the Eighth Army on the map. . . .

I think it is high time for me to be getting out. . . . I do not want you to believe that I am going to risk myself any more like I did during the last week. This was a special raid that required special action. I found out from a photographer who was with us, a captain from GHQ, that they did not order any photographers on this expedition saying that it was a suicide mission, but they did allow volunteers. Of course that was only the reaction of the Signal Section, but it shows how people felt towards this operation. . . .

Joe Swing is going to be very sorry to come under any other unit. I am going to recommend the 11th Airborne Division for a Presidential Citation.

February 9, 1945

After breakfast we packed and shortly we were off down the road to Nasugbu. This ride was without incident although . . . there are still a lot of Japanese in that country. The ride (in the C-47) down from Nasugbu to Mindoro was very rough. When we reached Mindoro there was a great gathering. . . . There were Woody, Jens Doe, Whitehead of the Fifth Air Force, . . . Eddie Edwards, who had been up to Lingayen and Subic Bay, . . . and many others. We had a grand luncheon and some conferences. . . . They were all very enthusiastic over our dash into Manila.

Eddie said that the only people who were not delighted . . . were those of the Sixth Army. He said that your palsy-walsy went up to the Big Chief and tried to get him to put the 11th Airborne under him as soon as we reached South Manila but the Big Chief turned him down cold.[10]

This was about the time we hit the outskirts of Manila. Eddie said he rode up and down over the Central Plains of Luzon in a cub and that everybody moved very slowly....The Sixth Army acted like they had nothing but time on their hands until suddenly we landed and even then they didn't take much notice because it was called a "reconnaissance in force." They came to life, however, when they found me chasing into Manila on the 4th day.[11]

The January 29th issue of one of the magazines shows old "Molasses in January" [Krueger]. If he is a great general or has any of the elements of greatness then I am no judge of my fellow man. Beyond a certain meanness, which scares those under him, and a willingness to work, he has little to offer. He doesn't even radiate courage, which is one thing we like to think a soldier has. Even up to the end, according to Eddie, he was way up near Lingayen Gulf with the Big Chief much farther forward.[12] I see where he has put across sixteen operations. The first three were dry runs — no Japs — in one of which the Australians at Goodenough were already in full possession. After that, until Leyte and Luzon, both of which the Big Chief handled under his personal command, he was usually from a hundred to five hundred miles away. This does not include several times when he went along as he did at Hollandia, stepped on the beach and then back on the boat. Personally I think that barring the force the Big Chief put behind him, he would have made a miserable failure of Leyte and perhaps Luzon. Down those long highways in Luzon with no opposition on the left he just crept along. In one twenty-four-hour period he had no casualties in the XIV Corps, and in another period two were wounded. In that time he proceeded very slowly. I know the Big Chief was disgusted and so was everyone else up there except perhaps his own staff.

I do not tell you these things to make you bitter, but they are all true. ...Of course history will show the battle of Luzon as a great victory. That is the way all histories are written, but people on the inside know the truth.

Whitehead...told me that the Big Chief is to be the number one Army man in the Pacific and that he has been so notified. If this is true I shall be delighted. He will have three armies[13] to play around with.

February 10, 1945
Brigadier Anderson, who is on my staff here, told me a funny story about Montgomery that made me laugh. He said that the King, on a visit, insisted that Eisenhower tell him how he liked Montgomery, and Ike finally said, "Your Majesty, he is one of your greatest generals, but since you insist, I must say I feel he is trying to get my job away from me." The King then said, "I am glad to hear that, because I had thought he was trying to get *my* job."

Late this afternoon we received quite a surprise when we were invited by General MacArthur to attend the formal entry into the City.... I hope they do not have the ceremony until all those Japanese stop shooting from behind those stone walls. If you could have seen me taking cover some of those times down in South Manila you would certainly have been proud of me.[14]

February 11, 1945

Sir George [Kenney] thinks I should have dropped the 511th on Nichols Field, but in view of those concrete emplacements I believe they would have been murdered. I do not think I could have gotten a corporal's guard out alive. No one will take a bigger risk than I will if I feel I have a reasonable chance, but I do not believe that would have been a fair show. I would not have minded dropping them in the vicinity of Imus, which is almost down to Manila, because there were practically no Japanese there. My force was so ridiculously small because I only landed with four battalions and one of these ... had to hold the base, which left me with three battalions; and one had to hold Tagaytay Ridge, which was a very commanding terrain feature, so I would only have had two battalions to march towards Manila if I had not dropped the three battalions from the air on Tagaytay Ridge. There were only seven battalions in the whole division. Personally I think we pulled one of the most daring feats of the war.

February 12, 1945

I started out with an early conference of my own staff, telling them of our drive up to Manila from Nasugbu. It seems as fantastic as a fairy tale.

I had intended to land at Subic Bay, but when they told me it would come under your palsy-walsy ... I backed out. This was particularly necessary since I had to be at Nasugbu to make two decisions: (1) To decide whether or not to change the "reconnaissance in force" into a real landing, and (2) if it was desirable to drop the 511th Parachute Regiment on Tagaytay Ridge....

I see there is a great deal of discussion in the press whether or not the Big Chief is going to be the number one Army man in the Pacific. I have a feeling that he has been so notified, and if so I believe he will use his three armies to leapfrog. Sometime of course Buck [Lt. Gen. Simon B. Buckner, Jr.] will get his little boys back[15] and he will be ready for an operation of his own. He belongs to a very rich family where they have been accustomed to everything. They do not know what it is to be poor like our soldiers in this theater; therefore they cry when they have to eat a few Aussie rations that we have had to live on for years. I let [Gen.] Johnnie Hodge know what I thought about his crybaby attitude. This of course I was able to do since he is still under my command....

It is my big hope that out of this conference that is going on in the

Black Sea area[16] that Honest Joe will agree to throw his Siberian troops into this fight. We have been fighting for some time the Japanese Divisions which have been withdrawn from Siberia, and these are their best troops. They have always used their worst troops against the Chinese. I hope that when Germany quits, and that must come soon, that Japan will be ready to do so also providing that Russian troops have crossed the Amur River and pushed down into Manchuria. Then we can all go home for good.

February 14, 1945

I went down by boat early this morning to inspect the 7th Division.... I made a talk... telling them that the boys from the POA were our rich cousins. We are unloading boats which contain new equipment, from trucks and guns to clothes throughout. I told them we would be awful glad to get their castoff things.... We have had patches on our clothes ever since we came out to this theater. Of course if the Big Chief gets command of all the Army troops in the Pacific he may change some of that.

Last night late Steve Chamberlin called to tell me that the parade into Manila had been put off indefinitely.... I do not believe anybody expected the Japs to make a house-to-house defense of Manila, so instead of coming in by way of Fort McKinley and wiping out resistance there, our troops in the north infiltrated down to the Pasig River and then it was announced that Manila had been captured. About that time the strength of the Japanese began to develop. They are raising hell up there.

Clovis and I have just returned from a grand dinner with Sir George. He ... said he has been hammering the Big Chief to get me in the big picture. When he was up at Tarlac at GHQ and the Big Chief was complaining about the delay he told him, "You will never be able to get any speed until you put Eichelberger in command." The Big Chief replied, "I would hate to have to retire an old man like that and send him home."

George is definitely batting on our team. According to George your old Leavenworth friend has had his trials and tribulations, not only because of his social friends, but also in the way he has dealt with people in Washington when he has been there. George says that Dick has wanted to command an army — he has lost a bit of caste now.

February 15, 1945

There was a letter from Joe Swing... written yesterday which I know you will appreciate. Joe said among other things:

> "Shorty says that if they have good communication back where you are, to radio Nimitz and tell him the 11th Airborne has found the Japanese Navy everyone is wondering about — it's on Nichols Field!"

... He said also that he was attacking Fort McKinley today. I am glad to see that because I thought they should have done that even earlier. There was also a successful landing today on the south edge of Mariveles Peninsula across from Corregidor. While the fight for Manila has been a pain in the neck and a time consumer, I do not believe there is going to be any big battle for Bataan, and that will allow the harbor to open up. The big thing is to get a fine harbor like Manila Bay where our boats will be protected.

February 16, 1945

In thinking over the fact that the war with Germany will soon come to an end, I wondered this morning whether or not they would try to run in some [American] leaders from France. I do not believe now they will attempt that. I am not thinking of the Big Chief himself, but the Army commanders here. It is true that Buck has never been in combat nor has his staff. One of my division commanders who really belongs to Buck brought that fact out as a matter of regret. But the Sixth and Eighth Armies have been in combat against the Japanese and therefore I believe the Big Chief would fight against any attempt to bring the European crowd over here even if they should desire to do so. My personal hope is that the Japanese will quit if and when Stalin begins to push down along the Manchurian railway. They will realize they cannot hope to stand up against that pressure. Certainly the question of Stalin participating in this war must be a matter of thought with "the powers that be." If we ever get Russia on our side out here the Japanese will be in a horrible position and therefore I think they will quit before having their towns bombed out.[17]

Today a lot of the staff took my two planes and went up to see certain events about which you will read in the papers.[18] I hope they have a good time. ... The work involved in many of these moves is tremendous. ... It involves endless conferences, particularly between the pick and shovel boys of the Navy, Air and Army.

We had planned to land the 41st Division behind Joe if conditions warranted it, and we actually did land two battalions of one of the regiments in Fred's old outfit to guard the base and line of communications to Tagaytay. We found, however, that the 41st was not needed and that it was almost impossible to land combat craft on the beach at Nasugbu. Too shallow — what we call wet landings because we had to walk ashore through the surf.

The last few days before I went aboard the boat were very hectic ones for me. I had to go in there with only one division and yet it had been put up to me in such a way that it demanded my personal leadership. I knew too that if I did not go in there they would immediately put that outfit under the Sixth Army and we would get no credit for it. It all really worked out fine and I enjoyed the open road. As you know, I thrive on these things.

Our real written orders ... were to establish ourselves on Tagaytay Ridge and stabilize conditions in that part of Luzon. My only directives about going to Manila were oral ones, and more of a nature of permission to go rather than a directive.[19]

February 18, 1945

This morning I saw the announcement of the capture of Bataan.[20] It had been my impression that there were some strong Jap forces there yet. However, we shall see. ... I am impressed again with the fact that the "On to Tokyo" release was a bid for further high command beyond the Philippines.

With reference to the fight for Manila I must say that I never heard anybody predict that any such fight would ever take place. We knew that a lot of defenses had been erected, but it was generally expected that the Japanese would declare Manila an open city or would evacuate.[21]

We do feel that our position in many ways is better than it ever has been out in this theater. The pick and shovel boys at GHQ are very friendly, but I do not believe the tigers will ever change their spots much. It is too soon for me to worry about what will happen to my army because we have some hard jobs ahead of us in the more or less immediate future.

Notes

1. Robert M. White to Mrs. Eichelberger, 21 June 1945.

2. Concern over the possibility of a Japanese kamikaze attack against his own ship was probably increased by the recent Japanese attack against the light cruiser *Nashville* during the Mindoro landings. The crash of one kamikaze killed over 130 on Admiral Struble's flagship, including several high-ranking military and naval officers. Gen. Dunckel lost his chief of staff and was himself wounded. Robert Ross Smith, *Triumph in the Philippines* (Washington, 1963), p. 46.

3. In order to avoid redundancies, this letter is actually recast from two separate letters to Miss Em dated 30 January 1945.

4. Many of the fire support ships in the Nasugbu landings had initially supported the landing of XI Corps on the west coast of Luzon two days earlier. This would account for the late arrival of the "big boat," which was probably the light cruiser *Denver*. Samuel Eliot Morison, *The Liberation of the Philippines Luzon. Mindanao. the Visayas. 1944–45*, Vol. 13, *History of United States Naval Operations in World War II* (Boston, 1959), pp. 187-190.

5. "Two dropping operations of the 511th Parachute Regiment were successfully carried out in the morning [of 3 February] with very light operational casualties and no battle casualties. Drop was entirely too dispersed and dropping grounds were missed by a considerable margin." Eichelberger Diary, 3 February 1945. The 1,750 troops had been dropped for the purpose of securing Tagaytay Ridge.

6. Gen. Byers reached Gen. Eichelberger's Command Post late on the afternoon of

5 February. "Several conferences were held...and approval was given to the program he presented for future operations." Eichelberger Diary, 5 February 1945.

7. Gen. Eddleman was G-3, Sixth Army Headquarters.

8. "Once again no information was obtainable from the Sixth Army concerning the ground position of their troops. A radio was sent direct to GHQ asking for an explanation. For the first time since the beginning of the action I did not go forward. A reply from GHQ...indicates the Sixth Army has been sending regular reports, however these have not gotten to us." Eichelberger Diary, 7 February 1945.

9. One battalion of the 148th Infantry, Thirty-seventh Division, crossed the Pasig River late on the afternoon of 7 February and successfully established a bridgehead; the following day the division completed the occupation of the north bank of the river as far as the Malacañan Palace and expanded the bridgehead. Walter Krueger, *From Down Under to Nippon* (Washington, 1953), p. 264.

10. In his memoirs, General Krueger writes of "the difficult problem" of coordinating the actions of his First Cavalry Division and Eichelberger's Eleventh Airborne. "The difficulties of coordination increased by the failure of GHQ to designate any boundary between Sixth and Eighth Armies. They were not removed until GHQ placed the 11th Airborne Division under my command on 10 February...." Krueger, *From Down Under to Nippon*, p. 248.

11. Although it may have appeared this way to Edwards as he "rode up and down over the Central Plains of Luzon in a Cub," it should be noted that late on 2 February Gen. Krueger ordered Gen. Griswold, the XIV Corps Commander, "to drive on to Manila with all possible speed." This was one day before the parachute drop on Tagaytay Ridge. Smith, *Triumph in the Philippines*, p. 217.

12. Headquarters Sixth Army had been established at Calasiao, a few miles from the beach at Lingayen, on 23 January. Gen. Krueger recalled "During this and succeeding days, I visited various parts of the front...to see for myself how everything was going." Krueger, *From Down Under to Nippon*, p. 232n.

13. The Sixth, Eighth, and also the Tenth, commanded by Gen. Buckner, a part of which was on Leyte being reequipped for the forthcoming Okinawa campaign.

14. This last passage is taken from Gen. Eichelberger's letter to Miss Em dated 11 February 1945.

15. The XXIV Corps was being completely reequipped before its departure for Okinawa. "The re-equipping of General Hodge's troops was something of a revelation to the veterans of the old Southwest Pacific Area.... [A]ll of us marveled. We had never seen such wonderful gear.... Equipment turned in by the XXIV Corps was stockpiled and the serviceable items were later issued to various Eighth Army units." Eichelberger, *Our Jungle Road to Tokyo* (New York, 1950), p. 183.

16. On 4 February 1945, leaders of the United States, Britain and the Soviet Union met at Yalta to discuss allied strategy "and related political issues."

17. Gen. Eichelberger's hope for Russian military intervention in the Far East stands in contrast to the postwar claims of Gen. MacArthur and his entourage that "by 1945 such intervention had become superfluous." Maj. Gen. Charles A. Willoughby and John Chamberlain, *MacArthur, 1941–1951* (New York, 1954), p. 285.

18. They went to observe parachute landings on Corregidor by the 403rd Parachute Regiment. Eichelberger Diary, 16 February 1945.

19. Because no official documents giving Gen. Eichelberger authority to change his mission from a "reconnaissance in force" to a dash against Manila apparently can be found (see Smith, *Triumph in the Philippines*, p. 230 and note), the following extracts from Eichelberger's Diary are of special interest.

"January 26 [1945]. On the 26th Gen. Byers telephoned Chamberlin G-3 GHQ and told him he thought I would take personal command if the situation warranted it in the advance from Nasugbu. Chamberlin said in that case he would have to take the matter up with Big Chief because it was contrary to Big Chief's policy to have an army commander take personal command of troops ashore. I called him back and told him that I would not take personal command but I would either have Swing take command or send in Sibert (X Corps) with a small staff at the time the 41st would go ashore. He told me the chances of the 41st going ashore were about 90-1. In taking this action I felt that if the question were presented to the Big Chief he would back up Chamberlin and I would not go ashore, and I did not want things bawled up that way. . . .

"January 27. Chamberlin came about 0900 and went into some detail about his future plans. He said he thought he would throw in the 41st in any case in southern Luzon to clean out that area, although it might be possible to land it at Mindoro and hold it there for future operations if it were not needed in Luzon. I told him how indefinite my plans had to be. My orders from GHQ require that I make the decision about whether or not the 187th Regimental Combat Team would be put ashore at Nasugbu after the 188th had come ashore under the directive "reconnaissance in force." I explained to him also that Gen. Whitehead had said he would not order a dropping on Tagaytay Ridge unless I gave him my personal word. I told Chamberlin in the presence of Byers that the question of whether or not I stay ashore temporarily would depend on the amount of resistance that is met. . . . If it looked as though there were no Japs there or only a small number, I would go ashore and watch the rapid advance to Tagaytay, since I could not afford to be on a boat 20 hours en route to Mindoro. Chamberlin said he believed that Gen. Mac-Arthur would want to make a very rapid advance . . . into Zamboanga, Borneo or Palawan soon after the fall of Manila since there would be a lot of combat craft available and that he was particularly anxious that I not use more than one battalion of the 24th Division at Nasugbu so that the bulk of the 24th would be available for another operation. He felt that the 503rd Parachute Regiment should be held available to be dropped in the vicinity of Manila if necessary [but see p. 215]. Chamberlin also brought out the point that if Manila was captured before the landing and resistance there had collapsed, that it might be well for me to send a column to Batangas to secure that area for a temporary naval base. These statements were all witnessed by Byers and showed how indefinite the plans were because they were dependent upon whether Big Chief could make a rapid advance into Manila or whether he would be held up at the Pampanga line. Also our plans are depending to a large extent on whether or not the Japanese had evacuated southern Luzon and particularly the Balangan, Nasugbu, Tagaytay Ridge area."

20. The union of elements of the First Infantry and 151st Infantry at Bagac on 21 February severed the Bataan Peninsula and virtually ended the campaign. About 1,000 Japanese remained on the northern portions of the peninsula, but these "presented no threat to Allied control of Bataan, and most of them died of starvation and disease" Smith, *Triumph in the Philippines*, p. 334.

21. In point of fact, Gen. Yamashita had no intention of presiding "over the destruction of Manila." He wished to hold it long enough to move much needed supplies to northern Luzon and to delay Allied occupation of the city. The decision to defend Manila, which ran contrary to Yamashita's expressed desires, resulted "from a series of compromises among Japanese Army and Navy commanders in the Manila area." Ibid., pp. 240-241.

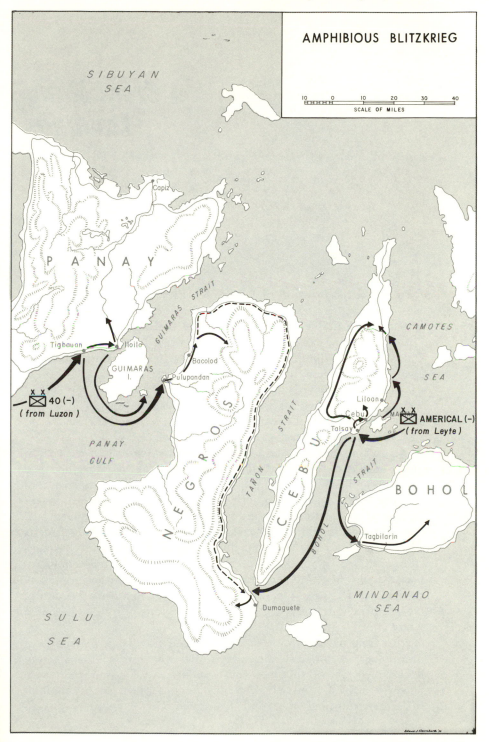

AMPHIBIOUS BLITZKRIEG

SCALE OF MILES

SIBUYAN
SEA

Capiz

P A N A Y

Tigbauan   Iloilo

GUIMARAS
I.

40 (-)
(from Luzon)

PANAY
GULF

SULU
SEA

GUIMARAS   STRAIT

Bacolod

Pulupandan

N E G R O S

TAÑON   STRAIT

Dumaguete

CEBU

Liloan

Cebu

Talisay

Tagbilarin

BOHOL   STRAIT

AMERICAL (-)
(from Leyte)

CAMOTES

SEA

B O H O L

MINDANAO
SEA

MAP 5

CHAPTER TWELVE

A Great Many Landings

Even before the invasion of Luzon, the Eighth Army was involved in operations to clear the Visayan Passages. Mindoro and Marinduque, which had been seized in the preliminary stages of the Luzon campaign, passed to the control of Eighth Army on 1 January. On 19 February units of the Americal Division established themselves on northwestern Samar and adjoining islands and the next day landed on Biri Island a few miles to the north. By the end of the month, organized resistance on northwestern Samar had ended, and early in March the Americal Division seized other islands to clear the eastern entrance to the Visayan Passages.

Meanwhile, units of the Twenty-fourth Division, based on Mindoro, assaulted Verde Island, dominating the passage between Mindoro and Luzon, and the Lubang Islands, guarding the western entrance. On 11–12 March, other elements of the Twenty-fourth Division invaded Romblon and Simara Islands in the Sibuyan Sea, east of Mindoro, and on 3 April the Fortieth Division launched its assault on Masbate, the last major island in the Visayan Passages still controlled by the Japanese. By 5 April Eichelberger could report that the Eighth Army had concluded its operations to secure the Visayan Passages. Operations on the Bicol Peninsula bordering the north of the Sibuyan Sea were the responsibility of the Sixth Army.

Next came Palawan, one of the bypassed islands in the southern Philippines. A long, slender island, Palawan formed the western boundary of the Philippines and was strategically important as a potential airbase from which planes could support an invasion of Borneo and blockade the South China Sea. On 28 February a combat team from the Forty-first Division landed on Palawan and quickly seized control of the area around Puerto Princesa. The rest of the Forty-first Division was employed on the Zamboanga Peninsula, where a landing was made on 11 March, and as soon as the situation on Zamboanga was brought under control the Forty-first Division began a series of small landings to win back the Sulu Archipelago, an island chain that stretched southwest nearly to Borneo. By the end of April Japanese resistance here also had been broken.

While these operations were in progress, the Eighth Army struck also at the southern Visayas. The Fortieth Division landed on Panay on 18 March and quickly drove the Japanese defenders into the hills. On 26 March the Americal Division began its assault on Cebu, while three days later a regimental combat team from the Fortieth Division landed on Negros Occidental. The fighting on Cebu was especially fierce and provided many anxious moments before the Japanese were driven from their defenses in the hills north of Cebu City.

For Eichelberger these were busy and exciting days. Scarcely forty-eight hours went by without some fresh landing, and his letters to Miss Em contained news of one victory after another. General MacArthur described the Visayan campaign as "a model of what a light but aggressive command can accomplish in rapid exploitation." To a proud soldier, as anxious to earn praise as he was to bestow it upon his own subordinates, this meant that his army not only had been successfully launched: it was already "riding on the crest of the waves."

February 19, 1945

Dearest Emmalina,

I am going up today to watch some small landings we are making on some neighboring islands. For some time I have been rather chained here mentally waiting for the word about that grand entry [into Manila]. As I pointed out . . . yesterday, the place where the speaker's stand was to be is in possession of the Japanese, and I think a large part also of the two principal boulevards over which the parade was to be held. I think the Bataan boys had already picked out their offices . . . and I believe they visualized going right back there to find conditions as they were when they pulled out. You know the story of how the Big Chief walked out of his apartment with just a suitcase, leaving flowers on the table, all his cherished possessions, including souvenirs of his father, his scrapbooks, all their wordly goods. . . . If it is not burned . . . the furniture will be gone, toilet fixtures looted, and it will be just in a hell of a fix.

The big question in our minds is still whether or not our Chief will continue on the drive to Tokyo.... When we finish cleaning out the Philippines there will be two armies here, but I imagine if the Big Chief is to stop here they will take away a lot of the divisions and therefore it would be feasible that at least one of the Army staffs will be put in the POA or disbanded. The latter doesn't seem reasonable because it will take a lot of troops if there is to be an actual attack on the Japanese ... or on the Chinese mainland. The Big Chief has such a high standing in the hearts of the people back home that they would not look with complacence on having some untried man commanding big armies and the Big Chief eating his heart out in Manila.

The thing that makes me feel good is the fact that I am now practically within leave distance of my forty years.... These are all idle thoughts, but it is always nice to feel that there is an "out" if I get mixed up in the peculiar battle of personalities which goes on in all theaters.

February 20, 1945

Yesterday afternoon I went out in the "Miss Em" [B-17] to witness the landing on an island off the northwest coast of Samar.[1] We passed the little fleet en route up there. It consisted of about six PT boats and a bunch of small landing craft, so we had to float around nearly an hour before they landed. There were Navy planes around to do the strafing and the preliminary bombing, so we rode out over the straits and along the coast of Luzon. The San Bernardino Straits have always been a very strategic area in all military discussions concerning the Philippines. Since the Japanese still hold that Luzon peninsula and also have a number of holdings in northwest Samar, we were of course armed and ready for trouble. Right behind us on our right rear came my B-25 with those fifteen machine guns, so my entire air fleet was out for the afternoon.

The landing was made at a small town, so we helped out their bombardment by cruising up and down the coast at low altitude to give all the gunners a chance to fire. They got a great kick out of this. We flew about a hundred yards out and about a hundred and fifty feet in the air and at times we flew right over the town. There was no indication of the enemy until they started firing about the time the landing commenced. It was a beautiful day and I thoroughly enjoyed everything.

I know you are going to laugh when you hear about the boys getting a chance to shoot up the Japs. All the crew were perfectly delighted and there were a number of my staff present.... Some of these have never seen anything since they arrived from the States, and they got a tremendous thrill out of their trip. The things which would have furnished enough excitement to have lasted a month in the old piping days of peace are now quickly passed over as other things approach.

I think I shall go up to Mindoro tomorrow to make a pep talk to some men up there.

February 21, 1945

Clovis and I saw Dick Sutherland down at his camp. . . . Dick seemed to be in good spirits and said he had been going out constantly investigating conditions of frontline units.

According to Dick, Bonner Fellers and some friend of his who is a wealthy Manila man have been going out gaining information about the position of our troops within the city of Manila and making recommendations to the Big Chief. Dick said some of these recommendations have enraged the Chief and he has had to calm him down to keep him from dismissing division commanders, or at least that is the inference I got. He said the Big Chief has been in a very bad mood for a while but now he is feeling better again.

Dick . . . said he and the Chief got a great kick out of my dash into Manila. They realized that we ran into tremendous power in the Nichols Field area. He said your old palsy-walsy was trying to lean back in the traces about turning some of his troops over to me for my coming operations, but that they would run the steamroller over him.

I asked him whether the Chief had heard what would happen to him after Luzon and he said he didn't think he had. I rather believe this is true because one of his announcements was a clear indication to give him more and higher command.

I understand the big parade has been called off, which suits me fine because I didn't know how I was going to get in and get out. . . . Your old Leavenworth friend blames Bonner for the premature announcement of the capture of Manila and Bataan. Some people think though that the Big Chief was anxious to get out the announcements while the big conference was going on in the Black Sea area.

February 22, 1945

After the usual morning conference today I went down to our own hospital which is nearby and inspected a great many wards of wounded. All too many of them were boys of the 11th Airborne. Most of those to whom I talked were wounded in the attack on Fort McKinley after the fall of Nichols Field. . . . One boy from the 11th with whom I talked was shot yesterday, and four hours later he was in our hospital on Leyte. They flew him out . . . from Nichols Field. . . . Of course that is hard work for me, as you can well understand.

Your old Leavenworth friend told me that he had recommended to the Big Chief during the recent fighting that your palsy-walsy be sent home and that his outfit be given to me or to Chink. He said that his tactics were all wrong and that he did not put enough power in his fast moving flank in order to push into Manila.

He also told me that he was worried about Sarah. He said he felt that she had made the biggest mistake of her career in having her family already on the way to join her. He said there were certain alterations in the ship which might be seized upon by unfriendly columnists. He said when he questioned Sarah that she threw him out.

February 23, 1945

We have ... taken all of that group of islands immediately off the coast. The Japs had defenses there to deny the straits to our ships.

I imagine there will be a lot of ill-feeling towards the Filipinos who are accused of being collaborators because the destruction of so much of Manila will create a lot of bitterness. We had a number of collaborators in our pen at Paranaque.

February 25, 1945

We are off tomorrow morning at daybreak to watch the bombing of Palawan, which is being put on for our benefit. ... I shall be taking a great many similar rides in the near future.

We are making a great many landings, large and small. ... Some of the troops we have used were drawn from operations up in Luzon without any time to rest, and of course I can't expect your palsy-walsy to turn loose his best outfit. Certainly he is not overly generous in his dealings with the other fellow. I always like people who occasionally pull one of their four feet out of the trough.

February 26, 1945

It was one of the most unsatisfactory days I have ever spent. We got up in the dark ... to go to Palawan to witness a special type of bombing, which means we travelled 1200 miles over the water ... and then found that nothing happened. Just where the American planes were I do not know. We stayed there about an hour and a half and except for some Japanese firing, which was way short of us ... I didn't see any other firing of any kind. A few American planes finally came over but didn't do anything.

Another thing which annoyed me this morning was the fact that the officers which I had permitted to go in my B-25 failed to show up in the dark and we waited a half hour for them, so I have lots of people to cuss out and that is always a pleasure.

There is a little island in the Camotes group off Ormoc Bay on which the Japanese killed every Filipino in there because they were said to have rescued some American aviators. I forwarded the investigation within the last few days. I doubt if those facts will ever be given out because some day I suppose we will want to settle down and be big friends again.

February 27, 1945

I shall try to describe my day. ... I was awake at six o'clock and took calisthenics until 6:20. Then, since it was too early for Dombrowski, I shaved with cold water and went over to the office to do some desk work. . . . Jens Doe and Ken Sweany were here and after breakfast they stayed for our usual officers' conferences, during which the different chiefs of section bring out the happenings of the previous day. I worked on my papers until nine-thirty and then I made a talk at a conference attended by a lot of Air Corps and Navy men and members of my staff. In effect, my talk was a plea for speed in fighting. [M]*y remarks pertained particularly to the need for rapid advances and the avoidance of any of the sit-still-and-patrol method. Also stressed importance of complete cooperation between the services.*[2] I worked in the office until lunch time. . . . They have finally started off for home and I am going to work on my papers which have accumulated.

After dinner we went to the outdoor theater where we heard first the Eighth Army choristers. Irving Berlin joined in with them for several songs and it was very nice entertainment with a full moon. By request, Berlin sang some of the songs which he has written. . . . Then we saw the four reels of the Army-Navy football game. . . .

Tomorrow morning I am going in my B-17 to watch a landing on an island which will be announced long before this letter reaches you. . . . If things go well . . . I think I shall go up about forty-eight hours later to Luzon to see the Chief and shortly thereafter I am going to make an investigation of some of the questions raised in those old songs, such as the existence of monkeys' tails,[3] virgins, etc. . . .

Believe it or not, we are still getting opposition out in western Leyte. Twice in the last week we have had Japanese planes strafe our troops there during the fighting and that is getting to be a rather rare thing south of Manila.

February 28, 1945

We arrived back here about 2:30 from a fine trip to Palawan where we had a successful landing today. . . . Those things are always a very inspiring sight with the Navy, our ships and many planes in the air. It isn't nearly as much fun for the doughboys down on the ground, however. . . . We have those trips down now so that they are very little trouble. . . . Late reports from Palawan indicate that we are having no trouble. The LCT's are unloading at the dock and although the town of Puerto Princesa had been largely destroyed I think there are a number of houses there that can be used as warehouses. The dock was in fine shape.

This afternoon I have talked to Kenney and Chamberlin who are just back from up there [at GHQ]. They say that the answer to the $64.00 question has not yet been given but that the Big Chief is trying to smoke out the people back home and make them state one way or another. . . .

I notice that the Marines intend to emphasize their losses and difficulties in fighting. Bill Dunn said the newspaper people were horrified when the capture of Manila was announced, since that spoiled their stories. As soon as that announcement went out, their directives from the home office to send in broadcasts dropped off immediately. They just begged Diller[4] to try to get the Big Chief to withdraw his announcement about the capture of the city, as they saw numerous stories coming out of the street fighting.

I have been put in command of all the guerrilla forces south of Luzon. This is more of a job than it would seem because we must not only supply them and fight them, but we must also muster them into the Philippine Army. . . . I have just been talking to the head guerrilla[5] from another big island. He has come to secure from Uncle Sam more benefits than they have yet received, although he has been given a great deal of money and considerable supplies. He looks like a number one cutthroat to me, and I may have to cut his before I get through.

We have cleaned out a large part of the Verde Island Passage and the San Bernardino Straits with a minimum of losses and . . . of troops.

March 1, 1945

Last night a telegram came from the Big Chief saying that he would be delighted to see me . . . so I shall arrive at his Command Post at 11:00 on the . . . 3rd. I want to find out the answer to the $64.00 question (who commands from here on out) and also to talk . . . about our coming operations. He may want to find out whether monkeys have tails also, and I would be glad to have him come along.

The entire day has been taken up with conferences, including three with big guerrilla chiefs. At breakfast I had Peralta and since that time I have talked to Fertig and Cushing.[6] The latter two are American mining engineers who have been in the guerrilla business since Corregidor fell. Peralta is a thirty-year-old Filipino, a college graduate and a hard looking baby if I have ever seen one. My list of acquaintances grows day by day.

Billie Bowen was at GHQ last night for a conference and the question came up about a certain task up in southern Luzon which will act as a supplement to a little job we have already put on in the San Bernardino Straits. Your old palsy-walsy wants to have a great fleet and a big bunch of men. Bill said Steve Chamberlin and a number of others said, "Give the Eighth Army a couple of squads and they will do it," and a big yell went up. That isn't a bad reputation for us to be getting.

March 2, 1945

We are off tomorrow . . . and will fly up by way of the west coast of Samar, the Ticao and Burias Islands, Marinduque, Verde Island, Balayan

Bay, Tagaytay Ridge and Manila, landing at Clark Field. This will allow us to stay away from Japanese ack-ack. Over Ticao and Burias we will have the benefit of a little air fleet — a bunch of Navy planes — which will be guarding the landings we are going to make tomorrow morning on those islands. The only possible trouble will be the fact that there are a few Japanese planes on various islands, probably reconstructed out of ones that have been partially destroyed.... It will not be long now, however, when all Japanese air will disappear from the Visayas. According to our latest information, there are still four fields in operation on Negros with perhaps a dozen planes. I do not know why we can't take these out.

Our Palawan landing came off all right. Up to date they have had only two men killed and those were due to booby traps....

I was just talking to Steve Chamberlin.... He said he is crazy about the Eighth Army because we don't ask for a tremendous force whenever we have things to do, and he added that that is the way everybody else at GHQ felt. He said he laughed about Verde Island, because after we had sent a small force in there to take it we later had to send a small mortar squad to take out the Jap artillery which we had discovered there. This we did without any fuss. He also said, "You people do things." He said things were boiling up north about the $64.00 question. He thinks I will learn a lot tomorrow. He says the Big Chief is putting things squarely up to them.

March 4, 1945

Yesterday morning we were off at 8:30 to see the Big Chief.... We went first along the west coast of Samar to watch some landings on Ticao and Burias Islands made by a battalion of the Americal Division....[7] Then we swung over Balayan Bay and Tagaytay Ridge. We almost knocked the roof off of the Annex to the Manila Hotel. From there we followed the concrete highway ... to Nichols Field and we circled around south Manila a number of times. The walled city is entirely gutted. There are no roofs on any of the houses. They are mere shells. Then we went north.... Stotsenburg is only partly destroyed. The valley looked beautiful. I was amazed at the amount of Japanese fortifications and also the number of Jap planes that had been destroyed. After we landed, Clovis, Chuck Downer and I went ... to call on the Big Chief, who is living in a sugar plantation about midway between Tarlac and Cabanatuan. I spent about two hours with him....

The Chief was very frank and most pleasant. The $64.00 question has not yet been answered but he was told it would be settled at a meeting of the Joint Chiefs of Staff in a few days. He has tried to smoke them out in every way possible. At one time George Catlett Marshall hoped to get overall command of the Pacific with Nimitz, Arnold and the Big

Chief commanders under him, but King objected to that since he and G.C.M. have strategic overall command already.[8] The Big Chief thinks now that G.C.M. will swing back to him for overall command of the ground forces. Buck . . . has an operation coming up [Okinawa] and the Big Chief doesn't want to command that one. In fact, the Big Chief says if Buck ever comes under him he would bust him because he has sold out to one of our sister services. Of course he doesn't mean that. He hopes to wind up all the fighting in the Philippines and to the south as rapidly as possible and then announce to the world that his mission is over and ask for further instructions. He says the Navy put out propaganda against him by saying he wanted to quit when he took Manila. Of course he said that wasn't true. He said, "I have fulfilled one of my missions and the other is just as important."

He said Nimitz is trying to get rid of your old Leavenworth friend and that the former is not the guileless person he appears to be, but is very *ambitious* and *shrewd*. I told the Chief that my desire to have him as overall Army commander in the Pacific was not based on selfishness, because I feel the Eighth Army will be used by whoever takes command, but I felt that he was the man best suited to do the job and gain victory.

The Big Chief seemed very delighted with the work I have been doing and said, "From now on you will be treated with absolute parity with reference to the Sixth Army or any other army." I asked the Big Chief about Gris and he said he had done better than he had expected him to. He thinks the 1st Cavalry is the best outfit he has and the 11th Airborne comes next. *In speaking of the bravery of Mudge[9] [of the 1st Cavalry], who was hit by a grenade in an attack on a pillbox, he said from now on his high ranking officers would be frontline generals and that he personally had observed quite a lot at the front.[10]* I told him I was often criticized by certain office boys because I had been exposed to enemy fire and that I had on a number of occasions felt like swinging at several people. He said that if anyone ever criticizes me again for exposing myself he would court-martial them, and he added that he was going to make all of his officers become frontline leaders. What a change![11]

The Big Chief suggested that I go in and see Manila. . . . As soon as we crossed the river . . . we found there was practically nothing that hadn't been entirely knocked down and in ruins. Down Taft Avenue they were still killing Japanese and . . . the Manila Hotel, the Army and Navy Club, the Elks Club, the University Club and the High Commissioner's home . . . were completely destroyed. All those apartment houses along Dewey Boulevard were gutted. Every beautiful public building is in ruin, and there is not a roof on any building in the Intramuros. It is all just graveyard. The Japanese barricaded themselves in all permanent buildings and these were all knocked down by our artillery. In addition to this, great sections were burned by the Japanese. . . .

In other words, Manila in effect has ceased to exist except for some places that the Japanese thought were not worth defending or where our American troops got in by surprise.... I cannot tell you how sad all this made me feel.

This morning... we flew over Corregidor at a very low altitude, passing those caves some of which the Japs are still holding. It is just shambles....

I leave for Mindoro on the 7th where I go aboard a big boat.... When I return I should be able to tell you whether monkeys have tails.

March 5, 1945

I was amazed to see that the Big Chief writes a lot of these announcements himself. For example, he was actually writing in longhand the release about our capture of Ticao and Burias Islands in the steamer lane just south of Luzon while I was there. I had passed over those islands in the morning and gave him the details which he took from me.

March 7, 1945

I left Tanauan airstrip for Mindoro at 0915 to join V-4 convoy....[12] After luncheon we drove through that terrible dust down to the beach where the Admiral's barge was waiting for me. We were glad to get on the water....

I like this Navy crowd. They are most hospitable and pleasant. Jens is aboard, and Ken Sweaney, Chief of Staff.[13] I find they are a bit full of the guerrilla reports of Jap strength at the place to which we are bound. I found up in Luzon that I could divide their reports by anything from 3 to 10 to get anything like proper strengths. I am afraid I shall need the same big club I used at Biak. At any rate that is the one big reason I came. We may find a lot of guns in there but I expect that our Air and Navy will take about all of it out.

March 8, 1945

We put to sea at seven this morning.... Long before this letter is mailed you will know that we have landed in Zamboanga — not the one you know about, because it will be burned and bombed out.... Of course the Japs got those places at the surrender just as they were and we will have nothing but ruins when we get through pounding the Japs out of them. That will be true of all places not already in the hands of the guerrillas. Of course we now go along blacked out.

No reaction from Jap air so far and fortunately we are in the dark of the moon — we may get some during and after the landing from Jap planes down Borneo way. We will have air cover during the day and lots of bombers over of every type.

March 9, 1945

We will be off our target area at daylight and I shall get up early to see it. We are going to get opposition, both gun and small arms, but how much I do not know — we shall have heavy air support and as soon as we get our artillery ashore we will get a lot of support from that. Also very heavy Navy gun support.... We have tanks and buffaloes [amphibious tanks] which should hurry things up, and a number of cruisers which can give supporting fire. Also the usual smaller protecting craft of all kinds....

All this is very interesting — how I wish I could have you see it through my eyes. Of course things can go wrong and I may have to bring in the reserve, which I hold at Mindoro. Also, of course, things may go slowly and that wouldn't be too good as I have many future uses for these troops. I have had to put out a lot of propaganda because most of these officers believe the guerrilla figures, which are as a rule grossly exaggerated.... Maybe I can get away about the 12th for Leyte.... At any rate I am an optimistic cuss.

March 10, 1945

This morning I was awakened at six o'clock.... We were just moving in then, opposite the beach which leads to Zamboanga. There followed the usual Navy fire and bombing by heavy bombers, followed by strafers. As a result, there was no opposition when our troopships beached, although there was plenty of wire and trenches to indicate preparation for heavy defense. The troops got ashore in good shape because the beach is not bad. The beach is quite deep and all the amphibious craft can go up against the shore.... There is a lot of rough gravel which forces construction of a road leading from each boat. This, however, can be done very quickly with bulldozers.

I finally went ashore at one o'clock. In spite of the propaganda I put out, the advance was slow and cautious, although satisfactory. The contrast with the 11th Airborne, however, was very evident.

My own feeling is that under the terrific Navy fire support and air support, one should move quickly before the Japs get over being dazed.

I talked to two prisoners who looked well nourished but quite ragged according to our standards.

There has been quite a little very poorly aimed mortar fire landing in the water — or perhaps some of it is gunfire or maybe 75 mm. A shell finally hit one of our landing craft. All the men quit work. Admiral [F. B.] Royal ["a grand chap"] is extremely angry and is using some of that profanity for which the Navy is famous.

I shall hope to return on Monday as I wanted to go up to Lingayen to talk to Rapp,[14] and that cannot be put off if I am to see him in the near future.

Of course, I realize that everything seems confused the first day on the beach, and I believe that I have put out enough propaganda to keep them moving reasonably fast.

One regiment established a rather shallow bridgehead and another regiment, which I think is a very fine one, landed under the protection of that beachhead and then will advance today about half the way to Zambo. Personally, I think they should have gone all the way in because the Japs are liable to come back and occupy their abandoned trenches.

No monkeys — with or without tails — a dead horse and a live one. Some dead Japs, I guess, but I didn't see any. . . . Was on the bridge to see us put to sea just at sundown — cruisers and other types flying around. Destroyers up near the beach throwing shells up into the hills — cubs flying around directing fire. The most impressive thing though is to watch the heavy bombers when they drop their 1000 pound bombs. I wish those mountains didn't come so near the shore.

I wish I could see you tonight and talk all this over — it won't be long until we have others like this. A lot of them, large and small.

No Jap air today — I rather expected it.

March 11, 1945

We were at sea last night — when I finally opened the black-out steel door we were coming into the harbor — cruisers, destroyers and lesser craft of all kinds. A destroyer going at very high speed cut across our bow — a beautiful sight. The whole Zamboanga peninsula is beautiful in spite of the Japs. . . .

Things went better today — Bill went ashore early but I didn't land until just after luncheon. Then we went on foot down the road until we were only about a mile from the center of Zamboanga. . . . We made a thorough inspection of the Jap defenses. At 4:00 this afternoon we were in Zambo — tanks and doughboys with destroyers lying just off the pier. . . . I saw today some strange sights, e.g., a square heavy reinforced concrete box opening with an aperture for a gun on the sea side. A complete dummy native type house had been built around it so that I had passed within 4 paces of it and missed it. The gun had been hit by one of our Navy shells. A dead American soldier was lying just inside — his head blown off by a booby trap.

There were many concrete or coconut log bunkers — and I mean many — with connecting trenches and barbed wire. The roads leading to them were heavily guarded with land mines and sunken bombs.

Zamboanga must have been beautiful at one time, but after our planes and guns got through today . . . there was not much.

March 12, 1945

This morning I went in early on the Admiral's barge to Zamboanga town. It has been entirely destroyed by our bombing and ... naval and artillery fire. Our incendiary bombs burned out a good many blocks. . . . The concrete piers are in almost perfect condition and a Liberty ship could dock there tomorrow. . . . On the way out, an underwater mine or a very big shell went off a few feet from our boat. The big fragments went way up in the air and we got away before they came down.

We had luncheon on the Admiral's ship and then got on a Cat to come back here. My, how I hate those planes.

I am getting up very early in the morning to go to Lingayen Gulf where I shall see Rapp Brush and give him a little pep talk.[15]

March 13, 1945

Rapp was fine — he is fed up though and says he will retire as soon as possible after the war. He dislikes your palsy-walsy very much and those who serve with him. They hurt his feelings by messages, etc. . . . Coming back we ... learned that Leyte was shut in with visibility almost zero, and rain. I then wired Woody and he just had time to meet us. We had a nice supper, a staff conference and saw some war films.

March 14, 1945

The Palawan landing has gone well but there has not been much speed there. For about ten days they were looking for the 1700 Japanese which were reported to be there and most of them I do not believe existed except in guerrilla reports. In fact my *bête noire* is going to be guerrilla reports.

March 18, 1945

We pulled off another operation this morning at Iloilo, on Panay. . . . After an early breakfast we took off for Iloilo in my B-25. The round trip, including the flying around we did over the target area, made up a total of perhaps 650 miles. . . . Reports later this afternoon from Iloilo indicate that a grand place to go ashore has been found and that the advance on the town had started. They say fires are going up so I imagine the Japanese are destroying the place.

I presume that in the papers you have been able to check off the places we are taking. . . . In addition to our two landings in Luzon, we have cleaned out the strategic passages south of Luzon from the San Bernardino Straits to Lubang Island. We have taken the Camotes near Leyte, the Romblon Islands east of Mindoro, Palawan, Zamboanga, and now we are ashore on Panay. You can see what we have left to do, but the big fight of course is ahead of us yet. You have studied this theater too carefully not to know what that big one will be.

March 19, 1945

This morning I talked with an Associated Press man who has come from Manila. He says the impression up there is that your palsy-walsy will be put in command of both the Sixth and Eighth Armies. I doubt if the Big Chief will try to do that before he leaves the Philippines. It might be just another example of his attempting to show that he has a high command ready to go forward if called upon or, in other words, it is another attempt to needle the people in Washington into putting him in over-all command of the Army troops in the Pacific. If your palsy-walsy is put over me I shall . . . withdraw myself from this picture. . . . I have done my duty for a person of my age. I have been in close combat more times than I could possibly remember and . . . I do not intend to put up with any more of your palsy-walsy's insults, because after all life is a wee bit short and I do not think I could take any more. . . . This sounds rather gloomy but I do not really feel that way.

Tomorrow I am going to fly in a Cat to Iloilo. . . . About the 23rd I shall go to Manila to see the Big Chief. That will be between operations. We have a lot of fighting to do yet right in that area where we struck yesterday and then harder work to the south. If we have luck in Mindanao I will be pretty well finished by the middle of June.

March 20, 1945

Just to let you know that I can be conservative, we had an escort of two Lightnings, which circled over the plane all the way over. We landed on the water . . . and we went ashore almost at once. At one time nobody thought we had a chance of taking Iloilo today.

We rode down in jeeps to Rapp's headquarters, which was in a beautiful town market. . . . Just before we went ashore, Rip's [Rear Admiral A. D. Struble] Intelligence Officer told us that one of his little Navy planes had seen civilians waving the Flag in the town and that they had written on the sand "Japs have left city!" That gave me a grand excuse to push things a wee bit.

Peralta was at Rapp's headquarters. . . . He is the guerrilla leader who has scared them all a bit. One of General MacArthur's Staff Officers had come down to Panay to urge Peralta to release some of Osmeña's men whom he had in the hoosegow. Peralta spent a week at my headquarters and we get along very well. He wanted to come along and see if we could not get into Iloilo, so Rip, Rapp, Bill, Peralta and I started right after lunch. A half hour later we were in the center of the city and the whole population had gone crazy.

About two-thirds of the city had been destroyed, partly by our bombs, partly by the Japs in the early days, and partly by the Japs in the last week. . . . After we had gone clear through the city, we went out to the north for about six miles, where our soldiers were chasing some remnants of the Japs. Then we came back to Peralta's headquarters. . . . There we had a ceremony in which I decorated him with the Distinguished Service Cross.

There had been some question whether we would arrest him or decorate him, but it is evident he had decided to be a good Indian.

Tomorrow morning I am going ashore to talk to Rapp some more about future plans and then I shall take off in the Catilina for home. . . .

Everything is going fairly well at Zamboanga — not too fast but satisfactorily. The losses which Doe is taking do not indicate much heavy fighting. He is a very ponderous fighter — not brilliant in any way. He has one regiment which is outstanding.

March 21, 1945

Things are moving along fast — by June 15 I hope to have this all over. By that time we will know whether General MacArthur will be the over-all Army Commander. I think he will.

March 22, 1945

Just now I was talking to Colonel Fertig about the setup on Mindanao. He will prepare for me a place for an advanced Command Post at Camp Keithley, which is on the shores of Lake Lanao. This place is in possession of the guerrillas now but it is too soon for me to go down there. . . . At present Fertig is spending quite a lot of his time up here with me. He . . . is practically a member of the family. . . . He is the head of all the Mindanao guerrillas. . . .

As you know I am going to Manila tomorrow morning. . . . There is nothing particular that I want to find out there except to talk to General MacArthur to see if he has any new information that he wants to give to me.

One of our amphibious ducks just now came out of the water and is now a truck.

March 24, 1945

Yesterday morning the "Miss Em" took off on the minute at seven as planned. . . . Flying high we decided to ignore the Japs so we went in over Batangas Bay and then across Lake Taal . . . and down that concrete road to Manila. . . . Sedans were waiting and we drove down to the GHQ offices which are north of the river. . . . On all sides . . . there was complete desolation. . . . En route . . . we went . . . down to our old house, where I got out and looked around. There is not a vestige of the house, but a great big embankment which the Japanese put up for protection. The gate is still there. Across the street . . . there was a truck with two dead Japs under it.

I talked to the Big Chief for about two hours. He is very pleased with what we have been doing and said it would have been impossible for your palsy-walsy's outfit to do that. He said they are mentally incapable but if given tremendous forces they are able to advance ponderously and slowly to victory. He said that your palsy-walsy had tried to keep the Eighth Army from ever being formed, although when asked he had no suggestion about anyone else commanding it. MacArthur said that his army is jealous of the Eighth Army and that they are trying in every way to keep troops and bullets from coming to me. He said his staff are fully aware of this and are angry about it and that they will fight for us.... His discussion of your palsy-walsy's unit occupied at least twenty minutes.

I told the Big Chief that since he had brought the matter up I want him to know that I never intend under any circumstances to serve under Krueger again. That at the time of the formation of my army I took certain insults because I knew my freedom was in sight, but I never intend to take them again from anybody. He said he would never force me to do so and that he didn't intend to have an army group commander....

He explained how the promotion happened[16] by saying that George Catlett Marshall asked his advice and gave him a list of names, including Patton. The Big Chief objected to this list and said he thought Sir George was the best air man in the Army and ... that your palsy-walsy's rank and victories should give him the call over my classmate [Patton], who could do brilliant things but was erratic to say the least. We discussed my plans at great length and he seemed to approve of everything. I told him what I had done and how I have had to beat down the guerrilla reports in Luzon and down at Zamboanga as well as Iloilo.

The Big Chief asked me to go to luncheon with him and I rode out with him in his car. He came out of his office with his arm around me and I looked around to find all kinds of motion picture and still cameras, as well as a great crowd of people at the door. He is living in the Japanese Ambassador's house and it is beautiful. Nothing had been disturbed and it was there that he found his silver. Jean said that her silver and her mother's silver ... had disappeared.... He said if he could find the Jap Ambassador he would try him for theft. He said he also intended to treat the Japanese prisoners just as they treated our prisoners. They march publicly through the streets to their work and do not receive very good treatment. I was glad to find out he was doing this as the Japs had murdered so many of our people.[17]

March 25, 1945

At the luncheon table ... I was telling him how valuable the white soldiers and officers have been who took to the hills at Mindanao [in May 1942], and what a help it would have been had all of our troops with their radios, stores, arms, etc. gone into the hills. He said, "I ordered them to keep on fighting and Skinny [Wainwright] ordered them to surrender while he was a prisoner. It was not a very creditable thing."[18] He pointed out too that one of Skinny's officers under Japanese guard came down to insure that the surrender took place and to state that anybody who failed to surrender all equipment would be court-martialed. It is all a very peculiar thing and I do not know how history will deal with it. Of course the reason Skinny directed the surrender was because the Japanese would not agree to accept the surrender of Corregidor unless he surrendered everything in the islands. . . .

One thing the Big Chief said . . . was that I would need more troops for my big show. This was with reference to the fact that your palsy-walsy had hogged everything. He said, "You need more artillery," and I said, "Yes, possibly so, but when there were 17 extra battalions of medium artillery your palsy took 16 of them and would have taken the 17th except that it had no guns." As a matter of fact, I hope to get through with some of these other shows which will leave some extra divisions available. I have six now, and can get more if I need them. The shipping is the vital thing because it takes a perfectly enormous amount of ships to put a division afloat, but if Jens cleans out his area promptly then I will have his troops to use, or at least most of them. . . . I have the 24th, 31st, 40th, 41st, 93rd and Americal divisions. I also have a couple of extra regimental combat teams for good measure. Of course every division has its organic four battalions of artillery and we have some extra now. . . . The Big Chief said, "You know when he gave you Brush he gave you what he thought was his worst division." I said, "I agree he thought he was giving me the worst division but he didn't, because I like the 40th Division. Furthermore, while I was talking to Rapp down there he received a letter of commendation dripping with honey from every pore." And I added, "Brush took it and slapped it down on his desk and said, 'He has ruined my career and then he sends me this!'"

The Big Chief said, "My God, did he lower himself to do a thing like that?"[19]

Steve Chamberlin is now one of our greatest boosters. Steve was very angry over the fact that a tank destroyer outfit sent down for me to use in a coming operation had about half of its vehicles incapacitated. They are flying in the spare parts, but they are all extremely angry that your palsy-walsy didn't give me one of the best they had. Of course these things do not help your palsy-walsy's standing very much.

I realize that a great many people blow hot and . . . cold with the wind, but nevertheless it is better to have people rooting for you than "agin ya."

March 26, 1945

You would have been interested if you could have been with me this morning *to make a reconnaissance flight over the Cebu landing....* The plane was in the air at exactly nine. In a surprisingly short time we were looking down into the Ormoc Valley and then were over the Camotes at a rather low level. In one of the Camotes the Japanese massacred the entire Filipino population.... We were over our boats in thirty-five minutes from the time we took off.... On a plane we can move around easily, switch seats and talk.... We ... circled over our many ships a lot of times.

We had to be very careful in order to keep out of the path of our cruiser fire but finally were able to pass over the beaches and saw everything was all right. We were over the target area for forty minutes and during that time we watched some heavy bombing of Cebu City by B-24's as well as some strafing and bombing by B-25's. The Japanese are reported there in some strength (roughly 14,000 on the island) but I doubt if the reports are accurate. Returned in time for luncheon.[20]

I am going over tomorrow in a flying boat to try to put some speed into that operation. Unfortunately like Zamboanga the hills come down very close to the beach and that makes defense easy for the Japs.

(later)

Things are going all right at Cebu but up to date they have not been able to find a place to beach the larger landing craft. As you know, the largest of these are over three hundred feet long. We were, however, able to get ashore with the use of Alligators and Buffaloes, which are amphibious tracked vehicles.

March 27, 1945
5:30 A.M.

I am off ... for Cebu — the reports from there indicate some progress. We have no way of telling how many troops are in Cebu or Negros because the guerrilla reports are so poor. The Japs were burning Cebu City yesterday — I do not think they can stop us. We did have a hard time getting ashore as the beaches are very poor.

March 28, 1945

We landed at 11:00 yesterday morning.... Duke Arnold[21] of the Americal Division met us at the beach and we started for Cebu City at once. ... As we got into the southern outskirts... we were stopped by a tremendous number of our own 1000-pound bomb craters which unfortunately in a number of cases had hit right on the road. We went back to Duke's Command Post and had some field rations for luncheon and then we started again. This time we found that we were able to get a jeep through the craters. We went on into Cebu and found the town almost destroyed.

Duke Arnold is doing a fine job and I am delighted with his rapid capture of the city. The Japanese had made tremendous preparations. The beaches were entirely lined with wire and there were land mines in four rows at about two-yard intervals. These mines varied from anti-personnel mines to small airplane bombs up to a hundred pounds. A number of our Buffaloes were knocked out by them. Back of that came the largest number of tank traps and tank barriers that I have ever seen. The latter were railroad irons set in concrete and the others were terribly deep ditches.

All of this the Japanese abandoned with hardly a fight, although much of the wire was so new that it must have been laid within the last two or three weeks. I didn't find any of the numerous bunkers that were knocked out by Navy fire so they could have stayed there right where they were. Many of the bunkers were of reinforced concrete with little native houses placed over them for camouflage.

Cebu must have been beautiful at one time and I am very sorry that it was destroyed. It had wide boulevards and beautiful homes which are now a mass of wreckage due partly to our bombs and partly to the Japanese fires. *The Japanese had dispersed their ammunition throughout most of the buildings in the city and when they fled they detonated these dumps, destroying the buildings at the same time.*[22]

Just before dark, one lone Jap plane came over and dropped three bombs. We were a short distance offshore and the bombs fell between us and the shore, narrowly missing some of our combat craft.

This is just another operation which has started most successfully and which I believe will be cleaned up promptly.

March 29, 1945

I am glad that you are pleased with the rapid advance at Zambo. As you have guessed I did have to use a bit of propaganda, but only because the reports of the Japanese troops had been terribly exaggerated. I also had to push Rapp a bit, but there was no necessity of pushing the Americal Division in the capture of Cebu City. They went to beat h_____. One of the two regiments ashore (I am holding one in reserve back here) is commanded by Dunn,[23] who was with me in the 77th. When I asked him what he proposed to do he said, "I am closing in on them."

You understand, of course, that when I go in on these operations I do not assume personal command. I merely land there as an Army commander. Of course what I want done is done, but I try to keep out of the tactical handling of troops. It would not be right for me to take personal command of a small force.

We are making a fine combat record. . . . No one can laugh off the fact that we have had about twenty-five successful amphibious landings during the last two months in addition to killing a tremendous number of Japanese in the battle for Leyte.

We are landing today on Negros, and that may be the worst of all, as even MacArthur estimated 15,000 there. Rapp is taking his 5 battalions in. Fred is fighting the battle of Leyte and Samar with Rapp's third regiment, reinforced by the 1st Filipino regiment which was trained in the USA.

March 30, 1945

The Hearst papers ... are campaigning for the Big Chief to get the high command in the Pacific. This is something that I think by all means he should get and this irrespective of whether I have anything to do with it or not.

There is so much to be thankful for. ... At least at Cebu I didn't get defeated, I didn't get shot, no bombs dropped on my boat, and I have had a continuous series of victories. This morning, for example, we landed on Negros and we were lucky enough to secure a great big bridge which I was worried about because I would not have had the bridge material to rebuild it if it had been wrecked.

This successful landing on Negros is a great break. The Big Chief has been worried about it and offered me some of the Sixth Army troops if I wanted them. ... The Big Chief warned me that I would meet 15,000 Japanese and Steve Chamberlin said 19,000. Up to this time I have only put five battalions ashore there but I have another regiment in addition to a parachute regiment ready if I need them.

It is true that the publicity is all on the European side or about others out here. Nevertheless, I get a great deal of quiet pleasure out of the fact that I have been in command of the landings at Zamboanga, Iloilo, and Cebu and that I had such a big hand in the capture of Manila. The hardest fight is still ahead of me. In the meantime, we are continuing to turn in one victory after another. ... This fighting is not a personal proposition. My duty to my country requires me to lick these Japs and that is what I intend to do. If I do a quick and thorough job, the word will get around. As a matter of fact, there has been nothing in this theater that faintly compares to the way we have been cleaning up the Visayas and Sulu Archipelago. For example, when I saw the Big Chief last he said, "What do you plan to do about Negros?" When I told him I would land on the 29th using the same troops with which I had just captured Iloilo he was perfectly astonished and said, "That is the way I like to see things done." I imagine he thought we would have to rest a month before doing anything.

I can see why you were worried about the Zamboanga landing, because you thought it was our intention to take Mindanao. That landing ... was for the purpose of securing the airfields at the end of the Zamboanga Peninsula and to eliminate the Japanese garrisons in the Sulu Archipelago. This we propose to do with speed. Most of the Zamboanga

Peninsula is in the possession of the guerrillas now and we used a guerrilla airfield at Dipolog, which is in the north part of that peninsula,
for our fighters during the Zamboanga landing. This permitted them to
stay much longer over the target because the trip from Mindoro . . . would
have been a long one. The bombers have such a tremendous range that they
do not enter into the picture. I had a nice letter from Jens Doe a few
minutes ago and it indicates that the situation is well in hand on Zamboanga — the fighting has practically ceased. He is fighting off a request
that nurses be sent there, saying he does not want any gals around.

Rapp did a grand job on Panay from every angle. We are unloading
ships at the docks; the hospital is in good shape, the electric lights are
on and the water is running, and the city of Iloilo is being cleaned up
rapidly. We pulled all of our troops out of there except one battalion of
infantry and service troops. The Filipinos are unloading the ships and
. . . doing it well.

Clovis left . . . this morning for Manila and may stay overnight. He
has some matters to discuss there about the Philippine Army. Bill Bowen
left by flying boat for Negros as our reports from there have not been too
complete. There has been quite a bit of fighting but we are maintaining
the upper hand.

My desk is a mess. I seem to get more work piled up every hour that
I stay here. I guess the best thing for me to do is to go off on another
operation. . . . It has not been definitely decided how I shall travel. . . .
Probably a cruiser.

March 31, 1945

This morning I got up at five o'clock and came over to the office early.
The papers seem to pile up. . . . This is particularly so since I have a lot
of people who want to come in and talk. . . . For example, just now I
received a telephone call from Harold Riegelman, who was our Chemical
Officer at I Corps. He is en route to the States for duty with the War
Department. . . . He claims he has a long story to tell of conditions up
there at I Corps. He stated that a new Chief of Staff and a new G-3
were forced on Palmer who, like all others, is not happy.

Bill Bowen came back from Negros after dark last night in a flying
boat. Rapp is acting in the best traditions of the Eighth Army. He first
landed a platoon at that big bridge which I was so anxious to get and
it annihilated a Japanese column just at daybreak and killed the guards
on the [Bago] bridge before they could pull the switch. It was a five
span, steel truss bridge, and each span is 130 feet long. I would have
had no way of replacing that bridge as I am saving all the pontoon
bridging that I have. Rapp then pushed on and took the capital, Bacolod,
in which there has been very little destruction. En route, he captured
every bridge and also three fine Jap airplanes intact on one of the air-

strips. His reconnaissance troops have branched out many miles into the interior trying to flush them out and find out where they are.

I give you the picture . . . to indicate how lives can be saved by speed. If we had gone slow we would have had to fight our way across those bridges, and Bacolod would have been destroyed. . . . Bill said the inhabitants seemed very apathetic as to our arrival. And there were no flowers, cheers, etc. as we found in Iloilo, so apparently that section was to a large extent pro-Japanese.[24] You must realize that not all the Filipinos are friendly towards us. The Japanese have managed to raise quite a sizable force to help them.

When Bill came back with his story I sent one of my personal telegrams to the Big Chief and I know he is going to be very happy over the situation in Negros. It has been a matter of worry to everybody except the Eighth Army.

April 1, 1945

Clovis came back yesterday afternoon full of enthusiasm. He had a grand talk with the Big Chief. He had received and wanted me to know first the answer to the sixty-four dollar question. You can guess what it is. . . . He found the most extreme enthusiasm for the Eighth Army and . . . what we have been doing. The Big Chief told Clovis that your palsy-walsy was incapable of doing what I have been doing. Steve Chamberlin told me yesterday also that a board of officers out here from Washington were popeyed while they were watching what I have been doing in the last ten days.

We certainly are riding high when it comes to turning in military victories. . . . You have been in my thoughts all the time — I am very anxious that you get a kick out of our operations and not too much worry. Don't see why I cannot get home next summer if my luck holds out.

April 2, 1945

Yesterday morning I left by flying boat for Negros, intending to return by water with Rip Struble. The trip over . . . was perfectly beautiful. . . . I decided that since it would take him two days to get home and it is only an hour by air that I would fly back. I rewarded the young Navy pilot by taking him with me when I went into Negros. It was the thrill of his life.

We landed at Pulupandan . . . [where] the 40th Division landed the other day. We then proceeded about 20 miles by jeep down that long concrete road to Bacolod. The Japs have been more or less pushed out of the way and although they greatly outnumber us we have the advantage of air support, tanks and artillery.

Rapp tells me he captured a Japanese house of prostitution with 60 girls and he is having a real problem there. Some of the girls were Japanese and some Filipinos. I told Rapp he should have first choice but he said he is not interested.

After a lunch of field rations...I decorated Rapp with the Silver Star. I thought he was going to cry, because he was pushed around so much up in Luzon.

Fred Irving has landed on Masbate using first a boat load of guerrillas whom we are now reinforcing before the Japs lick them. That will be a small operation. As you can see from the map, Bohol is about the last island on which we have not landed in the Visayas. Of course we have plenty of Japs to kill on Cebu and Negros.

In the next big operation I am going to treat myself to the luxury of riding on a cruiser....Many important things lie ahead of us unless the war ends suddenly or I lose my good humor and health....Jens has some things to pull off which you will read about long before this letter reaches you.

April 3, 1945

Of course you haven't probably remembered it, but today is our wedding anniversary, making a total of 32 years of married life interspersed with a couple of wars. You know so well how I feel about it all. I still manage to get just as homesick as I did when I first came over.

Yesterday afternoon...the Governor of Palawan, who is of course a Filipino, arrived to spend the night....This little Filipino is as bright as a whip and very much overcome by his being treated courteously by an American general....I could see that he was quite ragged so I fitted him out in some government shirts....He has been in the hills for nearly three years. You will recall that it was on Palawan that the Japanese murdered the American prisoners who had been working on the airfield there. This happened last fall. We do not know the exact number but...only about five escaped. Our investigation indicated that some had been burned and some...shot. We have been very anxious to capture any of those Japs on Palawan, but without much success. One prisoner made quite a good drawing of the Japanese positions before he tried to escape.[25]

Yesterday Lee Van Atta received a telegram from the INS asking for a 300 word interview with me which they want to release as soon as the war with Germany is over. This they want to do to offset the feeling back home that the entire war is over. We are going to have a difficult time keeping our men happy when they realize that the men are pouring home from Europe. While I do not make any comparison between fighting in a jungle and fighting in Europe, I do feel that those boys over there have a much more interesting time on one of their leaves than we have here. Now that we are so far away from Australia there is no place we can send these boys for a leave.

Bill Bowen left today for Cebu and the B-25 went down to Tawi Tawi, which is south of Jolo, where we are continuing our mopping up of the Sulu Archipelago. A landing was made there yesterday.[26] We have also made a landing on the island of Masbate. A surprise attack was made by a bunch of guerrillas led by an officer on my staff, and Fred Irving left yesterday with a couple of boats to consolidate the landing. In about six days we will have quite a force ashore there and we will wipe out that island, which unfortunately is quite large. I think the Japanese there are mostly refugees from Negros, Panay, Cebu and from the battle of Leyte. A few of them got ashore from boats that were sunk in the various battles in these waters. We are beginning to search the seas with PT boats now in the daytime for Japs disguised as Filipinos who travel in small boats.

April 4, 1945

Last night ... Al Wedemeyer[27] called from GHQ. He was there with some Air Corps general on his way to China. Clovis and I drove down to see him and he was very interesting. Al was very friendly as always and outlined the situation in Washington for us, including the future plans for this area.... Some of the operations planned here have not been definitely approved by the Joint Chiefs of Staff. Insofar as we are concerned we have nothing definitely approved beyond the operations in the Sulu Archipelago and those for the capture of Mindanao.

April 5, 1945

Yesterday afternoon I ... talked to a Lt. Commander of the Japanese Navy who had been captured by the guerrillas down in Mindanao after being torpedoed by one of our submarines. He didn't know a lot as he has been a captain of a small transport and ... a prisoner since last September up in the mountains....

Fred is back, having made a successful landing on Masbate, and I know you have read ... about the landing the Eighth Army made on Tawi Tawi ... about thirty miles from Borneo. That leaves Bohol the only island in the Visayas on which we have not landed. Of course there are still a number in the Sulu Archipelago and, as you have so wisely remarked, we haven't taken Mindanao by a long shot.

The Cebu fight is the hardest of them all and that is something we had to find out by actual combat. There were no guerrilla reports or other things that I read that would so indicate. We are putting reinforcements into Cebu and expect to take them out very soon. Of course what we want to do is scatter them into the hills so that the guerrillas will kill them, but every time the Japanese advance on those little brown beggers they are inclined to take off with speed and discretion. The finest thing I know about the Filipinos has been the warmhearted care they have given our aviators who have been shot down.... They have literally saved hundreds of our lives. Even that Jap commander said that they treated them well. I asked him if he had not been afraid of having his throat cut, because that is what the Japanese have been doing to the guerrillas. He seemed to think though that the cruelties are all limited to the Japanese.

April 6, 1945

There will be a great deal of committee meeting now at GHQ to decide how they are going to build up the staff of the new command which gives General MacArthur overall command of the Army forces in the Pacific. I am sure of one thing and that is that he will want to finish this job off as quickly as possible, and whether or not I am a part of the final fight I am anxious to have it over with. I have a feeling that I have done my bit.

I think you are wrong when you think that George Catlett Marshall has no idea of what is going on. From things that Wedemeyer said I imagine they are well informed, but there has been little that they have been able to do about it. For example, the attitude of Nimitz toward your Leavenworth friend[28] is interesting, and the fact that G.C.M. asked that he not be sent to Washington to represent this area anymore was very interesting too.

Tomorrow morning . . . we expect to . . . fly to Bacolod. . . . We will see Rapp . . . then we are going to fly to Cebu and see how the fighting is going above that town. That is the worst spot I have right now and I am throwing Duke Arnold's third regiment in there to help him out. He found a tremendous cave full of guns and equipment on the captured airfield. . . . The airfield isn't much good to us yet because they are still bringing 20 mm fire to bear on it, but we are putting an airstrip on Mactan Island which is directly opposite the city.

April 7, 1945

This morning I took off in a Martin Mariner . . . for Bacolod. Lt. Gen. Styer and Brig. Gen. Wiley from Service Forces, Washington, went along. Gen. Styer, who is the number two man for Summervell, wanted to . . . look into the shipping question (why so many boats are sitting around in harbors). That isn't my problem except at Eighth Army supply points such as Zamboanga, Iloilo and Cebu City. It is perfect at these points from the standpoint of supply — 3 days at Cebu and 4 at Iloilo, which is wonderful. *Gen. Styer and Gen. Wiley expressed themselves as greatly impressed and pleased with the trip we gave them and the information we had available about our different supply points.*[29]

April 8, 1945

Fred went to Manila the day before yesterday to see the Big Chief and came to see me last night. He had a grand talk with the Big Chief who promised him he would make him a division commander on the recommendation of anyone except your palsy-walsy. It is evident that the Big Chief does not trust your palsy-walsy to be fair to Fred.

I told Fred that I would recommend him for the first vacancy which might come up in division commanders. Of course I am delighted, because I think a great injustice was done. The Big Chief told Fred that he realizes that his division did make a fine record and that he is sorry that the action was taken. I have been throwing more and more responsibility on Fred through what we call the Eighth Army Area Command, which is really a sort of rear area Army corps. In addition to rear areas he now has direct command of operations on Leyte and Samar as well as Masbate, and I shall extend his responsibilities from time to time. . . . I think it has been my friendship which has brought him through these troubles. Clovis and I have noticed that the Big Chief never violates his spoken word, and if he promises to do something he will do it.

Please do not allow yourself to take the Hearst papers too seriously. They were launching a campaign to have the Big Chief put in command of the Army troops in the Pacific. They will later undoubtedly launch a campaign to make him President if he is alive and well a couple years from now.

If I would get all the publicity you would like to have me receive I would never get the chance to fight in the battle of Japan, and you know that is a fact.

(later)

I have just seen Steve. He tells me that the Big Chief was offered some famous names for future operations, both staff and command, and that he said in effect: "No, thank you. They [MacArthur's subordinate commanders] have been with me all this time and I do not intend to see them superseded. Anyone who comes over must be junior to them."

April 9, 1945

I believe I do not exaggerate when I tell you that the Eighth Army is riding on the crest of the waves. Steve said that everybody in Manila from the Big Chief . . . on down are praising the Eighth Army. *Steve said that the history of the Visayan campaign would some day be considered a classic.*[30]

I gathered that they are going to do some of the things that I wanted for the next operation (near future). They plan in the big picture (many months away) to have your palsy-walsy make a landing at one place . . . while the Big Chief with two units such as mine, but with more divisions, makes the main attack on another island. . . . (This would be where I would come in.)[31]

Joe E. Brown [A popular comedian] arrived shortly after luncheon yesterday and . . . at 4:00 Joe went with me to our own hospital nearby which is chucked-full of wounded boys. Joe made a great hit there. I distributed a lot of Purple Hearts and talked with many of the men. Joe claims he saw me crying a number of times but I do not think he is correct, although I felt like it. Some of the wards where they have the serious cases are full of boys in casts with their arms and legs up in the air, one man with a broken neck, another with a broken back, etc. This is very hard for me to take, and when I get through with a couple of hours of that I am ready to quit, especially if the wounded have been serving under my command. Joe has a troupe which will start out to tour the Eighth Army areas. . . . By the time they get to Cebu City I hope the Japanese will be pushed back far enough so that they won't get shot.

April 10, 1945

We landed at Jolo yesterday without opposition, and at almost the same hour we made a landing on Busuanga Island . . . in the northern part of the Palawan group. . . . Both of these landings were successful. We have only one more landing to make in the Visayas and that is at Bohol. We have plenty of troops ashore at Masbate so I am not worrying a bit about that. The real fight we are having is at Cebu.

You will notice from the attached communique that we are getting most of our opposition on Negros, but that is not accurate. The best Jap troops I have seen for a long time are above Cebu City. They came down the night before last and blew up one of our big ammunition dumps by killing themselves.

This morning we . . . made a fast trip direct to Nichols Field. . . . A sedan met me and I went at once to GHQ. . . . When I went in to talk to the Big Chief I never received so many bouquets in my life. He said that my operations in the Visayas, Zamboanga and the Sulu Archipelago had been handled just the way he would have wanted to have done it had he been an Army commander — speed, dash, brilliance, etc. He said that your old palsy-walsy is the old-fashioned Army general who wants to do everything by the rules. If he is given a certain number of troops to do a job with, he wants twice that number. The Big Chief said that if he had been trying to take the Visayas he would just now be preparing to attack Palawan (where we landed late in February) with an army corps (we used one regiment). He said he would not have dared to take in less than a division on any of these landings. He said he was the type like Meade, the Union general in the Civil War who used to make Grant so angry. You will recall that it was Meade that let the Confederates get away after Gettysburg.

He said he wanted to have the Eighth Army make the initial landing in the big blow, wherever it might fall. He said that he had been offered a lot of big names, including Omar and Georgie, and that he had accepted certain ones but has turned down the high ranking ones in as diplomatic a manner as he could. He said that if Omar came over he would have to accept a lesser job than he has been handling, as he intended to command the armies in the big show himself. He said if the War Department did not relieve your palsy-walsy that he would give him the type of job for which he was fitted — one which would require him to land and take up something in the nature of a defensive position. He said that he probably would organize something in the nature of two area commands, one with Richardson and one with Styer... and that Jimmy Frink would then command the forward supply work.

I told the Big Chief that I was going in on another operation and that I would not see him for a while. He said he was coming down to make a personal inspection of the places I had captured and that he would like to have me present if possible.... He was anxious to have us complete our fight at Cebu as he wanted to give this campaign the greatest amount of publicity of any that have taken place in the SWPA. He does not think he should do so until the Japs at Cebu have been scattered. I think that would be good psychology.

The Big Chief let me read all his telegrams and it is evident that it was quite a struggle to put him across. Also he seemed to think, and I agreed with him, that there would be some who will try to prevent him from acting in accordance with his directive... that although he has been designated the top man there will be attempts to keep him from being it.

Oh yes, I forgot to say that the Big Chief, in talking about your palsy-walsy, said that he was all infantryman. He would tolerate the artillery and hate the Navy and Air Corps; could not get along with them. (Your palsy-walsy's propaganda in the old days against me was that I was just a good-natured fellow that everybody liked and that it took a tough hombre like himself to really handle the other services!)

There is one thing you may be sure of and that is if I am to have a big position in this war from now on it will have to come from the Big Chief. The War Department did their best for me in 1943 but now they have their own fairhaired boys fresh from their fights in Europe.... Grand work is being done in many parts of the world and I am very happy over these many successes.

April 13, 1945

Yesterday I interviewed here a little Jap officer who was captured in Masbate island.... He was on Capul the day we landed. He saw that big silver plane shooting at them but claims he wasn't one of those who shot back. You remember how the "Miss Em" helped out that landing. He was a sad little fellow, about half starved, but he still believes Japan will win.

9:30 A.M.

While at breakfast with the governor of Samar, the news came of the passing of the Commander in Chief [FDR]. We were all shocked, but I am *not* surprised. He has looked terrible for a long time, but particularly since before the Honolulu Conference.

April 15, 1945

We are headed for the Malabang-Cotabato area of Mindanao. The convoy as always is beautiful — great lines of ships as far as you can see. The routine has become very familiar to us all.

This morning...we went to the brief service held for President Roosevelt. Our routine is mostly to read and sleep. Clovis has now started a book I finished called *Rivers of Glory,* a romantic historical novel of the Revolution.

All these ships have had quite a history. I do not know what the writers of the future will do about Army-Navy history because there has been more naval fighting and amphibious landings in one small section of the Pacific than in the whole prior history of the Navy.

I can imagine the terrific excitement back home following the death of the President. I think everybody dreaded that a bit. It seemed so evident from his pictures that he was not a man who could live through another term as President, but I was horrified when he died so quickly. Of course it is a remarkable thing that a man of his health and affliction could have lasted over three terms in that terrible job.

April 16, 1945

The guerrillas have captured the town of Malabang where we expected to land tomorrow, so we are changing our objective to Parang, about 20 miles down the coast — it isn't far from Cotabato, which is our immediate objective.... The rest of the crowd are working on the revised field order for tomorrow.

In a message to Sibert I urged a rapid advance inland and stressed the importance of not sitting down and sending reconnaissance parties out, but of pushing forward in full strength.[32]

Notes

1. This is a reference to the landing of elements of the 182d Infantry on the southern tip of Capul Island, in the San Bernardino Straits.

2. The passage in italics is taken from the Eichelberger Diary, 27 February 1945.

3. The reference here is to phrases in songs popular with the old army: "Monkeys have no Tails in *Zamboanga,*" and the "ten year old Virgin" whose home was *Cebu City.* Being familiar with the words to these songs, Miss Em would know where to expect the next amphibious landings.

4. Press relations officer at GHQ.

5. Col. Marcario L. Peralta, commanding the Sixth Military District on Panay. Eichelberger Diary, 28 February 1945.

6. Col. Wendell W. Fertig commanded the guerrilla forces on Mindanao; Lt. Col. James M. Cushing commanded guerrillas on Cebu.

7. First battalion, 132d Infantry.

8. This is denied emphatically by Dr. Forrest Pogue, General Marshall's biographer. Personal information.

9. Lt. Gen. Oscar W. Griswold commanded XIV Corps; Maj. Gen. Verne D. Mudge commanded the First Cavalry.

10. The sentence in italics is lifted intact from Eichelberger's Diary and inserted here for a more faithful reconstruction of the conversation.

11. MacArthur "said he felt that Eisenhower's curve had gone down since last summer and he is not now considered the great leader he formerly was. He also agreed with me that the American public would not give the American Army on the Rhine credit for these victories but would give it to the pressure of the Russian troops from now on." Eichelberger Diary, 3 March 1945.

12. This statement is taken from the Eichelberger Diary, 7 March 1945.

13. Maj. Gen. Jens A. Doe commanded the Forty-first Division in the liberation of Palawan, Zamboanga, and the Sulu Archipelago. The 186th Regimental Combat Team had landed at Palawan on 24 February; the rest of the Forty-first comprised the assault force for *Victor IV*.

14. Maj. Gen. Rapp Brush commanded the Fortieth Division, which was slated to capture Panay and western Negros.

15. Gen. Eichelberger's Diary for the following day reveals the nature of this "pep talk." "Discussed the V-I operation [liberation of Panay and western Negros] with Gen. Brush and made the following points: no credence to be given guerrilla reports and tactical decisions are not to be affected by them. Also the need for speedy and aggressive action and the constant maintenance of contact was stressed."

16. Krueger's promotion to full general, with rank from 5 March.

17. The remainder of this account of Gen. Eichelberger's conversation with Gen. MacArthur is taken from the letter to Miss Em dated 25 March 1945.

18. Professor Morton suggests that in making this judgment Gen. MacArthur "was probably unaware of the circumstances which had dictated Wainwright's course of action...." Lt. Gen. Jonathan M. Wainwright, who had assumed command of U.S. forces in the Philippines on March 20, 1942, ordered troops in the southern Philippines to surrender for fear the Japanese would kill the 11,000 troops recently taken on Corregidor. Louis Morton, *The Fall of the Philippines* (Washington, 1953), p. 575. "It was only after General Wainwright was released from a Japanese prison camp at the end of the war and signed up to write a serial for the newspapers that General MacArthur took him to his bosom, stood him beside himself on the deck of the *Missouri* along with the British General who had surrendered at Singapore (without too much credit to himself). It was then that General MacArthur recommended promotion and the Medal of Honor for Wainwright. General Malin Craig, a former Chief of Staff, told my wife in Washington while I was in the Pacific that the War Department had wanted to give Wainwright a Medal of Honor at the time they gave General MacArthur his, but MacArthur would not agree." Eichelberger Dictations, 27 October 1945.

19. In May 1948, Gen. Eichelberger appended the following note to the entry in his Diary for 20 March 1945: "It should be noted that Krueger tried to get Griswold, Commanding General XIV Corps to relieve Brush in Luzon. Transferred his 40th Division to Chink Hall's XI Corps and tried to get Chink to relieve him. Both refused. Chink told me that when he went up to see Brush west of Stotsenburg and told Brush he was directed to relieve him, that Rapp told him that neither Krueger nor his staff had ever been up to see him fight. Then Chink refused to relieve Brush. Gris said he told Krueger, 'You can relieve me if you wish but I won't recommend Brush to go.' Both Griswold and Hall told me this story."

20. Eichelberger's information was more accurate with respect to actual Japanese strength on Cebu than in many of his other operations. In his official report he stated that there was a total of 11,500 Japanese in the areas ... Cebu, Bohol, and Negros Oriental," with an estimated 10,500 on Cebu, 8,750 of which were in the vicinity of Cebu City.

Report of the Commanding General Eighth Army on the Panay-Negros and Cebu Operations: Victor I and II, p. 58. But because many troops had filtered in from Leyte and some service elements had not been detected prior to contact, the actual strength of the Japanese was roughly 14,500, with all but 2,000 deployed near Cebu City. Robert Ross Smith, *Triumph in the Philippines* (Washington, 1963), pp. 608-609. Sentences in italics came from Eichelberger Diary, 26 March 1945.

21. Maj. Gen. William H. Arnold, commanding general, the Americal Division.

22. Sentence in italics comes from Eichelberger Diary, 27 March 1945.

23. Colonel Floyd E. Dunn commanded the 182d Infantry.

24. The Diary speaks of "the unusually cool reception given the troops by the Spanish civilians." Eichelberger Diary, 30 March 1945.

25. Five years later Eichelberger had still not lost his anger over this atrocity. "On December 14 the Japanese occupation troops herded the Americans into air-raid shelters they themselves had built. Then the prisoners were saturated with gasoline and blazing torches were thrown into the tunnels. Most of the Americans burned to death; others, trying to escape the flames, were shot down.... Eleven men managed to break through the end of one of the tunnels.... They were the only survivors.... I record for infamy the name of the Japanese unit responsible — 131st Airfield Battalion, 4th Flying Division." *Our Jungle Road to Tokyo* (New York, 1950), p. 206.

26. By the Forty-first Division.

27. Lt. Gen. Albert C. Wedemeyer commanded the China Theater.

28. On 23 March 1945, Gen. MacArthur confided to Eichelberger: "I think the Navy is giving in with reference to me, but they want to get Sutherland. I understand Nimitz objects to Sutherland being in the picture." Eichelberger Diary, 23 March 1945.

29. Sentences in italics are taken from the Diary, 7 April 1945.

30. Sentences in italics are taken from the Diary, 9 April 1945.

31. Gen. Chamberlin stated "that they were having great problems in the redeployment of troops. They expect to get a total of about 45 divisions out here counting what we now have and what is in the central Pacific. Gen. Krueger will command one landing on [Kyushu] and Gen. MacArthur will command an Army group consisting of the 8th and 10th Armies on [Honshu] — the main show." Eichelberger Diary, 8 April 1945. In the original diary the bracketed names were left blank; Eichelberger added them after the war.

32. Sentence in italics is taken from Eichelberger Diary, 16 April, 1945.

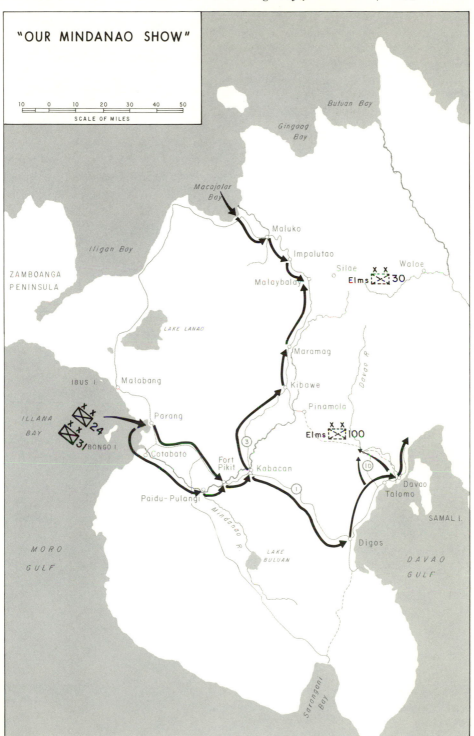

MAP 6

CHAPTER THIRTEEN

Mindanao — A Long Way from Buna

Although it was not obvious at the time, with the grim prospect of an invasion of the Japanese homeland and its attendant risks and possibilities, the Mindanao campaign was to provide a proper climax to the rise of the Eighth Army.

Initially this rugged and inhospitable island, second only to Luzon in size and lying southernmost in the archipelago, was to have been the site of MacArthur's return to the Philippines, but the steady erosion of Japanese air and shipping strength made it possible to bypass Mindanao in favor of Leyte as a naval and logistic base. There remained, however, some 55,000 Japanese in eastern Mindanao (including over 12,000 civilians) even after the landings west of Zamboanga City in March, and no one at Eighth Army headquarters was taking the task of rooting them out lightly.

Because the enemy forces were concentrated and well entrenched in the area around Davao, Maj. Gen. Franklin C. Sibert's X Corps went ashore on the west central coast, where Japanese defenses were known to be weak. On 17 April the Twenty-fourth Division, now commanded by Maj. Gen. Roscoe B. Woodruff, landed on two beaches and, utilizing the Mindanao river as well as Route 1, pushed swiftly into the interior. Fort Pikit, thirty-five miles inland, was reached on 21 April, and the vital road junction at Kabacan was seized the following day. By this time most of the Thirty-first Division, under Maj. Gen. Clarence A. Martin, was also ashore and moving up to free the Twenty-fourth Division for the dash across the island to Davao Gulf, which was reached 27 April. Turning north, the Twenty-fourth took Davao on 3 May — the same day that advance elements of the Thirty-first Division, which had been fighting its way north along the Sayre Highway, entered Kibawe.

The speed and success of the advance upon Davao far exceeded expectations. "Part of my personal aggressive policy in Mindanao . . . was based on erroneous intelligence of the Japanese strength," Eichelberger admitted after the war. "Had I known that the Japanese strength at Davao was more than it was supposed to be in all of Mindanao, less Zamboanga, I would not have been at the head of the column with . . . [the Twenty-fourth] division strung out for a least 50 miles."

Fortunately the speed of the advance seemed to paralyze the Japanese, and while the fighting along the Sayre Highway and in the hills above Davao was brutal, bloody, and desperate, the ultimate success of the operation was hardly in doubt. On 10 May the 108th Regimental Combat Team landed at Macajalar Bay and linked up with the Thirty-first Division on 23 May, marking the end of enemy resistance along the Sayre Highway. There remained fanatical resistance in the hills to the east, near Malaybalay, and above Davao until late June, by which time the campaign had entered the phase known all too well as "mopping up."

As these letters to Miss Em reveal, the fight on Mindanao occurred at a time when there was a behind-the-scenes struggle between MacArthur and the Navy for leadership in the final drive against Japan. "Therefore, the speed and success with which the Eighth Army operated pleased MacArthur to the nth degree. The fact that we crossed from Moro Gulf to Digos in ten days when he had predicted three or four months would indicate why he should have been pleased. It was very evident during this fighting that he was appreciative. He would show me consideration beyond what I have ever seen him show other officers, e.g., he walked out to put me in my car at various places, and sent officers out to the airfield when I would leave him in Manila to put me aboard the plane. . . . ('If Bob gets into trouble in his advance into Davao,' he assured Gen. Byers on one occasion, 'I'll throw every man I have in to help him.')"[1]

It was a long way from Buna.

April 17, 1945

Dearest Miss Em,
We were up this morning at 4:45 to get ready for the landing. The guns of this cruiser opened up at 6:00. . . . We were all on the top bridge, which is about five flights up, and there we stayed during the bombardment until 10:00 when we went ashore. Of course the noise is terrific and at one time a couple of five-inch guns fired just below the admiral's chair in which I was sitting. Bill Bowen claims I jumped a yard in the air.

Franklin[2] came aboard to go ashore with me. There was the usual struggle through the heavy sand and then we walked up a long hill. Finally we picked up a jeep, but our travels were brought to an end when we reached one of those long wooden bridges which the Japs had set afire.

We came back here for lunch and then this afternoon started out in a PT boat which traveled at almost fifty miles per hour. We went up to Malabang where there had been another landing and looked over those beaches.... The whole day was intensely interesting although I did not hear a hostile shot fired. I imagine the Japs are back in the hills waiting for us to come after them.

One of the interesting things to me was to see the Moro guerrillas for the first time. They look about the same except that they have highly colored headdresses of various types. I imagine those Moros are going to be hard to lick now that they have arms. It would not surprise me if the Filipino government will have many a headache in years to come.

It is always quite a thrill ... to come into a hostile shore for the first time, without much knowledge of what is ahead.

April 18, 1945

Only killed three Japs so far in the battle of Mindanao proper. That was up to 3 yesterday afternoon. There is a big booming from air and fleet right now at 7:00 A.M. Cotabato is catching it — we could go in there easily except for the bridges.

(later)

This morning, accompanied by a choice collection of admirals and newspaper men, we went ashore again at Parang and went up to Woody's Command Post and Franklin's Command Post. The troops were advancing slowly because the bridges are out, but a bunch of them made a movement by small craft which went up both branches of the Mindanao River. One of these groups captured Cotabato at nine this morning.

When we left this afternoon we took a PT boat ... to the mouth of the river and then a small landing craft for an hour or more up the broad stream. We are hoping to establish a new type of warfare in the SWPA with troops and supplies moving up the river for sixty or seventy miles before they hit the road. Maybe we can do it.

Tomorrow afternoon we will return to Leyte where I shall probably spend about five days. Then I shall return to Mindanao, stopping en route to see Colonel Fertig at Camp Keithley on Lake Lanao. The fighting at Cebu is very severe and that worries me.... The Americal [Division] has already taken fourteen hundred casualties from a bunch of Japs who are firmly entrenched in concrete fortifications. At Tawi Tawi, Jolo, Zamboanga and Iloilo, the fighting has died out. This is also true on Bohol, Leyte and Samar. We do not look for a hard time on Masbate either. Rapp is having some hard fighting on Negros but I do not think he is up against good troops there. I suspect we are up against regular infantry above Cebu City, but I am hoping for good luck.[3]

April 19, 1945

If I were writing a "My Day" column[4] it would read about as follows:

Up at six and breakfast at seven; about nine a big Martin flying boat circled over the harbor and landed near our cruiser....

We took off at once and went north, circling over Malabang town and Malabang airstrip...a strip 7,000 feet long built by the guerrillas. Then we went north over the narrow part of Mindanao with the weather perfect.... By eleven o'clock we had passed over Bohol to see where the fighting was going on there and then landed on the water near Cebu City. A fast Navy crash boat picked us up and took us to Duke Arnold.... As soon as I saw his face I knew that my fears were unjustified, because he told me the Japanese positions had been broken and they have scattered into the hills. He had already counted 5,000 dead Japs.

The area the Japs had been defending was a mass of caves and tunnels, many of them interlocking and most of them filled with food, ordnance, *as well as a lot of loot.... No accurate count has been made so far but it would be an understatement to say that there were 500 of these caves. In some, antiaircraft guns of about .50 cal. size had been placed which had command of the entire terrain below it right to the straits.... It is understood that these fortifications were made by Formosan and Korean labor, and that the local people were denied permission to enter the entire area. At one place, there was an entire underground Command Post made of reinforced concrete. This was right above Malubug airfield and the guns from this post swept the entire field.*[5]

A lot of Japanese officers committed hari-kari and the one whose saber I brought home had a pet monkey on his shoulder at the time he blew himself up with a grenade. We only saw a small part of the Jap positions as they had a width of almost 3 miles, with many ridges, and a depth of about 4 miles. You can imagine how happy it made me to have that fine victory following the successful landings at Parang and Cotabato.[6]

April 20, 1945

We went to both Negros and Cebu today.... Rapp and his men are in fine spirits. They were attacking the Japanese over a front of about five miles and I could see a lot of it through some very powerful Japanese telescopes. You can see from this that I was being good and staying out of fire.

April 21, 1945

You should have seen the tremendous preparations the Japs made above ... [Cebu] city. Every yard of the way was subjected to flanking fire from neighboring ridges out of prepared caves and pillboxes. I am sorry that the newspapermen go in on landings and then take off to some city. ... so that they can file their dispatches readily.

As you now know, it was the hope of Steve Chamberlin and the planning boys that I take an army into Java, but it had never been approved by the Joint Chiefs of Staff. As it stands now, for obvious reasons, that is off. From now on, after Mindanao, things will go slowly because certain things are not done in a day. The uninitiated may think things are done in a couple of months, but that is not the way things work out.

I am not worried about anything except the Mindanao show. At present our troops are pushing in rapidly by road and river with very little opposition. That is a temporary situation. We will get into a big fight later. . . .

You may be sure that I shall demand things when it becomes necessary. It has been necessary for me to be very diplomatic to get by. As a consequence, the Chief realizes now that I get along unusually well with the Navy and Air Corps as well as with his own staff. As long as our [Eighth] Army had not been tried in combat they were reluctant to give us credit for what we had done.

April 22, 1945

Yesterday Clovis received a letter from Bonner Fellers dated 19 April and the first paragraph reads as follows: "Congratulations to you and your able chief. You'll have all the Philippines south of Luzon cleared before the Cagayan Valley [in northern Luzon] falls. That's an achievement which no one can fail to appreciate, even if he doesn't want to — if you follow my attempt to be expressive." Of course he was referring to your palsy-walsy. . . .

I am afraid that I am not going to get much amphibious help in Mindanao because of the great use for transportation. I am sure I can bring all the troops I need into the area where we are fighting now. As a matter of fact, our troops are already in the vicinity of Pikit, which is getting quite near to Kabacan, the junction of Highway No. 1 and the Sayre Highway, which goes south ... through the Del Monte airfields. Kabacan lies almost directly east of Cotabato, inland about 60 or 70 miles.

The only fighting in the Zamboanga-Sulu Archipelago campaign is at Jolo and that is developing rapidly into a chase through the hills, with the Japanese on the receiving end of the bullets.

April 23, 1945

Yesterday I sent you General MacArthur's message. We were all very pleased with it since he doesn't give out anything like that very often. ...A letter received from Steve Chamberlin yesterday...read: "Certainly the Eighth Army is going great guns. I do not know how they happened to work the rabbit foot so hard on Cebu and succeeded in killing so many Japs in such a short time, but I suspect it is because of a little bold and aggressive action which sometimes has been lacking from our operations...." Our reputation for hospitality and friendliness has made us many friends. Joe E. Brown says that he has never seen such an army in all his travels around the world....

Woody...is pushing rapidly into the central part of Mindanao and has already reached the Kabacan area. We shall have great supply troubles there, but the Japanese are probably confused about where to send their troops. They are afraid to desert the Davao area because we can land there if they do, and if they put all their troops in Davao we can run them out of central Mindanao. If they show any sign of withdrawing from the Cagayan area at the head of the Sayre Highway...I shall put some troops in there and start moving south. All in all, it is not a bad picture. Clarence [Martin] will join Franklin [Sibert] soon....

Brisbane Billie and Tubby Burgess are off for Manila tomorrow to stay for quite a period. These are our two key men. Think that over.

April 26, 1945

This morning...we took off [from Zamboanga] at seven-thirty. We headed directly east and flew almost over Davao to where our foot troops are, only ten miles out of Digos. *Flew around the Kabacan area for about an hour and then back to Malabang Field, where we landed.... Went to Sibert's headquarters and was handed a telegram just received from Woody saying that he would take Digos that day and would march on Davao tomorrow.*[7] Of course I am delighted to be so far along, because we didn't expect to get there for a couple of months. We are going to push in all we can and my staff is meeting this afternoon to discuss this. We really haven't met those Japs in force yet — they may have abandoned Digos.

I would like to wipe out that [Japanese] colony before the rainy season comes.... We have quite a large body of troops there now and I will put more in. The road and river were crowded with troops moving eastward. It was a very grand sight in the early morning.

April 27, 1945

Yesterday, following my return, I had a lot of work to do and I am still busy with our plans for the fight for Davao Gulf. Frankly Woody has moved faster than we have thought possible. In fact we rather expected the

Japanese to make a big fight for the Kabacan area...where the Sayre Highway...runs into Highway 1 going east. There is a lot of pretty rolling country there under cultivation.... After submitting my plan to GHQ for the shifting of additional reinforcements into Mindanao, I received a telegram about eleven o'clock last night...from the Big Chief, which said, "Heartily approve your plan...."

Regarding your questions, I found that I could not get enough ships to carry a corps into Davao Gulf in one big landing. This is why we landed in the comparatively peaceful area around Parang and Cotabato. They thought we would take several months to get where we are now — it is only 10 days since the Parang landing.

We do not know much about what lies ahead of us in Mindanao because the Japanese have not yet fought us in any force. I telegraphed General MacArthur today that I propose to find them and then fight them. You won't mind if I get a wee bit swanky, I know.

April 28, 1945

This morning...we left for Manila at 8:00 in the B-17.[8]...I had about an hour and fifteen minutes with the Big Chief. The praise from him and everyone up there is really embarrassing. Of course it was a grand psychological moment for me to go there since the flashes had come through this morning that we were in Digos on the Davao Gulf. Now I am going to push power in there right away.

The Big Chief said he approved heartily my recommendations about the reinforcements that I want to send into Mindanao and that anything else I wanted would be done.... He told me about the trouble he was having with certain people who have received a directive making him the number one Army boy but who give this order only lip service. He and others think that their object is to control all overseas positions after the war, using the Marines, and using the Army as a sort of home guard. He has beaten them before and I do not doubt that he will do it again. ...He says that if the Navy idea of piddling around for a long time before doing anything against the Japanese homeland carries through, he still wants me to go into Java rather than have my troops sit around and stagnate. In this I think he is dead right. Actually, the opinion of everybody seems to be that the Navy wants to end this war with Japan without the help of the Big Chief by landing in China and forming a ring around Japan and conducting bombings by the Air Corps under their control.

A telegram just received indicates that about half of Woody's outfit has reached Digos. When it is all there, there is not enough Japanese strength in Mindanao to throw them out. I know the Navy will be glad to cooperate in opening that place up now that we have it.

April 29, 1945

This morning we heard that elements of the 31st Division have moved as far as Santa Cruz, while other elements have moved down and captured the airstrip south of Digos. That will give them about 16 miles along the water line already. They captured coast artillery guns, which were booby trapped, as well as antiaircraft guns, so it is evident that our rapid advance fooled them a bit. They are fixing up an airstrip so that I will be able to fly there within the next two or three days....

May 1, 1945

News came late yesterday afternoon that Woody is only ten miles out of Davao City. I think that has been a perfectly remarkable campaign so far. I am only hoping that the Japs do not all run away into the hills. That has been the standard Jap pattern for some time. Although there are a lot of Japs down there we have the feeling that they are in poor condition. A captured Jap nurse said that at least 20% had malaria.

I imagine Woody will be in Davao City by tomorrow and then his big fight will probably occur above the city. Clarence Martin[9] has been advancing north of Kabacan on the Sayre Highway and I would like to keep those two Japanese forces separated. That Japanese colony in Davao was a menace when I was G-2 out here. When World War II opened up I believe they had about 40,000 civilians in Davao and many of them have gone into the Army.

May 2, 1945

The last report I got last night was that we were four miles out of Davao City and that the 31st Division advanced ten more miles up the Sayre Highway against quite a bit of opposition.... I do not know how good your map is. We couldn't even find out whether that road from Kabacan to Digos was open or whether it would be possible to get through. That is one reason I am so delighted that we were able to cover 125 miles in ten days in spite of the bridges being burned out. The threat of Japs around every turn also slows a timid man down a lot.

May 3, 1945

[Yesterday] we landed on Padada airstrip without a bounce and I know it was the first four-motored plane that ever came there.... It is a big strip with many revetments and barracks, storehouse, concrete pill-boxes, etc. Franklin, with a lot of jeeps, met us.... It was a long ride to Woody's Command Post and we passed through many villages. I thought I could recognize a lot of slant-eyed babies as the result of the Japanese colony being there so many years.... It was 41 miles from Padada strip to Davao City. The Japs have been attacking our trucks there a bit and we found a number that had been burned. We must have had a dozen MP's in jeeps guarding us.

After a hasty luncheon we went forward to try to get to Davao City, which our advance elements had entered via a foot bridge. Fire was coming across the road from two directions so we went back to camp where . . . I talked to some war correspondents in praise of the 24th Division. . . . I must have had eight and one-half hours sleep in spite of heavy artillery fire.

[Today] after an early morning breakfast . . . we took off for Davao City and crossed a very swift river on a very precarious foot-bridge which consisted mostly of slanting planks. I pinned the DSM on Franklin. . . . This town of course has been to a large extent destroyed. Then we went up to the 21st Infantry where Colonel [William] Verbeck, a four times wounded officer, stood off Jap attacks all night and killed a lot of them.

We then drove to Santa Cruz where our amphibious craft were unloading supplies. . . .

We are following the end of the war in Europe with great interest. I realize that with Hitler dead things should close down very quickly. Now we are going to see what plans they adopt for the war against Japan.

May 4, 1945

We have a choice of a number of methods of fighting those fellows [on Mindanao], but if GHQ will approve my plans I am sure that we can lick them with some speed. I have just put a regiment, the 162nd Infantry from Jens' outfit, into Parang for use in the rear areas up to Kabacan. That will allow Clarence to push his men full strength forward. He has many engineer problems because the Japs have destroyed all of the bridges.

I can imagine how excited you have been over our rapid advances into Davao City. Believe me I have been excited myself. We need every man we can get in there, but I imagine the Japs are not going to like it if Martin pushes some of his strength down on them from the northwest. . . . They are all hoping that I finish up that Mindanao campaign by the 1st of July. This I hope to be able to do, particularly if I can throw in all the extra troops I can spare from other places. The question of moving troops by water is always a great problem because of the lack of transportation.

May 5, 1945

Unfortunately, Bill [Bowen] agreed to give up my Zamboanga troops for training for future operations much earlier than I would have agreed, and that applies to the 40th and American also. . . .

Rapp feels now that his Japs are beginning to break a bit. The Japs are launching a lot of banzai attack which are a prelude to defeat. In some of these banzai attacks they jazz themselves up with sake or dope of some sort. When our soldiers meet a banzai attack they certainly have a field day. Once in a blue moon these attacks succeed, but it has been very seldom in this theater, and a successful one is almost impossible against veteran troops armed with automatic weapons.

I ran into Bill Sibert again down there with the 24th Division. He was hot, dirty and covered with mosquito bites. The perimeter of his regiment had been under constant attack . . . during the night, including automatic weapons and mortars. Bill told me he would much prefer to fight in Europe than in the jungle, and he is an expert since he was wounded three times in Europe. . . .

We have a lot of heavy artillery around Davao City now and I'll bet the Japs love the sound of those big shells coming over. This is no military secret because the Japs can hear them without any effort and can feel them too. Bill Bowen is the one who insisted on taking those eight-inch howitzers in there and I laughed at him but finally gave in. They actually brought them all the way across that island.

I see by the San Francisco news this morning that they are all hell-bent for releasing our veterans out here. I can remember when the Japanese could have won the first fight I was in if they had gone out during the night and pounded on tin pans. Now they can't lick us with anything they have. I hate to see . . . the vets go and I hope as many as possible volunteer to stay.

I am not a very good swimmer but I have found out how to handle myself in rough water. . . . Joe E. Brown went in the other night in the moonlight without any trunks on, leaving his towel on the beach. He came out finding some eager young officer sitting on his towel with a girl, and that I think is quite a joke.

May 6, 1945

A letter from Bill indicates that the planning is going on merrily, particularly with reference to your palsy's part, which will presumably be the first. Of course no plan has yet been submitted for this area and we do not know whether we are going right at the Japs or whether we are going to piddle around on the outskirts. Until these conflicting views are settled we will not know much.

May 7, 1945

After the officers' meeting this morning, at which I cussed everybody out including myself, I went in the B-17 to Negros and Cebu. . . . Rapp had told me that we couldn't land at his airstrip, but we fooled him.

Clovis and Bill came back with renewed expressions of the fine reception they received from everybody. . . . The various things I asked

for were granted. . . . Clovis' best rumor so far he obtained from Bonner
Fellers, who said definitely that Ike would not be Chief of Staff and
that George Catlett Marshall thought that he had been giving in too
much to foreigners. The favorite name is Bradley, who had done well with
foreigners, and he said my name was the next one up. I hope you get a
good laugh out of that.

May 8, 1945

TODAY IS V-E DAY

  Before breakfast I was listening to the radio and it told of a point system that will be used to send men home — those with lots of children
(OK by me), overseas service, combat, decorations, etc. will be high up
to go home. A recruit newcomer with no combat or decorations would
have to stay to fight. Clovis thinks it is OK, but no one but . . . old Uncle
Sam would send home the veterans and fight with recruits.

May 9, 1945

We have another little show coming up tomorrow. . . . I shall fly over
there to watch the landing and then the following day I expect to land in
a flying boat and go ashore. After that I expect to go down to see Franklin and Clarence. I have insisted that Clarence be allowed to hold his
force together and not split it here, there, and every place. In that way
he ought to do well. At one time he had 48 bridges out that he was
trying to get to work on, and that means that it is almost impossible
to get vehicles up until the engineers have done their stuff. Woody of
course has his troops concentrated and they are able to unload his supplies nearby.

  While our eyes already turn to other directions, it is a long time off.
. . . I know that I will be in the middle of the fight because the Big Chief
and I see eye to eye on the question of going after these little fellows.

The letters written from 10 to 14 May appear to be missing, but the
diary indicates the nature of General Eichelberger's activities during
the next several days.

  On 10 May he flew in the "Miss Em" to northern Mindanao to
observe the unopposed landing of the 108th Regimental Combat
Team at Macajalar Bay, from which point a fresh drive could be
launched southeast along the Sayre Highway to link up with General Martin's Thirty-first Division as it fought its way up from the
south. "The forces that went into Macajalar Bay consisted of the
108th RCT of the 40th Division and one battalion of the 164th of
the Americal," he explained to Miss Em several days after the landing. "Of course a regiment and a battalion never gives the true picture because there are always engineers, hospitals, tanks, port com-

panies, etc. Then of course there is artillery too, and in that case the battalion that ordinarily serves with the 108th plus one battery went in with the extra battalion."[10]

The day following the landing General Eichelberger drove along the Sayre Highway for several miles. He confessed in his diary that he was impressed by the "very strong defense positions which the Japanese had abandoned," and he ventured the opinion "that one company could have held us up for about a week, had the Japs stayed." The country was "beautiful, with high mountains and very deep canyons on each side of the highway." As he drove south he passed many doughboys: "All of them looked fine."

On 14 May General Eichelberger returned once again to Mindanao to keep a watchful eye on the closing pincers along the Sayre Highway.[11]

May 15, 1945

Dearest Miss Em:

We got away promptly at eight and at nine we joined a couple of Marine fighters at our rendezvous point over Macajalar Bay. It had been my original intention to take a circuitous route around by Malabang, but the way was so clear that we just hightailed it down the Sayre Highway, passing over a lot of Japanese airstrips and the headquarters of *the 35th* Japanese Army. Of course we did not fly close enough to be within effective ack-ack range, although I am not too sure just where the Japanese are in that valley.

Colonel Downer made a fine landing on the grass Maramag airstrip which had been captured two days ago by the 31st Division.[12] Shortly before I arrived the Japs launched a two-way attack against one of our battalions located about a half-mile south of the strip. They very proudly displayed for my edification 72 dead Japs, ten machine guns, and a lot of other booty. This would be a horrible sight for most people to look at but they do not bother me a bit.

Tomorrow I expect to go to one of the Del Monte airfields where the 108th is fighting southward.

May 16, 1945

The Japs are only about two miles from the airstrip where we landed and a fight was going on at the time. As a matter of fact, our artillery was in back of the airfield and they had to cease firing to let us land.

Our men were held up in a canyon where the road curls down through narrow passages and comes up on the other side. The Japs are in caves down there and since the vegetation is thick it is going to be hard to get them out. A battalion of men waded across the river and came up the other bank of the canyon where they were in position on the other side of a young mountain. From the observation post on the side of the canyon I could look all around with my glasses and watched the tanks shooting into the caves.

The usual jeeps were there filled with arms and men and we went at once down to where the fighting was going on. It really is not very serious. The commanding officer is a very fine officer and a very courageous one, but I can see that he does not like to have his men hurt. Therefore, he will be slowed up quite a bit. If necessary, I shall send Bob Shoe over there, since he is the number two man in the 40th Division and the fighting on Negros is about over.

May 17, 1945

We have been having a terrible fight above...Davao City, and I have thrown everything into it that I can get. Right now my chief weapon is to send replacements. Remembering my experiences at Buna, I am sending every man I can get my hands on into that fight to the exclusion of other islands and units because it will raise their morale very much to realize that new men are coming in in such quantities. When a Jap gets wounded or sick there is no new man to take his place.

From Mindanao word has come that Clarence Martin has advanced as far as the airfields at Valencia, although up until today he had not been able to get his artillery across a certain river which I inspected with him. The Japs have an Army headquarters at Impalutao, which is near Malaybalay...about half way between Clarence and the 108th, which is below Del Monte. There is still a gap of about fifty or sixty miles. Maps are unreliable down here.

You thought Woody's troubles were east of Davao City, but we haven't seriously tried to pass far to the north. There has been quite a bit of fighting on that island just outside Davao City, which the guerrillas told us was unoccupied.[13] Our fighting is up that road that leads up above Davao City into the interior. Clarence holds one end of it and when he gets through with the Japs up above I am going to send him down that road. I could use another division of troops but I am guarding a lot of the supply lines with other units such as antiaircraft gun battalions which we do not need anymore because there are no more Japanese planes.

I have an eternal yearn to keep traveling while that fight is going on. ...I take plenty of chances but I do it with my eyes open and I do not like to take unnecessary chances. This would make some of my officers laugh but it is true.

May 18, 1945

I am about to send the B-25 over to Negros to pick up Bob Shoe so he can go down to the Del Monte area with me tomorrow. I am going to have him take over command of the task force which landed at...

Macajalar Bay and is now moving south toward a junction with Clarence's troops. By doing this I feel that Colonel Stratta,[14] the Commanding Officer of the 108th, can devote his undivided attention to his regiment. Most of his troops are now beyond the canyon which I described to you the other day. . . . They have been doing all right, but I think they could be a little more aggressive in moving forward.

Franklin has built up some fine supply bases down there on the southern coast of Mindanao, but I do not believe he has put enough people up where the roads make the going tough due to the destruction of all the bridges. I am referring particularly to Clarence's engineering problems. I really believe he could move some of his manpower up there to help these boys out without hurting his rear areas. As it is, Clarence's advance elements have to rely on air droppings for their food and other things.

(later)

A communique yesterday just about ended our war in Mindanao, but actually the fight is just going fine at Davao City and we have not yet met the main Japanese force in central Mindanao.

It looks as though the Japs are beginning to break above Davao City. If they pull out of their present positions they will give up something they have been preparing for years. We have a threat on their backs as Martin has sent one battalion down the road from Kibawe southeast toward Davao City. This is more of a trail than a road, and does not show on most maps. . . . I am moving every available engineer I can get up to that Kabacan-Valencia road, the large part of which is corduroy.

May 19, 1945

I was up at five this morning and we took off promptly at seven for Del Monte, arriving down there shortly after eight. The 108th Regimental Combat Team, reinforced by a battalion of the Americal Division and other units, is doing very well. The thing that is holding us up is the construction of a steel bridge across a canyon which the Japanese blew up. It should be finished by tomorrow morning as we are working night and day. First we had to defeat the Japanese before we could get to the bridge.

From Del Monte we took off for Maramag. . . . I was met . . . by Franklin, Clarence Martin, and Colonel Fertig, and we settled a lot of points. I then took Franklin with me to . . . Libby airdrome at Davao City. We had been warned that it was dangerous and we were the first American plane that has ever landed on that strip. In order to approach the field we had to circle over the Japanese positions and that was the most dangerous thing. Franklin and Woody had the field surrounded by a mass of tanks, self-propelled artillery, MP's and a bunch of infantrymen. They were afraid that some ack-ack from a distance would be fired at the strip after the Japs saw the plane land, but no shots were fired all day. They were also afraid of the ever-present suicide infiltrations.

Woody is doing a grand job there and he is pounding them with a tremendous amount of artillery under our new Brigadier General, Hugh Cort, and this artillery includes eight-inch howitzers and 155 [mm.] guns.... There are lots of Japanese troops down there and of course a tremendous civilian colony, but I do not believe the Japanese can do anything but get thoroughly licked. If I were the Japanese general I would go way back into the mountains and wait until our troops go off to some other war, but of course that means sickness, starvation, and eventual death.

We returned the same way we went. Chuck worried me a bit because he insisted on riding up the whole length of the Japanese Army on the Sayre Highway...at the height of about 2000 feet. Those Japs must think that we are crazy. We may have had troubles...but...the Navy dive bombers were working the Japs over in the Malaybalay area as we passed by and I think that is why they didn't fire at us. Mindanao from the air today was unbelievably beautiful.

I have had almost my share of fighting and almost my share of the tropics. It will soon be three years....Rumor has it that I will take over the entire Philippines soon, so your palsy can busy himself with other things. Personally, I hope it will not be so, because the rainy season is about to start up in Luzon and there is an awful lot left to do.

May 20, 1945

A telegram just received indicates that Clarence's advance elements are only three miles south of Malaybalay....I feel they have gone into the hills without making a very serious fight but I do not believe that northern force has a terrible amount of power. Eventually I shall have to move down the Kibawe-Davao trail and clean them out in there....

Bob Shoe goes down tomorrow to take over command of the northern task force which...has been moving a little too slowly to suit me. They must have about seven or eight thousand troops....

Bill came back tonight and...thinks I must go up to Manila on Tuesday for a conference with Krueger and MacArthur regarding my taking over Luzon. Krueger always tries to put something over on me — I will be on the watch.

May 21, 1945

It seems that I am going to take over up in Luzon some time around the 1st of July. By that time I shall have Mindanao in good shape. As a matter of fact, the northern column on the Sayre Highway finally got that big steel truss bridge constructed over the river down at the bottom of the canyon and now tanks and heavy vehicles are moving on to the south. The two columns are about 30 miles apart. Last night Clarence entered Malaybalay. . . . I wish the Japs would come out and fight. I would relish it but I am afraid they are not going to give us that satisfaction.

You can imagine what a satisfaction it is to me to know that my plans are going so well in Mindanao and I can assure you that the plans have really been mine except for the fact that I was forced to make the original landing at Parang when I really wanted to make a landing on Davao Gulf, which I could have done without too much trouble. The power of the Japs on Davao Gulf has been overrated through the years and the Navy and GHQ were afraid of it. The coast line is about 75 miles long and there are many places where we could have landed that didn't have any defenses.

May 22, 1945

The northern column is moving some now since the big bridge has been put in across the gorge, but we are airdropping today to the forward elements so it is evident that there is another bridge out. Our method is to wade the rivers and push on even beyond artillery range while the bridge is being built. During this time we supply these troops with food and ammunition by dropping them from the air. We are carrying on quite a modern war down there.

Woody is not moving very fast now, but things are shaping up very well. I am sending him another bunch of replacements to keep him up to strength. Woody is at a tremendous disadvantage on account of the vegetation everywhere, which is very dense and over everyone's head. That is the thing that does not appear in the picture. I do not think for a minute however that the Japs are having any fun. They have no airplanes to drop food and they have no boats to bring in replacements, so they are distinctly worse off than we are.

We have captured an enormous amount of Japanese naval guns and field pieces, but of course they have a lot more that we have not yet knocked out. The Japs are afraid to fire much because Hugh Cort can locate the guns by the flashes and then pour an irresistible amount of our artillery on them.

Some of these fights that we have had seem just like a dream to me, particularly Cebu and Negros. Duke Arnold (Americal Division) estimates there are only 4,000 Japs left of the original 14,000 on Cebu[15] and these are scattered and poorly equipped. Rapp's show on Negros is not a difficult one anymore except that the mountain which the Japs are backing up into as they gradually withdraw is over 8,000 feet high.

The day after tomorrow we expect to go and see the Sultan of Sulu. I am going to present him with a nice carbine at the expense of Uncle

Sam. This does not worry me because we have been giving thousands of them to the guerrillas, who spend their nights firing in the air because they think they see Japs. Those guerrillas are a thin reed to lean on, but they do give the Japs the impression of operating in enemy territory and are available to furnish some sort of protection to bridges in rear areas.

May 24, 1945

This morning we were up early and off to Jolo at seven-thirty.... The distance is approximately 500 miles, so we made a round trip of... approximately the distance from Florida to Panama. We had grand weather throughout....

The strip at Jolo can hardly be dignified by that name, but Chuck, after circling a few times, landed there without any trouble. When we came back there at two-thirty, however, the wheels had sunk into the ground where Chuck had parked the plane, and it was necessary to get a couple of tractors before we could pull the "Miss Em" out on the runway. Then we had to keep moving or she would have sunk in the runway proper.

We drove out about twelve miles to call on the Sultan of Jolo, or Sulu as he is usually called. He was expecting us and had a bunch of datus (leaders) waiting at the house. Also a bunch of women and children, some of whom were very nice looking. After some pleasantries I presented him with a carbine and a citation ... thanking him for his services to the U.S.A., to which we affixed a gold seal with a ribbon.... He presented me with some kind of a beaten silver jewel box for you and a beautiful Moro barong (heavy blade knife) and a kris to match. A kris, as you know, has a wavy blade.

We then drove quite a few more miles to visit the Governor, who was also a Moro and surrounded by datus and quite good looking women. At both places they laid out an elaborate feast.... The Governor presented me with another barong and another kris.... He also gave me a very fine spear. Now I wonder what I am going to do with all these damn things....

Among other points of interest today was a Japanese prisoner being led along by some Moros and the prisoner kept making signs for us to shoot him. He evidently thought he was about to be tortured.

When we took off we promised the Sultan we would fly over his house. Chuck, who had a grandstand seat, said he saw at least fifteen or twenty of the Sultan's family watching us as we circled.... The house is about as follows: There is a very fine bamboo fence thickly woven to keep out the Jap infiltrators. Inside the compound is a sunken fort to protect the women while the men did the fighting. The house was on a raised bamboo platform well off the ground, and there were no steps near the ground so that no animals and dogs could get in. The Sultan's room

... was lined with a sort of Persian rug on the ceiling and walls. There was also some matting. Apparently most of the family slept on the floor on bamboo beds. The Sultan had a big double bed. They say he is 72 years old and had another child the other day, although I am not too sure about that story.

May 25, 1945

The communique for the 25th of May puts Mindanao in the mopping up stage.... My personal feeling is that we have more Japanese alive on Mindanao than there are on Luzon and in much better condition.[16] The reports indicate that the Japs on Negros are in pitiful condition — half starved and many without arms. Within the last few days we have killed six hundred more Japs on Leyte and taken about forty prisoners without any losses to ourselves, which indicates that they ... have lost all semblance of a military force. In fact, on Leyte a couple of days ago they found some Japs eating another Jap. This has not been uncommon since my early days on Papua. They are much nearer the animal stage than one would suspect who has only traveled through Japan and seen the beauties of the place.

Franklin has done quite well but his big error has been in building up a tremendous supply base at Parang which will shortly be subjected to heavy southwest monsoons. His road from Parang to Kibawe is almost impassable, and I have directed that they supply the 31st Division from Macajalar Bay on northern Mindanao.[17]

Del Monte is about fifteen miles south of Macajalar Bay on the Sayre Highway. About ten miles further on is Valencia and then about two-thirds of the way down to Kabacan comes Kibawe. From Kibawe a road or trail runs southeast to Davao City. I want you to remember that. Don't worry about our situation in Mindanao. I know you are worried about Woody's sector, but you can take my word for it that I have built up a power house down there not only in artillery of all types, but I have kept Woody's division filled up full strength. The Japs run down hill pretty fast under those conditions. The Japanese hospital organization is never good.

May 26, 1945

Today has been another busy day.... We ... flew first to Macajalar Bay, where we circled for some time, and then to Del Monte airstrip. ... From there we flew on to the Malaybalay strip where we again circled for some time, finally landing at Valencia. I did this in order to let General Styer, who joined me at the plane, have a chance to see what a grand training area that would be down here.... On the plateau there are just miles of rolling country covered with grass and just occasional clumps of trees, but with streams and all other types of obstacles for training.

From Valencia we took off about ten o'clock for ... Davao City. As we approached we could see various artillery concentrations and a bunch of planes dive bombing the Japs, one of which failed to come out of the dive.... Again there were many tanks and men at the field to protect us.... The vegetation is so thick around there that Woody said a Jap with a machine gun got in there yesterday morning at the corner of the field and caused a lot of trouble.

Before we left the field I decorated Woody with three medals, the first he had ever received.... By the time the third appeared he was overcome.

You may take it from me that the fighting on Mindanao is not over and that Woody is having a very hard fight. However ... Hugh Cort has a tremendous concentration of artillery which he slaps at them at any and all occasions. The Japanese haven't anything that faintly compares with it, and when he finds out where they are he knocks them groggy.

May 27, 1945

Rapp has the Japs licked on both Panay and Negros and Duke Arnold is chasing them all over northern Cebu. There are, however, lots of Japs left, so that any recruits that come in within the next few months will have good training ahead of them patrolling against actual live Japs.

I am going to take a rest for a couple of days, because I have been moving almost constantly.

May 28, 1945

Today some officer was here from the Operations Division of the War Department and I guess that is the beginning of a long line. In fact it wouldn't surprise me if some of those birds up in Manila would come down to see this fight. Charlie Willoughby has not seen a thing since Leyte and Pat Casey, the engineer officer at GHQ, is the only visitor we have had. How ... the signal officer at GHQ could turn down our signal officer's promotion to Brigadier General is more than I can understand, because he has never been around to see his work. For example, on a map around Malaybalay and Valencia the ground looks just the same as the ground around Davao City. The former, however, is rolling hills and open for twenty miles in all directions, while around Davao City one is not able to see more than ten feet in any direction as the car goes along the road.

May 29, 1945

The fighting ... in the central plateau of Mindanao ... I have brought on myself by directing Franklin to seek out the Japanese. The advances which Woody has made above Davao City have been slow but steady. It is only a question of time until the Japanese there will go into the hills.

We will have to keep troops in there for quite some time to watch them. My best weapon on Mindanao has been to get reinforcements and keep moving them in there.

Tomorrow is Memorial Day and I am going to make two speeches. One here in camp will be at the dedication of a memorial to a famous man who died recently [President Roosevelt]. I am not enough of a hypocrite to want to get too effusive on that score. The second speech will be made at the dedication of a cemetery.

May 31, 1945

I am going to try sending my letters through the open mail, but I will not be able to be as frank in them as I would otherwise. . . .

Rapp and Duke are fine. I also do not worry about Woody or Clarence. Your beau is a very lucky person because I could have been whipped on a number of occasions.[18]

Good fortune has always followed me in my fighting against the Japanese. No commander operating on a shoestring has ever been treated better by his enemies. In Negros we landed with five battalions against a Japanese force estimated to number from fifteen to twenty thousand.[19] Our surprise bewildered them so that we were able to win a quick victory.

Our Mindanao show continues to go better than I could have anticipated. The Japanese have prepared for years for that fight down there and their numbers in the beginning were approximately equivalent to . . . our own. We did the unbelievable thing of marching a division in column down the shores of Davao Gulf and into their big city . . . and on the hills above there was a Japanese division looking at them as well as naval units and other combat units of all types.

June 1, 1945

This morning I was . . . in the air at seven-thirty and off to Del Monte. . . . I think things are going fine.[20] Arriving back here about two-thirty I found Bill had returned, bringing Rapp. The latter is very much disturbed over the possibilities of serving with palsy again and states that he will ask for retirement rather than do so. Of course it has not been definitely decided whether palsy will get the outfit. It will depend on whether palsy is going to be the first one up to bat or comes up at the same time I do.[21] I will be interested in knowing what Sarah will say when she knows that Rapp doesn't want to stay.

Just now I have been perfectly astounded to hear that a good many of my staff are eligible to be sent home on the point system. I did not imagine that anybody would be eligible since they just arrived here last summer, but of course many of them have been in the Army since the beginning of induction. They get a point a month for that and some have children too.

June 2, 1945

Rapp has just left to return to his station. He looks very bad and is quite skinny. He is seriously considering the question of asking for relief from this theater, but I have told him to wait and find out whether or not he [is] to continue with me. That question has not yet been definitely settled. . . . I have advised Rapp to take a leave of absence effective about the 15th of June. Jens is already home and Duke Arnold is going about that same time. . . . I would like to be on my way also.

As things stand now I shall establish a command post at Baguio [Luzon] on or about the 20th of June, but I do not expect to stay there very much of the time. The most serious job I have right now is the Mindanao fighting. While most of the Japanese are still alive they have given up their powerful position on Davao Gulf without a very creditable fight. They are being pushed further and further back up into the mountains and that is also true of the fighting in central Mindanao. East of Malaybalay we have run up against resistance, which is just what I wanted. I want to kill as many of them as possible. They are perfectly capable of living for some time in the mountains with the food and supplies they must have stored up — for years in fact, although any force in that condition would gradually lose its offensive value. What I want to do is whittle them down so that the successors to the guerrillas, the Philippine Army units, can handle them. They will relieve us for future operations.

Last night I went out to see a movie . . . called "Molly and Me," with Monty Woolley and Gracie Fields. It really had some good laughs and was quite a relief after the many poor movies which we have been sent lately. I think the people in the War Department misjudge the taste of the soldiers. . . . I believe soldiers enjoy a good movie as much as anyone and do not like one that is on the order of a Mack Sennett comedy. . . .

I must say that I am not looking forward to that trip [with MacArthur] tomorrow, but I guess in the end I shall enjoy it. My knowledge of what my fellow traveler will want to do is rather limited. If you will recall those schedules at West Point, they did not want to leave a man five minutes to sit down and drink a Coca-Cola. In most places a visitor is killed with kindness.

June 3, 1945

I had a mixed feeling with reference to the declaration that Mindanao was in the "mopping up" stage. Of course I realized that it was not so, but on the other hand we have definitely taken the initiative away from the Japanese and are confining their space of living to a comparatively small part of Mindanao.

It is true that a lot of our publicity is sappie. Dick Bergholz (Associated Press) said yesterday that it was all designed to publicize one person. Insofar as it helped build him up into a great General I think Sarah is right. I do think that it tended to make our Chief a big frog in a small puddle, and that a different type of advertising would have been more efficacious. However, I do not know. Certainly the Big Chief is one of our great generals, and this country would lose a lot if anything were to happen to him.

Notes

1. *Report of the Commanding General Eighth Army on the Mindanao Operation: Victor V,* pp. 23–79; Robert Ross Smith, *Triumph in the Philippines* (Washington, 1963), pp. 620–648; Robert L. Eichelberger, *Our Jungle Road to Tokyo* (New York, 1950), p. 223; Eichelberger Dictations, 21 March 1955.

2. Maj. Gen. Franklin C. Sibert, commanding X Corps.

3. According to the official history, the reverse would almost appear to be the case. Of the 13,500 Japanese in northern Negros, about 4000 were trained combat effectives, but these "lacked many essential items of supply." At Cebu, on the other hand, "trained ground combat strength was low." There were 14,500 Japanese on Cebu, of whom 2,550 are described as combat troops, and 1,700 as noncombatant civilians. These, in contrast to the forces defending Negros, defended elaborate fortifications and had an ample supply of small arms and ammunition. Smith, *Triumph in the Philippines,* pp. 605, 609–610.

4. A reference to the syndicated column by Mrs. Roosevelt.

5. Passages in italics are taken from the Eichelberger Diary, 19 April 1945.

6. In May 1948, Gen. Eichelberger added the following to his Diary. "The flight ... to Cebu City was because certain of my staff thought the Americal was taking a licking. Gen. Arnold had visited the Eighth Army Command Post while we were at Parang or perhaps the day before and some of my staff thought he was licked. However, Col. Art Thayer, Deputy Chief of Staff, made a hurried visit to Cebu and thought Arnold was doing a fine job. The 164 Infantry had been sent by Arnold into the Jap rear area road and trail 27 miles. This threat on their rear caused their retreat, although they could have held out quite some additional time. From that day they lived in the mountains until after the surrender following the atomic bomb."

The 164th attacked on 13 April; the Japanese commander ordered a withdrawal the night of 16 April. According to a Japanese colonel who survived the war, "The Americal Division had been inordinately slow in mounting envelopments.... The frontal attack in the center had been wasteful of time and lives and ... the Americans would have done better to execute an early, strong envelopment of the Japanese left...." Smith, *Triumph in the Philippines,* p. 616.

7. Passages in italics are taken from the Eichelberger Diary, 26 April 1945.

8. Passage in italics is taken from the Eichelberger Diary, 28 April 1945.

9. By this time a major general, this former member of Eichelberger's staff from Buna days was in command of the Thirty-first Division.

10. Eichelberger to Miss Em, 20 May 1945.

11. Eichelberger Diary, 10, 11 May 1945

12. Passage in italics is taken from the Eichelberger Diary, 15 May 1945.

13. "The false reports about Samal Island were caused by the guerrillas who claimed they went over it and found nothing there. Then we had a company go over there and it got pinned down by heavy fire, and we also received naval gunfire in Davao City from there, so it finally took a battalion to drive the Japanese off or to kill them." Gen. Eichelberger to Miss Em, 24 May 1945.

14. Lt. Col. Maurice E. Stratta.

15. This, it turned out, was an optimistic estimate, for over 8,500 Japanese surrendered on Cebu after V-J Day. Smith, *Triumph in the Philippines,* p. 617.

16. This is an exaggeration. Japanese strength in eastern Mindanao before the American landings was 43,000, with an additional 12,850 Japanese noncombatant civilians. In contrast, a month after Gen. Eichelberger wrote this letter, the Shobu Group in Northern Luzon still had 65,000 men, while the Shimbu Group southeast of Manila still had a strength of nearly 26,000 at the end of May. Smith, *Triumph in the Philippines,* pp. 419, 579, 621–622.

17. This decision paid off within a week. On 3 June, Gen. Eichelberger wrote: "I am grateful to Lady Fortune that I forced Franklin into shifting our supply point to Macajalar Bay. He told me when I saw him two days ago that rains have practically closed down Kabacan and the rains will get worse." Eichelberger to Miss Em, 3 June 1945.

18. The next two paragraphs are taken from Gen. Eichelberger's letter to his brother George, 30 May 1945, and are included here because of the views expressed about Japanese leadership on Negros and Mindanao.

19. According to the official history, there were about 14,800 Japanese troops on Negros, of which about 4,000 were trained combat effectives. Smith, *Triumph in the Philippines,* p. 605.

20. Passages in italics are taken from the Eichelberger Diary, 1 June 1945.

21. This refers to the order in which the Sixth and Eighth armies were to be thrown into Japan.

CHAPTER FOURTEEN

Old Haunts and New Horizons

On 3 June 1945, General Eichelberger flew to Manila and boarded the cruiser Boise in company with General MacArthur and several members of his military family. For the next ten days they visited the scenes where the Eighth Army had been fighting in the central and southern Philippines and talked of future operations, particularly the plans for the invasion of Japan that were even now beginning to take shape.

For MacArthur it was also a trip back through time. One of his motives was to retrace all of his flight from the Philippines during those dark days in 1942, and Eichelberger observed as they steamed past Corregidor on the first evening that the chief "was under very evident stress as he remembered these historic events."[1]

June 4, 1945

Dearest Miss Em,

As we came aboard there was the usual ceremony. I have the Admiral's suite.... The Big Chief is on the other side in similar accommodations....

It was very dramatic as we passed Corregidor because the sunset was ... beautiful. [MacArthur] talked a lot about looking at similar sunsets and of his departure, which he said was the low point of his life. He said that he called Palsy and told him to throw power in after breaking through at Balete Pass and move rapidly on Aparri, but that Palsy says his men were too tired. He said: "If you don't do it by July 1st I shall bring in Eichelberger and he will do it for you." Bonner [Fellers] had already told me this. Don't you know that this burned up Palsy. The orders are out for me to take over on 1 July.

He said, "I may have to make you my Chief of Staff. I have looked over the list and you are the only one who can do it. Dick has been sick ... but was up again and at work and that may explain the crazy things he has been doing for the last six months. Think this over and so shall I....." He would have to take me away from the Eighth Army, but ... I would have a broader field as Group Chief of Staff with him. I wouldn't want that job, although I shall do whatever I am ordered to do except to serve under Palsy. I hope it doesn't come up.[2]

Dick told me yesterday that the Navy have threatened to bust Buck — he doesn't see how they can do it when there are a lot of admirals in the chain of command above Buck. Ain't that sumpin!

It is a funny world, Baby, with a lot of funny people. You and I are the real sensible ones.

June 5, 1945

Quite a day today. Up at 5:20 A.M. and when I finally got on deck we were in beautiful Macajalar Bay. Franklin, Clarence and others came aboard and at 8:00 we were ashore en route to Del Monte and Malaybalay. At Del Monte we wasted time trying to find where the Big Chief had lived en route to Australia. There wasn't a trace.

All the boys assumed that he would fly from Del Monte to Malaybalay to avoid that terrible road. I told them he wouldn't, *and he didn't*. I rode in the rear seat of his jeep all day.... About 120 miles altogether. It was a terrible pounding and the Big Chief stood it fine. The war correspondents say they will write their dispatches standing up.... I am bruised from head to feet, but by the gods I didn't get hurt....

Had luncheon at Malaybalay. Only unpleasant feature was that Big Chief refused to inspect a guard of honor and bawled Clarence out for having one.

We had come in from that long ride in jeeps and suddenly Martin sprung on us that great big escort with a band and three companies of soldiers. Well away from the center of them, at least a hundred yards, there was a place taped off for the Big Chief to stand. He took the salute, said a few words in a low voice to the commanding officer, and then got back in his jeep [before] ... the Star Spangled Banner was played. The driver jumped out and saluted but the Big Chief remained seated and did not salute. Being caught in the jeep with him I did the same thing.... It was after the Star Spangled Banner was over that he bawled out Clarence by saying: "Honors in the field are contrary to Army regulations and I don't like it, Martin." Without any break I started right in chatting to Martin about unimportant things as though nothing had happened and I think that helped to break up the embarrassment. From then on the Chief was neither angry nor unusually pleasant.[3]

Believe me, the Old Man can take it.

June 6, 1945

At 2:00 P.M. we were back aboard the ship and ready to start for Iloilo.
. . . We shall go by PT boat to Bacolod and after seeing things at Negros
will go back to Iloilo and look that over.

It was a fine day. . . . We drove about 30 miles north of Cebu City
along good roads after landing at the docks in crash boats. Lots of guards,
steel scout carts, baby tanks, etc. . . . We also went up to see where the
fighting had gone on and then drove through the destroyed city to Duke's
house. . . . When we tried to go back aboard the ship it was very rough
and I was afraid the Big Chief would break his neck. It took him about
10 minutes to get on the ladder. . . . The Big Chief got a good scare.[4]

June 7, 1945

That big cruiser lay way off Iloilo because it was afraid of the water
around Bacolod. Then we went hell bent by PT boat to Bacolod 40 miles.
. . . Rapp met us at the little pier. . . . We three rode in the Packard and
I never had a smoother trip — only about 2 miles by jeep. We went up
to 3000 feet to an observation post where the Big Chief could see what
had gone on.

When Filipinos recognized the Big Chief they went wild. The Chief
enjoyed seeing where the fighting took place and he complimented Rapp
very highly. Rapp is crushed with the knowledge that he will come back
under Palsy on 1 July.

I had a very indifferent feeling about who would do things in the future
— a "don't give a damn" attitude, and for that reason seemed to please
the Big Chief. The Big Chief said . . . that they are trying to force him
from Washington into various indefensible things. E.g., George Catlett
Marshall asked him to write a letter for a Congressional Committee
giving his views on Universal Training. He refused — said it was controversial and that the others gave *secret* testimony while his letter would
be published. Also asked him to have Negro troops come over to be mixed,
platoon by platoon, with white troops. He refused that too, and asked
for definite data on where that was done in Europe.

June 8, 1945

Looking back on my trip I have a very funny reaction. I know that everybody was most friendly to me, including the Big Chief. For some reason
though I seem to get fed up on things myself. I do not know whether it
was the fact that so little publicity was given to the people that did the
fighting or what. I know the way that lies ahead of us is a very difficult
one and that there will be very hard fighting unless the Japanese quit. I
wish I cared more for those for whom I must fight. Of course one fights
for one's country and not for individuals, and, as you know, I have asked
for little. It does get one's goat a bit when you realize that our fighting,

man for man, on Cebu has been as hard and more bloody than that at Okinawa[5] and yet there is little credit given for that terrific fight that was put up there. Those Japs that we licked there were just about our equal in numbers. It wasn't any question of a terrific group of ships and materiel against a comparatively small bunch of entrenched Japanese. Of course up there the Navy has been subjected to suicide attacks which have been taboo to discuss until the Navy broke it at Okinawa. The losses have been heavy. . . . The Japs put a lot of half-trained men into obsolete planes and start them going, and one plane may seriously damage a battleship or sink a smaller boat.

Some people think that the Japs will quit and at one time the Big Chief thought so also, but when I asked him the other day he said "no" very emphatically. The little fellow is a mean enemy because he does not surrender. One does not get long lines of thousands of prisoners like they secured in Germany.

Did I tell you that Bonner Fellers said that Dick [Sutherland] tried to get the Big Chief to give him your palsy's outfit during the Luzon fighting? It may be possible that at some previous time he tried to get my outfit but I think he abandoned that idea a long time ago.

June 9, 1945

It looks like I shall have to get rid of Franklin sooner or later. He is good but not good enough.[6] The Chief never seems willing to throw anybody out on his back side, but I do not feel that way.

June 10, 1945

The sunrise this morning was . . . surprisingly beautiful, and with the Miss Em riding about five hundred yards off the beach and about ten big bancas going by with varicolored sails it was quite a sight. . . . We are expecting . . . a General Gairdner (whom the Big Chief calls "Churchill's spy")[7] and tomorrow I am going to take him to Davao City and leave him with Woody. . . . General Stilwell . . . arrived at 1700. . . . He seemed to be anxious to find out what the score is out here.

June 12, 1945

The Big Chief and party were back from the Borneo landing, which . . . was successful. Tomorrow morning we reach Davao City and after spending the day there will leave for an overnight run to Zamboanga. This is not so easy, Baby, as you would suspect.

I talked with George [Kenney] for a couple of hours this afternoon. . . . He has his troubles with Hap in Washington[8] and doesn't like to have Spaatz come out to the Pacific.[9] After a fine dinner . . . the Big Chief talked for at least 1½ hours about coming events and even said that Palsy, for a certain type of frontal advance, was equal to anyone in our military history. Some stronger statements...indicate that Palsy will get forces out of proportion to the importance of his landing.[10] Incidentally, I have seen indications that he will get the best of the divisions, or at least the ones he prefers....However...I will just keep rolling along.

Joe Stilwell told me last night what a dirty deal he got from Chiang and from the husband of the woman I escorted around Australia [i.e., President Roosevelt]. Chiang promised unlimited troops and all he got were 3 divisions. They all have had their troubles...but in the end things seem to work out for us.

June 13, 1945

George Kenney and I had a lot of nice talks and I know his problems. He is very good company. His B-17 came in...this morning, so when we dropped anchor...George took off for Manila. Franklin and Woody came out in small craft and we went ashore...to see dive bombers and an artillery shoot.

The Big Chief told me tonight what units (8) that I will have plus *all* the armor, so you see I rate a bit. *He said he wants me to be the one who lands in the north and pushes across the Tokyo plains....In this discussion he did not mention again his hope of making me Chief of Staff, but talked about me entirely in terms as Army Commander of his moving flank. He told me that he had turned down Bradley to come over here and reemphasized the fact that he had offered Richardson an army, which he had refused....*[11] There are 5 corps commanders coming from Europe with their staffs such as Ridgeway, Gillem, Joe Collins, etc....He expects Courtney to come to the Philippine Islands but he said he told George Catlett Marshall he didn't want him right now.[12]

June 14, 1945

We were up early today and dropped anchor off Zamboanga. We then made a tour over very wet roads....Just about noon the "Miss Em" came floating in over the sea and I left the Big Chief en route back to his ship. He went away very happy....

I am to make the fast dash into Japan....Your palsy will land someplace several months before I do but it will not be the main blow.[13] That is a job that will be saved for myself, Courtney (Hodges) and Buck. Bonner still hopes that this preliminary blow...by your palsy will not come off and that the time will be shortened up by some months by just having one big blow. In fact it will almost be time for my birthday [March 9] before we go in because it will take a long time to get supplies, equipment, troops, etc....

I returned...to find Joe Stilwell here....One statement by Uncle Joe was very interesting to me, and that was that the Flying Tigers were a bunch of "mercenary bums." They flew P-40's against a lot of very poor Japanese crates during the early months. When the chance came for them to go into the Army only two accepted.

He had some very bitter things to say about Chiang and FDR also.

June 15, 1945

Rapp is leaving at once for the States, and I advised him to wait ... to decide whether or not he wants to come back, for it is not necessary to make a quick decision. He is of course all broken up over the fact that he will serve with Palsy again, and if I were he I would get out even if it were necessary to invoke the question of tropical fatigue. Rapp's service after taking Panay and Negros is on a very high curve and I have recommended him for the DSM, so he need not worry about the future....

Today I celebrate my 40th year in the U.S. Army. Personally I think it has been a long time, and I know you will agree with me when I tell you that from now on I do not intend to accept anything but courtesy out of anybody out here....

We have had a lot of conferences.... Gris, with the 6th, 37th, 38th and 32nd Divisions will come under me on July 1st. He will be down for a conference on Monday. He is quite old, Bill [Bowen] says, and broken up over the way he has been treated, but glad to get back with me.

June 18, 1945

We talked to an extremely bright Jap officer prisoner this afternoon — he is the brightest we have seen yet, and everyone got a kick out of him. He told us frankly everything we wanted to know. He did say that there was neither malaria nor dengue among the Japs on Negros, where he surrendered, but that they were nearly starved to death.

June 19, 1945

This morning I was up early and talked to Mr. [Henry] Luce [of *Time* and *Life*] and Mr. Schroth, who owns the Brooklyn Eagle, for about an hour and a half before we ate breakfast.... I think they understand the situation much better than they did. I think they all thought there was little or no fighting in the southern islands, but when they realized the losses of some of the regiments and the hard poundings they took they were perfectly amazed.

We were shocked to hear about Buck this morning.[14] He has been on my mind all day, and I cannot realize that that big husky fellow has been killed. When I think the number of times I have run that risk it makes me realize how lucky we have been.

June 20, 1945

Insofar as Woody is concerned I would like very much to get him a corps, particularly if he is going to serve under me. If I finally find that a certain corps commander [Gen. Franklin C. Sibert] is going to serve under me it will be necessary for me to ask for his relief, and then I shall ask for Woody. This corps commander is good but he is not good enough. Woody is a fighter and he has a good head.

June 21, 1945

This morning we were up early and took off at 8 o'clock for Cebu. . . . We had a grand trip back and arrived to find Gris here and delighted to be in our family. His voice really almost broke when he spoke to me. He told me this great *secret:* Sarah called him in the other day (following Buck's death) and showed him a telegram in which he had recommended Gris [Lt. Gen. Oscar W. Griswold] for Buck's job, and in the succession of command Woody for corps commander and Fred Irving for division commander. The later two were in accordance with my recommendation to the Big Chief. Isn't that something to think about? Grizzy told me, however, that it did not go through as the job had been given to Stilwell, who was caught on his way home.

Gris has had a very hard time and he said he feels that Rapp Brush and Duke Arnold of the Americal will fall under the axe before long. He also says that Joe Swing is scared to death that he'll get the axe from Palsy when he gets them under him. . . .

June 22, 1945

The announcement came last night that Joe Stilwell will take command of the Tenth Army. From what Gris told me I know that the Big Chief's recommendations were for Gris, Woody and Fred Irving, because Gris saw the telegram. That is certainly a hard break for everybody. I think if we can pull old Tut-Ankh-Amen out of his tomb there on the Nile maybe we can make him into a leader. This bright remark was not aimed at Joe particularly, because I have a very great admiration for him, but in the general setup I am just about the real kid of the whole bunch and as you know I am just a little older than Rip Van Winkle. Every time I take a step I watch out for that long grey beard that ought to be there, to keep from stepping on it.

June 23, 1945

The point system . . . applies to officers and men. Divisions like the 81st that have not been in the Pacific very long will not lose very many men or officers, while other divisions, like the 24th, which have been out here a long time will lose a great many men. Fortunately I have kept the 24th filled up with recruits and they will emerge as a veteran *young* division. Woody's outfit is really overstrength right now, although that does not necessarily mean that they are overstrength on the firing line, since many men are usually sick and wounded. . . . In my own staff . . . I am going to lose about 20% of my officers.

Woody's men captured a whole bunch of prisoners yesterday . . . and they say the Japs are in bad condition above Davao City. They are hungry and running out of ammunition, and of course are separated in many cases from their medical supplies. I understand that they said the Japs are only giving food to the men in good health and that the badly wounded are being killed. It is certainly a queer army.

Do not worry any more about Mindanao. That situation is in good hands and the Japanese have been thoroughly licked.

Naturally I am sorry about Gris, because it would have solved my problems with reference to Woody and Fred very easily. I do not doubt that the order for Joe must have come from Washington and ... that they will protect him. I imagine that Joe will not let the Navy run over him and he will probably bring out his own publicity *until he comes here* [italics added].

You may be sure that I realize all the implications of the lack of publicity which followed my winning of the Visayan and the Sulu Archipelago-Zamboanga campaigns. ... A certain great leader not only wants to be a great theater commander but he also wants to be known as a great front-line fighting leader. This would be very difficult to put over if any of his particular leaders were publicized. ... By not publicizing the Eighth Army he leaves the impression with the people back home that he has been the one who has been doing the frontline fighting. This does not mean that he does not appreciate what I have done or that he does not give me a lot of mental credit. He just wants all of it for himself. Unless one understands this dual feeling on his part of wanting to be a great strategic ... and also a frontline leader it will be impossible for anyone to understand the setup here. You can readily appreciate why he did not want Omar [Bradley] to come as a group leader because he wants to be his own group leader and I believe he will do a grand job. ... Uncle Sam ... will not suffer, because Big Chief will get a lot of victories.

I do feel that some time it will backfire on him. ... There are many writers who would like to write these things up and will someday probably do so. ... In comparison the leaders out here have lost ground because there has been a tremendous amount of publicity for the European leaders. By the time we get home there won't be anything in the nature of a reception.

June 25, 1945

This morning ... we wanted to get into the air by 7:45 on our trip to Davao. ... This time we took off almost directly south and hit Butuan Bay. From there we followed the Agusan River ... and flew over some of our troops who are making a move up the river to cut off the Japanese, who are retreating from in front of Clarence.[15]

Woody met us at the airstrip and we rode up to his new Command Post. ... The ridge that he is on is one that was even beyond artillery range when I was there last with the Big Chief.

Hugh Cort, Woody's artillery officer, is giving the Japs hell and Woody feels that there are only about 2000 combat troops left in front of him, with about 2000 more mixed troops in addition to a bunch of civilians. ... Unfortunately Colonel "Jock" Clifford was killed yesterday by Jap mortar fire. He commanded the 19th Infantry, which advanced from Digos to Davao City and was with me the day I went into the city. ... He had done grand fighting all away along the line and although of the class of '37 he was about in line to get a Brigadier General if his good work kept up.

June 27, 1945

Quite a few Japanese civilians with children are coming in now to surrender to Woody. This has all been within the last week and some have been shot trying to get through the lines. Woody does not think too highly of the Japanese that are left above Davao City and I am sure that Clarence will have no difficulty with his forces. What I am anxious to do is to have the guerrillas, or rather the Philippine Army which will take over the guerrillas, assume the burden of killing off the Japs. The 31st and 24th must get ready before very long for future operations. These divisions I have are filled up with recruits that have had experience and I would place them very high up on my list as desirable outfits. I have no confidence in green troops in fighting the Japanese, who are very savage and fanatical fighters. When our boys get up against the Japanese in the dark their views about their superiority over the Japs die down a bit.

June 30, 1945

In your letter yesterday ... you seemed to be still worried about whether or not your palsy might be made a group commander and placed over me. If I were you I wouldn't worry about that because I have no intention of serving under him. ... I couldn't afford to, because my name has been used so many times to urge him on to greater speed that he would cheerfully and willingly cut my throat if the opportunity ever offered. It wouldn't hurt my feelings a bit to tell officially why I wouldn't serve under him. ... If a group commander were appointed for a certain future operation it ... would probably be Joe, since ... [he] is senior. Certainly everybody out here would prefer Joe; in fact, most of us would prefer Yamashita. ... Palsy is going to be a lone wolf and his work will be important, because it will be the first test of a certain kind. As always he will have plenty to do it with. There is a board going to meet to take up the question of the elimination of retired officers, but they won't get him because he just suits the Chief in many ways. Also, the Chief will fight for any of his boys. Walter has no glamour and that is certainly a recommendation for him out here.

Bill Bowen got back last night. ... Bill said that some opposition has developed in Washington against the Chief acting as his own group commander. Personally I do not think that this opposition will take a very tangible form because the Chief has always seemed able to ... get what he has wanted.

Bill and Tubby [Burgess] say that the units up north that are coming under the Eighth Army on July 1st are pathetically glad. This applies to division commanders, Gris and others. Bill went up the Cagayan Valley to see Beightler[16] and the Ohio boys. Palmer [Swift] was there on an inspection and he didn't seem very happy.... Bill says that Beightler and all the others are going home because they do not like the fact that they were given little credit for their fight in Manila, at Baguio and up the Cagayan Valley.... Gris told me that Palsy ordered him not to recommend Beightler for a DSM but that he did so anyway.

Bill says your old Leavenworth friend is going home on a 45 day detached service status.... My medico tells me he hasn't been well.... Possibly some of Dick's sickness has been due to the fact that he realizes his status is not as good as it was.

While I would hate to walk out on that crew in time of war ... I have served nearly three years in the tropics with only one very short vacation. Unless the Japs quit the way ahead will not be an easy one. In the past the Japanese have been the easiest part of my service in this combat area. They have been considerate enough to die promptly, or at least they have not been able to inflict any defeats on me.... I don't know why it became my fate to land among some elderly gentlemen whose motives are not always as nice as I would like to have them be.

July 1, 1945

Last night a telegram came from Franklin which, according to him, practically ends the fighting down in Mindanao....[17] There remains, however, a place called Sarangani Bay, into which I have been trying to stick Franklin's nose for some time.

I also sent a telegram to Franklin ... asking him to come up today to talk things over. He goes off on a sidetrack every once in a while and I have to pull him back on the main line.

We assumed command of the remaining fighting in Luzon as of midnight last night. I do not anticipate any trouble. Gris will have four divisions (6th, 32d, 37th, 38th) plus operational control of certain portions of Walter's divisions.... Down in the Visayas we will still have the use of Walter's new divisions....

In my moods I have my ups and downs. Sometimes I get perfectly amazed at the way news is shelved about my outfit. Then I get astonished, like this morning, when they mentioned the Eighth Army in connection with Mindanao. I could see no particular reason for its mention at this time.... I usually do not stay in a bad mood very long.

Frankly, I have given a lot of thought to that question of Dick's job and I do not believe I should take it under any conditions. Having settled that in my mind, I feel fine today.

Notes

1. Eichelberger Dictations, 11 December 1952.

2. "I asked (Colonel) Roger Egeberg if he had heard the Chief of Staff talking of a new job for me. He said yes...." Eichelberger Diary, 3 June 1945. The next day Col. Egeberg elaborated upon Gen. MacArthur's reasons for dissatisfaction with Gen. Sutherland, which were largely of a private nature, and ventured the opinion that he "does not think Big Chief will throw Dick out although he would like to." That evening Gen. MacArthur commented: "When the war is over I am going to try to make you Chief of Staff." Ibid., 4 June 1945.

3. This paragraph is taken from Gen. Eichelberger's letter to Miss Em dated 26 June 1945, but is included here because of its contents.

4. The last sentence is from the letter of 7 June 1945.

5. The Americal Division lost 410 men killed and 1,700 wounded on Cebu, while the Japanese lost roughly 5,500. Robert Ross Smith, *Triumph in the Philippines* (Washington, 1963). p. 617. On Okinawa the two Marine Divisions by the end of May had lost 1,718 killed and 8,852 wounded, plus 183 missing. The official history of this campaign claims that here "Casualties on the American side were the heaviest of the Pacific War." On Cebu, however, the Americal Division incurred over 8,000 nonbattle casualties as compared to a little over 14,000 by the six divisions on Okinawa. Ibid., p. 617; Roy E. Appleman et al., *Okinawa: The Last Battle* (Washington, 1948), p. 384.

6. The comment that General Sibert "is good but not good enough" probably reflects Eichelberger's desire to have subordinates who shared his belief in the need for a rapid advance against the Japanese. He had been dissatisfied with certain of Sibert's logistical arrangements on Mindanao, and, for the forthcoming invasion of Japan, he evidently would have preferred General Woodward, whom he later recommended for corps command. Eichelberger always respected Woodward, and he probably regarded him as a more adaptable leader and somewhat easier to work with.

7. This clause is inserted from Eichelberger's letter of 9 June. Lt. Gen. Sir Charles Henry Gairdner visited Gen. Eichelberger at Tacloban, while Gen. MacArthur and his party observed the Australian invasion of Borneo. Eichelberger, *Our Jungle Road to Tokyo* (New York, 1950), pp. 242–243.

8. Gen. Henry ("Hap") Arnold, Commanding General, Army Air Forces.

9. Lt. Gen. Carl Spaatz, commander of U.S. Strategic Air Forces.

10. "The Big Chief was talking in the dark because the door of the office was standing open and the ship was blacked out. He told me the number of divisions that would be given to Krueger (13 I believe) and said he had so arranged the maneuver that Krueger would have to make a double envelopment. He said he thought he was one of our greatest generals for a frontal assault. (The Big Chief has often told me that Krueger could not do the quick and brilliant things that have been done by the Eighth Army.) The Big Chief outlined his strategy for the movement on Japan. A landing on the island of [Kyushu] would be followed by a final blow on the island of [Honshu]." Eichelberger Diary, 12 June 1945. At the time of this entry, Gen. Eichelberger left blank the names of the two islands.

11. Passage in italics is taken from the Diary entry dated 13 June 1945.

12. Lt. Gen. Matthew Bunker Ridgeway, Maj. Gen. Alvin C. Gillem, Jr., and Maj. Gen. J. Lawton Collins each commanded a corps in Europe. Lt. Gen. Courtney H. Hodges was commanding general, First Army, European Theater of Operations.

13. "After Krueger's Luzon operation, General MacArthur told me that he had considered relieving Krueger many times during the march from Lingayen to Manila. I interpreted this to be because of slow progress, rather than anything wrong in Krueger's battle plans. (In fact, the first time I flew up to see Manila, he had his headquarters at a sugar central about half way to Manila while Krueger had his headquarters still back in the vicinity of Lingayen.) ... MacArthur told me that he couldn't trust Krueger to command the main blow against the Kanto Plain in Japan because "he will not advance a yard as long as any Japanese are alive behind him." Eichelberger Dictations, 11 December 1952, 4 November 1960.

14. Gen. Buckner was killed early on the afternoon of 18 June by a Japanese artillery shell that exploded above a forward observation post where he was watching the fighting.

15. On 25 June a battalion combat team of the 155th Infantry was sent up the Agusan River aboard LCM's, reaching Waloe, fifty-five miles upstream, two days later. Smith, *Triumph in the Philippines,* p. 644.

16. Maj. Gen. Robert S. Beightler commanded the Thirty-seventh (Ohio) Division.

17. "Actually, fighting against organized bodies of Japanese continued after that date, but there can be no doubt that by 30 June the main ends of the campaign had been realized." At a cost of about 3,700 casualties, the Eighth Army and attached guerrillas had killed well over 10,000 Japanese, with another 2,325 Japanese killed between this date and the end of the war. Smith, *Triumph in the Philippines,* p. 647.

CHAPTER FIFTEEN

On Top of the World

In the exhilarating and fast-moving days ahead, Eichelberger had reason to feel even better about the war and the contributions of the Eighth Army to the victory that was just around the corner.

July 3, 1945

Dearest Miss Em,
The way things stand now I will be leaving here early Thursday morning for Manila. I plan to pay my respects to the Big Chief and then will go on . . . to visit the divisions that came under us on July 1st. . . . We are going to take Ventura along on this trip with the hope that he will be able to locate his parents at Laoag. He has not seen his mother and father for some seventeen years. . . .

July 6, 1945

On the plane yesterday morning . . . we saw in the clear air an 8000 ft. volcano near Legaspi. . . . A perfect, sharp lava cone with smoke rolling out — our left wing passed about 100 feet distant from the top. What a beautiful sight.

Went in to see Big Chief but was told by Bonner . . . that the Big Chief was "busy and asked to be excused." Didn't like that much, as Clovis and I thought he might have stuck his head out. At any rate we went into another office to see your old Leavenworth friend.

The latter was very jovial and said: "If one army is going to do that job[1] (you can imagine what), it will be the Eighth Army. If two, it will be the Eighth and First Armies.[2] If three, it will be the Eighth, First, and Tenth Armies in that order. If Nimitz wants that army [Tenth] he can have it and we will get another, but the Eighth Army will always be first." He volunteered this and ... Clovis and I at once decided that it had been discussed and to a larger extent settled or he wouldn't have been so ready to volunteer so much. After thinking this all over I decided this morning ... that they couldn't afford to have the coup de grâce delivered by Joe [Stilwell] or F.H.B.[3] Courtney because then they would get most of the credit. Therefore, it had to be some one of his own gang. ...

I am going to have a hide like a rhinoceros from now on — there is no genuine gratitude — just whatever is best for them. A couple of cold selfish babies if I have ever seen any, so what the h____ ...

At 8:00 A.M. after a fine breakfast ... we took off for Bagabag near the north end of Balete Pass. ... There we met [Maj. Gen. Charles E.] Hurdis, who commands the 6th Division, and drove up number 4 highway about 20 miles into the mountains. The Japs have taken a licking up there and we passed one of the biggest [Jap] supply dumps I have ever seen. I finally reached the scene of the fighting. Up there are the Ifiegaos, who ... wear nothing but a fancy breechcloth, knapsacks of deer skins, spears and knives. They have killed lots of Japs and are beautifully built. ... There were 175 wrecked Jap trucks in one section of road, mostly destroyed by air attack. They have killed 4000 Japs in northern Luzon in my first five days and taken a lot of prisoners.

We had luncheon at the 6th Division in Bagabag and then rode up here to Tuguegarao. Another rough trip but only 100 miles by air. ... There Beightler and his Ohio crowd met us. ... Gris is here with us. ... They all hate your old palsy. Bill Gill said he had joined the Fuller club of those who couldn't serve another day with him. Beightler is sore because his division has received so little credit. He did most of the fighting in central Manila. ...[4]

July 7, 1945

We had a very cool night's sleep in the Command Post of the 37th Division. ... After we finished eating (breakfast) I talked to the staff for a while. They all feel very disgruntled because they have received little praise. They never got credit for capturing Baguio, although they were here two days ahead of the 33rd Division and had put up a sign welcoming the others ... when they arrived. ...[5]

About 8:30 we took off straight north in Gris' C-47. ... At Naguilian we left dear old Gris ... and started up the mountain on Highway No. 9. ... All along the road of course there were signs of a lot of fighting, particularly Japanese caves which they build very industriously and fill up with supplies. ... After we capture the caves the Filipinos loot them. ... Baguio had ... been knocked flatter than a pancake by our industrious bombers. ...

It is evident that the honest Filipinos and also some soldiers looted this place thoroughly. I doubt if the Japs took much because they were in too great a hurry to get out of here....

July 9, 1945

We had a fine luncheon at Palmer's in his beautiful home right on the edge of Baguio....We discussed everything, although of course I laid off my great and good friend....I find that he spent most of his time up where the fighting was going on. He told me that in the great battle for Tuguegarao there were only six Japs killed. He was present and knows that to be a fact.

Palmer feels that the Japs in these mountains will all be dead by the end of the rainy season. He says they will get hungry and go in groups of two or three to rob the native gardens and the mountain savages will kill them, or they will die from exposure to the cold and rain.

I still can't make up my mind whether the Big Chief's excusing himself when I asked to see him the other day was because of his being so busy, or whether he was sore at something that I had done.

July 10, 1945

This morning...we had a very smooth ride to Nielson Field, where [Maj.] General [William C.] Chase of the 38th Division...met us.... After a nice luncheon we went out to inspect some troops, including a hospital and the front line.... This is a grand division and will not be hurt very much by the point system because it has not been out in the Pacific so very long. *After dinner I...wrote MacArthur about my trip, telling him that I had inspected all four divisions on Luzon and found the strengths of each division very encouraging. Divisions are up to strength on enlisted men but short on officers. The morale of each outfit was very high.*[6]

July 12, 1945

This morning Bill Bowen came over to talk things over...before... leaving in the B-25 for Sarangani Bay to watch the landing.[7] General Chamberlain and Summerall, from the Operations Division of the War Department General Staff...went along. They are...evidently very much impressed with what we have done. They can tell the boys all about it when they go back home.

Yesterday I got a very nice letter from Joe Swing which reads in part as follows:

I stopped in to see General MacArthur the other day and he said that the Eighth Army had certainly done a bang-up job in the Visayas and Southern Islands. I love to hear such words of course, but the speech that warmed the cockles of my heart was said by Chamberlin, to wit: "The Eighth Army in all its operations has certainly shown that in landings we need not give so much consideration to the Jap reaction nor be as conservative in our ground operations when once landed as some of our other troops have been. Eichelberger has demonstrated that we can afford to take chances...."

You can readily understand the desire of the whole outfit to take part in an operation in which some dash will be injected and movement is the word.

We are still wondering just what divisions I will have after Courtney gets out here. Naturally I am anxious to retain some of the divisions with which I have fought in the past.

July 13, 1945

After a hectic morning I finally got away at 1 o'clock for Manila.... I went first to see Steve Chamberlin, who went over future plans with me. There is no question about my place in these plans....

The Big Chief was very friendly but seemed to be depressed over the fact that he is having quite a difficult time with the sister service getting them to cooperate. He talked of Ike Eisenhower and the reception he had had and said there was no question in his mind now that he could have Chief of Staff if he wanted it. He remarked that he couldn't understand why we have received such an unfriendly press. He said there were three stories that he thought would make a tremendous hit with the public — the Visayan publicity, the Mindanao publicity and the northern Luzon. He said the communique on the latter was the only one that had received any play up ... and he asked me to write an article which I suggested should go out under somebody else's name.

We talked at length about my divisions and he said he thought a great error had been made in trying to make two wars out of this World War II. A situation has been created in which all the men feel entitled to go home.

It was 6:30 before I got out to Dick's home.... He had brought in a lot of extra boys, china and good food and the dinner was fine. In addition to Lord Louis[8] there were an admiral, a general, and Horace Fuller. Horace had taken some before he arrived and he felt very sorry for himself. He cried when I praised him and ... the last thing he told me was that he would gladly serve under me as a colonel if he could get back here.

I sat across the table from Lord Louis and then sat beside him until about midnight. He is a tall, very handsome, unassuming chap who would be quite a glamour boy if he were in Hollywood. He has a nice voice and a very quiet manner. They had flown all the way from China and yet he did not seem to be tired in spite of being on the go all day. We talked on a great variety of subjects. It was evident that Dick was happy to have me there.

One thing the Big Chief spoke about to me was the fact that nobody in this theater had had their faces on *Time* and *Life* for a long period of time, while they put those in the European theater on again and again. Of course a lot of this makes me laugh....

July 14, 1945

Our Sarangani Bay landing has been entirely successful although they have not located very many Japs. My own feeling is that there are not very many in that area and that the few remaining ones are hiding out.[9] The same was true in our push up the Agusan River valley. According to guerrilla reports there was a large force of Japs there retreating from Clarence Martin's troops. As a matter of fact, they have made practically no contacts.

July 16, 1945

The Big Chief told me when we were on our trip that he would call off the Philippine campaign around about July 1st. You understand of course that we are not having any trouble with the Japs. The rainy season and the guerrillas will help to kill them and I do not anticipate any real difficulty. However, if our troops get careless here and there they will lose lives. For example, I was told this morning that some new unit going into Cebu did not put out the proper guards and the Japs went in and killed several.

July 17, 1945

Tubby Burgess and Hosmer of Bill Bowen's section have been up in Manila looking among other things for a good place for an advance Command Post for me in the Manila area when things really get hot (I mean planning). Hosmer has come back and Bill gets the impression from him that Joe [Stilwell] and I are the ones to be used and that F. H. B. Courtney will be the one to remain here after we go. Of course these things can be changed any time. The reasons they would want to use me are many, one of them being that they think I can do the job and another the fact that I am more or less a member of the family.

I have given a great deal of thought to the question of my going home. If I ask I am afraid it is going to arouse instant suspicion that I want to go home and have a parade. A question like this is intimately linked up with the matter of publicity. The question of who will be selected to command certain things rests on a very delicate balance. Therefore I am in quite a quandary....

July 18, 1945

We are off ... for Mindanao and Morotai. Lindesay Parrott and Frank Kelley of the New York *Times* and *Herald Tribune* respectively are going along.... We sat out on the veranda and talked until after ten o'clock last night. They both think that the publicity out here is very poor and that it has resulted in the lack of popularity with the G.I.'s. They say they haven't been able to get out a story for a long time because, with the announcement of the conclusion of the Philippine campaign[10] there is nothing to write about.

Colonel Verbeck, who has been Woody's Chief of Staff lately and who commanded the 21st Infantry during most of the Mindanao show ... told me that he had a young company commander who was due to go home at the conclusion of years of foreign service, so he pulled him out of combat and sent him down to sleep on the seashore near Woody's camp. ... A Jap got in with a grenade and killed him. That leaves only three of his original company commanders. There were a number of Japs and they killed and wounded a number of our men before they were killed. The undergrowth is so heavy down there that it is almost impossible to prevent infiltrators from getting in. Personally, I think they should surround those Command Posts with a double apron iron fence with plenty of tin cans on them. He said that some of the Japs were dressed as women. That will be a good lesson for the other boys ... but I am afraid it will result in some little Filipino girls being shot when they may only be looking for romance.

Many people think that George Catlett Marshall will become Secretary of War and Ike Chief of Staff. Not a bad combination if [President] Truman will do it.

July 19, 1945

We were in the air promptly at eight, headed south and the weather was beautiful.... By nine we were on the ground at Del Monte, where I was met by Clarence and Franklin.... Among other things I urged Clarence to take a leave but he is one of those chaps that hates to leave his work. He has not been home for three years.

When we took off about ten-thirty we flew down the plateau to Valencia and then cut straight across over the mountains to Davao. This of course included going over the places where the remaining pockets of Japanese are still living. I could see some fresh clearings up there in the mountains which might indicate that the Japs are building shacks and preparing to make some gardens.

We landed ... at Davao City ... where Woody met us. He is fine and we went down to have a grand luncheon at his Command Post....

We were in the air again at one, heading south for Morotai.... About three o'clock we were on the ground and then I inspected Harry Johnson's 93rd Division (colored).... I have never seen so much snap in my life. They had every vehicle polished, the engines were cleaned up fine, and every colored boy saluted as far as he could see you. When a car stopped they would all jump out and salute. There are no disciplinary cases in the division and their kitchens are as clean and as neat as a pin. Johnson certainly has done a fine job. . . . It is apparent that he knows just how to handle these colored boys and I must admit I was amazed, although I had heard from my inspectors that the division is fine. . . .

For the present the Philippine fighting has been washed off. That is to show that the famous campaign is over. In this particular case I do not think it is a bad idea. While there are perhaps 25,000 Japs in Luzon and 12,000–15,000 in Mindanao, these Japs are not in a position to do anything of an offensive nature.[11]

July 21, 1945

You would be interested in the reports which I received this morning from Negros, where Rapp was. After the 40th Division left me and went to Panay I had nothing left there but the 503rd Parachute Infantry, which is a small outfit, and guerrillas. The latter are outstanding in that particular island for their willingness to eat rather than to fight and as a consequence the Japs have come down out of the mountains where they were once quite starved and now are beginning to fatten up again because they have robbed the native gardens. They have no great supply of ammunition; in fact probably only one out of four has a firearm that will function. We are going to train the guerrillas a bit and maybe they will fight better. Personally, I would be inclined to tell them, "No fight, no soup." On the other hand, a young West Pointer named Volckmann[12] has some guerrillas up near Bontoc that are outstanding. I understand that during his guerrilla days Volckmann would take no foolishness and if necessary would take a fellow out and shoot him. Therefore his guerrillas are scared to death of him and do what he tells them. In many localities the civilians are more afraid of the guerrillas than they are of the Japanese but no generality will cover the whole situation. Many pilots and airmen shot down by the Japanese have been rescued by the guerrillas and treated with extreme kindness over long periods of time. Many others have maintained radio sets throughout the Philippine Archipelago.

Sometime the question will be raised in history as to why Sharp and others surrendered on the order of Skinny Wainwright after he became a prisoner. The Big Chief told me that he ordered Sharp to keep on fighting and that Sharp was not under the orders of Wainwright. Certainly he was not under Wainwright's orders after Wainwright was captured. The other side of the picture of course is that the Japs probably told Skinny they would kill all the prisoners unless he secured the surrender of those down in Mindanao. They finally surrendered everything they had including radios and equipment of all kinds, intact.[13]

July 22, 1945

Yesterday I looked over a history of World War II from '41–'44 inclusive, prepared by the Military Intelligence Division in Washington and given distribution by the *Infantry Journal* on their mailing list. The general picture in the Pacific was that the South West Pacific Area has been just a flank guard for the Navy's advance. Buna was just mentioned by name while there were pages on the Navy's advance. The fighting from Aitape to Biak inclusive was summarized as the acts of the 41st Division. In this, the 32nd and 24th were not mentioned. As you know, I commanded about 55,000 troops at Hollandia, of which the elements of the 41st Division at that point comprised about 10,000. This presentation may be the result of enmity against General MacArthur or it may have resulted in part from the fact that our publicity has played down on our own accomplishments and has failed in the past to give organizations and a clear picture. . . . I hate to see the Army giving out what amounts to propaganda for the Navy.

I rather imagine if I am every going to see anything faintly approximating the truth concerning these operations I shall have to write it myself. A lot of the reason for our poor publicity has been the centralization of publicity around one man. While it has made him a big figure in the puddle, the puddle in turn has been so small that the frog could jump across it. It hasn't been exactly fair for the many brave men who have died in winning these victories.

July 24, 1945

So far as my going home at this time is concerned I have a very honest doubt whether I should do so. The trouble is that a great many people, probably 50%, feel that Japan is about to fold up. I would feel very strange to be caught away from here if a sudden movement were ordered for the occupation of Japan.

July 25, 1945

So many believe that the Japs will quit if Russia comes in, and I hope they do. In the meantime, Halsey seems to be destroying the last of their merchant marine and fleet. They have a few more battleships, destroyers, carriers and cruisers some place — perhaps off the coast of Korea.

July 27, 1945

Just after I finished reading your letters I received a telegram from Manila ordering me back there tomorrow to discuss a possible readjustment of the point system. At present the enlisted men are entitled to go home with 85 points and of course that means that the ones going home are the non-coms and the veterans. If the figure is lowered it will mean that the rest of the non-coms and . . . veterans will go. I do not suppose there is an army in the history of the world that discharged its veterans just before a big battle. Will argue against going lower than 85.

July 29, 1945

As you can imagine, the main interest now focuses around the plans for the movement into Japan should they quit. It would be terrible if no such plans were made. Of course your palsy's plans are already drawn and there is no great rush to complete the final plans and details of our movements should Japan *not* quit. Approval in principle has already been given for the final blow should Japan not quit and those plans are quite well under way. For example, Steve [Chamberlin] was able to give me the information on just what units I shall have in either case.

August 1, 1945

General Greer from the Public Relations Office in the War Department . . . took off for Del Monte and Davao this morning. Greer is a very bright hombre and before he left he made some very interesting remarks about the publicity from out here. He said the newspapermen in Manila are very outspoken in their complaints . . . and he found out that the Big Chief writes his own communiques. . . .

Right after lunch I had a nap before going over to hear a fine planned talk by a General Borden from General Marshall's office in Washington on the subject of experiments that have been made in the United States about taking out caves. He had lots of interesting data to offer and also had been at Okinawa to see the caves there. Okinawa and the troops there came under General MacArthur on the 1st of August. One of his abbreviations is CINC AFPAC, which stands for "Commander in Chief, Army Forces in the Pacific. . . ."

August 4, 1945

It is obvious that I cannot get home now. Yesterday we received the first draft of our orders from AFPAC concerning what we are able to do if Japan quits. Out of all these conferences, such as that one in Potsdam, must come either the early entrance of Russia into the war or a threat to Japan by Russia that she will enter the war if Japan does not quit. It is clear that Japan cannot fight the world and that her industrial life is being destroyed by our air attacks. If it were any other country but Japan I would say that early surrender would be in sight, but the very traits of character that make them fight to the death in a hopeless fight might make them continue to fight as a nation, particularly as the public mind in Japan has hardly been prepared for a defeat. . . . At the present time naturally I must be here as we will from now on be planning night and day. . . . The whole tempo of our life will be stepped up. . . .

August 7, 1945

We went down to see various friends. . . . I went to GHQ and talked to General MacArthur. *This conversation . . . indicated his now firm belief that the Japanese would surrender as the result of the atomic bombing which was announced in the morning and because of the prospective entry of Russia into the war. He affirmed his original statement that the 8th Army would be the one to take over the big push in case of a military occupation and would handle the job in case of a nonmilitary occupation. General MacArthur was very friendly throughout.*[14]

August 8, 1945

Our plans in case the Japs quit in a hurry have again been changed. . . . They are now talking about letting me serve with the outfit I was with in early February [XI Corps]. If they quit we will all fly up and land as a preliminary force but only after agreement with the Nips. Of course your friend Sarah will go along.

August 9, 1945

Of course you can imagine the excitement here with the news of the new atomic bomb followed by the entrance of Russia into the war. I had understood for a long time that the official date was August 15, so Russia really beat the gun by about a week. I think probably the atomic bomb did that. Russia was probably afraid Japan would quit without Russia getting into the fight. Tonight we heard that another bomb had been dropped on Nagasaki. It would have been better if they had dropped it on the naval base right next to Nagasaki. . . .

You can imagine what is going around in our minds now because most of us believe Japan is going to quit soon and this is the first time we have really believed it. Of course it will be a great break if we do not have to fight our way ashore as I never thought that would be easy.[15]

August 10, 1945

There is an increasing tempo of conferences . . . which will rise to a high point if Japan quits. . . . Tubby Burgess told us over the phone last night that things were red hot but no new plans had been advanced. . . .

(later)

At nine-thirty (P.M.) we returned here to hear the news that Japan has decided to accept the terms of the Potsdam conference with minor exceptions *(with the proviso that the Emperor and his prerogatives would be retained)* which I believe will be accepted. We are a bit excited. . . .

Now I think we will go in to Tokyo as soon as we can get ready. The AFPAC boys (GHQ) are caught partially with their panties down and with their Chief of Staff away, but not entirely so. The plans have been partially prepared and for two days they have been working on the idea of sending in the 11th Airborne Division with part of the Eighth Army and an advance detachment of AFPAC (General MacArthur) by air. *More telephone calls from General Bowen and Colonel Burgess indicated the necessity for being in Manila early the following morning.*[16]

August 11, 1945

Everyone is excited here at GHQ as you might suspect. Most of the boys were awake all last night and I understand there was plenty of shooting excitement and I suppose quite a lot of free-for-all drinking. It now appears that I will be connected for this job with the group who took me into Manila, which is fine and dandy with me. From what I can learn in this uproar, and on a day when no one really is sure of anything, I may be on my way in about a week. I'll know more about that before I get back to Leyte.... I have just learned too that the Big Chief has been nominated as the one to accept the capitulation and that seems entirely proper to me.

(later)

Have just come out from talking to Big Chief and there is no doubt that I am the one to go to Tokyo and it will be either with the Big Chief or before him.... When I tried to congratulate the Big Chief, he said: "How about yourself and what the Eighth Army has done."

The Big Chief was in fine spirits this morning but very busy. I only stayed about twenty minutes. He has now definitely committed himself that I am the army commander among the four who will go to Tokyo.

Joe Swing came under me tonight. Plans are of course in the state of flux and subject to change, but when I tell you that they are thinking of staging Joe into Okinawa within the next two or three days you can see how fast things are moving.... These plans have not been approved yet in Washington, D.C., insofar as I know.... I can merely tell you the trend of thought. As a matter of fact, no one has accepted Tokyo's surrender and I do not believe it will be accepted in the form it was presented. It may be necessary to drop some more bombs. I do not want them too uppity when I go in.

General MacArthur stated that the Navy was trying to horn in and were almost planning a landing of their own on Japan. He also said that pressure was being brought by British circles to have General MacArthur made the supreme commander in the Japanese occupation.... While our plans call for the partitioning of Japan between the various armies in the Pacific, he had no assurance that Russia would not come in from the north or that Britain would not send in a delegation.[17]

August 12, 1945

I want to emphasize what the Big Chief told me yesterday. He said: "I have always been afraid of that drive up from the south into the Tokyo area. That was the main blow and of necessity it had to be practically a frontal attack. You were to get it. The First Army movement in from the coast southeast of Tokyo was merely a token since the terrain did not permit a real blow from that area. The proposed attack north of Hodges' area was the one I had hoped to give to you because it would permit rapid movement, but we found that the beaches would not permit a landing."

The Big Chief added: "The main blow would have been a deadly thing because the Japanese are fine in defending against what would have amounted to a frontal assault. Krueger's landing on Kyushu was a cinch and he would not have suffered over 15,000 casualties."

From this you can see that you and I are lucky that the operation "Coronet" did not come off. I do feel flattered that my army fought its way into the number one position. . . .

August 14, 1945

The latest information is that the air trip is off. As of yesterday it was planned that I should accompany a certain person on a boat and that . . . someplace we would receive a number of goggle-eyed little bucktoothed birds and there settle things. Of course the best laid plans may go awry if someone else is made supreme commander or designated to accept the peace terms. . . .

It looks as though . . . it's going to be a very interesting spectacle up there leading up to the surrender.

August 15, 1945

The radio has just announced President Truman's statement on the acceptance of the terms by the Japanese, also the announcement of General MacArthur as supreme commander. . . . I imagine the sequence will be something like this. . . .

First, monkeys will come to Manila where final peace terms will probably not be signed; second, MacArthur will meet the Japs on a battleship off Japan and there he and certain representatives of the Allied powers will sign the peace treaty. Shortly thereafter, as soon as the bomb craters are filled, we will fly in. I may be fooled about this. Joe [Stilwell] has been entirely eliminated as anything but a supply man according to the rumors. Even the corps which may go to Korea will be under GHQ. F. H. B. Courtney doesn't enter into the picture at all. . . . There is a rumor that the reason Joe is not going to Korea is that Chiang says he will not allow him to set foot on Chinese soil. I have also heard that Joe is in a hospital in Manila.

Billy . . . says that a warning order has gone out for us to hold ourselves on 24-hour alert for movement to Okinawa. That means that the advance detachments of GHQ and Eighth Army will take station there ready to move right on. We will have two divisions going in by air. Personally, I would like to accompany General MacArthur on the battleship. . . .

August 16, 1945

Yesterday was surrender day. . . . At 1:30 we were off in the *Miss Em* for Manila, arriving at 3:30. . . .

I saw Steve Chamberlin for a little while at GHQ and he intimated that George Kenney was trying to steal the show by landing early. About that time George got me on the telephone and wants to see me so I can tell him what parts of Tokyo I want to occupy. I told him it was impossible for me to answer until I knew what parts he had destroyed. . . .

Then I saw Charlie Willoughby for a moment about some Japanese interpreters of the type I would want to use personally for confidential conversations. He had already sent me 16, varying from captains to sergeants. . . .

Then I saw the Chief, who was jubilant. . . . He said: "They haven't gotten my scalp yet, Bob!" I congratulated him on being supreme commander and he said, "Bob, we'll let a few paratroops drop and perhaps a battalion of infantry land, and then you and I are going in. You're going to command the troops and I want you near enough so I can yell 'Bob' when I want to talk to you. This is a great day and a real miracle." He said he had been trying to radio Tokyo for representatives to come here at once but the Japanese refused to answer his radios. He has so informed our government. The Emperor's statement to his people sounds like he's just a good-hearted fellow who had been trying to bring peace to the world.

(later)

We were trying to determine where we want to land. The photographs are not up to date and not too clear. . . . I am responsible for the planning and execution of the whole thing and Kenney and the Navy and everything else have been ordered to report to me for instructions. That is no small job for a country boy whose great ambition is still to put his feet on the railing of Mrs. Eichelberger's front veranda, wherever she may be living.

August 17, 1945

This morning I was up early going over a field order that Bill Bowen worked on nearly all night. . . . Things are still in a state of flux. The Japanese representatives have not yet arrived. The word Bill gets about the Big Chief's movements northward is at a great variance with what he told me. It seems obvious to me however that if he wants to get into the heart of Tokyo from some airfield on the outside it is going to be a difficult proposition. We will have to rub a magic lamp suddenly and have the ruins of a destroyed city removed, bridges repaired, dead removed, electric lights and water turned on, food installed, service, etc. As an alternative I am going to propose that I guard him into some palace or large home on Sagami-Wan, which is the great bay south of Tokyo. . . . Another plan would be to let him land and go aboard a battleship. Another would be to have him wait.

In view of the fact that we did not defeat that army and it is still intact I am anxious to handle that whole situation through them, and with ease and tact I think we can land a small force by air and not go knocking people around. . . . We have given the Japanese a chance to save face by keeping the Emperor and government. Therefore we must use them.

August 18, 1945

This has been another busy day. There was a conference this morning and then . . . luncheon. About 4 o'clock Clovis and I went down and had a grand visit with Jean [MacArthur]. She of course is all excited and is busy packing up her hubby's heavy clothing. Their house is really even more beautiful than I had realized.

After we left there I went over to a cocktail party given by General Gairdner.[18] There I ran into about everybody — Blamey, . . . a choice collection of American and British admirals, . . . Chink Hall, and last but not least, your palsy. He looked awful sad to me and was acting like he had been spanked. I don't suppose he likes the idea of the Eighth Army going into Tokyo.

Palsy is the head of a board of officers which meets Monday and I am on it.

You understand, of course, the setup here. The Eighth Army is in command of the movement into the eastern part of Honshu and all of Hokkaido, including Tokyo. After our advance elements get in, Krueger is to move into the western areas. . . . My principal worry, although not a serious one, is that some incident may occur when the Big Chief lands and I shall take every precaution to guard against that. . . . The Eighth Army is sitting on top of the world. At least, everybody wants to go with us.

August 19, 1945

I understand that the Japanese have requested that we keep out of Tokyo and other large cities and allow them to disarm their own troops. I feel that a very careful study should be made of the Japs. Their official announcements do not sound like a people willing to admit mistakes and defeats. They will be alert to the possibilities of resuming hostilities at some future time, just as Germany did in World War II.

It will be very easy for the Japs to become hysterical. They must have suffered terribly in the bombing of their cities and, having been fed a lot of blabber by their government, they have not realized that they were suffering defeat until just the end. The mental readjustment must be very difficult at this time.

Personally, I am no great proponent of this flying troops in there. I would have preferred an armed landing similar to the one we were going to put on under fire.

(later)

The plan to go down to the seashore rather than to try to go into Tokyo is apparently going through and that is a great relief to me. The Jappies are not behaving too well up there. Some of our photographic planes in the Tokyo area received ack-ack attacks and attacks from Zeros. I think this belligerent attitude will go pretty rapidly after their forces in China and Manchuria begin to surrender. As long as their armies are intact they feel their strength a bit. I notice that the new premier has cautioned the Japanese that they have been defeated. Most of their announcements up to date have indicated that they have received a setback but not a defeat.

Beginning at 10 tomorrow morning I shall start meetings on that General Officer [Readjustment] Board. I am sure that Sutherland, Frink, Kenney and I can hold Palsy down a bit. I do not intend to have him railroad anyone like Fred Irving, whom I admire.

August 20, 1945

This has been a hard day because it has been something of a row.... While I cannot go into the details we have been busy rating the officers out here and ... you can imagine how much your pal and I agree when it comes to Fred Irving and your Panama friend. Of course we had a very friendly atmosphere there but they were all for rating most of the people on the GHQ staff, whose names came before them, very low.

I had expected to get away about day after tomorrow, but I understand it has now been put off three days ... in order to let the little monkeys withdraw out of the area before we go in. The Navy seems to want to get hold of most of the area where we want to go in. The emissaries said that the only places down on Sagama Bay that haven't been destroyed are around Kamakura and Hayama. Of course that's where the Navy want to go in. Their maps are probably a whole lot better than ours.

General Bowen reported at breakfast concerning the interrogations of the evening before. He reported the Japanese delegation consisted of 3 Army, 2 Navy and 3 Air Corps officers, the remainder of the 15-man group being held in a room at City Hall.... The Japs proved to be a typically ill-dressed and scrawny looking group of staff officers ...

and apparently were entirely unknown to each other. The envoys were introduced to their interrogators by General Willoughby, who weighed in at about 220 and is 6′ 3″ in his stocking feet, making a fine contrast. The MP's guarding them were also a selected group of better than average size soldiers.

Bill said that ... he was asking one of the little Japs some questions and the Jap spoke good English, having been stationed in Washington. One question was how much damage had been done in Tokyo. The little Jap said, "Blown to hell."

Many of my predictions were borne out in the testimony. . . . Part of the Sagami Wan coast has been battered badly. The area into which it has been decided to take the SCAP and other higher headquarters, i.e., Kamakura, is 80% intact. The Jap soldier is not fully sold on the surrender. The Japanese claimed they were not prepared to discuss the surrender in detail but were under the impression their presence was merely to arrange an armistice. They have asked that the task of disarming the Japanese armies be left in their hands. Their attitude is definitely not one of a defeated nation but they regard the defeat as a setback and nothing more. As a result of the conversations the landing date has been postponed from the 25th to the 28th. . . . The forces landing on that day ... shall be in the guise merely of security troops for the presence of the SCAP.[19]

August 21, 1945

I worked on my records for that board meeting until nearly twelve o'clock last night. . . . We have been meeting all day. . . .

In our deliberations a great many of the old guard came off second best. By that I mean the Bataan boys. Your Leavenworth friend was not a part of the meeting but seemed to approve of our deliberations very much. In one or two cases he did not agree with our action on certain people but there wasn't much he could do about it. What surprised me was the way he puts somebody that works in his office clear down at the bottom of the list. I came out very well with Clovis, Bill and Fred Irving, but I had to be prepared for a row every minute.

August 22, 1945

You would be surprised ... how that board looked upon staff men. The fact that a man had had a big staff job during the war did not appeal to them at all. I am referring now to the recommendations for who should be on the brigadier general eligible list. Some of the reactions were perfectly surprising. Some of Sarah's great pals were recommended for *demotion.*

August 23, 1945

The $64 question concerns how the Japs will behave. We know of course that the great mass of them will be docile but there are a lot of young army hotheads, particularly among the young officers. I refer to the type that assassinated so many members of the cabinet in the years leading up to the war. The SCAP's refusal to guard himself may prove to be an embarrassment. When we first go in we shall have only a few troops and it will take about six days to get the two divisions in there by air.

August 24, 1945

Clovis told me that he had a very interesting discussion with our friend Steve Chamberlin this morning. . . . He told Clovis that he had had a tremendous amount of difficulty with my air friend George [Kenney] and that he had already had to go to Dick about their refusal even to attempt to comply with instructions. He had told Dick at that time that the cooperation of the Sixth and Eighth Armies had been outstanding. In fact, said Steve, "Never in all my service have I seen anything that approaches the Eighth Army for brilliance of leadership, intelligence and coordination down to the lowest point in staff work or the individual ability of the various staff chiefs. *You people took what was given you, asked no questions and completed one of the most brilliant campaigns in American history almost before we here at headquarters knew you had started. When you people first took over a year ago I had serious doubts about your ability to handle the situation. So you have achieved this opinion the hard way."*[20] He finished with, "I can't tell you what it's meant to me. It has been the finest thing I've ever seen."

A phone call came from GHQ extending me my invitation to attend the surrender ceremony, stating I could not take anyone with me, not even an aide, as the space would be very limited. In talking to Dick today I find he has arrived at the same feeling I have had all the time. He said, "Let the Japs run their own government and merely tell them what we want done rather than to try to run around shooting this man and trying to arrest that man and bringing on a fight." Dick's ideas as a rule are very good.

August 25, 1945

We got away this morning from Nichols Field. . . . It was very interesting coming in along the west coast of Okinawa. . . . I was impressed with the fact that the hills are not as high as I expected, but there is no question about the severity of the terrain and of the fighting.

After we got settled I went down to see Joe Stilwell, who is sorry as the dickens because he is not going to be allowed to go to China, although one of his corps will go but not under his command. He says he doesn't blame Chiang Kai-shek so much for objecting to his coming but he blames our authorities for allowing Chiang to keep him out of Manchuria and Korea when China has no control over those countries. Maybe he blames Mac for not fighting for him — I don't know.

August 26, 1945

Just now I have been talking to a couple of scientists who are generals. They have had something to do with bringing the atomic bomb out here and they want to take a big planeload of scientists in with me. I have compromised by agreeing to take one and to let the rest come in later. I find I am getting to be a great compromiser in my old age.

August 27, 1945

The soldiers with whom I talked this morning[21] are mostly recruits. Even in the artillery I found the recruits had been trained as infantry. They are fine looking lads and make me realize that we were not getting any of the cream in the Southwest Pacific in the old days. All those fine appearing, trained infantrymen were going to Europe and we were getting the culls as replacements when we got any at all.

I am glad I do not have to take this bunch of recruits into a real row — I doubt if they could lick veteran Japs until after they had been man-handled a few times under fire.

August 28, 1945

Since I inspected the 27th Division yesterday I have been giving it a great deal of thought. Out of perhaps a hundred soldiers with whom I talked there was hardly a veteran combat man in the bunch. The combat veterans have been sent home under the point system. As a consequence I would have had to go into the worst fight of the war with a bunch of well trained men who had not been in combat. The older officers had all gone home. In one regiment there was only one man of field grade besides the colonel. Therefore, again I feel I am very lucky. . . .

August 30, 1945

Sorry I had to put it off until I am so tired because I wanted to write a good letter today. This morning I was up at 4:30. . . . We were in the air in that beautiful big plane by 7 o'clock and I have never seen a smoother ride than we had for the next five hours. It was beautiful and clear and we could see Fujisan for a hundred miles.

Although we expected the field to be congested we did not circle at all but came right down. One of the most thrilling parts though was when we first began to go low over Japanese territory. We passed just over Kamakura and it had not been badly destroyed. In fact, I was surprised at the small amount of destruction all the way up to the airstrip.

I only had about an hour and a half to get ready for General MacArthur and there had not been much done. Before he arrived there must have been 200 newspapermen and cameramen there, including a lot of Japanese. When he finally emerged from the plane he had that big long corncob pipe in his face. He walked down the ladder and I saluted him. We then had famous remarks of famous people on famous occasions — he said, "How are you, Bob."

After all the pictures were taken we went to the cars and about that time George Kenney, Spaatz and a lot of other Air Corps men arrived. . . . It struck me that there were a lot of sightseers there.

The procession started off with truckloads of soldiers before and behind, but I give you my word there were thousands of Japanese gendarmes and military police and soldiers lining the road all the way into Yokohama. . . . I noticed that the soldiers' rifles looked so much better than they had down where I have been fighting them. They were new and the bluing was still on them. I rode with General MacArthur and Sutherland and it was a very dusty ride of about an hour and a half.

It was not until we were almost in town that we began to see signs of the destruction. Yokohama was to a large extent burned down, not knocked down. Tremendous sections of the city showed the effects of recent fires. . . .

It really has been a very thrilling day. Certainly one that I shall remember for the rest of my life.

September 2, 1945

This morning I was up at 5:30 and we took a destroyer out to the *Missouri,* arriving there about 8 o'clock. There were foreigners of all nationalities and I had a chance to talk to them all. Russians, Chinese, French, Aussies, etc., were all there. We were lined up according to diagram. My place was on the front row of the Army section about five paces from the nearest Japanese.

In the front row was the Japanese premier and on his left was the chief of staff. The premier is quite lame and had to use a cane. He was dressed in tails, striped trousers and top hat with gloves. There were a couple more civilians and a bunch of high ranking Army and Navy officers.

I wore one of those tropical worsted suits today without tie. General MacArthur wore neither tie nor ribbons[22] but most of the foreigners wore a lot. I thought the Big Chief looked very fine today and certainly not over 57. He was a bit nervous and the paper shook as he talked over the radio.

The ceremony was extremely impressive. I thought that General MacArthur's gesture in having Wainwright and Percival[23] . . . stand with him when he signed was an unusually fine one.

Just after the ceremony ended hundreds of our planes dashed over the *Missouri* . . . which . . . is a sight in itself.

In Halsey's cabin is the most beautiful saddle I have ever seen. It is a donation from some town in Oklahoma and is cowboy type with a great deal of sterling silver. He said it cost $2,000. . . . The saddle of course is to use when he rides the Emperor's white horse (if and when). I got a kick out of seeing Halsey when he scowled at the Japs as he stood behind Nimitz when the latter was signing the surrender document.

It requires no imagination to appreciate the thoughts of all present for the ceremony on the Missouri. Perhaps General Eichelberger's sentiments on this day, signifying the end of a terrible war and the peak of his career as a field commander, find the most lofty expression in the formal statement he was directed to issue upon entrance to Tokyo.

Today as we proudly reach the Tokyo area my mind turns back nearly three years to the first ground force victory in the bloody swamps of Buna. Once more my memory recalls those wonderful Australians who fought side by side with us in those bitter days and contributed so much toward that victory. I live again the advance along the New Guinea axis followed by the swift liberation of the Philippines. Again I see the countless amphibious landings, the doughboys fighting in the steaming jungles or digging the enemy out of mountain strongholds. Down the long trail which ends today we see our indomitable Commander in Chief, General MacArthur, with clear-cut, courageous directives pointing for us the straight road to victory. Gratefully we thank the Air, the Navy, and all the services without whom no successes would have been possible. Reverently we pay tribute to those who gave life or health along the way. Any exultation we might feel now should be stilled at the thought of them and only gratitude for their courage and selflessness remain. I know I speak for every man in the Eighth Army — and for every other American — when I say Thank God we come in victory — and in peace.[24]

And to the faithful and loving Miss Em, who had shared his fears, his hopes, and his most intimate thoughts every step of the long way, he wrote one week after the surrender.

Of course no one has suffered more than you have through these years and no one has followed the situation more carefully, so you appreciate the historical significance of these things. What I have always tried to have you avoid is to let your dislike of certain people influence your personal judgment about their ability. I imagine if one knew Napoleon or Julius Caesar or any of the great leaders of history there would have been a good many personal characteristics one would not have liked.

This would also probably have applied to Grant, Sherman, etc. History is still in the making right here and I want you to see all sides of it.[25]

Notes

1. The invasion of Honshu. Eichelberger Diary, 5 July 1945.
2. The veteran First Army, commanded by Gen. Courtney H. Hodges, was being redeployed from Europe to the Pacific.
3. F.H.B.=Fair Haired Boy — a favorite expression used by Gen. Eichelberger to indicate someone who currently was in favor at GHQ. Eichelberger always spoke of Gen. Hodges in this fashion.
4. This is true if casualties mean anything: the Thirty-seventh Division lost 3,000 killed and wounded in the fight for Manila, which is twice the amount suffered by any of the other divisions involved. Robert Ross Smith, *Triumph in the Philippines* (Washington, 1963), p. 307.
5. It is only fair to Gen. Krueger to point out that in his memoirs he does credit the Thirty-seventh Division with capturing the city, even though at the time the general commanding the division and his staff apparently thought otherwise. Walter Krueger, *From Down Under to Nippon* (Washington, 1953), p. 304.
6. Sentences in italics are taken from the Eichelberger Diary, 10 July 1945.
7. The last battalion of the Twenty-first Infantry, Twenty-fourth Division, landed at Sarangani Bay, some seventy-five miles southwest of Davao. They encountered no opposition at the beach.
8. Admiral Lord Louis Mountbatten, the Supreme Allied Commander in the South East Asia Command, which was established in August 1943.
9. There were roughly 2,000 Japanese troops, a fourth of them naval personnel, at Sarangani Bay at the time Gen. Eichelberger wrote this letter. Their defensive positions were ten miles inland and so the main body of Japanese were not encountered for several days yet. The fighting throughout was light: losses were thirteen killed and a like number wounded. The Japanese lost 450 killed. Smith, *Triumph in the Philippines*, p. 647.
10. On 5 July 1945, Gen. MacArthur had announced the official end of the Philippine campaign. The previous month he had told Eichelberger that he was going to call off the Luzon operation on 1 July, "no matter what the situation might be." Eichelberger Dictations, 24 September 1953.
11. Roughly 50,000 Japanese troops surrendered on Luzon after the end of the war and over 22,000 Japanese turned themselves in on Mindanao, so Eichelberger's figures are a little optimistic here. Smith, *Triumph in the Philippines*, pp. 579, 647.
12. Col. Russell W. Volckmann had refused to surrender in the fall of the Philippines and had organized a force of guerrillas known as the U. S. Army Forces in the Philippines (Northern Luzon). Volckmann had graduated from the Military Academy in 1934.
13. According to one eminent historian, "It was the fear of what would happen to the 11,000 men on Corregidor which had forced Wainwright to accept Homma's terms. Wainwright believed, as did many of the American officers on his staff, that the Japanese would kill their prisoners in cold blood if the commanders in the south did not surrender." Louis Morton, The *Fall of the Philippines* (Washington, 1953), p. 575. Gen. MacArthur in his *Reminiscences* gently scoffed at the notion that he blamed Wainwright for the surrender. "For three years he had imagined himself in disgrace for having surrendered Corregidor. He believed he would never again be given an active command. This shocked me. 'Why, Jim,' I said, 'your old corps is yours when you want it.' The emotion that registered on that gaunt face still haunts me." General Douglas MacArthur, *Reminiscences,* (New York, 1964), pp. 271–272.
   This is not in accord with Eichelberger's own recollections after the war. According to Eichelberger, "it was only after General Wainwright was released from a Japanese prison camp at the end of the war and signed up to write a serial for the newspapers that Gen. MacArthur recommended promotion and the Medal of Honor for Wainwright. Gen.

Malin Craig, a former Chief of Staff, told my wife in Washington while I was in the Pacific that the War Department had wanted to give Wainwright a Medal of Honor at the time they gave Gen. MacArthur his but he (MacArthur) would not agree." Eichelberger Dictations, 27 October 1954.

14. Sentences in italics are taken from the Eichelberger Diary, 7 August 1945.

15. The dropping of the atomic bomb caught Gen. Eichelberger completely by surprise. Therefore, his reactions as expressed to Miss Em represent his first thoughts on the matter. As a general under orders to prepare his army for the main blow into Japan across Sugami Beach, with the mission of capturing Yokohama and Tokyo, he often had cause later to reflect what this historic and controversial event probably meant for him.

"Having inspected the hidden defenses during my period in Japan and having demobilized that great veteran Japanese Army, I am in a position, looking backward, to realize what a terrific task had been assigned. Through the years I have been inclined to believe that I should have a very grateful attitude towards the atomic bomb and its use at Hiroshima and Nagasaki. The dropping of these bombs ended the war quickly and turned my mission from an armed invasion of Japan into a mission of taking the Eighth Army into a country which had agreed to surrender.

"...I am not at all certain it would have been successful because my training on Sugami Beach after the war has indicated that there were sand bars which would have made the use of our landing craft extremely difficult. The Japanese defenses were almost impregnable and the defenders would have been well disciplined and fanatical." Eichelberger Dictations, 10 December 1954.

16. Eichelberger Diary, 10 August 1945.

17. The passages in italics are taken from the Eichelberger Diary, 11 August 1945.

18. Lt. Gen. Sir Henry Gairdner of the British Army.

19. Passages in italics are taken from the Eichelberger Diary, 20 August 1945.

20. The sentences in italics have been taken from the Eichelberger Diary, 24 August 1945, where the remarks of Gen. Chamberlin are quoted more extensively.

21. Gen. Eichelberger spoke to several battalions of infantry in the Twenty-seventh Division.

22. "When I first arrived in Australia...MacArthur...always wore a great mass of decorations....However, a bit later when photographs came back of Gen. Eisenhower in Africa showing him without ribbons, General MacArthur shed his ribbons and necktie. From then on, throughout the war years...he did not wear ribbons or tie." Eichelberger Dictations, 5 September 1955.

23. Lt. Gen. Sir Arthur Ernest Percival commanded the British and Imperial troops that surrendered at Singapore on 15 February 1942.

24. Quoted in Gen. Eichelberger to Miss Em, 26 August 1945.

25. Gen. Eichelberger to Miss Em, 9 September 1945.

Index

About the Author

Jay Luvaas is Professor of History at Allegheny College. He received
his M.A. and his Ph.D. from Duke University. Professor Luvaas' other
books include *The Civil War: A Soldier's View* (1958), *The Military
Legacy of the Civil War* (1959), *The Education of an Army* (1964), and
Frederick the Great on the Art of War (1966).

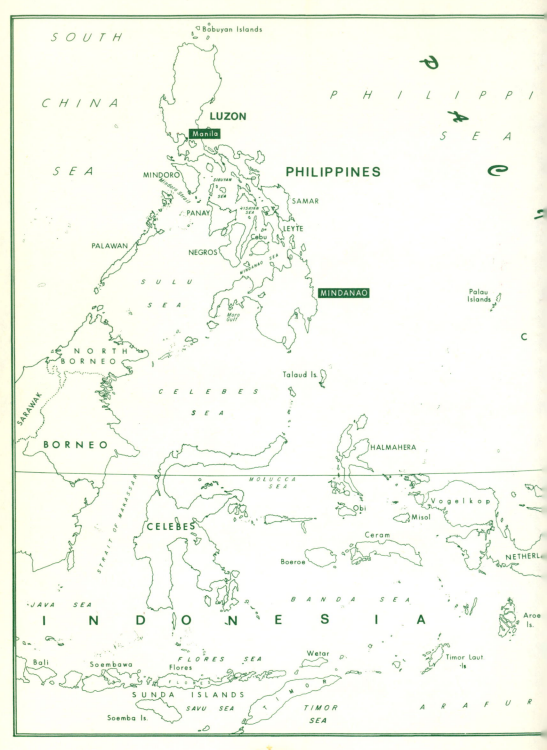